with best
Javaid
(June 2005)

MAIN LENDING **3 WEEK LOAN** DCU LIBRARY

Fines are charged **PER DAY** if this item is overdue.
Check at www.dcu.ie/~library or telephone (01) 700 5183 for fine rates and
regulations for this item type.

ISLAMIC STATE PRACTICES, INTERNATIONAL LAW AND THE THREAT FROM TERRORISM

In the post '9/11' legal and political environment, Islam and Muslims have been associated with terrorism. Islamic civilisation has increasingly been characterised as backward, insular, stagnant and unable to deal with the demands of the twenty-first century and differences and schisms between Islam and the west are being perceived as monumental and insurmountable. The 9/11 terrorist attacks have unfortunately provided vital ammunition to the critics of Islam and those who champion a 'clash of civilisations'.

In this original and incisive study, the author investigates the relationship between Islamic law, State practices and international terrorism. It presents a detailed analysis of the sources of Islamic law and reviews the concepts of Jihad, religious freedom and minority rights within Sharia and Siyar. In eradicating existing misconceptions, the book provides a thorough commentary of the contributions made by Islamic States in the development of international law, including norms on the prohibition of terrorism. It presents a lucid debate on such key issues within classical and modern Islamic State practices as diplomatic immunities, prohibitions on hostage-taking, aerial and maritime terrorism, and the financing of terrorism.

The book surveys the unfairness and injustices within international law—a legal system dominated and operated at the behest of a select band of powerful States. It forewarns that unilateralism and the undermining of human rights values in the name of the 'war on terrorism' are producing powerful reactions within Muslim States: the 'new world order' presents a dangerous prognosis of the self-fulfilling prophecy of an inevitable 'clash of civilisations' between the Islamic world and the west.

Islamic State Practices, International Law and the Threat from Terrorism

A Critique of the 'Clash of Civilisations' in the New World Order

Javaid Rehman
University of Ulster

·HART·
PUBLISHING

OXFORD AND PORTLAND, OREGON
2005

Hart Publishing
Oxford and Portland, Oregon

Published in North America (US and Canada) by
Hart Publishing c/o
International Specialized Book Services
5804 NE Hassalo Street
Portland, Oregon
97213-3644
USA

Hart Publishing is a specialist legal publisher based in Oxford,
England.
To order further copies of this book or to request a list of other
publications please write to:

Hart Publishing, Salter's Boatyard, Folly Bridge,
Abingdon Road, Oxford OX1 4LB
Telephone: +44 (0)1865 245533 or Fax: +44 (0)1865 794882
e-mail: mail@hartpub.co.uk
WEBSITE: http//www.hartpub.co.uk

British Library Cataloguing in Publication Data
Data Available
ISBN 1–84113–501–1 (hardback)

Typeset by Hope Services (Abingdon) Ltd.
Printed and bound in Great Britain by
MPG Books, Bodmin, Cornwall

'The best form of Jihad is through persuasion'

Hadith of Prophet Mohammed, the Prophet of Islam
(Peace be Upon Him)

Acknowledgements

This book is a result of my personal and longstanding interest in the field of international human rights law and Islamic law. After the terrorist attacks of 9/11 Islam and Muslims have increasingly been associated with international terrorism. It is nevertheless surprising to notice the lack of legal scholarship that deals directly with the possible relationship between Islamic law, Islamic State practices and international terrorism—a subject which in the post 9/11 legal and political environment has taken centre stage, and deserves a critical and detailed examination. Furthermore, in any such debate it is important to take account of the position of legal scholars from the world of Islam. While aiming to adopt an objective view of international law, the present study aims to reflect the positions, values and concerns emanating from Muslim legal scholars and jurists.

The immediate incentive for working on a book project was provided through a grant made by the British Academy in June 2002. I am grateful for the generosity of the Academy for this award. The award allowed me to conduct very concentrated and detailed research into this area and to have the privilege of excellent research assistance. I was also able to conduct research visits, consult documentation and in some cases interview experts on the subject in a number of countries.

Many individuals and institutions have supported me in developing my ideas and for completing of this work. Special thanks are due to Professor John Bell (Cambridge University) for his kind support and encouragement during all these years. I would like to thank my colleagues, in particular Professor Christine Bell, Dermot Feenan, Jacinta Miller, Aisling Norrby and Ivan Topping from the University of Ulster for their time and support. I am grateful to the Library at the University of Ulster (Magee Campus) for providing me with all the relevant documentation. In this regard, I would like to thank Janice McQuilkin (the Law Librarian at Magee) who has very patiently and generously supported me, addressing all my enquires.

I am very thankful to Professor Abdullahi Ahmed An-Na'im and Professor Martha Fineman (both at Emory University, USA) for their kindness and generous support. I am also very thankful to colleagues at the International Islamic University (Malaysia), Dhaka University (Bangladesh), Peshawar University (Pakistan) and Cornell Law School (United States) for their invitations and for allowing me to benefit from their research resources. I am grateful to Professor Danielle Conway-Jones (Hawaii Law School), Mr Kamran Arif (Peshawar University) and

Mr Saman Mosafi (an Iranian scholar based in London) for their comments and support in the completion of this book. I am extremely thankful to my research assistants Daisy Cooper, Patrick Ferrari and Rocio de la Calle Porta for their hard work and enormous support. I am enormously grateful to Richard Hart, Mel Hamill and other colleagues at Hart Publishing for their generous support and for agreeing to publish this book at very short notice. Finally, and most importantly, I would like to thank my family for their patience and understanding while I have been working on this difficult, complex and potentially controversial project. I would like to thank Maleeha, my parents, my sisters and their families for their love, kindness and support. I undertake responsibility for any errors and omissions. I have been able to take account of law and information available to me up until the end of October 2004, although minor amendments have been possible at proof stage.

Javaid Rehman
City of Derry, Northern Ireland
February 2005

Contents

Acknowledgements   vii
Table of Cases   xiii
Table of Treaties   xv
Glossary   xix

Introductory Reflections and the Scope of the Study   1

Scope of the Study   3
Structure of the Book   4
The 'Clash of Civilisations' and the 'New World Order'   7

1 The Sources of *Sharia* and the Ethos of an 'Islamic' Identity   10

Introduction   10
The Sources of the *Sharia* and *Siyar*   11
Secondary Sources of *Sharia*   14
Understanding the Content and Scope of the *Sharia*   15
Extrapolating Legal Norms from Religious Sources   17
Permutations of Legal Schools of Thought   18
Surveying Islamic State Practices   21
Impact of European Imperialism upon the Muslim Peoples   24
Modern Islamic States and Issues of Islamic Identity   26
The Organisation of the Islamic Conference (OIC)   27
Institutions of the OIC   28
Subsidiary Organs of the OIC   30
Affiliated Insitutions   33
Additional Institutions   37
Specialised Institutions and Organs   37
Standing Committees   40
Conclusions   42

2 The *Sharia* and *Siyar* in the Development of the Law of Nations   44

Introduction   44
Sharia and the Law of Nations   45
Jihad, Violence and International Terrorism: Articulation of Legal
     Principles   51
Contextualising *Jihad* and the Use of Force: Intertemporal Law and
     Compatibilities with Modern Norms of International Law   53

The Use of Force and Religious Tolerance   60
Ideology of Tolerance and Modern State Practices   65
Conclusions   69

3 Conceptualising Terrorism in the International Legal Order 71

Introduction   71
The Definitional Issues   73
Recent Developments on Definitional Issues   77
Review of Comparative Regional Perspectives on Terrorism   79
Examining the Substance of Terrorism in the Development of
    International Law   83
International Efforts to Formulate Legal Principles Prohibiting
    All Forms of Terrorism   85
Dealing with Specific Terrorist Activities   92
Conclusions   95

4 Hostage-Taking in International Law and Terrorism   97
against 'Internationally Protected Persons'

Introduction   97
Hostage Taking: Denial of Fundamental Human Rights and the
    Breach of Peremptory Norms of International Law   98
Islamic Perspectives on the Convention   101
Internationally Protected Persons and International Law   112
The New York Convention and Internationally Protected Persons   113
Islamic Perspectives on the Protection of Diplomats   117
Articulation of the Rights of Internationally Protected Persons
    Under Islamic Law   119
The *Sharia* and Hostage-Taking of Internationally Protected
    Persons   123
Abuse of Immunity by Internationally Protected Persons   126
Conclusions   129

5 Aerial and Maritime Terrorism   130

Introduction   130
Aerial Terrorism   131
Combating Aerial Terrorism   132
Dealing with Aerial Sabotage   136
Islamic Treaty Ratifications on Aerial Terrorism   139
Incidents of Conflict and Islamic States   141
Judiciousness and Approaches to Accountability   142
Accountability for Terrorist Offences   151
Maritime Terrorism   152

The *Achille Lauro* Incident and Islamic State Practices   153
Examining the Legitimacy of the US Use of Force   155
The Adoption of the Convention   155
Human Rights Concerns   157
Islamic States' Involvement with the Maritime Convention   159
Conclusions   161

6 Financing of International Terrorism   **163**

Introduction   163
The United Nations and Attempts to Curb Financing of
   International Terrorism   165
Combating Financing of Terrorism: The International Convention
   for the Suppression of the Financing of Terrorism (1999)   168
9/11 and Implications for Islamic Communities and Institutions   183
Curbing the Financing of Terrorism and Islamic State Practices   186
Conclusions   189

7 The OIC and Approaches to International Terrorism   **191**

Introduction   191
Terrorism, Antagonism and a Lack of Trust Amongst Islamic States 192
The Establishment of the OIC: Reacting to External Aggression   194
Aggression and Terrorism versus the Right to Self-determination:
   Cases of Crises   200
The OIC and Legal Instruments Combating International
   Terrorism   210
The Role of the OIC and its Member States in the Aftermath of
   11 September 2001   217
Conclusions   220

8 Concluding Observations   **221**

Positioning Islam within the Context of International Terrorism   221
Rationalising the debate on a Culture of Conflict and the 'Clash of
   Civilisations'   223
11 September 2001, Islamophobia and the Future for Muslims   227

Select Bibliography   231
Index   247

Table of Cases

767 Third Avenue Associates v Permanent Mission of the Republic of Zaire to
the United Nations 988 F 2d 295 (1993)... 126

Abbasi (R on application of) v Secretary of State for the Foreign and
Commonwealth Office [2002] EWCA Civ 1316 229
Aden and Others v Council and Commission T–306/01 R1 185
Aerial Incident of 3 July 1988 (Islamic Republic of Iran v United States
of America) [1989] ICJ Rep 132 144–5
Al-Megrahi v HM Advocate, Opinion in Appeal against Conviction,
14 March 2002 (Appeal No c104/01) 150
Arbitral Award of 31 July 1989 (Guinea-Bissau v Senegal) [1990]
ICJ Rep 64 25

Barcelona Traction, Light and Power Co (Belgium v Spain) [1970]
ICJ Rep 3 197

Case Concerning the Aerial Incident of 3 July 1988, Islamic Republic
of Iran v United States of America, 22 February 1996, General
List No 79 145
Case Concerning Questions of Interpretation and Application of the 1971
Montreal Convention Arising from the Aerial Incident at Lockerbie
(Libyan Arab Jimahuriya v United States of America) 10 September
2003, General List No 89 151
Case Concerning United States Diplomatic and Consular Staff in Tehran
(United States of America v Iran) Request for the Indication of
Provisional Measures [1979] ICJ Rep 7 121–2

East Timor Case (Portugal v Australia) [1995] ICJ Rep 90 197
El Salvador v Honduras (Nicaragua Intervening) [1992] ICJ Rep 351 25

Frontier Dispute Case (Burkina Faso v Republic of Mali) [1986]
ICJ Rep 554 25

Her Majesty's Advocate v Megrahi, No 1475/99 (2001) 40 ILM 582 150

Legal Consequences for States of the Continued Presence of South Africa
in Namibia (South West Africa) Notwithstanding Security Council
Resolution 276 [1971] ICJ Rep 16.. 197

Legal Consequences of the Construction of a Wall in the Occupied
  Palestinian Territory (2004) <http://www.icj-cij.org/icjwww/
  idecisions.htm> 208
Libya v UK; Libya v US Question of Interpretation and Application
  of the 1971 Montreal Convention Arising from the Aerial Incident
  at Lockerbie, Order of 14 April 1992 [1992] ICJ Rep 3 148
Libyan Arab Jimahuriya v USA [1988] ICJ Rep 115 149

Nicaragua Case (Merits) [1986] ICJ Rep 14 166

Questions of Interpretation and Application of the 1971 Montreal
  Convention arising from the Aerial Incident at Lockerbie, Libyan
  Arab Jimahuriya v United Kingdom [1998] ICJ Rep 9 149

Rann of Kutch Arbitration (1968) 50 ILR 2 25

South West Africa Cases (Second Phase) [1966] ICJ Rep 6 196
Sovereignty over Certain Frontiers (*Belgium v the Netherlands*)
  [1959] ICJ Rep 209 25
State Bank of India v The Custodian of Evacuee Property, West Pakistan
  (1969) PLD, Lahore, 1050 50

Taba Award (*Egypt v Israel*) (1989) 80 ILR 224 25
Temple of Peach Vihear Case (*Merits*) (*Cambodia v Thailand*) [1962]
  ICJ Rep 6 25

United States Diplomatic and Consular Staff in Tehran (*United States*
  of America v Iran) [1980] ICJ Rep 3 .... 99, 121, 123

Western Sahara Case [1975] ICJ Rep 12 197

Table of Treaties

1535 Treaty of Alliance (Between Sultan Sulayman, the Magnificent
of the Ottoman Empire, and Francis I, King of France) 48
1648 Treaty of Westphalia 7
1937 Convention for the Prevention and Punishment of
Terrorism 75, 86
1944 Chicago Convention 144
1945 Agreement for the Prosecution and Punishment of Major
War Criminals (London Agreement) and Charter of the
International Military Tribunal (Nuremberg) 86
1945 Charter of the United Nations 53, 60, 174, 208
1945 Statute of the International Court of Justice 13, 14
1948 Convention on the Prevention and Punishment of the Crime
of Genocide 67
1949 Geneva Convention I for the Amelioration of the Condition
of the Wounded and the Sick in Armed Forces in the Field 105
1949 Geneva Convention II for the Amelioration of the Condition
of the Wounded, Sick and Shipwrecked of Armed Forces
at Sea 105
1949 Geneva Convention III Relative to the Treatment of Prisoners
of War 229
1949 Convention IV Relative to the Protection of Civilian Persons
in Time of War 105–7
1950 Agreement between India and Pakistan Concerning
Minorities 68
1958 Convention on High Seas 152–3
1961 Vienna Convention on Diplomatic Relations 112, 119,
122, 125, 126–9
1963 Vienna Convention on Consular Relations 112, 122–3, 129
1963 Convention on Offences and Certain Other Acts Committed
on Board Aircraft 79, 93, 132–3, 136–7, 142, 212
1964 Universal Postal Union Convention and the Postal Parcels
Agreement banning insertion of explosives, flammable or
other dangerous substances in the mail 94
1965 International Convention on the Elimination of All Forms
of Racial Discrimination 196
1966 International Covenant on Economic, Social and Cultural
Rights 101, 177
1966 International Covenant on Civil and Political Rights 66

1969   Vienna Convention on the Law of Treaties 25, 176
1970   Convention for the Suppression of Unlawful Seizure of
       Aircrafts 79, 80, 82, 93, 134–9, 142, 156, 159, 169, 212
1971   OAS Convention to Prevent and Punish Acts of Terrorism
       Taking the Form of Crimes against Persons and Related
       Extortion that are of International Significance 93
1971   Convention for the suppression of Unlawful Acts against
       the Safety of Civil Aviation 79, 80, 82, 93, 136–8,
                                            140, 142, 144–6, 156, 159, 169, 212
1972   Charter of the Organisation of the Islamic Conference 194–5
1972   Convention on the Prohibition of the Development,
       Production and Stockpiling of Bacteriological and Toxin
       Weapons and on their Destruction 94
1973   International Convention on the Suppression and Punishment
       of the Crime of Apartheid 196
1973   Convention on the Prevention and Punishment of Crimes
       against Internationally Protected Persons, including
       Diplomatic Agents 79, 82, 92, 97, 112, 113–7,
                                                        125, 129, 156, 159, 169, 212
1977   European Convention on the Suppression of
       Terrorism 80, 93, 97
1977   Protocol Additional to the Geneva Conventions of 12 August
       1949, and Relating to the Protection of Victims of International
       Armed Conflicts (Protocol I) 106
1977   Protocol Additional to the Geneva Conventions of 12
       August 1949, and Relating to the Protection of Victims of
       Non-International Armed Conflicts (Protocol II) 106
1978   Vienna Convention of State Succession in Respect of
       Treaties 25
1979   International Convention against the Taking of
       Hostages 77, 79, 92, 99, 103, 108, 129, 159, 161, 169, 212
1979   Convention on the Physical Protection of Nuclear Materials 79
1979   Convention on the Elimination of All Forms of Discrimination
       against Women 178, 222
1980   Convention on the Physical Protection of Nuclear
       Material 93, 169, 213
1981   African Charter on Human and People's Rights 101
1982   Law of the Sea Convention 152–3, 213
1987   SAARC Regional Convention on Suppression of
       Terrorism 82, 94
1988   Protocol for the Suppression of Unlawful Acts of Violence
       at Airports Serving International Civil Aviation, supplementary
       to the Convention for the Suppression of Unlawful Acts
       against the Safety of Civil Aviation 93, 138, 140, 156, 169, 213

1988   Convention for the Suppression of Unlawful Acts against
       the Safety of Maritime Navigation 79, 93, 155–7, 157–9, 169, 213
1988   Protocol for the Suppression of Unlawful Acts against the
       Safety of Fixed Platforms Located on the Continental
       Shelf 79, 93, 169, 213
1989   United Nations Convention on the Rights of the Child 177
1991   Convention on the Marking of Plastic Explosives for the
       Purpose of Detection 93, 142, 213
1993   Convention on the Prohibition of the Development,
       Production, Stockpiling and Use of Chemical Weapons
       and on their Destruction 94
1997   International Convention for the Suppression of Terrorist
       Bombings 92, 169, 213
1998   Arab Convention on the Suppression of Terrorism 79, 93
1998   Rome Statute of the International Criminal Court 108
1999   OAU Convention on the Prevention and Combating of
       Terrorism 81, 93–4
1999   Convention of the Organisation of the Islamic Conference
       on Combating International Terrorism 186, 191, 210–20
1999   International Convention for the Suppression of the
       Financing of Terrorism 93, 165, 167, 168–183
1999   Treaty on Co-operation among States Members of the
       Commonwealth of Independent States in Combating
       Terrorism 94
1999   Agreement between the Netherlands and the United Kingdom
       Concerning a Scottish Trial in the Netherlands 149
2000   African Union, the Constitutive Act 25

Glossary

Ahal al-kitab	The Peoples of the Book
Allah	God, the Creator
Amân	Pledge of security and safe conduct
Dar-ul-Harb	The enemy territory; the territory at war with Islam
Dar-ul-Islam	Territory of Islam
Dhimmi	A member of one of the Peoples of the Book
Fiqh	The science of law, jurisprudence
Hadd (Had)	Limit; A crime against the Law of God for which prosecution and punishment in case of guilt is mandatory
Hadith	Saying; Event; Tradition (ie Tradition regarding the Prophet Muhammad). A literary form that communicates a *Sunna* of the Prophet Muhammad
Haram	Forbidden
Hawala	'to change or transform'; 'trust'; 'transfer of money between two persons through a third person'; 'reference'
Hirabah	Making War
Hudood	Plural of *Hadd (Had)*
Ijma	Consensus of qualified legal scholars
Ijtihad	General process of endeavour to comprehend the divine law; independent legal reasoning to formulate an opinion or view
Isnad	Source or Chain of narrators of *Hadith*
Istihsan	Equity; Juristic Preference
Jizya	Capitulation tax; Poll tax
Kafir	Non-Believer
Madrasas	Religious schools
Matin	Substance of *Hadith*
Millet	Nation
Mjutahid	One who engages in *Ijtihad*
Naskh	Abrogation
Qadi	An Islamic Judge
Qisas	Crimes against the person (murder, homicide, maiming, serious bodily harm) for which retaliation or compensation (*Diyya*) is due
Qiyas	Application by analogy or deduction
Qur'an	The Holy Book; the principal source of Islamic Law
Riba	Usury
Salaat	Prayer

Salem Aleikum	May Peace be on you
Selm	Peace
Sharia	Islamic law; the right path; literal meaning 'the road to the watering place'
Siyar	Islamic international law; branch of *Sharia* dealing with international relations
Sunna	The tradition and practices of Prophet Muhammad (PBUH)
Surahs/Surras	Chapters of the Holy Book, the *Qur'an*
Tahkím	Mediation
Taqlid	Imitation; Legal conformity
Tazir	The literal meaning is to admonish or to punish (with a view to correcting). Refers to offences against public welfare, morals and safety and those against private and personal interests which can be categorised as neither *Hudood* nor *Qisas* and for which prosecution and punishment is discretionary
Ummah	A community having a common religion. The Muslim community
Usul	Roots or Source of the Law
Waqf	Pious endowment; a charitable trust dedicated to some pious, socially beneficial purpose
Zakat	Legal Almsgiving, calculated on the basis of one's wealth

Introductory Reflections and the Scope of the Study

We must be aware of the superiority of our civilisation, a system that has guaranteed well-being, respect for human rights—and in contrast with Islamic countries—respect for religious and political rights. Islamic civilisation is stuck where it was fourteen hundred years ago.[1]

It gives us great credibility to say to the Muslim world: Where have you been since 9/11? Where are your voices of reason? You humbly open all your prayers in the name of God of mercy and compassion. But when members of your faith, acting in the name of Islam, murdered Americans or committed suicide against 'infidels' your press extolled them as martyrs and your spiritual leaders were largely silent. Other than a few ritual condemnations, they offered no outcry in their mosques; they drew no moral red lines in their schools. That's a problem, because if there isn't a struggle within Islam—over norms and values—there is going to be a struggle between Islam and us.[2]

ISLAM AND ISLAMIC law (the *Sharia*) continue to be the subjects of intense debate and controversy.[3] Since the events of 11 September 2001, and the subsequent military interventions in Afghanistan and Iraq by the United States and its allies, Islam and Islamic legal principles have become the focus of world attention. Critics of Islam argue that Islam per

---

[1] Italian Prime Minister, Silvio Berlusconi, comments made in Berlin, 26 September 2001. These comments have been cited extensively: see A Palmer, 'Is the West Really Best' *Sunday Telegraph* 30 September 2001 at 14; A Osburn, 'On the Brink of War: Reaction—Scorn Poured on Berlusconi Views—European and Muslim Leaders Express Disgust' *The Guardian* September 2001 at 4; BBC News 'EU deplores "Dangerous" Islam Jibe' <http://news.bbc.co.uk/1/hi/world/middle_east/1565664.stm > (9 October 2004).

[2] TL Friedman, 'Noah and 9/11' *New York Times* 11 September 2002 at 33.

[3] AA An-Na'im, *Toward an Islamic Reformation: Civil Liberties, Human Rights and International Law* (Syracuse NY, Syracuse University Press, 1990); FM Denny, *An Introduction to Islam* (New York, Macmillan Pub Co, 1994); AE Mayer, *Islam and Human Rights: Tradition and Politics* 2nd edn (Boulder, Col, Westview Press, 1995); CG Weeramantry, *Islamic Jurisprudence: An International Perspective* (London, Macmillan Press, 1988); R Landau, *Islam and the Arabs* (London, George Allen and Unwin Ltd, 1958); MA Baderin, *International Human Rights and Islamic Law* (Oxford, Oxford University Press, 2003); R Afshari, 'An Essay on Islamic Cultural Relativism in the Discourse of Human Rights' (1994) 16 *Human Rights Quarterly* 235; PJ Riga, 'Islamic Law and Modernity: Conflict and Evolution' (1991) 36 *American Journal of Jurisprudence* 103; J Entelis, 'International Human Rights: Islam's Friend or Foe? Algeria as an Example of the Compatibility of International Human Rights regarding Women's Equality and Islamic Law' (1997) 20 *Fordham International Law Journal* 1251; SS Ali, *Gender and Human Rights in Islam and International Law: Equal Before Allah, Unequal Before Man?* (The Hague, Kluwer Law International, 2000).

se is an aggressive religion advocating recourse to violence, terrorism and destruction.[4] In order to reinforce their prejudices against Islam they point to a lack of constitutionalism, abuse of power, political manipulation and violations of fundamental human rights in many Islamic States. Doubts have also been expressed as to whether the *Sharia* is capable of accommodating global economic policies and dealing effectively with the challenges of modernisation. Classical Islamic banking with the prohibition on usury has been castigated as antiquated and impractical.[5] Islamic financial institutions have, since 11 September 2001, been increasingly linked with terrorism and significant curbs have been placed upon schemes such as the *Hawala* system.[6]

More fundamentally, Islam as a religion has been equated with the wars of aggression, fanaticism, intolerance and violence.[7] Islam is labelled as 'a religion of the sword [that glorifies] military virtues'.[8] The 'violent origin' of Islam, according to one commentator, is 'stamped in the foundations of Islam'.[9] Islamic civilisation has been symbolised as backward, insular, stagnant, unable to deal with the demands of the twenty-first century.[10] The terrorist attacks of 11 September 2001 have unfortunately provided vital ammunition to those who had hitherto been restrained though deeply suspicious of Islam and Muslims. 'Islamabophia', a term of art, now finds a firm place both in societal discourses and in the psyche of State practices.[11]

---

[4] 'Many horrific acts have been, and continue to be carried out in the name of Islam, just as they have been in the name of Christianity. But unlike Islam, Christianity does not justify the use of all forms of violence. Islam does.' P Sookhdeo, 'A Religion that Sanctions Violence' *Daily Telegraph* 17 September 2001 at 22.

[5] See I Bantekas, 'The International Law of Terrorist Financing' (2003) 97 *American Journal of International Law* 315 at 320; B Zagaris, 'Financial Aspects of the War on Terror: The Merging of the Counter-Terrorism and Anti-Money Laundering Regimes' (2002) 34 *Law and Policy International Business* 45; J Rehman, 'Islamic Perspectives on International Economic Law' in AH Qureshi (ed), *Perspectives in International Economic Law* (The Hague, Kluwer Law International, 2002) 235–58.

[6] See Report by the International Bar Association's Task Force on International Terrorism, *International Terrorism: Legal Challenges and Responses* (Ardsley NY, Transnational Publishers, 2003) at 119.

[7] JL Esposito, *The Islamic Threat: Myth or Reality?* (Oxford, Oxford University Press, 1992) at 5; A Cassese, *Terrorism, Politics and Law: The Achille Lauro Affair* (Cambridge, Polity Press, 1989) at 1.

[8] SP Huntington, *The Clash of Civilizations and the Remaking of World Order* (London, Simon & Schuster, 1996) at 263.

[9] JL Payne, *Why Nations Arm* (Oxford, Basil Blackwell, 1989) at 127.

[10] Conor Cruise O'Brien echoes these views in a highly insensitive and offensive manner. He writes, 'Muslim society looks profoundly repulsive . . . It looks repulsive because it *is* repulsive . . . A Westerner who claims to admire Muslim society, while still adhering to Western values, is either a hypocrite or an ignoramus, or a bit of both . . . Arab and Muslim society is sick, and has been sick for a long time'. CC O'Brien, 'Sick Man of the World' *The Times* 11 May 1989.

[11] Muslim minorities in Europe and North American have been made victims of 'Islamophobia'. Concern for the Muslim diasporas in Europe and the United States has been so grave that in its fifty-ninth session the Human Rights Commission requested the Special

The operatives of terrorism have invoked religion—chronicles of human history testify to the tragic involvement of religion with wars, violence and terrorism. In that sense, Islam, as an instrument of exploitation is no different from other religions and philosophies. Muslim history is littered with instances where acts of violence, terrorism and negation of human rights have been conducted ostensibly to promote Islam, the *Sharia* or the Islamic ideology.[12] Many dictatorial regimes have thrived on the pretext of establishing an Islamic social and legal order.[13]

SCOPE OF THE STUDY

The present research is not an exercise in theology, nor is it an examination of the history and politics of Islam. The focus of this research is upon those aspects of Islamic law (the *Sharia*) and the *Siyar* (Islamic international law) that relate directly to international terrorism and violations of human rights. In conducting such an examination the fundamental objective is to eradicate existing misconceptions that have linked the Islamic legal systems per se with international terrorism. The study takes the view that notwithstanding considerable ideological and conceptual deviances, modern Islamic State practices are broadly in agreement with international laws prohibiting acts of terrorism. Indeed, in a number of instances, Islamic States have taken the lead in developing international

Rapporteur on the contemporary forms of racism, racial discrimination, xenophobia and related intolerance to examine the situation confronting Muslim and Arab peoples all over the world regarding physical assaults and other forms of attack against their places of worship, cultural places, businesses and properties since the events of 11 September 2001. See Commission on Human Rights, Sixtieth Session, Annotations of Provisional Agenda E/CN.4/2004/I/Add.1 para 29; for further analysis see J Rehman, 'International Terrorism, Sharia and Muslim Minorities in Europe: Islamophobia after 9/11' (2005) 3 *European Yearbook of Minority Issues* 217.

[12] Some of these harrowing memories emerge inter alia from the seizure of the Holy Grand Mosque in Mecca on 20 November 1979 by a dissident extremist faction with the apparent objective of 'cleansing' Islam—see 'Saudi Arabia—Occupation of the Grand Mosque' *Keesings Contemporary Archives* 16 May 1980, at 30247; the seizure of the American Diplomatic and Consular Staff in Tehran (1979)—see L Gross, 'The Case Concerning United States Diplomatic and Consular Staff in Tehran: Phase of Provisional Measures' (1980) 74 *American Journal of International Law* 395; K Grzybowski, 'The Regime of Diplomacy and the Tehran Hostages' (1981) 30 *International & Comparative Law Quarterly* 42; the attack on the Twin Towers (2001); and the Bali Bombing (2002)—see J Aglionby, 'Smiling Bomber to Face Firing Squad for Bali Blasts: Relatives in Court Cheer and Weep—But Fear Execution will Create a Martyr' *The Guardian Unlimited* (8 August 2003) <http://www.guardian.co.uk/international/story/0,,1014406,00.html> (19 September 2004). For a useful summary of terrorist attacks see B Davies, *Terrorism: Inside a World Phenomenon* (London, Virgin Books, 2003) at 93–127.

[13] J Rehman, 'Accommodating Religious Identities in an Islamic State: International Law, Freedom of Religion and the Rights of Religious Minorities' (2000) 7 *International Journal on Minority and Group Rights* at 139; J Rehman, 'Minority Rights and Constitutional Dilemmas of Pakistan' (2001) 19 *Netherlands Quarterly of Human Rights* 417.

norms in combating terrorism. Therefore, as the thesis advances, Islam or the application of *Sharia* are not the most critical elements in the presence or escalation of terrorism emanating from the Islamic world; terrorism is a product of and a reaction to a whole host of factors, not least the presence of real or perceived exploitation and abuse.

Much of the debate centres around modern Islamic State practices, although in order to conduct a fruitful analysis a number of conceptual and historical factors have been assessed. It is important to have a basic understanding of the sources of Islamic law, the *Sharia*. The *Sharia*, as the study reveals, does not represent a monolithic body of legal regulations. The complex and amorphous nature of the Islamic legal systems has allowed a variety of interpretations. It is argued that while a narrow, insular view of the *Sharia* is antithetical to international law, there are considerable possibilities of reform and conformity within existing structures.

While the focus of this book is upon Islamic States, their practices in combating terrorism can only be evaluated and assessed in the light of contemporary international legal standards. These standards, reflected through both customary and treaty law, are analysed in significant detail. There is also a critical examination of the contributions of Islamic States in formulating these standards and advancing international law towards effective implementation.

STRUCTURE OF THE BOOK

The study consists of the present introductory comments and eight additional chapters. Chapter 1 provides a basic understanding of the primary and secondary sources of the *Sharia* and *Siyar*. It also examines the meaning and substance of a number of key concepts such as *Jihad*, freedom of religion and rights of minorities within *Sharia* and *Siyar*. The issue of identity for the Muslim world has been of critical significance. There is a highly charged debate as to the basis and rationale for claiming an Islamic identity. What makes a State 'Islamic'?[14] Is the proportion of population claiming to practice a particular philosophy or religion the key indicator in determining the identity of the State they inhabit?[15] To what extent do minorities or other ethnically and racially differing communities have a role in forming this identity?[16]

[14] See M Kahf, 'International Trade Patterns of the Muslim Countries' in Islamic Council of Europe (ed), *The Muslim World and the Future Economic Order* (London, Islamic Council of Europe, 1979) 199–222; N Yalcintas, 'Trade and Co-operation among Muslim Countries', *ibid*, at 223–41.

[15] J Rehman, 'Accommodating National Identity: New Approaches to International and Domestic Law—Concluding Reflections' (1999) 6 *International Journal on Minority and Group Rights* 267.

[16] The identification and definition of 'minorities' itself has been a complex subject of international law: see J Rehman, 'Minority Rights in International Law: Raising the

During the colonial phases, Muslim communities remained under the shadow of alien rule, their sense of identity having being modified and manipulated by European encroachments. In the modern, post-colonial phase Islamic States have found it difficult to forge an identity. Having emerged from the rubble of colonisation, their geographical and political landscapes bear substantial marks of European imperialism. In their existing incarnation, the Islamic States, have to accept the dominance of western industrialised world. Their limited and frequently ineffectual position is evident in the workings of politically powerful and resourceful executive institutions such as the United Nations Security Council.

Although of relatively recent origins, a number of States have asserted an Islamic identity both at the domestic and international scenes. In emphasising upon an Islamic identity, these States have relied inter alia upon the role of the *Sharia* in their constitutional and legislative processes, religious beliefs and sentiments of their populations as well as their leanings and membership of international organisations that promote this identity.[17] The principal organisation, with a specific agenda of promoting the economic and political interests of Islamic States is The Organisation of Islamic Conference (OIC).[18] With its exclusive focus on promoting the interests of Muslims, the OIC and its Member States project a unique Islamic identity. In the light of this commitment of the OIC Member States towards forging an Islamic identity, the present study focuses on the practices of these States.

In order for a proper assessment of Islamic State practices, an overall conceptual understanding of international terrorism remains of critical importance. Chapter 3 of the study is dedicated to an examination of the conceptual and definitional issues of terrorism in general international law. An engagement with this subject, however, reveals substantial complexities. There is no consensus definition of 'terrorism'. Perceptions vary in differentiating a 'terrorist' from a 'freedom fighter'.[19] The conceptual disagreements have not only proved an impediment in drafting substantive legal provisions in combating terrorism, but they also impinge upon the extradition and trials of perpetrators of terror.

Conceptual Issues' (1998) 72 *Australian Law Journal* 615; J Rehman, 'International Law and Indigenous Peoples: Definitional and Practical Problems' (1998) 3 *Journal of Civil Liberties* 224.

[17] H Moinuddin, *The Charter of the Islamic Conference and Legal Framework of Economic Cooperation Among its Member States: A Study of the Charter, the General Agreement for Economic, Technical and Commercial Co-operation and the Agreement for Promotion, Protection and Guarantee of Investments Among Member States of the OIC* (Oxford, Clarendon Press, 1987); Rehman, n 5 above, at 235–58.

[18] Moinuddin, *ibid*.

[19] See G Levitt, 'Is "Terrorism" Worth Defining?' (1986) 13 *Ohio Northern University Law Review* 97; JF Murphy, 'Defining International Terrorism: A Way Out of the Quagmire' (1989) 19 *Israel Yearbook of Human Rights* 13.

Chapter 4 evaluates the implications of terrorist acts of hostage taking and other violations on the rights of internationally protected persons. The study confirms that the protection of diplomats and the inviolability of their persons and properties is a principle enshrined within classical *Sharia*. Islamic States have been key contributors to developing norms of diplomatic immunities.[20] In so far as the issue of hostage-taking is concerned, while there has been considerable involvement of Muslim States in the drafting the Convention on Hostage Taking, differences have surfaced over the exceptional position of National Liberation Movements (NLMs).[21]

The phenomenon of Aerial and Maritime terrorism is considered in chapter 5 of the study. Aerial terrorism represents a troubling feature of modern civil aviation and in the aftermath of 11 September 2001 it is of absolute necessity to reassess the value of existing regulations on air transportation. While analysing the *Lockerbie* and the 11 September cases, the study highlights the difficulties in accountability for acts of terrorism.[22] The seizure of the *Achille Lauro*, and killing on board the ship of a disabled elderly hostage represents the most significant incident of maritime terrorism. The chapter investigates the details of the incident and assesses its implications upon international maritime law.[23]

Chapter 6 deals with the convoluted though crucial area of financing of international terrorists. The debate on financing terrorism has been volatile and international law of late has adopted stringent mechanisms to ensure banning of all forms of financial and economic support to those invoking violence and terrorism.[24] However, as the study explains, the detection of all the financial avenues through which terrorism can be

---

[20] MC Bassiouni, 'Protection of Diplomats under Islamic Law' (1980) 74 *American Journal of International Law* 609 at 610.

[21] See J Lambert, *Terrorism and Hostages in International Law: A Commentary on the Hostages Convention 1979* (Cambridge, Grotius Publishers, 1990); E Chadwick, *Self-determination, Terrorism and the International Law of Armed Conflict* (The Hague, Martinus Nijhoff Publishers, 1996); WD Verwey, 'The International Hostages Convention and the International Liberation Movements' (1981) 75 *American Journal of International Law* 69.

[22] See SE Evans, 'The Lockerbie Incident Cases: Libyan-Sponsored Terrorism, Judicial Review and the Political Question Doctrine' (1994) 18 *Maryland Journal of International Law and Trade* 21; A Klip and M Mackarel, 'The Lockerbie Trial—A Court in the Netherlands' (1999) 70 *Revue International de Droit Penale* 777; R Black, 'Analysis: The Lockerbie Disaster' (1999) 3 *Edinburgh Law Review* 85.

[23] See A Cassese, n 7 above; MD Larsen, 'The Achille Lauro Incident and the Permissible Use of Force' (1987) 9 *Loyola of Los Angeles Journal of International and Comparative Law* 481; M Halberstam, 'Terrorism on the High Seas: The Achille Lauro, Piracy, and the IMO Convention on Maritime Safety' (1988) 82 *American Journal of International Law* 269.

[24] See E Rosand, 'Security Council Resolution 1373, the Counter-Terrorism Committee, and the Fight Against Terrorism' (2003) 97 *American Journal of International Law* 333, at 334; M Levitt, 'Iraq, US and the War on Terror: Stemming the Flow of Terrorist Financing: Practical and Conceptual Challenges' (2003) 27 *The Fletcher Forum of World Affairs Journal* 59.

supported remains problematic. An overzealous approach, as reflected in recent State practices of the United States and the United Kingdom, can result in undermining Islamic financial institutions and the rights of communities which have been reliant upon those institutions.

The position of the OIC, the premier Islamic organisation, is assessed and evaluated in chapter 7. As the chapter elaborates, the OIC has played a prominent role in resolving inter-State disputes such as the *Lockerbie* crisis.[25] The OIC was also at the forefront of condemning the terrorist attacks of 11 September. In the aftermath of the tragedy in the US, the OIC made all possible efforts to mediate between the Taliban government and the United States administration for the extradition of Usama Bin Laden. At the inter-governmental level, the OIC has developed a detailed and comprehensive treaty on international terrorism. The chapter examines the various provisions of the OIC Convention on Terrorism. There is also a survey of the legislative and administrative practices undertaken by individual Member States of the organisation. The final chapter, chapter 8, advances a number of concluding observations on this subject. The involvement of modern Islamic States in international laws on the prohibition of terrorism has evolved over time. Evidence of this intercourse is reflected in the plethora of international, regional and national instruments.[26]

THE 'CLASH OF CIVILISATIONS' AND THE 'NEW WORLD ORDER'

There have been many phases in the modern developments of international law. Legal historians and analysts have varyingly classified the Treaty of Westphalia, the Congress of Vienna, the League of Nations, the establishment of the United Nations and the collapse of the Berlin Wall as milestones of international law.[27] The present study advances the view that in a world under the domination of a single superpower, the most profound event has been in the form of terrorist attacks on 11 September 2001. The nature of these attacks was evil and horrific, and the international

[25] See A Aust, 'Lockerbie: The Other Case' (2000) 49 *International & Comparative Law Quarterly* 278, at 284.

[26] The most significant instruments can be located through a variety of sources. See United Nations Treaty Collection, Conventions on Terrorism <http://untreaty.un.org/English/Terrorism.asp> (9 October 2004).

[27] On the development history of international law see SC Neff, 'A Short History of International Law' in MD Evans (ed), *International Law* (Oxford, Clarendon Press, 2003) 31–58; L Gross, 'The Peace of Westphalia 1648–1948' (1948) 42 *American Journal of International Law* 20; MN Shaw, *International Law* 5th edn (Cambridge, Cambridge University Press, 2003) 1–41; A Nussbaum, *A Concise History of the Law of Nations*, revised edn (New York, Macmillan Co, 1954); M Koskenniemi, *The Gentle Civilizer of Nations: The Rise and Fall of International Law, 1870–1960* (Cambridge, Cambridge University Press, 2002).

community congregated in support of the United States to condemn and punish those involved in these atrocities. 11 September however allowed the United States to give up all its pretensions of working within the established framework of international law. Henceforth, the 'war on terrorism' would dominate international relations and development of laws. Arguments based on humanitarianism or human rights would be ineffective when dealing with perceived threats from terrorists. Since those engaged in the aerial attacks on 11 September were Arabs and Muslims, many individuals from the Islamic communities were stigmatised. The United States legislature preying upon its prejudices devised new laws and administrative policies, which targeted Arab and Muslims; thousands were arbitrarily arrested, detained and deported from the United States.[28]

The United States also embarked upon an expansionist and imperialist agenda. The invasion of Iraq took place in March 2003, and the United States deployed a range of arguments to justify its position.[29] Notwithstanding overwhelming opposition from world public opinion, the United States insisted upon the righteousness of its decision to invade Iraq. The United Kingdom government, and a number of other western leaders, unfortunately provided full support to the American administration. The consequences of this invasion, and its impact upon both the peoples of Iraq and the wider international community, it would appear, were not thought through rationally.[30] The aftermath of the Iraq invasion has raised question-marks over the ability of the United Nations to act as an organisation effective in its role of saving 'succeeding generations from the scourge of war, which . . . has brought untold sorrow to mankind'.[31]

The action from the United States has also tragically unleashed immeasurable forces of reaction and opposition in the Islamic world. Emerging

---

[28] See Amnesty International's Annual Report on the United States of America. The latest report details the violation of rights conducted by US authorities. AI Report, United States of America 2004 <http://web.amnesty.org/report2004/usa-summary-eng> (4 September 2004). According to Human Rights Watch, '[Since 11 September 2001 the USA] has witnessed a persistent, deliberate, and unwarranted erosion of basic rights against abusive governmental power that are guaranteed by the US Constitution and international human rights law. Most of those directly affected have been non-US citizens. Under Attorney General John Ashcroft, the Department of Justice has subjected them to arbitrary detention, violated due process in legal proceedings against them, and run roughshod over the presumption of innocence'. Human Rights Watch 'United States: Presumption of Guilt—Human Rights Abuses of Post-September 11 Detainees' <http://www.hrw.org/reports/2002/us911/USA0802.htm#P86_1667> (5 October 2004).

[29] See below chapter 8; see D McGoldrick, *From '9–11' to the 'Iraq War 2003': International Law in an Age of Complexity* (Oxford, Hart, 2004) 47–86.

[30] 'Blair "lacked post-Saddam plan". The Daily Telegraph published leaked papers suggesting the prime minister was warned in 2002 that an invasion could lead to instability' BBC News <http://news.bbc.co.uk/1/hi/uk_politics/3668776.stm> (18 September 2004).

[31] Preamble to the Charter of the United Nations 1945; Charter of the United Nations (signed 26 June 1945, entered into force 24 October 1945) 59 Stat 1031, TS 993, 3 Bevans 1153, UNTS xvi (892 UNTS 119), UKTS (1946) 67.

news of exploitation and abuse of the thousands of men, women and children in Iraq, Afghanistan and elsewhere has shattered the trust and belief of Muslims. The continuous violations of the rights of Palestinians, and an occupation of their lands by Israel is being perceived as a United States driven imperialist agenda. It is now firmly established in the minds of many Muslims all around the globe that in the twenty-first century, the principal colonial ambition of the United States is the invasion of Islamic holy lands, an occupation of Muslim nations and undermining of their values and traditions. The 'new world order' presents a dangerous prognosis of the self-fulfilling prophecy of an inevitable 'clash of civilisations' between the Islamic world and the west.[32]

---

[32] See AA An-Na'im, 'Upholding International Legality Against Islamic and American Jihad' in K Booth and T Dunne (eds), *Worlds in Collision: Terror and the Future of Global Order* (London, Palgrave, 2002) 162–72, at 164.

1

The Sources of Sharia and the Ethos of an 'Islamic' Identity

INTRODUCTION

ISLAM MEANS 'SUBMISSION' or 'surrender' to the Almighty and the one who surrenders is called a Muslim.[1] Islamic law is often referred to as the *Sharia*. The concept of *Sharia*, however, is not confined to legal norms, but conveys a more holistic picture; the Arabic translation of *Sharia* is 'the road to the watering place'.[2] Furthermore the *Sharia*, unlike Canon law or *Kirchenrecht*, does not simply represent religious laws, but covers a wide range of secular laws and ordinances.[3] These include areas as diverse as international commercial law, criminal law, constitutional and administrative law, humanitarian and human rights law.[4] The aspects of *Sharia* which regulate international law and the conduct of States

---

[1] FM Denny, *An Introduction to Islam* (New York, Macmillan Pub Co, 1994) 67; I Manzoor, *Lisān Al-Arab* vol XII (Beirut, Dar Sader, 1955) 293; DF Mulla, *Principles of Mahamedan Law* 18th edn (Lahore, PLD Publishers, 1990) xiv; HAR Gibb, *Mohammedanism: An Historical Survey* (London, Oxford University Press, 1949) 1; Bassiouni makes the pertinent point that Islam's 'derivation is from the word *Selm* or peace; wherefore the traditional Islamic greeting of *As Salam Aleikum*—May peace be on you'. MC Bassiouni, 'Sources of Islamic Law and the Protection of Human Rights in the Islamic Criminal Justice System' in MC Bassiouni (ed), *The Islamic Criminal Justice System* (London, Oceana Publications, 1982) 3–54, at 6.

[2] R Landau, *Islam and the Arabs* (London, George Allen and Unwin Ltd, 1958) 141; AA Oba, 'Islamic Law as Customary Law: The Changing Perspective in Nigeria' (2002) 51 *International & Comparative Law Quarterly* 817 at 819; AR Doi, *Sharíah: The Islamic Law* (London, Taha Publishers, 1997) 2; LW Adamec, *Historical Dictionary of Islam* (Lanham, Maryland and London, The Scarecrow Press, 2001) 241.

[3] H Moinuddin, *The Charter of the Islamic Conference and Legal Framework of Economic Cooperation Among its Member States: A Study of the Charter, the General Agreement for Economic, Technical and Commercial Co-operation and the Agreement for Promotion, Protection and Guarantee of Investments Among Member States of the OIC* (Oxford, Clarendon Press, 1987) 6; J Rehman, 'Islamic Perspectives on International Economic Law' in AH Qureshi (ed), *Perspectives in International Economic Law* (The Hague, Kluwer Law International, 2002) 235–58, at 236.

[4] S Mahmassani, 'The Principles of International Law in the Light of Islamic Doctrine' (1966) 117(1) *Recueil des cours de l'académie de droit international* 205 at 229; A Rahim, *The Principles of Muhammadan Jurisprudence According to the Hanafi, Maliki, Shafi'i and Hanbali Schools* (London, Luzac, 1911); GM Badr, 'Islamic Law: Its Relations to Other Legal Systems' (1978) 26 *American Journal of Comparative Law* 188.

towards each other are termed *Siyar*.[5] The *Siyar*, as we shall analyse, has been based on sources identical to the *Sharia*.

The present chapter has three fundamental objectives. Firstly, it examines the primary and secondary sources of the *Sharia* and the *Siyar*. As the present research establishes, extrapolating legal norms from the labyrinth of religious sources has been a taxing and complicated task for Islamic jurists and States in their practices. Secondly, the chapter aims to demonstrate that the *Sharia* and *Siyar* do not represent a monolithic system. Thirdly, there is the complex issue of an 'Islamic' identity. In their historical progression, many of the regions (where Islam survived and expanded) have undergone a metamorphosis; the transition into the period of modern international law has been difficult.[6] During this period, peoples within the Islamic faith had to accept changes in their legal and political status. Muslim Empires went through a phase of domination by European colonisation, and many of their religious and cultural values were undermined. The chapter addresses the question of Islamic 'identity' in this new world order.

THE SOURCES OF THE *SHARIA* AND *SIYAR*

A variety of primary and secondary sources constitute the *Sharia* and *Siyar*.[7] At the apex is the primary source of *Qur'an*,[8] which is accompanied and interpreted by the *Sunna* of Prophet Muhammad (Peace be Upon Him).[9] As we shall examine in due course, in addition to the primary sources *Ijma*, *Qiyas* and *Ijtihad* represent the secondary sources. Amongst these secondary sources for *Siyar*, jurists have also added the practices of Islamic rulers and caliphs, their official instruction to commanders and statesmen; constitutional laws and internal legislation of Islamic States both in the historic as well as in the modern era.[10]

---

[5] M Khadduri, *The Islamic Law of Nations—Shaybānī's Siyar: Translated with an Introduction, Notes and Appendices by M Khadduri* (Baltimore, Maryland, Johns Hopkins University Press, 1966) 5.

[6] See A Nussbaum, *A Concise History of the Law of Nations*, revised edn (New York, Macmillan Co, 1954); CH Alexandrowicz, *The European-African Confrontation: A Study in Treaty Making* (Leiden, Sijthof, 1973).

[7] NJ Coulson, *A History of Islamic Law* (Edinburgh, Edinburgh University Press, 1964) 9–20.

[8] On every occasion that the study mentions the *Qur'an*, reference to the terminology (the Holy Book) shall be assumed.

[9] On every occasion that the study mentions Prophet Muhammad, reference to the terminology (Peace be Upon Him) shall be assumed.

[10] Bassiouni regards the consistent practice of Muslim Heads of State (*the Khalifas*) as secondary sources of Islam. See MC Bassiouni, 'Protection of Diplomats under Islamic Law' (1980) 74 *American Journal of International Law* 609 at 609; M Hamidullah, *Muslim Conduct of State: Being a Treatise on Siyar, that is Islamic Notion of Public International Law, Consisting of the Laws of Peace, War and Neutrality, Together with precedents from Orthodox Practices and Precedent by a Historical and General Introduction* (Lahore, Sh Muhammad Ashraf, 1977) 28; M Khadduri, *War and Peace in the Law of Islam* (Baltimore and London, Johns Hopkins University Press, 1955) 44; I Hussain, *Issues in Pakistan's Foreign Policy: An International Law Perspective* (Lahore, Progressive Publishers, 1988) 100.

The *Qur'an*, according to the Muslim belief, represents the accumulation of the verses revealed by God to Prophet Muhammad.[11] According to the Muslim faith, every word of the Holy *Qur'an* is divine and cannot be challenged. Neither Prophet Muhammad nor any other human being had any influence over the divine book, save for its structuring and the names of the *Surahs* (chapters) which were established in the years that preceded the Prophet's death.[12] While meticulously noted down, and revealed in stages during the lifetime of the Prophet, the *Qur'an* was produced as an authentic text only during the currency of the third Caliph *Hazrat* Uthmān.[13] The *Qur'an* is aimed at establishing basic standards for Muslim societies and guiding these communities in terms of their rights and obligations. At the time of its revelation, it provided a set of progressive principles. It advances such values as compassion, good faith, justice and religious ethics. The *Qur'an*, however, is a religious text and is not a legal document per se. In reiterating these points, two leading comparative lawyers note that:

> [o]nly a few of the statements in the Koran constitute rules of law capable of direct application. It consists mainly of precepts of proper ethical behaviour too generally phrased to have the precision and point of legal rules. For example, the Koran prescribes that a Muslim must act in good faith, that he must not bribe judges, and that he must abstain from usury and gambling, but it does not specify what legal consequences, if any, attach to a disregard of these commandments. Furthermore most of the rules of behaviour contained in the Koran concern the rituals of prayer, fasting and pilgrimage; even where it deals with legal problems in the narrow sense, such as those of family law, it does not offer an integrated system of rules but simply gives the solution of a few individual problems with which MUHAMMAD was concerned as a judge and prophet of the law.[14]

The Sunna, the second principal source of Islam, represents model behaviour and is referred to as the tradition and practices of Muhammad, the Prophet of Islam. The *Sunna* of the Prophet has been expanded through the practices of Prophet Muhammad's followers and other Islamic leaders.[15] The concept of *Sunna* had been in vogue long before the birth of Prophet Muhammad and was actively practiced by contemporary Arab communities. While maintaining its characteristics, the application of

---

[11] CG Weeramantry, *Islamic Jurisprudence: An International Perspective* (London, Macmillan Press, 1988) 26; Denny, n 1 above, at 63; Landau, n 2 above, at 25; CB Lombardi, 'Islamic Law as a Source of Constitutional Law in Egypt: The Constitutionalization of the *Sharia* in a Modern Arab State' (1998) 37 *The Columbia Journal of Transnational Law* 81 at 92.

[12] Denny, n 1 above, at 63.

[13] Mahmassani, n 4 above, at 229; Coulson, n 7 above, at 13; K Zweigert and H Kötz, *Introduction to Comparative Law*, 3rd edn (Oxford, Clarendon Press, 1998) 305.

[14] *Ibid.*

[15] See below.

Prophet Muhammad's *Sunna* took on board a more profound spiritual and religious meaning. It was to be, after the word of God, the most revered source of knowledge and legal acumen. The *Sunna* of Prophet Muhammad in the words of one scholar 'is an idea as well as a memory, and even it is an ideal for Muslim behavior. As such it is engrained in the lives of pious Muslims and handed down by example and personal teaching'.[16] The memorisation and transmission of the *Sunna* in a literary form is characterised as *Hadith*. The term *Hadith*, meaning 'occurring, taking place', represents the 'report' of Prophet Muhammad's *Sunna*.[17] The *Sunna* of Prophet Muhammad therefore is preserved and communicated to succeeding generations through the means of *Hadiths*.[18] While the *Qur'an* was recorded within a relatively short time, the recording of the *Sunna* took a much longer period.[19] There is a significant debate over the authenticity and accuracy of some of the *Sunna* and there have been comments as to the possibility of fabrication in the recording of the *Sunna*. Commenting on this subject, Coulson makes the point that 'the extent of [Muhammad's] extra Qur'ānic law-making is the subject of the greatest single controversy in early Islamic legal theory'.[20]

If the concept of the *Qur'an* as providing binding ordinances and the *Sunna* of the Prophet is taken as the source of Islamic legal jurisprudence, then significant analogies can be drawn between the sources of the *Sharia* and that of modern international law. Article 38(1) of the Statute of the International Court of Justice, representing the sources of modern international law, provides for both treaties and customary law.[21]

---

[16] Denny, n 1 above, at 159.

[17] Weeramantry, n 11 above, at 34.

[18] A *Hadith* consists of two parts. *Isnad* and *Matin*. *Isnad* refers to the link, the source or the chain of narrators of the *Hadith*. Hence a *Hadith* in its *Isnad* would report the person who acted as transmitters. The *Matin* contains the substance of the Prophet's sayings, deeds or actions. See Denny, n 1 above, at 160–1; SH Al-Mūsawi, *Manhajul-Fiqhil-Islami, A Course in the Islamic Jurisprudence* (Tehran, Islamic Culture and Relations Organisation, 1997) at 21–2.

[19] Mahmassani, n 4 above, at 229.

[20] Coulson, n 7 above, at 22.

[21] According to Article 38(1): The Court, whose function is to decide in accordance with international law such disputes as are submitted to it, shall apply:

(a) international conventions, whether general or particular, establishing rules expressly recognised by the contesting states;

(b) international custom, as evidence of a general practice accepted as law;

(c) the general principles of law recognized by civilized nations;

(d) Subject to the provisions of Article 59, judicial decisions and the teachings of the most highly qualifies publicists of the various nations, as subsidiary means for the determination of rules of law.

Statute of the International Court of Justice (1945) UKTS 67 (1946) Cmnd 7015 (adopted 26 June 1945, entered into force 24 October 1945).

SECONDARY SOURCES OF *SHARIA*

In addition to the primary sources of the *Sharia*, there are a range of secondary sources which include *Ijma, Qiyas* and *Ijtihad*. *Ijma*, meaning 'consensus', is an important secondary source: it provides the Islamic community with essential tools to reach agreements. It is a powerful source instrumental in the interpretation of the *Qur'an* and *Sunna*. Prophet Muhammad himself endorsed the validity of *Ijma*. According to one *Hadith*, the Prophet is reported to have said, 'My People will never agree together on an error'.[22] Pursuing a comparative vision, further analogies can be drawn between the sources of modern international law and Islamic law: taking into account the views of jurists, *Ijma* can be regarded as akin to Article 38(1)(d) of the Statute of the International Court of Justice which allows for 'judicial decisions and the teachings of the most highly qualified publicists'.[23] Difficult questions arise, however, when investigations are made to devise the basis of this consensus. It would be stretching the concept of *Ijma* were it to be regarded as analogous to modern day western liberal democracy. According to the classical jurisprudence, consent of the whole Muslim community is not required.[24] *Ijma* became a powerful force for conformity and gradually dominated Islamic jurisprudence among the *Sunnis*, for whom it provided stability and a constant source of authentication. *Ijma*, as a doctrine, represents the traditional relationship with the community, the *Ummah*. Despite the undoubted value of *Ijma* as a source of the *Sharia*, debate has centred around the constituency of the *Ummah*, and the form of consensus. Does the *Ummah*, for example, only represent Muslims, or is the modern Islamic State under an obligation to seek and consider the opinion of its non-Muslim citizens?

A useful operation is also derived from *Qiyas*, which means application by analogy or deduction.[25] In the absence of concrete answers from the *Qur'an* and *Hadith*, Muslim jurists would look for an analogous situation in which a decision had been made.[26] A further secondary source of the

---

[22] Ibn Majah, from his collection of Hadith, 'Fitan' section; also cited in Weeramantry, n 11 above, at 39.

[23] Statute of the International Court of Justice, n 21 above, Article 38(1)(d).

[24] Coulson, n 7 above, at 77.

[25] MH Kamali, *Principles of Islamic Jurisprudence* (Cambridge, Islamic Texts Society, 1991) 197.

[26] According to a well-recited *Hadith*, the role of *Qiyas* was confirmed at the time when Prophet Muhammad (while sending Mu 'adh b. Jalal to Yemen to take the position of a *qadi*) asked him the following question: 'How will you decide when a question arises?' He replied, 'According to the Book of Allah'—'And if you do not find the answer in the Book of Allah?'— 'Then according to the *Sunna* of the Messenger of Allah'—'And if you do not find the answer either in the *Sunna* or in the Book?'—'Then I shall come to a decision according to my own opinion without hesitation.' Then the Messenger of Allah slapped Mu 'adh on the chest with his hand saying: 'Praise be to Allah who has led the Messenger of Allah to an answer that pleases him'. 'Kiyas' in HAR Gibb and JH Kramers (eds), *Shorter Encyclopaedia of Islam* (Ithaca, NY, Cornell University Press, 1953) 267.

Sharia is *Ijtihad*. *Ijtihad* is a term that refers to the use of independent legal reasoning in search of an opinion. *Ijtihad* conveys a sense of exertion, a struggle and has the same origins as *Jihad*.[27] Inherent in this self-exertion and struggle are the fundamentals for reforming society and its legal norms. *Ijtihad* and *Qiyas* are often used interchangeably, although the former represents a wider, more general undertaking. One who exercises *Ijtihad* is known as a *Mjutahid*. There were phases within the Islamic history when it was deemed that all doors towards *Ijtihad* had been closed; this development led to *Taqlid*, 'imitation' and acceptance of authority without engaging in original *Ijtihad*. After the inception of Islam, for centuries, Muslim scholars remained reluctant to rely upon the doctrine, since such an exercise implied questioning the time-honoured (though static) principles of the *Sharia*.[28] In order to make Islamic societies more compatible with the rapidly developing times, many scholars advocated the doctrine of *Ijtihad*. Foremost amongst these was the Egyptian jurist Muhammad 'Abduh, who advocated a reinterpretation of the *Sharia* to introduce legal reform.[29] Muhammad Iqbal, an Indian Muslim poet and scholar, argued that reliance upon *Ijtihad* was not only required but was also a duty of the Muslims if Islam was to adapt to the modern world.[30]

UNDERSTANDING THE CONTENT AND SCOPE OF THE *SHARIA*

There are a range of misconceptions regarding the meaning, content and scope of the *Sharia*. The first of these relates to a belief that the totality of Islamic law, its interpretation and application is the ultimate expression of the Almighty.[31] Islamic scholars have often found themselves restricted in a debate surrounding the *Sharia* because of existing perceptions that the totality of Islamic legal system is the word of God. Any analysis or attempts to review the *Sharia* would be tantamount to heresy. Such assertions are,

---

[27] B Weiss, 'Interpretation in Islamic Law: The Theory of Ijtihad' (1978) 26 *American Journal of Comparative Law* 367.

[28] See discussion by J Schacht, *An Introduction to Islamic Law* (Oxford, Clarendon Press, 1964) at 69; Coulson, n 7 above, at 80.

[29] MAZ Badawi, *The Reformers of Egypt* (London, Croom Helm, 1978) 35–95; JMS Baljon, *Modern Muslim Koran Interpretation* (Leiden, EJ Brill, 1968); E Kedourie, *Afghani and 'Abduh: An Essay on Religious Unbelief and Political Activism in Modern Islam* (London, Frank Cass & Co Ltd, 1997); M Asad, *The Message of the Qur'an: Translated and Explained by Muhammad Asad* (Gibraltar, Dar Al-Andalus, 1980).

[30] MK Mas'ud, *Iqbal's Reconstruction of Ijtihad* (Islamabad, Islamic Research Institute, 1995); MA Chaudhri, *The Muslim Ummah and Iqbal* (Islamabad, National Institute of Historical and Cultural Research, 1994); Z Kauser, *Islam and Nationalism: An Analysis of the Views of Azad, Iqbal and Maududi* (Kuala Lumpur, AS Noordeen, 1994).

[31] AA An-Na'im, *Toward an Islamic Reformation: Civil Liberties, Human Rights and International Law* (New York, Syracuse University Press, 1990); '[t]here is often a traditional misconception about Islamic law being wholly divine and immutable' MA Baderin, *International Human Rights and Islamic Law* (Oxford, Oxford University Press, 2003) 33.

however, misleading since there exists a clear distinction between the Islamic legal system (which represents evolutionary processes and in common with other legal systems needs constant review and change) and the fundamental principles of Islam, which remain unalterable. Thus, notwithstanding the fact that the *Sharia* regards the *Qur'an* and *Sunna* as its principal sources, distinctions between divine ordinances and man-made principles regulating societies are inevitable. *Sharia*, in this sense, is in fact no more than the understanding of early Muslims of the sources of Islam.[32] The Muslim jurists who developed the *Sharia* during the second and third centuries did so in accordance with their personal understanding and comprehension of the word of God. It is arguable that *Sharia* represents the human endeavour to understand and implement the core values and principles specifically referred to in the principal sources of Islam. Thus while the man-made legal principles are not immutable, the word of God as contained in the *Qur'an* and expanded upon by the *Sunna* remains indelible, having been preserved for humanity.[33]

A related cause of significant confusion is the general belief that the *Sharia* is rigid, stagnant and cannot be made to apply to evolving situations.[34] As subsequent discussion establishes, there is the substantial possibility of evolution in the Islamic legal systems. The true essence of the *Sharia* is brought out by Parwaz, who notes that '[t]he *Sharia* refers to a straight and clear path and also to a watering place where both humans and animals come to drink water, provided the source of water is a flowing stream or spring'.[35] It is therefore, as another scholar agues, 'no slight irony and tragedy that the *Sharia*, which has the idea of mobility

---

[32] An-Na'im, *ibid*.

[33] Bernard Weiss makes the poignant remark that '[a]lthough the law is of divine provenance, the actual construction of the law is a human activity, and its results represent the law of God as humanly understood. Since the law does not descend from heaven ready-made, it is the human understanding of the law—the human fiqh—that must be normative for society' BG Weiss, *The Spirit of Islamic Law* (Athens, GA, University of Georgia Press, 1998) 116.

[34] The issue of human involvement and interpretation of the divine lines has been a subject of debate amongst both oriental and western scholars. Two leading scholars of comparative law make the point that '[o]ne of the consequences is that Islamic law is in principle immutable, for it is the law revealed by God. Western legal systems generally recognize that the content of law alters as it is adapted to changing needs by the legislator, the judges, and all other social forces which have a part in the creation of law, but Islam starts from the proposition that all existing law comes from ALLAH who at a certain moment in history revealed it to man through his prophet MUHAMMAD. Thus Islamic legal theory cannot accept the historical approach of studying law as a function of the changing conditions of life in a particular society. On the contrary, the law of ALLAH was given to man once and for all: society must adopt itself to the law rather than generate laws of its own as a response to the constantly changing stimulus of the problems of life.' Zweigert and Kötz, n 13 above, at 304.

[35] GA Parwez, *Lughat-ul-Quran: Lexicon of the Qur'an—In Four Volumes* (Lahore, 1960) at 941.

built into its very meaning, should have become a symbol of rigidity for so many in the Muslim world'.[36]

EXTRAPOLATING LEGAL NORMS FROM RELIGIOUS SOURCES

One substantial complexity facing the early Islamic jurists in formulating principles of the *Sharia* related to finding compatibility between the legally authoritative though competing injunctions of the *Qur'anic* verses and the *Sunna*.[37] The *Qur'an* is not a legal text and in fact there is little in the *Qur'an* with strict legal content. From over 6000 verses of the *Qur'an*, strict legal content is arguably attached to only around 120 verses.[38] Save for a few specific offences there is no indication of criminal sanctions.[39] Some detailed legal rules can be identified regarding civil law, for example on family law and inheritance, some of which have been the subject of intense debate and argumentation.

As noted earlier, particular complications have arisen in articulating legal principles from a range of Islamic legal sources, some of which overlap or are in competition with each other. A useful mechanism for dealing with competing norms and values has been through the adoption of *Naskh*. The principle of *Naskh* allows for a process of abrogation or repeal of the legal efficacy of a *Qur'anic* verse. The revelation of the *Qur'an* coincides with the metamorphosis undergone by the Arab community over a period of twenty-three years. During this phase, two broad processes are of particular significance in terms of the substance of the message contained in the holy book: the Meccan stage and the Medina stage.[40] The

---

[36] R Hassain, 'The Role and Responsibilities of Women in the Legal and Religious Tradition of Islam', paper presented at a biannual meeting of a Trialogue of Jewish-Christian-Muslim scholars on 14 October 1980 at the Joseph and Rose Kennedy Institute of Ethics, Washington, DC, USA at 4.

[37] There still remains controversy surrounding the marginal traditions in the *Sunna*. See An-Na'im, n 31 above, at 16.

[38] See GM Badr, 'Islamic Law: Its Relations to Other Legal Systems' (1978) 26 *American Journal of Comparative Law* 188, at 188. According to Ali the legal content can be considered to be only around 80 verses. SS Ali, 'The Conceptual Foundations of Human Rights: A Comparative Perspective' (1997) 3 *European Public Law* 261 at 266. Glenn makes the observation that 'the Koran has some law, but not much, and it's hard to find.' HP Glenn, *Legal Traditions of the World: Sustainable Diversity in Law* (Oxford, Oxford University Press, 2000) 159; 'the so-called legal matter . . . consists mainly of broad general propositions as to what the aims and aspirations of Muslim society should be. It is essentially the bare formulation of the Islamic religious ethic . . . In short, the primary purpose of the *Qur'an* is to regulate not the relationship of man with his fellows but his relationship with his creator'. Coulson, n 7 above, at 11–12.

[39] An-Na'im, n 31 above, at 20. Even in the context of the most serious crimes for which penalties are prescribed, the evidential requirements are stringent to ensure that punishment is awarded only in the absence of any doubt as to the commission of the crime by the accused through requisite mens rea. See generally Bassiouni, n 1 above, at 3–54.

[40] For further information on the content of the *Qur'an* and attempts at ascertainment of dates of the revelation of the various *surras* see Denny, n 1 above, at 138–43.

Meccan *Surras* are more charitable, while the verses revealed in Medina show the strains of actual governance, and are reflective of concrete legal and administrative problems that were confronted during that phase. Because of the changes in the context of Islam through violent disruption in the otherwise peaceful message of Islam, there are noticeable differences of approach in the Mecca and Medina stages. While the validity of the verses of the *Qur'an* remains intact and not in doubt, the concept of *Naskh* has been deployed to challenge the legal efficacy of those verses which are deemed as being out of context, and not suited to contemporary requirements.

The aforementioned consideration establishes that without challenging the authenticity of the *Qur'an* and *Sunna*, considerable jurisprudential disagreements have arisen as to legal content within a number of their provisions.[41] The process of distinguishing a body of positive rules proved a taxing exercise, leading to an emphasis upon *Ijtihad*.[42] To formulate a cohesive set of Islamic laws, differing weight was afforded to competing ordinances from the *Qur'an* and the *Sunna*, and jurists extensively relied on the techniques of analogy and deduction. Arguments about the application and the interpretation of the *Sharia* and *Siyar* nevertheless materialised, and over a period of time led to the creation of various schools of thought.[43]

PERMUTATIONS OF LEGAL SCHOOLS OF THOUGHT

Islam, like other major religions of the world, has witnessed differences and variations within itself. While opinions vary as to how many sects and segments can be found within this great religion, the two principal branches are represented through the majority *Sunni* and the minority *Shia* communities. The fragmentation between *Sunnis* and *Shias* represents a historic disagreement over the issue of succession, a friction that became apparent soon after the death of Prophet Muhammad. Prophet Muhammad died in 632 AD, and as he had no established or recognised heir-apparent, Muslims were left without a leader and had to make a quick choice regarding his successor. Within the community itself, there

[41] See AA An-Na'im, 'Religious Minorities under Islamic Law and the Limits of Cultural Relativism' (1987) 9 *Human Rights Quarterly* 1 at 15; Ali, n 38 above, at 266.

[42] B Weiss, 'Interpretation of Islamic law: The Theory of Ijtihâd' (1978) 26 *American Journal of Comparative Law* 199, at 200.

[43] Weiss elaborates upon the crucial distinctions in the interpretation of the *Sharia* between *Sunni* and *Shia* schools of thought. *Ibid* 210–12. For a consideration of the *Shia* school of thought see RK Ramzani, 'The Shi'i System: Its Conflict and Inter-action with Other Systems' (1959) *Proceedings of the American Society of International Law* 53; S Qureshi, 'The Politics of Shia Minority in Pakistan: Context and Development' in D Vajpeyi and Y Malik (eds), *Religious and Ethnic Minority Politics in South Asia* (Glendale, Riverdale Company Publishers, 1989) 109–38.

were disagreements. Prophet Muhammad himself had no surviving male offspring, and even if he did have one, it is by no means certain that without the exceptional attributes of his father he would have been acceptable as his successor. In this chaos, a small committee of Prophet Muhammad's followers assigned the role of *Khalifa* to Abu Bakar. This appointment and the whole issue of succession to *Khalafat* led to bitter disputes within the Islamic community. The *Shias*, the party of Alī, viewed the leadership of the Islamic community as a divine right, a right which they perceived as having been bestowed upon Alī by Prophet Muhammad. Others disagreed. Alī Ibn Abī Tālib ultimately became Caliph after Uthmān ibn 'Affān's death in 656 AD. Armies of Muawiya (the Syrian governor who refused to accept Alī's Caliphate and refused to step down in favour of his nominee) assassinated Alī in 661. After the death of Alī, his eldest son Hasan succeeded him for six months. However, later in 1661, Hasan abdicated his power to Muawiya, who ruled as Caliph throughout the Islamic world, forming part of the Ummayid dynasty.

According to *Shia* belief, Alī, the cousin and son-in-law of Muhammad, was appointed by the Prophet to be his successor, and succession was inherited by the heirs of the Prophet: Alī and his descendants.[44] Expanding on the distinctions between the *Sunnis* and the *Shias*, Professor Cherif Bassiouni makes the following observations:

> [t]he essential distinction between the Shiite and *Sunni* doctrines lies in the claim to the *Khilafa* (the succession) and the powers of the Imam. The *Shias* claim that Ali Ibn Abi-Taleb, cousin and son-in-law of the Prophet, had a more legitimate claim to the *Khilafa* than all the others and that it should have been inherited by the heirs of the Prophet, thus Ali and his descendants. Disagreement between *Sunnis*, who believe in an elective *Khilafa*, and the *Shias*, who believe in succession, was therefore mainly political and has remained so throughout the history of Islam.[45]

Additional disagreements that have arisen between the *Sunnis* and the *Shias* have also been of a political nature.[46] There are limited differences, in so far as the *Sharia* and interpretation of the principal sources of Islamic law are concerned. The most prominent law school amongst the *Shias* is the *Jaffari*, named after its founder, *Jafar al-Sadiq*, the sixth Imam. While believing in the two principal sources, the *Shias* translate the *Ijtihad* exclusively through the medium of Imams. Amongst the *Sunnis*, the larger, more predominant Islamic community, *Maliki*, *Hanafi*, *Shafi'i* and *Hanbali* schools of law have emerged.[47]

---

[44] Bassiouni, n 10 above, at 617.
[45] *Ibid*, at 617–18.
[46] See HH Halm, *Shiism* (Edinburgh, Edinburgh University Press, 1991); MS Kramer (ed), *Shi'ism, Resistance and Revolution* (Boulder, Colo, Westview Press, 1987).
[47] Glenn, n 38 above, at 179–83.

The oldest school is the *Hanafi*, which was founded by Abu Hanifa (d 767/150) in early *Abassid* times. The *Hanafi* school is the most liberal and flexible of the four *Sunni* schools. There is an emphasis upon *Qiyas* as a means of formulating legal judgments, a practice that was deployed extensively by Abu Hanifa himself. Indeed the practice of *Qiyas* and reasoning was prevalent to such an extent in Abu Hanifa's teaching that his followers were labelled 'People of Opinion' as opposed to 'People of the Tradition', the latter taken to mean relying upon traditions.[48] This endorsement of logic and reasoning allowed the followers of the *Hanafi* school of thought to carry out detailed investigations of legal sources prior to forming juridical principles.[49] Abu Hanifa and subsequently members of his school are accredited with formulating and developing significant principles of *Siyar*. In contemporary terms, the *Hanafi* school is predominant in Central and Western Asia (Afghanistan to Turkey), Lower Egypt (Cairo and the Delta) and the Indian Sub-Continent.

The *Malaki* school was established in Medina and the Hejaz by Malik ibn Anas (d 795/179).[50] Malik was a great collector of the *Hadith* and was a profound supporter of the 'living tradition of Medina'. In this regard Malik has been described as 'primarily a transmitter of earlier or contemporary doctrine, particularly the consensus of the Medinese jurists'.[51] The *Maliki* school has followings in North Africa and Upper Egypt. The adherents of the *Maliki* school regard juristic preferences (*Istihsan*) and public interests (*al-masalih al-mursala*) as key sources for juridical decisions.[52]

The *Shafi* school was established by Muhammad ibn Idris al-Shafi (d 820/204). Al-Shafi hailed from southwest Palestine (Gaza), and travelled extensively, meditating under Malik in Medina, teaching and practising law in Baghdad, and finally taking up residence in Egypt where he produced his major works before his death there. Al-Shafi's greatest contribution was his preference for the prophetic *Hadith* in contrast to the 'living tradition' of Medina that his teacher Malik had cultivated. This resulted in the Prophet's prestige and authority rising ever higher and being second only to the *Qur'an* in theory and in some cases higher in practice. The close relationship in Islamic law between the *Qur'an* and the *Sunna* of the Prophet was highlighted through the teachings of al-Shafi. Al-Shafi refined the practices of *Qiyas* curtailing its usage hitherto encouraged and relied upon by the *Hanafi* school. In addition to the established

[48] JL Esposito, *The Oxford Encyclopaedia of the Modern Islamic World* vol II (New York, Oxford University Press, 1995) at 457.

[49] A Sachedina, 'The Ideal and Real in Islam' in RS Khare (ed), *Perspectives on Islamic Law, Justice and Society* (Lanham, Md, Rowman and Littlefield Publishers, 1999) 15–31 at 17.

[50] See A Hassan, *The Early Developments of Islamic Jurisprudence* (Islamabad, 1982) 51; M Walliullah, *Muslim Jurisprudence and the Quranic Law of Crimes* (Lahore, IBS, 1982) 57.

[51] WB Hallaq, *Authority, Continuity and Change in Islamic Law* (Cambridge, Cambridge University Press, 2001) at 30.

[52] Sachedina, n 49 above, at 18.

Muhammad's *Sunna* as the second of the four 'roots' (*usul*) of law, al-Shafi defined *Ijma* in its classical form and invested it with the power that enabled it to oust *Ijtihad* from jurisprudence, except in the most limited sense. That is, *Ijma* came to be the principle as well as the procedure that the jurists of all the *Sunni* schools increasingly used in order to determine what was authentically Islamic. Thus *Ijma* extended even to the authentication of *Hadith*. It is in this context that the fateful *Hadith* attributed to the Prophet 'My people will never agree together in error' takes on meaning. If the earlier decisions of legal experts and judges were accepted through *Ijma* as definitive, then nothing more was to be attained from a survey of new cases save to utilise them for guidance as correct precedents. The *Shafi* school is predominant in Malaysia and Indonesia, Southern Arabia, East Africa, Lower Egypt and most of the Indian Ocean littoral.

The fourth school of thought, the *Hanabali* school, was founded by another contemporary of al-Shafi, Ahmad Hanbal (d 855/241) who carried Al-Shafi's enthusiasm to a new level. Hanbal was a thorough conservative and believed in a rigorous interpretation of Islam. He is regarded as a 'traditionalist and theologian, and his involvement with law as a technical discipline [was] rather minimal'.[53] His deep convictions of the *Qur'an* and *Hadith* led him and his followers to have a rigid interpretation of the *Sharia*. His independent-mindedness and resistant theological approaches led him to suffer imprisonment and persecution by the ruling Caliph.[54] While primarily a theologian, his teachings were based largely around religiously ordained *Hadith*, and only rarely articulated in strict legal jargon. Ibn Taimiya, the thirteenth century self-proclaimed *Mujtahid*, was a disciple of Ahmad Hanabal. More significantly the seventeenth century *Wahabi* reformation in Arabia was influenced by his thoughts. The *Wahabi* school has continued and flourished in the Arabian Peninsula. It remains the dominant legal school of thought in northern and central Arabia (modern Saudi Arabia).

SURVEYING ISLAMIC STATE PRACTICES

Within a century of the death of Muhammad, Muslim empire spread across the continents. However, these developmental processes and expansion were not without their problems. We have already considered the divide over the issue of succession. The two major sects of Islam themselves were to branch out further into smaller sects and schools of thought, undermining the orthodox Islamic vision of a singular unified *Ummah*. As Islam progressed, the expansion led to further decentralisation,

---

53 Hallaq, n 51 above, at 40.
54 See Weeramantry, n 11 above, at 54.

diversification and division sanctifying the hitherto unanticipated 'illegit-imacy of the Nation State'[55] under the classical Islamic vision of the *Ummah*.[56] No longer was the central base of Islam concentrated in Arabia. Under the *Ummayids* in the seventh century, the capital shifted to Damascus. The expansion of the Islamic empire had also meant coming into contact with non-Arabs: the Turks, the Persians, the Mongols and the Indians. Tensions were generated in the treatment of non-Arab Muslims, and their discrimination and exclusion were major contributing factors to the downfall of the *Ummayid* household (661–750). The collapse of the *Ummayids* and the rise of the Baghdad-based *Abassids* in the eighth century (749–1258) resulted in further fragmentation of a unified Muslim empire. During the tenth century, secondary caliphates emerged in Cairo and Cordoba. This significant decentralisation was an impinging factor on a coherent body of laws. According to two commentators:

> [I]n the course of time serious disagreements arose between [the then existing] schools of law. Individual scholars were originally allowed to make up their own mind on matters not foreclosed by the Koran and the Sunna, but the mem-bers of the different schools, which were geographically far apart, were influenced in their views by the style of life, the stage of development, and the legal practices of the surrounding population, so it was only natural that the schools should reach different views . . .[57]

As indicated above, the remnants of the *Ummayid* dynasty were able to establish themselves in Spain during the *Abassid* period. The Muslim rule in Spain lasted for over 500 years. In Egypt, a *Shia* dynasty, called the *Fatimids*, came to power in the tenth century, a rule which lasted in excess of a hundred years. The incursions towards Afghanistan and India that had commenced during the *Ummayid* and *Abassid* periods culminated in the founding of the Sultanate of Delhi in 1206. This not only marked the beginning of Islamic dominance over South Asia but also led to Islam's expansion to the Far East.

While the decentralisation of the Muslim empire continued, the mantle of caliphate itself was wrested away from the *Abassids* and shifted to the Turkish invaders. The Ottoman Turks, who had established their power during the fifteenth century with the capture of Constantinople (1453), swept across the Middle East and North Africa, establishing a new caliphate in 1517.[58] In addition to the medieval Islamic history that could be characterised as having under its umbrella the magnificent and versa-tile Ottoman dynasty of the Eastern Mediterranean, Asia Minor and South

---

[55] SP Huntington, *The Clash of Civilizations and the Remaking of World Order* (London, Simon & Schuster, 1996) at 177.

[56] *Ibid.*

[57] Zweigert and Kötz, n 13 above, at 307.

[58] Huntington, n 55 above, at 177.

Eastern Europe, it also included the *Mughal* empire of India and the *Safavid* dynasty of Iran. Although, technically under Muslim rule, each of these empires operated from differing ideological and political perspectives. The *Safavids* followed a vigorously *Shia* faith. The *Mughals* of India, as we shall consider, adopted a more benign and assimilationist approach. Thus the developmental processes of Islam with varied political, economical and ideological influences also produced divergent viewpoints on legal approaches towards *Sharia*. These divergences were evident not only in substantive areas such as the extent of prohibiting *riba* (usury) in commercial transactions, rules regarding the non-use of force, sanctions against trading with the non-Islamic world, and formulation of labour standard regulations for inter alia slaves, women and children, but also in the physical implementation of the *Sharia* itself. Politics also had a significant bearing on the development and application of the legal systems. The political elite showed an unwillingness to allow the judges or *qadis* to interpret *Sharia* that was detrimental to their own personal agenda. Commenting on the varied forms of interpretation and application, a scholar makes the following pertinent point:

> [t]hough the theoretical frame of the Siyar was derived from Koranic provisions and utterances of the Prophet, the manner of interpretation and the doctrinal development supported by legal and methodological arguments rendered by the jurists left flexible room for expansion or critique. Thus the exposition of the rules of Siyar . . . by Muslim jurists was dictated neither by the needs of the Islamic State nor officially promoted by it. On the contrary, it was the individual and independent effort of Muslim jurists . . . to expound the Divine Law. The Shariah was deemed binding on the rulers of the Islamic State, but they were free to give preference to the opinions of any one of the prevailing schools of jurisprudence. In practice the rulers deviated from strict adherence to the Shariah whenever political self-interest dictated such a course.[59]

In addition to the political self-interest noted in the above passage, as indicated already, there were many other factors contributing to differing interpretations of *Siyar* or deviations from it. The developmental phase of Islam and its interaction with other traditions also influenced the principles of *Sharia* and *Siyar*. Islamic practices absorbed and assimilated many foreign concepts and ideals. Firstly, the *Umayyad* Empire utilised the Byzantine Market inspectors as *amil as-suq* magistrates with limited jurisdiction.[60] From there emerged the office of *qadi*, a judge of a special kind. The office of *qadi* had a significant impact on developing the substantive law. In the application of local laws, the work and judgment of the *qadis*

---

[59] Moinuddin, n 3 above, at 38; according to Coulson 'the effective enforcement of the whole system of Sharia law was entirely dependent upon the whim of the de facto ruler' n 7 above, at 83.

[60] *Ibid*, at 28.

reflected enormous diversity. Secondly, because the *qadis* were able to apply personal opinions (*ray*) they were able to add to existing Islamic jurisprudence.[61] The *qadis* and subsequent jurists were also able to derive advantage from the apparently competing ordinances in the *Qur'an* and *Sunna*. The jurists in particular were sucessful in formulating subjective analogical deductions.

As Islam spread to territories alien to it, a number of influences became pre-eminent. While it was possible for many non-Arabic communities to embrace Islam, they were reluctant to give up their indigenous laws and norms of social and cultural interaction. In India, for example, the *Ismaili Khojas, Cutchi Memons* and *Bohras* continued to follow their practices of inheritance despite conversion to Islam. A similar pattern was followed in Java. In the face of some strong indigenous customs and traditions, the *Sharia* as well as the courts enforcing the *Sharia* had to make significant concessions.

IMPACT OF EUROPEAN IMPERIALISM UPON THE MUSLIM PEOPLES

The doctrines of Islamic legal systems were adulterated by disturbances of colonialism. In the context of the British and French territorial possessions, Islamic laws were relegated to the position of customary laws; disengaged from their jurisprudential bases they were framed in a colonial legal system and court structure.[62] In this process the classical structure of Islamic laws—established on divergent sources with flexible interpretations—were replaced by a law which assured the dominance of a colonial elite.[63] The *Tanzimat* reforms brought within the Ottoman Empire during 1839–1876 reflected a substantial influence of the French Commercial and Penal Code.[64] In order to apply these new codes *Nizamiyya* courts (a new set of secular courts) were established. The codification of law, based on European systems, led to further infiltration of European laws. Further changes were brought about when in 1926 Turkey implemented a criminal code, replicating Italian criminal law. Similar changes were also brought about in the territories which belonged to the Ottoman Empire.[65] With the imposition of imperial laws and values, and the consequent decline in the Ottoman and Mogul empires, the Muslims were submerged under European colonialism—a subjugation that produced political and legal undercurrents of enormous magnitude. Henceforth for considerable

[61] Moinuddin, n 3 above, at 30.
[62] Oba, n 2 above, at 819.
[63] J Strawson, 'Islamic Law and English Press' in J Strawson (ed), *Law After Ground Zero* (London, GlassHouse Press, 2002) 205–14, at 205.
[64] Coulson, n 7 above, at 151.
[65] *Ibid*, 151.

periods the Muslim communities remained under the shadow of colonisation and alien rule, their indigenous legal and political systems being
manipulated and modified by European encroachments. The imposition
of European law was evident in the application of Dutch laws in Indonesia
and the enforcement of the Indian Penal Code (1862) superseding Islamic
criminal law and the Penal Code (1898) in the Sudan. In the overall scheme
of things, Strawson's comment reflects a great measure of truth when he
notes:

> Colonialism bequeathed to the world's states legal systems, civil law and
> common law stamped with race, gender and the class discriminations of the
> European occupying power. International law emerged as colonialism and
> sought to legitimise conquest, slavery, ethnic cleansing, genocide and racism. In
> this process other systems of law became subordinate or were excluded. The
> legitimacy of current world order is compromised by this past. While we should
> not be held hostage to it, we do need to recognise it in shaping the new contours
> of legal discourse. This interactive task involves relocating privileged positions
> gained by political and military power but dressed as law.[66]

Much of the modern world was engineered and framed on doctrines
devised by European colonisers; the principle of *uti possidetis* was applied
in creating post-colonial States.[67] The end of colonialism and independent
statehood for a majority of the Islamic States was rarely accompanied by
political cohesion and economic stability. In the post-colonial phases,
political instability, economic mismanagement and policies of double-
standards have led to enormous disillusionment not only with the

---

[66] J Strawson, 'Introduction: In the Name of Law' in J Strawson (ed), n 63 above, at xix–xx.
[67] The origins of the principle of *uti possidetis* can be traced back to the early nineteenth
century, whereby the newly independent successor States of the former Spanish Empire in
South and Central America were considered to have inherited the administrative divisions
of the colonial empire as their new territorial boundaries. For an affirmation of the principle
see Article 3(b) the African Union, The Constitutive Act (adopted 11 July 2000); Principle III
of Final Act of Helsinki Conference 1975 (adopted 1 August 1975) <http://www.osce.org/
docs/english/1990-1999/summits/helfa75e.htm>(20 September 2004); Article 62 2(2)(a)
Vienna Convention on the Law of Treaties (adopted 22 May 1969, entered into force 1980)
1155 UNTS 331; 58 UKTS (1980), Cmnd 7964. Article 2 of the Vienna Convention of State
Succession in Respect of Treaties 1978 17 ILM (1978) 1488, 1946 UNTS 3 (adopted 22 August
1978, entered into force 6 November 1996). For judicial acknowledgement of the principles
see *Frontier Dispute Case (Burkina Faso v Mali)* [1986] ICJ Rep 554; GJ Naldi, 'The Case
Concerning the Frontier Dispute (Burkina Faso/Republic of Mali): *Uti Possidetis* in an African
Perspective' (1987) 36 *International & Comparative Law Quarterly* 893; *Temple of Peach Vihear
Case (Merits) (Cambodia v Thailand)* [1962] ICJ Rep 6, at 16; *Rann of Kutch Arbitration* (1968) 50
ILR 2, at 408; *Arbitral Award of 31 July 1989 (Guinea-Bissau v Senegal)* [1990] ICJ Rep 64; *Land,
Islands and Maritime Frontier Case: El Salvador v Honduras (Nicaragua Intervening)* [1992] ICJ
Rep 351, at 380; also see *Sovereignty over Certain Frontiers (Belgium v the Netherlands)* [1959] ICJ
Rep 209, in particular Judge Moeno Quitana's dissenting opinion, at 252; *Avis Nos 2 and 3 of
the Arbitration Commission of the Yugoslavia Conference*, 31 ILM (1992) 1497, at 1499; *Taba Award
(Egypt v Israel)* (1989) 80 ILR 224, in particular arbitrator Lapidoth's dissenting opinion; also
see J Klabbers and R Lefeber 'Africa: Lost between Self-Determination and *Uti-Possidetis*' in
C Brölmann, R Lefeber and M Zieck (eds), *Peoples and Minorities in International Law*
(Dordrecht, Martinus Nijhoff Publishers, 1993) 33–76.

governments but also with the State structures themselves. Many in the Islamic world perceive their governments as stooges of the 'west', with the 'west' having its own duplicitous agenda of exploitation, expansion and imperialism. It is in this environment, where peoples '. . . have no stake in government, no faith in the future, and harbor an easily exploitable discontent with the status quo'[68] that extremist and fanatical organisations such as Al-Qaeda have found a fertile breeding ground.

MODERN ISLAMIC STATES AND ISSUES OF ISLAMIC IDENTITY

A number of modern States purport to place reliance on the principles of *Sharia* in implementing their domestic constitutional law and conducting their international relations. These States represent diverse geographical, historical, political, economic and cultural features. Islamic States also differ widely in their history and political systems, the catalogue ranging from States such as Afghanistan with a poor record of constitutionalism to Malaysia, a growing and powerful democratic State. There is also the example of Turkey. As a Muslim majority State, Turkey has put in place modern secular laws and is currently a strong contender for membership of the European Union.[69] Notwithstanding their wide-ranging differences, all Islamic States are members of the United Nations, and have affirmed the modern principles of international law.[70] Whilst endorsing the *Siyar* principles, these States have entered into a range of bilateral, multilateral or regional agreements relating to international law, pointing to the lack of incompatibility between the two systems. Within the United Nations system, the Islamic States have advanced international law, with emphasis on political and economic sovereignty, the right to self-determination, devolution of rights and responsibilities, and a right to development.[71] Islamic States have also been heavily involved in the work of the United Nations regional commissions operating under the auspices of the Economic and Social Council (ECOSOC), and the more specialised organisations and institutions such as the United Nations Conference on Trade and Development (UNCTAD), the Food and Agriculture

[68] See the United States House of Representatives, Committee on International Relations, Sub-Committee on Africa, *Africa and the War on Global Terrorism: Hearing before the Sub-Committee on International Relations, House of Representatives, One Hundred Seventh Congress, First Session* (Washington, DC, United States, 2001) at 8.

[69] See JL Esposito, 'Contemporary Islam: Reformation or Revolution?' in JL Esposito (ed), *The Oxford History of Islam* (Oxford, Oxford University Press, 1999) 643.

[70] See M Khadduri, 'The Islamic System: Its Competition and Co-existence with Western Systems' (1959) *Proceedings of the American Society of International Law* 49, at 52; M Khadduri, 'Islam and the Modern Law of Nations' (1956) 50 *American Journal of International Law* 358.

[71] See below, chapters 4 and 7.

Organisation (FAO) and the United Nations Development Programme (UNDP).[72]

The compatibility of international law and modern Islamic State practices, however, does not remove the central question of identity. How can a State be identified as 'Islamic'? In other words what are the attributes of an Islamic State? It is extremely difficult to address the question of identity. Indicators may point to the proportion of Muslims in a State or the system of government that is operative. Some advocates of Islamic identity would rely upon the question of whether *Sharia* is enforced in a State, others may acknowledge Islamic identity simply through hortatory statements in constitutional and legislative provisions. At present fifteen constitutions name Islam as the official religion; five States have declared themselves Islamic Republics.[73] The present study, while acknowledging the significance of Islamic identity amongst modern State practices, adopts a pragmatic approach. For the purposes of the present research, Islamic identity is associated with membership of an organisation, the Organisation of the Islamic Conference, which identifies itself with Islam; its primary objectives are to promote Islamic solidarity and to work for the furtherance of the interests of Muslims across the globe.[74] While the membership of the OIC is not exclusively Muslim, a huge proportion of Member States do in fact have Muslim majorities. On the other hand, membership does not entail any obligations to implement the *Sharia* or have in place Islamic political, social or ethical frameworks.[75] The discussion that follows examines the role and achievements of the OIC as an Islamic Organisation.

THE ORGANISATION OF THE ISLAMIC CONFERENCE (OIC)

The OIC was established in Rabat, Kingdom of Morocco, on 12 Rajab 1389H (25 September 1969). Its establishment was a reaction against a Zionist arson attack upon *Al-Aqsa* in occupied Jerusalem on 21 August 1969. Motivated to defend the faith and integrity of the Muslim peoples, a large group of States united by this common cause covenanted in their first meeting held in Rabat to liberate Jerusalem and Al-Aqsa from Zionist occupation.[76] Now existing as an inter-governmental organisation

---

[72] See P Malanczuk, *Akehurst's Modern Introduction to International Law* 7th rev edn (London, Routledge, 1997) 224.

[73] Baderin, n 31 above, at 8 (see text accompanying n 33). According to an earlier study, there are twenty-three countries recognising Islam as the State religion. See IR al-Fariqi (ed), *Historical Atlas of the Religions of the World* (New York, Macmillan, 1974) 279 cited in JL Payne, *Why Nations Arm* (Oxford, Basil Blackwell, 1989) at 122–3.

[74] The reliance upon OIC membership as identification of 'Islamic' States has been adopted by a number of scholars and jurists: see eg Baderin, n 31 above, at 8.

[75] Moinuddin, n 3 above, at 101.

[76] Huntington, n 55 above, at 176.

numbering fifty-six states, the OIC continues to pool its resources and efforts in its endeavour to present a unified voice and protect the interests of Muslim peoples and the Muslim world community.

A permanent General Secretariat was created and a Secretary General was appointed at the First Islamic Conference of Ministers of Foreign Affairs. After the first epochal meeting in Rabat, the Islamic Conference of Foreign Ministers approved the Charter of the Organisation.[77] Pursuant to Article II of the Charter, the Organisation's objectives are:

- to promote Islamic solidarity among Member States;
- to consolidate co-operation among Member States in the economic, social cultural, scientific and other vital fields of activities, and to carry out consultations among Member States in international organisations;
- to endeavour to eliminate racial segregation, discrimination and to eradicate colonialism in all its forms;
- to take necessary measures to support international peace and security founded on justice;
- to co-ordinate efforts for the safeguarding of the Holy Places and support of the struggle of the people of Palestine, to help them regain their rights and liberate their land;
- to back the struggle of all Muslim peoples with a view to preserving their dignity, independence and national rights;
- to create a suitable atmosphere for the promotion of cooperation and understanding among Member States and other countries.

The Organisation is further impelled by the following principles:

- total equality between Member States;
- respect of the right of self-determination, and non-interference in the domestic affairs of Member States;
- respect of the sovereignty, independence and territorial integrity of each Member States;
- settlement of any conflict that may arise by peaceful means such as negotiation, mediation, reconciliation or arbitration;
- abstention from the threat or use of force against the territorial integrity, national unity or political independence of any Member States.

INSTITUTIONS OF THE OIC

The Conference is composed of main bodies, secondary organs, specialised institutions and standing committees. Pursuant to Article III of the

---

[77] The OIC Charter was approved and adopted in the third Islamic Conference of Foreign Ministers held in Jeddah in March 1972. The Charter was registered in conformity with Article 102 of the United Nations Charter on 1 February 1974. For the text of the Charter see <http://www.oic-oci.org/> (2 October 2004); also see P Sands and P Klein, *Bowett's Law of International Institutions*, 5th edn (London, Sweet & Maxwell, 2001) 148.

OIC Charter, the Organisation establishes three main bodies: (i) the Conference of Kings and Heads of State and Government, (ii) the Conference of Foreign Ministers, and (iii) the General Secretariat and Subsidiary Organs. The Conference of Kings and Heads of State and Government is the supreme authority of the Organisation. It compulsorily meets once every three years, and additionally when the interests of Muslim nations warrant it, to lay down and co-ordinate the Organisation's policy.[78] The Conference of Foreign Ministers meets once a year and whenever the need arises, to consider means of implementing its general policy and resolutions, to adopt new resolutions, and to examine the report of the Financial Committee and approve the budget.[79] The General Secretariat is the executive organ of the organisation. Headed by a General Secretary, the Secretariat is entrusted with the implementation of the decisions of the two aforementioned main bodies.[80]

A fourth main body is in the process of being created. The International Islamic Court of Justice (IICJ) will be located in Kuwait and will be the principal judicial organ of the OIC. It will consist of seven members elected by the Islamic Conference of Foreign Ministers (ICFM). The remit of the Court will be dispute settlement between Member States, the issuing of opinions as requested by the Islamic Summit, the ICFM or by any organ of the OIC with the prior approval of the ICFM, and the interpretation of the Charter of the Organisation.[81]

There are a number of secondary organs and institutions that collaboratively work towards the attainment of the Organisation's objectives: subsidiary organs, specialised institutions, affiliated institutions and standing committees (categorised by the degree of autonomy they each enjoy vis-à-vis the Organisation) have been proliferating steadily in both numbers and in terms of areas covered. Notably, by the third year of the World Decade for Cultural Development, an initiative inaugurated by the United Nations in 1988 under the auspices of UNESCO, the OIC had already built Islamic Colleges, and Cultural Institutes and Centres for the purpose of disseminating Islamic culture and proliferating the teaching of Arabic, the language of the Holy Qur'an, and other languages.

Several additional institutions have been established within the framework of the OIC and in accordance with the resolutions adopted by the ICFM. Member States automatically become members of these organs and their budgets are approved by the ICFM. As we shall consider shortly, these additional institutions include the Statistical, Economic, Social Research and Training Centre for Islamic Countries (located in Turkey),

---

[78] Article IV, OIC Charter.
[79] *Ibid.* Article V.
[80] *Ibid.* Article VI.
[81] For a critical examination see Hussain, n 10 above, at 90–117.

the Islamic Institute of Technology, the Islamic Centre for the Development of Trade in Casablanca, Morocco and the International Commission for the Preservation of Cultural Heritage.

The remit of subsidiary organs is both research and operational. Several of the organs are creating and publishing databases of information collected through surveys and research. In their operational capacity, the organs set up programmes for the dissemination of expertise, training, and resources for the benefit of all Member States. At present there are ten subsidiary organs. In establishing these agencies, the OIC commented that:

> The undermentioned Centres are established within the framework of the Organization of the Islamic Conference in accordance with a resolution adopted by the Islamic Conference of Kings and Heads of State and Government or the Islamic Conference of Foreign Ministers. Member States shall automatically become members of these organs and their budgets shall be approved by the Islamic Conference of Foreign Ministers.[82]

SUBSIDIARY ORGANS OF THE OIC

The Statistical, Economic, Social Research and Training Centre for Islamic Countries (SESRTCIC)

This Centre researches and compiles data regarding the economic and social structure of the Organisation's Member States. As well as exploring the potential for collaborative projects between Member States in the fields of commerce and industry, the Centre also examines social issues such as poverty, education, health and employment. Recent publications include the *Statistical Yearbook of the OIC Countries 2002*[83] and *Basic Facts and Figures on OIC Member Countries 2002.*[84]

The Research Centre for Islamic History, Art and Culture (IRCICA)

This Centre provides a venue for the collaborative efforts of scholars, historians and research institutions of the Member States and other countries throughout the world to study, and exchange knowledge and information regarding the history, art, science and culture of the Muslim peoples. As the Secretariat and executive organ of the International

---

[82] <www.oic-oci.org/english/main/subsidiary%20organs.htm> (20 September 2004).
[83] SESRTCIC Publications 2002.
[84] SESRTCIC Publications 2002.

Commission for the Preservation of Islamic Cultural Heritage (ICPICH), the Centre organises conferences and exhibitions, as well as training courses.

The Islamic Institute for Technology (IIT) (Formerly: Centre for Vocational and Technical Training and Research (ICTVTR)

Providing technical and vocational training to industrial, technical and mechanical instructors from all Member States, this Institute aims to improve human resources within, and technical co-operation between, States. The latter objective is achieved through the exchange of skilled experts and training programmes, and through publications and practical workshops. Through conducting its own research in these technological fields, the Institute provides advisory and consultancy services for the benefit of any government or international organisation.

The Islamic Centre for the Development of Trade (ICDT)

To promote trade between Member States, this centre provides both legal and practical advice as to how to proliferate both internal and inter-national trade. Moreover, the Centre's efforts are in abundance: not only does it promulgate trade information vis-à-vis publications and bulletins, the centre organises seminars, trade fairs and exhibitions designed to encourage States to adopt expedient strategies for trading.

The Islamic *Fiqh* Academy

The remit of this Academy is jurisprudential; it studies contentious contemporary issues and seeks solutions in accordance with the principles of the Islamic *Sharia*. Its findings are disseminated through the Muslim community using seminars and publications, and in doing so, the Academy endeavours to provide a proper understanding of the tenets of the Islamic faith.

The Executive Bureau of the Islamic Solidarity Fund (ISF)

This subsidiary organ provides emergency aid when Member States suffer natural or man-made disasters. Moreover, as its title suggests, the Islamic Solidarity Fund advances monetary assistance to Islamic communities in non-Member States for the purposes of religious, socio-economic, or cultural improvement. The Bureau strengthens its financial position by using its endowment, the *Waqf*, to acquire liquid assets; it also owns a number of fixed properties donated by the governments of Member States and by Muslim organisations.

Al-Quds (Jerusalem) Fund

The purpose of this fund is two-fold. Firstly, it supports the Palestinian struggle for independence in and around Jerusalem, and secondly, it strives to preserve the Arab character of this city. Like the ISF, the *Al-Quds* Fund seeks to improve its financial position by investing in liquid assets, whilst acquiring fixed properties donated by the governments of Member States and by Muslim organisations. As shall be examined in due course, since the events of 11 September 2001, States have placed substantial restrictions on what they perceive as terrorist funding operations. It is troubling to note that doubts have been expressed as regards supporting the Palestinian cause. In the light of these negative developments the existence of *Al-Quds* Fund itself remains doubtful.

International Commission for the Preservation of Islamic Cultural Heritage (ICPICH)

The Commission's mandate is to raise and then distribute funds to assist Member States, individually and collectively, in the preservation and restoration of items and places depicting Islamic cultural heritage, including the heritage of *Al-Quds Al-Sharif* (Holy Jerusalem). Such items and places include historic cities, libraries, manuscripts and monuments.

The Islamic University of Niger

The *Oum Al-Qura* University was established with financial assistance from the Islamic Solidarity Fund. In developing facilities for teaching higher education and for research in both the arts and the sciences, the intention has been that the University will provide an adequate response to the growing need for higher education of Muslims in an Islamic academic environment, throughout the countries of West Africa.

The Islamic University of Uganda

This University was established with the help of the OIC. In a fashion similar to the University of Niger, the University of Uganda was created with a view to developing facilities for higher education in both the arts and the sciences. Situated in Uganda, the University seeks to assist Muslims in the countries of Central and East Africa.

AFFILIATED INSTITUTIONS

The Affiliated Institutions of the OIC consist of international governmental, professional and societal institutions of Member States that were founded under the auspices of the Organisation. The OIC states that collectively:

> [t]hese group together entities or mortal persons. Membership to these institutions is optional and is open to institutions and organs of OIC Member States. Their budgets are independent of the budget of the Secretariat General and those of subsidiary and specialized organs. They were established under the auspices of the Islamic Conferences of Heads of State and Government or the Islamic Conference of Foreign Ministers. Affiliated institutions may be granted observer status by virtue of a resolution of the Islamic Conference of Foreign Ministers. They may obtain voluntary assistance from the subsidiary and specialized organs as well as from Member States.[85]

Located in different cities of the Islamic world, seven affiliated institutions have been established. They include the Islamic Chamber of Commerce, Industry and Community Exchange (ICCI) (Karachi), the International Association of Islamic Banks (Jeddah) and the Organisation of Islamic Capitals and Cities (Mekkah).

The Islamic Chamber of Commerce, Industry and Community Exchange (ICCI)

The ICCI was established as a result of a resolution adopted by the Tenth Islamic Conference which took place in Fez, in May 1979.[86] The General Secretariat of the ICCI is headed by the Secretary General. The Secretary General is appointed by the General Assembly, the governing body of the Islamic Chambers. As noted above, the ICCI has its headquarters in Karachi, Pakistan. Its objectives include inter alia to promote and encourage trade, industry and handicrafts among the Member States; to make recommendations for safeguarding the economic interests and commercial activities of the Islamic world; to promote co-operation between the Islamic Chambers and other international commercial, industrial and

---

[85] <www.oic-oci.org/english/main/Affiliated%20Institutions.htm> (20 September 2004).
[86] Resolution No 15/10–EC.

agricultural organisations; to promote the exchange of commercial dele-
gations and to organise trade fairs, exhibitions, seminars, lectures and
publicity campaigns; to promote investment opportunities and joint ven-
tures among the Member States and to provide for arbitration in the settlement of commercial and industrial disputes; and to promote exchange
of commercial, technical, industrial, management and scientific information and know-how among Member States.

The International Association of Islamic Banks

Under the umbrella of the OIC, another significant institution, the
International Association of Islamic Banks, was established on 21 August
1977. Its central offices are in Jeddah, Saudi Arabia. The primary objectives
of the Association are inter alia to promote Islamic banking, coordination
amongst Islamic banks and to resolve operational constraints of standard-
isation and the application of the *Sharia*.[87] The Association also undertakes
and facilitates research in Islamic economics, providing assistance in
manpower development, maintaining a databank of all Islamic financial
institutions and providing technical assistance in Islamic banking. The
Association aims to advance and enforce the ties and links amongst
Islamic financial institutions and to promote intra-co-ordination and intra-
co-operation. It is designed to ensure the institutions' Islamic observance
and character in pursuance of achievement of the common and mutual
goals.

The Organisation of Islamic Capitals and Cities

The Organisation of Islamic Capitals and Cities was created by virtue of
Resolution No 9/9–E which was adopted by the ICFM in Dakar, Republic
of Senegal during April 1978. The Statute of this Organisation was
approved by the ICFM in Fez, Morocco, on 8 May 1979. However it was
not until the First General Conference of the Organisation held in Al
Mukarramah in January 1980 that the Organisation of Islamic Capitals
was officially inaugurated. Its objectives are as follows:

1 Strengthening the bonds of friendship, brotherhood and solidarity among
Islamic Capitals and Cities;
2 Promoting, developing and expanding the scope of cooperation among the
Islamic Capitals and Cities;
3 Preserving the identity and heritage of Islamic Capitals and Cities;

---

[87] On the doctrinal issues regarding Islamic Banking see below, chapter 6.

4 Seeking to implement comprehensive urban, architectural plans which may guide the growth of Islamic Capitals and Cities in accordance with their actual economic, social, cultural and environmental characteristics;
5 Upgrading the standards of public services and utilities in the Islamic Capitals and Cities.[88]

The Sports Federation of Islamic Solidarity Games

This Federation was established pursuant to Resolution No 17/11–C of the Eleventh Islamic Conference of Foreign Ministers (held in Islamabad, Pakistan, in May 1980 (1400H)), and Resolution No 7/3–C of the Third Islamic Summit (held in Makkah Al Mukarramah Tarif in January 1981 (1401H)). Its objectives are as follows:

1 To strengthen Islamic solidarity among youth in Member States and promote Islamic identity in the fields of sports;
2 To inculcate the principles of non-discrimination as to religion, race or class, in conformity with the precepts of Islam;
3 To reinforce the bonds of unity, amity and brotherhood among youth in Member States;
4 To unify positions in Olympic International and continental conferences and meetings and to cooperate with all the international and continent sports bodies and organisations;
5 To promote cooperation among Member States on matter of common interest in all fields of sports activities;
6 To preserve sports principles and to promote the Olympic sports movement in the Muslim world;
7 To make youth in Member States aware of the objectives of the OIC.[89]

The Islamic Committee for the International Crescent

The Islamic Committee for the International Crescent was sanctioned during the Eighth Islamic Conference of Foreign Ministers which took place in Tripoli the capital of Libya, during May 1977. The Headquarters of the Islamic Committee are also established in Libya, in the city of Benghazi. The principal objectives of the Committee have been to alleviate the consequential distress and suffering of natural disasters, and war:

1 To provide medical assistance and to alleviate the sufferings caused by natural catastrophes and man-made disasters;
2 To offer all necessary assistance within its possibilities, to international and local organisations, serving humanity.

[88] <http://www.oic-oci.org/> (1 October 2004).
[89] *Ibid.*

The Islamic Shipowners' Association (ISA)

ISA was established and approved by a Statute at the Third Islamic Summit Conference held in Makkah Al-Mukarramah/Taif (Kingdom of Saudi Arabia). Its mandate is:

1 To coordinate and unify the efforts of the members in realizing cooperation among the maritime companies, in Member States, to maximize profit;

2 To encourage members to set up joint maritime companies and shipping lines between Member States;

3 To establish contact between the Islamic world and other countries within an integrated maritime network;

4 To develop periodical and regular freight and passenger voyages between Islamic and other countries;

5 To assist in drawing up a unified policy for the Islamic maritime transporters; and

6 To conduct studies and research in the various disciplines of maritime transport.[90]

The World Federation of International Arabo-Islamic Schools

The World Federation of International Arabo-Islamic Schools presents a useful example of the vision and foresight of the OIC. The establishment of the Federation was sanctioned at the Seventh Islamic Conference of Foreign Ministers, in Istanbul in May 1976. The Federation represents Arab-Islamic schools around the globe and the intention is to support and assist them. Amongst the principal objectives of the Federation are teaching of the Arabic language and the dissemination of Islamic culture and traditions. These objectives are attained inter alia through extending financial and moral support to the schools and cultural centres. The Federation has provided support for the setting up of many of the religious schools, the *Madrisas*. Whilst the objectives of the Federation are to be commended and applauded, there has been considerable debate regarding the role and contribution of *Madrisas* in enlightening the Muslim youth. Critics of the *Madrisas* have questioned the role of *Madrisas*. In particular there is criticism of the rigid, intolerant and stagnant version of the *Sharia* that is advanced in many of these *Madrisas*. In the modern phase of international law, a number of Islamic States have responded to this particular criticism by establishing a stricter regime of *Madrisas* and by developing a compulsory educational curriculum.[91] The Federation also has a signific-

[90] *Ibid.* Resolution 4/3 IS.
[91] *Ibid.* See *The Deeni Madirsa (Voluntary Registration and Regulation Ordinance)* 2002. For criticisms of the regulation see International Crisis Group, *Pakistan: Madrisas, Extremism and the*

ant role in the training of personnel capable of developing the Islamic ethos and culture in Arab-Islamic schools.

ADDITIONAL INSTITUTIONS

The OIC has also established a number of standing committees for economic and trade co-operation. The Ministerial level Committee was established to give effect to Resolution No 13/3–P (IS) adopted by the Third Islamic Summit, held in Mekkah in January 1981. The Committee is entrusted with the implementation of resolutions adopted by the Islamic Conference in economic and commercial fields, examining all possible means of strengthening co-operation in those fields among Muslim States and putting forward programmes and proposals likely to improve the capabilities of Islamic States in these sectors.

In addition to establishing agencies and affiliated institutions, the OIC has also taken significant steps towards economic co-operation through specific treaty arrangements. Two of these agreements are of particular importance. The General Agreement for Economic, Technical and Commercial Co-operation among Member States of the Islamic Conference was approved and adopted in the Eighth Conference of Foreign Ministers during 1977.[92] The second specific treaty agreement entered into under the auspices of the OIC is entitled the Agreement for the Promotion, Protection and Guarantee of Investments among Member States of the Organisation of the Islamic Conference.[93] The agreement is aimed at encouraging foreign investments and ensuring the securities of such investments against expropriation by the host State.[94]

SPECIALISED INSTITUTIONS AND ORGANS

Specialised institutions are defined by the OIC as those that:

are established within the framework of the Organisation of the Islamic Conference in accordance with a resolution adopted by the Islamic Conference

Military (Islamabad, Brussels, 2002) Report No 36; S Ahmed, *Pakistan's Unkept Promise: The Untamed Madrasas, International Herald Tribune, The IHT online* (Cedex, France, 26 January 2004) <http://www.iht.com/articles/126492.html> (12 September 2004); 'Lessons in Jihad for Pakistani Youth: Religious Schools Resist Law to Curb Extremism' *The Washington Post* 14 July 2002 at A19 <http://www.washingtonpost.com/ ac2/wp-dyn?pagename=article&contentId=A1568-2002Jul13&notFound=true> (5 September 2004).

[92] Doc ICFM 8–77/ICES-9.

[93] Doc Annex—I to ICMF 1281–E/D.6. The text of the agreement was finalised on 14–16 March 1981 and was approved by the Intergovernmental Conference of Foreign Ministers (ICFM) of the OIC held in June 1981 in Baghdad, Iraq.

[94] The Preamble of the agreement provides that the objective inter alia is *to provide and develop a favourable climate for investments*.

of Kings and Heads of State and Government or Islamic Conference of Foreign Ministers. Membership to these organs is optional and open to OIC Member States. Their budgets are independent of the budget of the Secretariat General and those of the subsidiary organs and are approved by their respective legislative bodies as stipulated in their Statutes.[95]

Four specialised institutions have been established and they are located within the Islamic World:

- The Islamic Development Bank (IDB), in Jeddah (Kingdom of Saudi Arabia);
- The Islamic States Broadcasting Organization (ISBO), in Jeddah (Kingdom of Saudi Arabia);
- International Islamic News Agency (IINA), in Jeddah (Kingdom of Saudi Arabia);
- The Islamic Educational, Scientific and Cultural Organization (ISESCO), in Rabat (Kingdom of Morocco).

The Islamic Development Bank (IDB)

The IDB is the international finance guild for the entire OIC.[96] Whilst offering services such as equity participation, non-interest loans and lease facilities, which contribute to the promotion of social and economic development within individual Member States and other Muslim communities throughout the world, the Bank also supports technical cooperation between Islamic Countries (TCIC). Moreover, like the Islamic Solidarity Fund (ISF), the Bank provides relief to Member States that suffer natural and man-made disasters.

The decision to establish the IDB originated from the efforts of Muslim Heads of State to establish a united Islamic economic and political bloc. The need for such a bloc was felt particularly strongly after the burning of the al-Aqsa mosque, the third holiest place for Muslim worship, during 1969. The al-Aqsa incident galvanised the Islamic community and prompted Muslim States to organise a series of conferences of Islamic Foreign Ministers under the auspices of the OIC. Two conferences were held in March and December 1970. These conferences proved to be precursors to the Cairo meeting of February 1972 in which an important document, 'the Institution of an Islamic Bank, Economics and Islamic Doctrine' (more widely known as the Egyptian Study) was approved.[97]

---

[95] <http://www.oic-oci.org/> (15 October 2004).

[96] For a detailed consideration see SA Meenai, *The Islamic Development Bank: A Case-Study of Islamic Co-operation* (London and New York, Kegan Paul International, 1989). Useful information can also be obtained from <http://www.isdb.org/> (7 May 2004).

[97] See A Saeed, *Islamic Banking and Interest: A Study of the Prohibition of Riba and its Contemporary Interpretation* (Leiden, Brill, 1999) 12–13.

The Egyptian Study proved instrumental in the drafting and ultimate adoption of the so-called 'Declaration of Intent for the establishment of the Islamic Development Bank' issued by the Conference of Finance Ministers of Islamic Countries (December 1973).[98] The inaugural meeting of the Board of Governors took place in July, and the Bank was formally opened in October 1975.[99] There are currently 53 members of the Bank, all of them States Parties to the OIC. The Bank performs wide-ranging functions. These include participating in equity capital and granting loans for pro- ductive projects and enterprises to institutions within Member States. The Bank also assists Member States in promoting foreign trade, especially in capital goods. It provides technical assistance to Member States. The assistance of the Bank, however, is not restricted to Member States but stretches to Muslims all over the world; it has established special funds to assist Muslim communities in non-Member States.

The activities of the Bank include the implementation of the task-forces on intra-trading, training, health and literacy. The Bank has also provided assistance to member countries in relation to the World Trade Organization (WTO) and the new multilateral trading systems. Assistance through the Bank has been given to Muslim communities in non-member countries, and the Bank has encouraged new initiatives to promote co- operation with national, regional and international organisations.[100] In addition, the Bank has invested resources in establishing such projects as the Islamic Banking Portfolio (IBP), the Unit Trust Investment Fund (UIF), the Infra-Structure Fund (ISF) and the Islamic Research and Training Institute (IRTI). These establishments, combined with recent structural and administrative changes, appear to have made the operations of the Bank significantly more effective.

The Islamic States Broadcasting Organization (ISBO)

By encouraging co-operation between Member States in the field of broadcasting vis-à-vis the exchange of radio and television programmes among the broadcasting organisations of these countries, the ISBO nurtures co-operation amongst OIC Member States and also stimulates the habituation of Member States with each other's religious and cultural heritage, and social and economic progress. It also encourages the feeling of brotherhood among Muslim peoples and aims to unite them in the development of Islamic causes. Importantly, the ISBO promulgates the principles of the Islamic Dawa (invitation to Islam) and encourages the teaching of Arabic and other languages spoken in the Member States.

---

[98] See the Second Annual Report of the Islamic Development Bank (1976–1977) at 4.
[99] See the Annual Report of the Islamic Development Bank (1999–2000) at 6.
[100] *Ibid*, at 36.

International Islamic News Agency (IINA)

The Agency was formally established at the third Islamic Conference held in Jeddah in March 1972. The principal objective of the Agency is to promote the exchange of information between news agencies vis-à-vis programmes of co-operation to ameliorate Member States' understanding of each other's political, economic and social situations. It also aims to raise the professional standards of the news media in all Member States in accordance with Islamic values.

The Islamic Educational, Scientific and Cultural Organization (ISESCO)

The original idea of establishing the ISESCO was considered at the Tenth Conference of Islamic Foreign Ministers. It was formally adopted at the Eleventh Conference when Resolution No 2/11–C approved the Statute of this newly created institution. The Organization's headquarters are situated in Rabat, Kingdom of Morocco. The ISESCO aims to promote co-operation between Member States in the fields of education, science, and culture. Regarding education, the Organization recommends that Islamic ethics and values should be integrated into the school curriculum. In the area of science, the use of modern technology and the development of applied sciences are encouraged within the boundaries of Islamic ideals, whilst cultural and educational exchanges are organised with a view to promoting world peace and security.

STANDING COMMITTEES

At present, there are four standing committees:

- *Al-Quds* Committee
- The Standing Committee for Information and Cultural Affairs (COMIAC)
- The Standing Committee for Economic and Trade Cooperation (COMCEC)
- The Standing Committee for Scientific and Technological Affairs (COMSTECH).

Al-Quds **Committee**[101]

The Committee was established as a consequence of Resolution No 1/6 –P adopted at the Sixth Islamic Conference of Foreign Ministers. The Islamic

[101] See discussion above on *Al-Quds* Funds.

Conference was convened on 12–15 July 1975. The *Al-Quds* Committee, also known as the Jerusalem Committee, was established with the following objectives:

(i) to study the evolution of the situation in Jerusalem;

(ii) to follow the implementation of resolutions adopted by the Islamic Conferences in this regard;

(iii) to follow the implementation of resolutions adopted by various international bodies on Jerusalem;

(iv) to make contacts with other international institutions that could play a role in safeguarding Jerusalem;

(v) to put forward proposals to the Member States, as well as all bodies concerned on measures to be taken to ensure the implementation of these resolutions and to face new situations;

(vi) to submit an annual report to the Islamic Conference of Foreign Ministers.

The Committee is currently chaired by King Mohamed VI of Morocco and comprises government ministers from sixteen of the OIC Member States: Bangladesh, Egypt, Guinea, Indonesia, Iran, Iraq, Jordan, Lebanon, Mauritania, Morocco, Niger, Pakistan, Palestine, Saudi Arabia, Senegal, and Syria. An annual report is submitted to the ICFM.

The Standing Committee for Information and Cultural Affairs (COMIAC)

This Committee, like its two counterparts (COMCEC and COMSTECH), was established in accordance with Resolution No 13/3–P (IS) adopted at the Third Islamic Summit held in January 1981; all three committees are ministerial level committees and consist of representatives from the OIC Member States. This Committee's responsibilities are two-fold: firstly, it must observe and ensure the implementation of the OIC's resolutions on information and cultural affairs; secondly, it must suggest means of improving the proficiency of, and co-operation between, Member States in these areas. For example, it examines the problems of childcare and the upbringing of youth in an Islamic environment. Most notably, the Committee reviews the progress of the OIC's 'presentation aid progress' action plan to promote Islam as a religion of peace and progress. The Committee's policy recommendations are submitted to the ICFM. Chaired by the President of Senegal, the Committee is open to all Member States and holds its meetings in Dakar.

The Standing Committee for Economic and Trade Cooperation (COMCEC)

As noted above, the Committee was established at the same time as COMIAC and COMSTECH. Its objectives include ensuring the implementation of the OIC's resolutions and encouraging co-operation between Member States, but it does so specifically in relation to the fields of economics and commerce: it develops guidelines for successful bilateral or multilateral agreements between Member States in economic areas such as agriculture, communication, industry, transport and tourism, in both the private and public sectors. On receiving reports from the appropriate subsidiary bodies, COMCEC provides feedback and recommendations for better progress. The President of Turkey chairs the Committee and its meetings are held in Istanbul. Its has held a series of meetings, the most recent being convened in 2003.

The Standing Committee for Scientific and Technological Affairs (COMSTECH)

COMSTECH was conceived at the same time as the two aforementioned Committees. COMSTECH ensures the implementation of resolutions adopted by the Islamic Summit and the ICFM, and encourages the development of capabilities in individual Member States, and co-operation between them, in the areas of science and technology. These fields include education, health, housing, meteorology, and academic and applied research. Chaired by the President of Pakistan, COMSTECH holds its meetings in Islamabad; the Committee is open to all Member States. Recently, its meetings have generally been on a biannual basis, the latest being held in 2003.

CONCLUSIONS

The present chapter has examined the sources of Islamic law—the *Sharia*, and Islamic international law—the *Siyar*. This exercise is fruitful for a variety of reasons. Firstly, this survey has highlighted the arduous processes and passages through which contemporary Islamic legal systems have evolved. Secondly, the analysis has refined our appreciation of the distinction between binding legal norms on the one hand and theological values and aspirations on the other. A systematic historical examination not only reflects the strength of Islam as a religion, but also affirms the tenacity of the *Sharia* which continues to flourish and 'be interpreted in the light of societal changes';[102] this tenacity and vibrancy of *Sharia* is also represented in the Islamic legal maxim *tatagayyar al-ahkam bi tagayaur al-zaman*, translated as 'legal ruling may change with changes in time'.[103]

Thirdly, a significant portion of the chapter has addressed the complex subject of Islamic identity. The issue of identity, particularly an identity based on a religious ethos, represents a vexed subject of general international law, where there is an increasing emphasis on secularism. In its attempts to configure and resolve the subject of identity, this study has placed reliance on the membership of an organisation which aims to promote the interest of Muslims and Islamic States. The critics of this study may advocate differing approaches. However, the present work advocates Islamic Identity of States to coincide with their membership of the OIC. We have examined the various institutions affiliated to the OIC, and its agenda in promoting the interests of Muslim States. A long-term, though improbable, aim of the drafters of the OIC Charter had been the economic and possibly political union of the Islamic States. This would have been a step towards forging an *Ummah*, which does not perceive boundaries between Islamic communities and does not validate the concept of nationality.[104] However, such idealistic conceptions are at present deemed impracticable and have not been addressed either by the provisions of the Charter or by the individual Member States. Short of major claims of economic and political union, the OIC nevertheless has a number of positive features encouraging economic co-operation through a range of diverse projects. Article II(A), 2 of the Charter represents the fundamental objective as being 'to consolidate co-operation among Muslim States in the economic, social, cultural, scientific and other vital fields of activities'.

Having been established with a religious as opposed to a regional focus, the OIC might appear limited when contrasted with, for example, the European Union (EU), the African Unity (AU), or the South Asian Association for Regional Cooperation (SAARC). Islam, the fastest growing religion in the world, nevertheless nurtures an overarching bond amongst its followers—the strength of this attachment is evident through the mechanics of this organisation. The OIC has played a critical role in dispute resolution amongst Islamic States themselves. As this study explores, it has also been instrumental in instituting mediation processes at the regional or global level. In so far as combating the scourge of terrorism is concerned, the work of the OIC requires a detailed analysis, a subject to be addressed in a subsequent chapter.[105]

---

[102] Baderin, n 31 above, at 30.
[103] *Ibid.*
[104] See generally CN Khan, 'Commonwealth of Muslim States' (1963) *Voices of Islam* 41; M Ahmad, 'Umma—The Idea of a Universal Community' (1975) *Islamic Studies* 27.
[105] See below, chapter 7.

2

The Sharia and Siyar in the Development of the Law of Nations

INTRODUCTION

OUR EARLIER EXAMINATION has highlighted the complexities inherent in enunciating absolute principles of the *Sharia* and the *Siyar*.[1] Notwithstanding complexities in formulating precise legal principles, it remains clear that *Sharia* and *Siyar* have been intimately involved in the growth of international law. Significant legal norms, as this chapter examines, have their origins in the Islamic world. Many contemporary laws establishing inter alia commercial, contractual and humanitarian norms are informed by *Sharia*.[2] There is concern and disappointment with the 'eurocentricism' that has meant a negation of the contributions which other civilisations have made in shaping the law of nations.[3] In the stereotypical negative images Islam is exclusively and invariably associated with destruction and violence. Insights into the profound spiritual and jurisprudential richness of the Muslim tradition are required to overcome existing preconceptions and prejudices towards Islam and Muslim States.

---

[1] See above, chapter 1.

[2] See MA Boisard, 'On the Probable Influence of Islam on Western Public and International Law' (1980) 11 *International Journal of Middle East Studies* 429; T Landscheidt, 'Der Einfluß des Islam auf die Entwicklung der Temperamenta Belli im europäischen Völkerrecht' (Göttingen, Unpublished Dissertation, 1955); MC Bassiouni, 'Protection of Diplomats under Islamic Law' (1980) 74 *American Journal of International Law* 609.

[3] Professor Abdullahi Ahmed An-Na'im has reiterated the position in the following terms. He notes: '[i]n my view, there can only be one international law, but it has to be truly international by incorporating relevant principles from different legal traditions, instead of the exclusive Euro-centric concept, principles and institutions of international law as commonly known today' Workshop on Islamic Law: Islamic Law and International Law, Joint AALS, American Society of Comparative Law and Law and Society Association, 2004 (Annual Meeting) <http://www.aals.org/am2004/islamiclaw/international.htm> 2–6 January 2004 (19 May 2004); see also MN Shaw, *International Law* 5th edn (Cambridge, Cambridge University Press, 2003) at 26; for a rare, though useful contemporary European perspective on Islam see S Ferrari and A Bradney (eds), *Islam and European Legal Systems* (Aldershot, Ashgate, 2000).

A second defect—which needs urgent rectification—is the stereotypical representation of the Islamic concepts of *Jihad*, freedom of religion and minority rights. There is much adverse publicity that Islam advocates violence and terrorism. There are tensions from within the Muslim community and jurists differ as to the precise scope of the application of *Jihad*. Having taken account of these strains and stresses, as this chapter explores, it would still be erroneous to assume that terrorism and aggression form an inherent part of Islamic State practices. The concept of *Jihad*, as Islam's *bellum justum*, it is contended, has been fully absorbed in the United Nations prohibition on the use of force. The implementation of the norms of religious tolerance and minority rights have arguably been more controversial. As this chapter explores, different approaches have characterised the practices of modern Islamic States.

SHARIA AND THE LAW OF NATIONS

Amidst the largely Christian oriented impressions which have been instrumental in formulating the principles of international law, there were a number of exceptions. One of the key exceptions was provided by the rise and spread of Islam.[4] The present analysis projects the view that the *Sharia* and *Siyar* have not only had considerable interaction with international law, *Siyar* has in many ways been instrumental in developing the law of nations. The *Qur'an* and *Sunna* have confirmed the sanctity of treaties and devised legal principles on the treatment of aliens, freedom of the high seas, diplomatic protection and expropriation of property.[5] The *Sharia* and *Siyar* have made invaluable contributions to modern environmental laws, and to the establishment of modern regimes of human rights law and international humanitarian laws.[6]

Within Islamic law, treaties are akin to contractual obligations governed by the following fundamental principles. Firstly, freedom to enter into treaties is subject to the proscription that the treaty must not contain

---

[4] See M Khadduri, 'Islam and the Modern Law of Nations' (1956) 50 *American Journal of International Law* 358; S Mahmassani, 'The Principles of International Law in the Light of Islamic Doctrine' (1966) 117(1) *Recueil des cours de l'académie de droit international* 205; S Verosta 'International Law in Europe and West Asia between 100 and 650 AD' (1964) 113(III) *Recueil des cours de l'académie de droit international* 491; CH Alexandrowicz, 'The Afro-Asian World and the Law of Nations' (1968) 123 (I) *Recueil des cours de l'académie de droit international* 121; HS Khalilieh, *Islamic Maritime Law: An Introduction* (Leiden, Brill, 1998).

[5] Mahmassani, *ibid*, at 227–73; also see J Rehman, 'Islamic Law and Environmental Regulations: An Analysis of the Rules and Principles contained in the *Sharia* and Modern Muslim States Practices' paper prepared for the University of Tezukayama (Japan), January 2004 (Unpublished, on file with the author).

[6] J Cockayne, 'Islam and International Humanitarian Law: From a Clash to a Conservation between Civilizations' (2002) 84 *International Review of the Red Cross* 597.

provisions contrary to Islam. Secondly, all treaty obligations must be respected and be followed in good faith, representing the modern international legal norm of *pacta sunt servanda*.[7] The *Qur'an* ordains Muslims 'to fulfil the covenant of God when you have a covenant and break not oaths after their confirmation'.[8] Indeed this law of respecting international obligations is so strong that it could even override traditional principles of *Jihad*. As the *Qur'an* commands, '. . . but if they seek your aid in religion it is your duty to help them, except against a people with whom ye have a treaty of mutual alliance'.[9] The tradition derived from Prophet Muhammad also confirms the sanctity and observance of treaty obligations. As the founder and head of the first Islamic State, Prophet Muhammad entered into a range of international agreements. He also emphasised the need for compliance with all aspects of these pacts and agreements.[10] The sanctity of treaties now forms part of the established code of the State Practices of the international community, including all the Muslim States. Thirdly, Islamic law ordains that there must be genuine consent among parties entering into a treaty arrangement and its provisions must not be coercive, unjust or oppressive towards one party. The practices of Muhammad as head of the State again provide the primary example. In his treaty with the Christians of the town of *Najarn* in Arabia, the Prophet cancelled the *riba* (usury) accrued to their debts that had accumulated since pre-Islamic times.[11]

The significance of international trade and commerce also forms an essential feature of *Siyar*. The *Siyar* confirms and develops international trade and commerce and has a particular bias towards *laissez-faire*. According to one authority:

> [a] dissertation has been written on the commercial language of the Koran, showing that the tradesman Prophet could not keep free of metaphors taken from his business. 'God' he repeatedly says, 'is good at accounts'. The Believers are doing a good business, the unbelievers a losing trade. Those who buy error for guidance make a bad bargain. . . . Even when he was sovereign at Medinah he did not disdain to buy goods wholesale and make a profit by selling them retail; while occasionally he consented to act as auctioneer.[12]

---

[7] 'The rule *pacta sunt servanda* is one of the fundamental principles of Islamic law' J Schacht, 'Islamic law in Contemporary States' (1959) 8 *American Journal of Comparative Law* 133, at 139. For the elaboration of the principle in general international law see JF O'Connor, *Good Faith in International Law* (Aldershot, Hants, 1991); MN Shaw, *International Law* 5th edn (Cambridge, Cambridge University Press, 1997) at 811.

[8] The *Qur'an* (16: 91).

[9] The *Qur'an* (8: 72).

[10] See HM Zawati, *Is Jihād a Just War? War, Peace, and Human Rights Under Islamic and Public International Law* (Lewiston, NY, Edwin Mellen Press, 2001) at 55–8.

[11] A Saeed, *Islamic Banking and Interest: A Study of the Prohibition of Riba and its Contemporary Interpretation* (Leiden, Brill, 1999) 30.

[12] DS Macgoliouth, *Muhammad and the Rise of Islam* (London and New York, GP Putnam Sons, 1905) 69.

From the *Sunna* of Muhammad, the interest of the Prophet in international trade and commerce becomes self-evident. It is well established that he had travelled and conducted business as a merchant in various countries.[13] He chose his first wife Khadija, the wealthy businesswoman and financier, and established his reputation as an honest and committed trader. Subsequent Islamic practices reinforced these principles of international trade. International commerce and trade acted as important tools for the expansion of the frontiers of Islam. Islamic ideals of commerce as well as commodities were exported from Arabia to the West to China and the Far East. According to Udovitch, the ports of Basra and Baghdad emerged

[a]s the hub of a flourishing international trade with goods as prosaic as paper and ink and as exotic as panther skin and ostriches streaming into Mesopotamia from the four corners of the globe. Here they were either sold, or transhipped by caravan to the Mediterranean coast or by caravan or ship on to further East. Sustaining long distance trade . . . regardless of its absolute volume, implies a fairly advanced degree of commercial techniques available to those engaged in this trade. Conversely, a clear understanding of the framework within which commerce was, or could have been carried out would offer us a valuable indicator of the level of this aspect of economic life.[14]

The advanced commercial techniques, as referred to by Udovitch, were based on laws and regulations, some of which had a substantial impact on subsequent developments within international and national commercial norms. In its interaction with the West, Islamic commercial law left a substantial imprint. Bills of exchange and assignments of debts, also referred to as *hawalah*, were practised by Islamic States as early as the eighth century AD.[15] The concepts and mechanisms derived from *hawalah* were introduced on the European continent during the twelfth century AD. The *Sharia* also developed the system of partnership laws, including the *mufawada* (unlimited, universal partnership) and *inân* (limited investment partnerships).[16] Islam impacted upon the development of trade and economic laws and commercial codes of the domestic legal systems of several European countries. Mahmassani alludes to French business transactions, pointing out that the concept known in France as *aval* is derived from the aforementioned term, *hawalah*.[17] The Islamic regulations of *inân*

---

[13] CG Weeramantry, *Islamic Jurisprudence: An International Perspective* (London, Macmillan Press, 1988) 3.

[14] AL Udovitch 'Commercial Techniques in Early Medieval Islamic Trade' in DS Richards (ed), *Islam and the Trade of Asia: A Colloquium* (Oxford, Bruno Cassirer, 1970) 37–66 at 38.

[15] GM Badr, 'Islamic Law: Its Relations to Other Legal Systems' (1978) 26 *American Journal of Comparative Law* 188, at 196. On the broad application and scope of *hawalah* see below, chapter 6.

[16] Mahmassani, n 4 above, at 271–2. According to Professor de Santillana, 'among our positive acquisitions from [Islamic] law, there are legal institutions such as limited partnerships and certain technicalities of commercial law'. D de Santillana, 'Law and Society' in J Schacht and CE Bosworth (eds), *The Legacy of Islam* (Oxford, Clarendon Press, 1974) 309–10.

[17] Mahmassani, n 4 above, at 265–6.

appear to have influenced the development of English commercial laws regarding 'occasional partnership'[18] and the doctrine of 'trust' has arguably derived from the *Sharia* principles of *waqf*.[19]

As we have already commented, the principles of *Siyar* were further elaborated and expanded into a distinct legal discipline by the great Muslim jurist and philosopher Abu Hanifa.[20] Abu Hanifa encouraged his disciples to engage in jurisprudential understanding of *Siyar*. Although for much of the subsequent centuries, *Siyar* as an independent legal discipline was not promoted, Islamic States nevertheless had to formulate a series of laws in their relations with the outside world. With the expansion of the Muslim empire, Islamic trade also expanded and blossomed. In the second millennium, there emerged a network of commercial relations between the Islamic world and the non-Islamic nations of southern and central Europe. In order to encourage international trade and commercial transactions, Muslim rulers provided substantial privileges. The Ottoman rulers are renowned for initiating commercial privileges and special concessions to European nations.[21] Once trade routes to India and the Far East were developed by the Europeans, resulting in a reduction in trade with the Ottoman Empire, the Ottoman Sultans provided liberal terms in their treaties to revive international trade and commerce. Thus the Treaty of Alliance between Sultan Sulayman the Magnificent and Francis I, King of France, signed in 1535, not only granted French subjects in the Ottoman territories the right to practise their religion but also accorded them exemptions from poll tax along with the right of trial in their consulates in accordance with their own laws. According to article 2 of the treaty, the King of France had the right to

> ... send to Constantinople or Pera or other places of the Empire a bailiff ... The said bailiff and consul shall be received and maintained in proper authority so that each one of them may in his locality, and without being hindered by any judge, qadi, soubashi or other according to his faith and law, hear, judge and determine all causes, suits and differences both civil and criminal, which might arise between merchants and other subjects of the King (of France) ... The qadi or other officers of the Grand Signior may not try any differences between the merchants and subjects of the King, even if the said merchants should request it, and if perchance the said qadis should hear a case their judgment shall be null and void.

---

[18] Mahmassani, n 4 above, at 265.

[19] Badr, n 15 above, at 196.

[20] See JL Esposito, *The Oxford Encyclopaedia of Modern Islamic World* vol II (New York, Oxford University Press, 1995) at 457. Also see above, chapter 1.

[21] See JC Hurewitz (ed), *The Middle East and North Africa in World Politics: A Documentary Record — European Expansion 1535–1914* (New Haven, Yale University Press, 1975); M Evans, *Religious Liberty and International Law in Europe* (Cambridge, Cambridge University Press, 1997) 60.

This network of contacts and commercial relations was so strong that it led one authority to argue that:

centuries of peaceful contacts and commercial relations between Islamic and non-Islamic States prior to the admittance of the Ottoman Empire to the European concert in 1856 had led to the emergence of a body of 'regional or Islamic' customary rules which provided the underlying basis of such relations.[22]

An examination of the *Siyar* also confirms that Islam developed international laws pertaining to diplomatic missions and immunities.[23] The subject of diplomatic immunities and the contributions of Islamic States in developing norms relating to diplomatic protection are particularly significant to our thesis. A detailed examination of this subject is reserved for a subsequent chapter.[24] However, in the overall context of Islamic law, a brief comment is nevertheless pertinent.

Within the traditional *Sharia,* diplomats enjoy immunities not dissimilar to the ones provided for in modern international law. Furthermore, in its initial phase classical Islamic law granted widespread concessions to foreign diplomats and emissaries and their arrival was often a ceremonious occasion. According to Mahmassani,

[within] Islamic practice, diplomatic agents were generally received with gorgeous ceremony. Similar ceremonies were observed on their departure. These ceremonies were often accompanied by great hospitality and the display of extravagant pomp and lavish processions, in order to give the emissaries the impression of the grandeur and power of the State.[25]

To facilitate international relations, and to provide adequate securities to foreign diplomats and emissaries, the *Sharia* also devised the concept of *amân*. The pledge of *amân* allowed non-Muslims safety of their person and property whilst resident within the territory of Islam, the *Dar-ul-Islam*. The rights under *amân* were extensive in nature, including the right to life and property, and remained enforceable by the heirs and legal guardians of non-Muslim residents. The concept of *amân* presents a remarkable example of an egalitarian principle, a principle which continues to be invoked by modern judicial systems to protect the rights of aliens. Thus, in one case, the Pakistan High Court had to place reliance on the *amân* doctrine to

---

[22] H Moinuddin, *The Charter of the Islamic Conference and Legal Framework of Economic Cooperation Among its Member States: A Study of the Charter, the General Agreement for Economic, Technical and Commercial Co-operation and the Agreement for Promotion, Protection and Guarantee of Investments Among Member States of the OIC* (Oxford, Clarendon Press, 1987) at 39.

[23] See Bassiouni, n 2 above, at 609.

[24] See below, chapter 4.

[25] Mahmassani, n 4 above, 265–6; M Hamidullah, *Muslim Conduct of State: Being a Treatise on Siyar, that is Islamic Notion of Public International Law, Consisting of the Laws of Peace, War and Neutrality, Together with precedents from Orthodox Practices and Precedent by a Historical and General Introduction* (Lahore, Sh Muhammad Ashraf, 1977) 151.

accord legal capacity to the successor of *enemy aliens* to successfully challenge the confiscation of their property.[26]

The Court specifically noted its inability to find similar principles within the statutory provisions and within the common law. Whilst elaborating on the *amân* doctrine, the Court stated that '*amân* is a pledge of security by virtue of which an enemy alien would be entitled to protection while he is in the dar-ul-Islam, [and] no procedural technicality can take away [these] rights'.[27] The *amân* concept is further strengthened by the *Sharia* principles relating to expropriation of foreign property. Whilst the *Sharia* does not prohibit expropriation of property per se, there remain the essential prerequisites of establishing compulsion of necessity, non-discrimination in acquisition and an obligation to pay compensation—points which are dealt with by the sole arbitrator, Dr Mahmassani, in the LIAMCO award.[28]

The concepts of arbitration, *tahkím* and mediation were developed by Prophet Muhammad and regulated by *Sharia* as important mechanisms for dispute resolution.[29] Both the *Qur'an* and the *Sunna* project mechanisms of dispute resolution, including arbitration and mediation. Prophet Muhammad himself acted as arbitrator in resolving disputes on numerous occasions. Arbitration was known in early Arabia among the various tribes. It was the chief form of justice among individuals in a society where right often depended on might. Islamic law recognised the legality of arbitration as a peaceful means of settling disputes in both civil and public law. Prophet Muhammad was appointed as the arbitrator by the tribal chiefs of Mecca to settle disputes which arose between them about the sacred Black Stone. There was also arbitration taking place during the reign of the fourth Caliph Alī Ibn Abī Tālib. According to an agreement, signed in year 37 H between Alī Ibn Abī Tālib and Muaiyah, the Governor of Syria, Caliph Alī appointed Abu Mua al-Ash'ari and Muawiyah appointed 'Amr Ibn al-'Ass as arbitrators to resolve a political dispute.[30]

In expanding on the procedures of *tahkím* within Islamic law, Zawati notes:

> According to Islamic law, *al-tahkím* procedure can be characterized as follows: first, the free selection of arbitrators; second, arbitrators must respect the rules of Islamic law; third, parties who agree to submit their dispute to arbitration must respect its ruling, and comply with its provisions; fourth, no arbitration in *al-hudūd* and *al-Qisās* (punishments stipulated in the *Qurān*); fifth, the award is

---

[26] *State Bank of India v The Custodian of Evacuee Property*, West Pakistan (1969) PLD, Lahore, 1050.

[27] *Ibid*, at 1062.

[28] (1981) 20 ILM 37 at 201. See RB Von Mehren and PN Kourides, 'International Arbitration Between States and Foreign Private Parties: The Libyan Nationalization Cases' (1981) 75 *American Journal of International Law* 478.

[29] Mahmassani, n 4 above, at 272–3.

[30] Zawati, n 10 above, at 70.

considered null and void in two cases: if the arbitrator is not chosen freely by the parties, and if he is a close relative to one of the litigants; and finally, the arbitrator must be a wise and just believer.[31]

Arbitration is now a key mechanism for dispute resolution both in the international law arena and within the domestic legal systems of modern States, including Islamic countries.[32]

JIHAD, VIOLENCE AND INTERNATIONAL TERRORISM: ARTICULATION OF LEGAL PRINCIPLES

There is considerable debate as to the extent to which *Sharia* and *Siyar* sanction aggression, violence and terrorism.[33] As indicated in the introductory sections of this work, critics of Islam regard it as promoting violence and aggression. Within the legal framework, the debate centres around the concept of *Jihad*. The terminology of *Jihad* is often erroneously applied as being synonymous with terrorism or violence. We have already noted that the term *Ijtihad* has the same origins as *Jihad*, *Ijtihad* meaning exerting one's faculties to form an opinion.[34] The term *Jihad* is adopted from the Arabic verb *Jahada*, which connotes exerting oneself, labour or toil. In essence *Jihad* is an expression of endeavour and struggle in the cause of Allah.[35] This exertion and struggle is primarily through passive means; the word of God is to spread through non-violent means with persuasion as the principal avenue. Expanding on the content of *Jihad*, Prophet Muhammad in his *Hadith* observed that the strongest form of *Jihad* is through persuasion. While forming an integral part of *Jihad*, the use of force represents only one aspect of *Jihad*. In elaborating upon *Jihad*, the principal source of the *Sharia*, the *Qur'an* makes the following observations:

> O Ye who believe! Shall I guide you to a commerce that will save you from painful chastisement? It is that you believe in Allah and His Messenger, and strive in the cause of Allah with your belongings and your persons. That is better for you. If ye have knowledge, He will forgive your sins, and will admit you to Gardens beneath which rivers flow, and to pure and pleasant dwellings in Gardens of Eternity. That is the supreme triumph.[36]

---

[31] *Ibid*, at 70.

[32] See AHA Soons (ed), *International Arbitration: Past and Prospects, A Symposium to Commemorate the Centenary of the Birth of Professor JHW Verzijl* (Dordrecht, Martinus Nijhoff Publishers, 1990); AM Stuyt, *Survey of International Arbitration 1794–1989* (Dordrecht, Martinus Nijhoff Publishers, 1990); JG Merrills, *International Dispute Settlement* (Cambridge, Cambridge University Press, 1998).

[33] SP Huntington, *The Clash of Civilizations and the Remaking of World Order* (London, Simon & Schuster, 1996) 263; JL Payne, *Why Nations Arm* (Oxford, Basil Blackwell, 1989) 121–33.

[34] See above, chapter 1.

[35] Zawati, n 10 above, at 13–14.

[36] The *Qur'an* (61: 11–13).

This broad vision of *Jihad* is further explained by Islamic jurists. Majid Khadduri, in his leading work, *War and Peace in the Law of Islam*, provides the following re-statement of *Jihad*. He notes:

> The term *Jihād* is derived from the verb jāhada (abstract noun, juhd) which means 'exerted'. Its juridical-theological meaning is exertion of one's power in Allah's path, that is, the spread of the belief in Allah and in making His word supreme over this world. The individual's recompense would be the achievement of salvation, since the *Jihād* is Allah's direct way to paradise ... *The Jihād, in the broad sense of exertion, does not necessarily mean war or fight, since exertion in Allah's path may be achieved by peaceful means as well as violent means. The Jihād may be regarded as a form of religious propaganda that can be carried on by persuasion or by sword.*[37]

In his recent study, Dr Hilmi M Zawati writes as follows:

> Linguistically speaking, the term Jihad is a verbal noun derived from the verb *jahada*, the abstract noun *juhd*, which means to exert oneself, and to strive in doing things to one's best capabilities. Its meaning is, in fact, extended to comprise all that is in one's power or capacity. Technically, however, Jihad denotes the exertion of one's power in Allah's path, encompassing the struggle against evil in whatever form or shape it arises'.

Another leading scholar, al-kāsāani, in examining the subject makes the observation that:

> according to Islamic law (al-Shar'al-Islami), Jihad is used in expending ability and power in struggling in the path of Allah by means of life, property, words and more.[38]

The *Oxford Encyclopaedia of the Modern Islamic World* notes that:

> Jihad in Arabic simply means 'struggle' and it came to denote in Islamic history and classical jurisprudence the struggle on behalf of the cause of Islam.[39]

---

[37]   M Khadduri, *War and Peace in the Law of Islam* (Baltimore and London, The John Hopkins Press, 1955) 55–6 (italics added, footnotes omitted). In another of his works, Khadduri reiterates the point that '[i]n technical language, it was an "exertion" of one's own power to fulfil a prescribed duty, and the believers recompense, in addition to worldly material rewards, would be the achievement of salvation, for the fulfilment of such a duty means the reward of Paradise. This participation might be fulfilled by the heart, the tongue, or the hands, as well as by the sword. The *Jihād* was accordingly a form of religious propaganda carried out by spiritual as well as material means'. M Khadduri, *The Islamic Law of Nations—Shaybānī's Siyar: Translated with an Introduction, Notes and Appendices by M Khadduri* (Baltimore, Maryland, The John Hopkins Press, 1966) at 15.

[38]   Alǎ al-Dān al-kāsāani, *Kitāb Badai' al-Sana'i fi Tartib al Shar'ia* vol 7 (Cario, al-Mtaba 'a al-Jamaliyya, 1910) at 97.

[39]   Zawati, n 10 above, at 13–14. In al-kāsāani's analysis 'according to Islamic law (al-Shar' al-Islami), Jihad is used in expending ability and power in struggling in the path of Allah by means of life, property, words and more.' Alǎ al-Dān al-kāsāani, n 38 above, at 97. JL Esposito, *The Oxford Encyclopaedia of the Modern Islamic World* vol II (New York, Oxford University Press, 1955) at 373.

CONTEXTUALISING *JIHAD* AND THE USE OF FORCE:
INTERTEMPORAL LAW AND COMPATIBILITIES WITH MODERN
NORMS OF INTERNATIONAL LAW

The present discussion aims to answer two key questions which have been the source of much confusion: the identification of primary components of *Jihad* and the debate surrounding the compatibility of *Jihad* with modern norms of international law, particularly the prohibition on the use of force.[40] Before we start our enquiry we need to remind ourselves of a number of factors. First, any analysis has to take account of the context in which Islam was revealed and was able to preserve its existence. Islam was proclaimed in the seventh century AD in Arabia in an extremely hostile and intolerant environment.[41] Violence was the norm, the Arabs being particularly intolerant when challenged upon religious and ideological positions.[42] There were few constraints on the manner and use of force in the international relations that existed at that particular time. In this sense it is to the credit of Islam and *Sharia* that it provided grounds for restricting the use of force, and regulated the conduct of hostilities with humanitarian value such as the ban on the killing of non-combatants, women, children and the elderly.

Having regard to the prevalent violence and terrorism, Islam, in its formative phases had to prepare for a difficult and uncertain future. Prophet

---

[40] The United Nations Charter prohibits the use of force in international relations. Article 2(4) provides—'All Members shall refrain in their international relations from the threat or use of force against the territorial integrity or political independence of any state, on in any other manner inconsistent with the Purposes of the United Nations'. The only exception to this prohibition on the use of force is provided in Article 51 according to which—'Nothing in the present Charter shall impair the inherent right of individual or collective self-defense if an armed attack occurs against a Member of the United Nations, until the Security Council has taken measures necessary to maintain international peace and security. Measures taken by Members in the exercise of this right of self-defense shall be immediately reported to the Security Council and shall not in any way affect the authority and responsibility of the Security Council under the present Charter to take at any time such action as it deems necessary to maintain or restore international peace and security'. Charter of the United Nations (signed 26 June 1945, entered into force 24 October 1945) 59 Stat 1031, TS 993, 3 Bevans 1153, UNTS xvi (892 UNTS 119), UKTS (1946) 67.

[41] See JB Glubb, *War in the Desert: RAF Frontier Campaign* (New York, WW Norton, 1961) at 31.

[42] Emphasising upon this point, Professor Abdullahi Ahmed An-Na'im makes the observation that '[t]he historical context within which *Sharia* was elaborated during the first three centuries of Islam was an extremely harsh and violent environment, where the use of force in intercommunal relations was the unquestioned norm. It was simply conceptually incoherent and practically impossible for *Sharia* regulation of intercommunal (international) relations to have been based on principles of peaceful co-existence and rule of law in the modern sense of these terms'. AA An-Na'im, 'Upholding International Legality Against Islamic and American Jihad' in K Booth and T Dunne (eds), *Worlds in Collision: Terror and the Future of Global Order* (London, Palgrave, 2002) 162–72, at 166.

Muhammad and his followers represented a community that faced extermination. Indeed, Muhammad himself was forced to migrate to Medina to avoid persecution and assassination, his migration marking the beginning of the Muslim calendar.[43] It was this betrayal, attempted humiliation, and disregard for kinship and obligations on the part of the Quresh of Mecca that disillusioned Muhammad and the beleaguered Muslim community. The *Qur'an* make the observations:

> How could there be a guarantee for the idolaters on the part of Allah and His Messenger, except in favour of those with whom you entered into an express treaty at the Sacred Mosque? So long as they carry out their obligations thereunder, you must carry out your obligations. Surely Allah loves those who are mindful of their obligations. How can there be a guarantee for the others, who, if they were to prevail against you, would have no regard for any tie of kinship or pact in respect of you. They seek to please you with words, while their hearts repudiate them; most of them are perfidious. They have bartered the Signs of Allah for small gains and hindered people from His way. Evil indeed is that which they have done. They show no regard for any tie of kinship or any pact in respect of a believer. If they repent and observe Prayer and pay the Zakat, then they are your brethren in faith. We expound Our commandments for a people who know.[44]

Against this backdrop of vulnerability and uncertainty it is to the credit of Islam that it adopted a balanced approach towards the use of force. A number of jurists and scholars have interpreted *Qur'anic* verses to advance the position that the classical *Siyar* advocates the necessity of the use of force to spread Islam as the primary expression of *Jihad*. The cited verses include:

> Fight in the cause of Allah against those who fight against you, but transgress not. Surely, Allah loves not the transgressors. Once they start fighting, kill them wherever you meet them, and drive them out from where they have driven you out; for aggression is more heinous than killing. But fight them not in the proximity of the Sacred Mosque unless they fight you there-in; should they fight you even there, then fight them; such is the requital of these disbeliveers. Then if they desist, surely Allah is most Forgiving, Ever Merciful. Fight them until all aggression ceases and religion is professed for the pleasure of Allah alone. If they desist, then be mindful that no retaliation is permissible except against the aggressors.[45]

and

[43] Weeramantry, n 13 above, at 4–5; J Rehman, 'Self-Determination, State Building and the Muhajirs: An International Legal Perspective of the Role of the Indian Muslim Refugees in the Constitutional Development of Pakistan' (1994) 3 *Contemporary South Asia* 111–29, at 113.

[44] The *Qur'an* (9: 7–11).

[45] The *Qur'an* (2: 191–94).

Warn the disbelievers of a painful chastisement, excepting those of them with who you have a pact and who have not defaulted in any respect, nor supported anyone against you. Carry out the obligations you have assumed towards them till the end of their terms. Surely Allah loves those who are mindful of their obligations. When the period of four months during which hostilities are suspended expires, without the idolaters having settled the terms of peace with you, resume fighting with them and kill them wherever you find them and make them prisoners and beleaguer them, and lie in wait for them at every place of ambush. Then if they repent and observe Prayer and pay the Zakat, leave them alone. Surely Allah is Most Forgiving, Ever Merciful. If any one of the idolaters seeks asylum with thee, grant him asylum so that he may hear the Word of Allah; then convey him to a place of security for him, for they are a people who lack knowledge.[46]

From an examination of these verses the following points emerge. The use of force is permitted against aggressors and in self-defence. Muslims are obliged to continue *Jihad* with the use of force until the cessation of aggression, or the vindication of their rights as the case may be. However, does vindication of rights incorporate an eventual supremacy of Islam over other religions? In other words, is it justified to use force in order to enforce the word of God? Some leading scholars take the position that classical *Siyar* sanctions the use of force to spread Islam and implement the *Sharia*. Majid Khadduri, for instance, makes reference to *Dar-ul-Harb* (the enemy territory) and *Dar-ul-Islam* (the territory of Islam), pointing to an eventual objective of classical *Siyar* to continue the *Jihad* until all the *Dar-ul-Harb* came under Islamic jurisdiction. There is also evidence that in jurisdictional expansion of Islam force was deployed, although aggression was not the sole motivating factor.[47] Indeed, religious zeal blended with a desire for egalitarianism and reform. Rom Landau's characterisation of the conquest of Damascus by Khalid-ibn-al-walid exemplifies the earlier phase of Islamic expansion. Landau notes:

[I]n an age when 'sack and pillage' was usual procedure followed by a victorious army on entering a conquered city, Khalid-ibn-al-walid's terms to Damascus were humane and very modest. In fact, it seems obvious that the Arab legions considered themselves as liberators of oppressed peoples as well as carriers of Islam.[48]

Whilst acknowledging the extraordinary nature of the religious-reformist zeal, differing academic interpretations have been advanced. Analysing the rationale for the use of force in this early period, Khadduri makes the point that:

---

[46] The *Qur'an* (9: 3–6).
[47] Khadduri, n 37 above, at 63.
[48] R Landau, *Islam and the Arabs* (London, George Allen and Unwin Ltd, 1958) at 41.

The *Jihād* as such was not a casual phenomenon of violence; it was rather a product of complex factors which Islam worked out its jural-doctrinal character. Some writes have emphasised the economic changes within Arabia which produced dissatisfaction and unrest and inevitably led the Arabs to seek more fertile lands outside of Arabia. Yet this theory—plausible as it is in explaining the outburst of Arabs from within their peninsula—is not enough to interpret the character of a war permanently declared against the unbelievers even after the Muslims had established themselves outside Arabia. There were other factors which created in the minds of Muslims a politico-religious mission and conditioned their attitude as a conquering nation.[49]

Elsewhere he has noted:

In theory the *dar al-Islam* was always at war with *dar al-harb*. The Muslims were under a legal obligation to reduce the latter to Muslim rule in order to achieve Islam's ultimate objective, namely, the enforcement of God's Law (the *Shari'a*) over the entire world. The instrument by which the Islamic States were to carry out that objective was *Jihād* (popularly know as holy war), which was always justifiably waged against the infidels and the enemies of the faith. Thus the Jihad was the Islam's *bellum justum*.[50]

In his examination, Professor An-Na'im acknowledges that the concept of *Jihad* could be used for a variety of activities in order to further the 'will of God'.[51] The primary meaning of *Jihad*, according to An-Na'im, is '"self-control" including checking any temptation to harm others'.[52] However his concern is that:

the term can also refer to religiously sanctioned aggressive war to propagate or 'defend' the faith. What is problematic about this latter sense of Jihad is that it involves direct and unregulated violent action in pursuit of political objectives, or self-help in redressing perceived injustice, at the risk of harm to innocent bystanders. . .[53]

Notwithstanding constant reminders that *Jihad* does not necessarily mean use of force, some scholars (principally from the western world) have insisted on adopting this narrow, rigid interpretation. Thus, for example, Roda Mushkat notes that:

Islamic law enjoins Moslems to maintain a State of permanent belligerence with all non-believers, collectively encompassed in the dar al-harb, the domain of war. The Muslims are, therefore, under a legal obligation to reduce non-Muslim communities to Islamic rule in order to achieve Islam's ultimate objective, namely the enforcement of God's law (the Sharia) over the entire world. The

---

[49] Khadduri, *War and Peace,* n 37 above, at 63.
[50] M Khadduri, 'Islam and the Modern Law of Nations' (1956) 50 *American Journal of International Law* 358, at 359.
[51] See An-Na'im, n 42 above, 162–72, at 163.
[52] *Ibid,* at 163.
[53] *Ibid,* at 163.

instrument by which the Islamic state is to carry out that objective is called the Jihad (popularly known as the 'holy war') and is always just, if waged against the infidels and the enemies of the faith.[54]

This image of *Jihad* as an instrument of aggressive war is relished by those who claim fundamentally divergent positions between the Islamic legal order and the non-Muslim world. Such a hypothesis forms the basis of apprehension, tensions and ultimately the so-called 'clash of civilisations'. Payne contrasts what he perceives as the 'western view of what religion is and ought to be, namely, a voluntary sphere where coercion has no place'.[55] with that of Islam. In this comparison:

[the] emphasis on non-violence is not the pattern in the Muslim culture. To the contrary, violence has been a central, accepted element, both in Muslim teaching and in the historical conduct of the religion. For over a thousand years, the religious bias in the Middle Eastern Culture has not been to discourage the use of force, but to encourage it.[56]

In engineering the 'clash', Huntington views Islam as 'a religion of the sword . . . glorify[ing] military virtues'.[57] In his perceptions '[t]he Koran and other statements of Muslim beliefs contain few prohibitions on violence, and a concept of non-violence is absent from Muslim doctrine and practice'.[58] This latter position of *Jihad* however remains contested and is largely inaccurate. Such a narrow and myopic view is a reflection of the narrow mindedness of the critics who (while disregarding the overall historical contextual picture) place exclusive reliance on limited and very specific instances.

It is also the case that a literal interpretation of any of the aforementioned verses of the *Qur'an* does not advocate a policy of *Jihad*, which endorses aggressions; there are substantial restraints and restrictions placed on the use of force. This latter restrictive view is acknowledged even by scholars such as Khadduri, who has advocated a more aggressive and expansionist form of *Jihad*. After making the observation which is noted above,[59] Khadduri acknowledges that 'the *jihād* did not always mean war since Islamic objectives might be achieved by peaceful as well as violent means. Thus the *jihād* may be regarded as intensive religious propaganda which took the form of a continuous process of warfare, psychological and political no less than strictly militarily'.[60] In a separate study, Khadduri accepts that the notion of Islam replacing other religions 'is not stated in the

---

[54] R Mushkat, 'Is War Ever Justifiable? A Comparative Survey' (1987) 9 *Loyola of Los Angeles International and Comparative Law Journal* 227.
[55] Payne, n 33 above, at 121.
[56] *Ibid*, at 122.
[57] Huntington, n 33 above, at 263.
[58] *Ibid*.
[59] Khadduri, n 50 above, at 359.
[60] *Ibid*, at 359.

Qurān'.[61] After an extensive review of the literature, another Islamic scholar, Dr Moinuddin, summarises his position by articulating the following four points on *Jihad* in so far as it relates to the use of force:

(a) that fighting in the cause of Allah is basically sanctioned by the Koran;
(b) that the permission to fight has been granted to the Muslims because they have been wronged or persecuted on the grounds of religion; hence warfare is permitted if Muslims are persecuted, because persecution is worse than slaughter;
(c) that sanction to wage warfare is, however, given against those who fight the Muslims; it is also conditioned by the stipulation that Muslims are not to begin hostilities or commit aggression;
(d) that fighting may be continued until persecution ceases or the persecutors desist.[62]

There is a further, more substantial constituency, which views *Jihad* as a technique of persuasion, fundamentally antithetical to violence and aggression. The concepts of *Jihad* on the one hand, and violence and terrorism on the other are described as being 'dramatically opposed to one another'.[63] According to one *Hadith* of the Prophet Muhammad, a true Muslim is one who hurts no one by word or deed.[64] In providing a commentary on this *Hadith*, Zaki Badawi makes the observation that the fundamentals of the Islamic legal system:

[a]re the protection of the community as a whole, the protection of life, property, honor and sobriety. The Muslim should commit the utmost effort towards self-improvement to be worthy and able to perform these duties. This is called Jihad, which in the mind of many people is equated with Holy war. Acts of violence are abhorred by Islam. War, a function of the failure of human nature, is permitted only in self-defence, and regulated by strict rule to limit its application exclusively to combatants.[65]

It may well be that in the chronicles of Islamic history, there are instances where the lines between violence pure and simple and *Jihad* are blurred; certainly, wars and other societal conflicts of early Islamic experiences by their very nature were destructive and bloody. Islam, as has been examined, in its rudimentary stages saw phases of considerable violence and terrorist activity. Prophet Muhammad was persecuted by the residents of Mecca prior to his *Hijrat*, with the shadow of death placed over him. The rule of both Uthmān ibn 'Affān, the third rightly guided Caliph (644–656) and that of Alī Ibn Abī Tālib, the fourth rightly guided Caliph (656–661) were brought to an end through their assassinations.[66]

---

[61] Khadduri, n 37 above (text accompanying n 16) at 59.
[62] Moinuddin, n 22 above, at 28; also See Y El-Ayouty, 'International Terrorism under the Law' (1999) 5 *ILSA Journal of International and Comparative Law* 485, 488.
[63] *Ibid*, at 489.
[64] Z Badawi, 'Are Muslims Misunderstood' *The Independent* 23 September 2001 at 19.
[65] *Ibid*.
[66] JL Esposito, *The Oxford Encyclopaedia of Modern Islamic World* vol III (New York, Oxford University Press, 1995) 439.

The trail of violence and terrorism has continued throughout the history of Islam. Within their domestic, internalised frameworks many Islamic States suffer from terrorism and violence. A whole host of reasons can be ascribed to such forms of terrorism: inter alia absence of constitutionalism and rule of law, exploitation and abuse of power, dictatorship and denials of fundamental human rights, negation of right of political and economic self-determination.[67] This catalogue of explanations could be extended. It is also the case that there are examples whereby political masters have perpetuated systematic abuse under the guise of 'Islamisation'.[68] In reality, however, there is no connection between the *Sharia's* principles and modern day acts of terrorism. To the contrary, there is substantial condemnation of acts of terrorism within the religious jurisprudence. Highlighting this abhorrence for acts of terrorism, Saudi Arabia, in a report submitted to the Counter-Terrorism Committee, noted that:

> In the Islamic Shariah, . . . crimes of terrorism are included among the crimes of *hirabah*. The severest of penalties area applied to these crimes in the Islamic Shariah, as set forth in the Holy Koran [Koran 5: 33]. The crimes of *hirabah* include the killing and terrorization of innocent people, spreading evil on earth (*al-ifsad fi al-ard*), theft, looting and highway robbery.[69]

Islamic legal scholars, in disassociating *Jihad* from terrorism, have condemned violence, genocide, and suicide bombings.[70] Reiterating Islam's opposition to genocidal warfare, Yassin El-Ayouty cites the *Qur'anic* verse which notes:

> whosoever killeth a human being for other than manslaughter or corruption on earth, it shall be as if he had killed all mankind, and whosoever saveth the life of one, it shall be as if he had saved the life of all mankind.[71]

On suicide bombing or other forms of self-sacrifice he makes the following points:

> [S]elf-sacrificing is a crime under Islamic law. The terrorists claim that Muslims who sacrifice themselves in car bombings and other acts of terror are martyrs and such martyrdom is a sure way to heaven. Islamic jurisprudence, as based on The Koran, says something completely different. Unless a Muslim is engaged in

---

[67] Islam is by no means unique in this regard. Other great religions and religious civilisations including Christianity and Judaism have gone through similar experiences.

[68] J Rehman, 'Accommodating Religious Identities in an Islamic State: International Law, Freedom of Religion and the Rights of Religious Minorities' (2000) 7 *International Journal on Minority and Group Rights* 139; J Rehman, 'Minority Rights and Constitutional Dilemmas of Pakistan' (2001) 19 *Netherlands Quarterly of Human Rights* 417.

[69] Report of the Kingdom of Saudi Arabia submitted pursuant to paragraph 6 of Security Council Resolution 1373 (2001) Concerning Counter-Terrorism S/2001/1294 at 5. Text available at <http://ods-dds-ny.un.org/doc/UNDOC/GEN/N01/722/76/PDF/N0172276.pdf?OpenElement > (7 October 2004).

[70] El-Ayouty, n 62 above, at 489.

[71] *Ibid*.

Jihad, . . . self-sacrifice is anti-Islamic. The Koran says 'be not cast by your own hand to ruin'. Here ruin means oblivious death. In the eyes of Islam, a Muslim killing himself, except in Jihad, dies an apostate or Kafir (non-believer).[72]

A further and final argument to note is that all Islamic States have accepted the provisions of Article 2(4) of the United Nations Charter.[73] There is also a renunciation of violence, aggression and terrorism. They have adopted this position without renouncing their Islamic credentials. This insistence upon the prohibition on the use of force in international relations therefore points towards a compatibility of the fundamental principle of international law with *Sharia* and *Siyar*. If there were any seeds of doubt invigorated by overzealous religious *Jihadists*, modern Islamic States conduct their relations on the basis of contemporary international law, with Article 2(4) as their central focus.

THE USE OF FORCE AND RELIGIOUS TOLERANCE

The emergence of Islam in Arabia in the seventh century and its growth at a phenomenal pace at one point threatened to overtake all other contemporary civilisations. Muhammad, the Prophet and founder of Islam, died in 632 AD. Within a century Muslim Arabs had conquered and were rulers of an area stretching from the borders of India and China to the Atlantic Ocean.[74] This was a huge empire which included much of North Africa, the Near East and Spain—'a collection of peoples under one banner greater than any before and a domain more extensive than the Roman Empire at its height.'[75] This was a remarkable achievement, unparalleled in human history. In the words of one historian:

This astonishing expansion had been achieved by a people who, if they were known at all to the great world beyond the Arabian peninsula, had been dismissed as ignorant nomads. They had overrun something above four-and-a-half million square miles of territory and changed the course of history, subordinating Christianity to Islam in its homelands in the Near East and in North Africa and Spain, forcing the Roman Empire of Byzantium onto the defensive and converting the Empire of the Persians into a bulwark of Islam. Human history tells of no other achievement comparable to this. Alexander had dazzled the ancient

---

[72] El-Ayouty, n 62 above, at 489.

[73] For the provisions of Article 2(4) UN Charter see n 40 above.

[74] Weeramantry makes the point eloquently when he notes '[t]he call of the muezzin from the minaret—"There is no god except God and Muhammad is the Apostle of God"—was, within a century of the Prophet's death, re-echoing in territories as far a field as Spain and China' Weeramantry, n 13 above, at 9; B Lewis, *The Jews of Islam* (Princeton, NJ, Princeton University Press, 1984) 16; Landau, n 48 above, at 45–6; MA Karandikar, *Islam in India's Transition to Modernity* (Bombay, Orient Longmans, 1968) 32–5; see also Khadduri, *War and Peace*, n 37 above.

[75] See R Landau, n 48 above, at 46.

world by his conquests, but he left behind him only legends and a few inscriptions. Where the Arabs passed they created a civilization and a whole pattern of thought and of living which endured and still endures, and they decisively determined the future history of Europe, barring the way to the rich lands of the East and thereby provoking—many centuries later—the voyages of exploration to the West and to the South which were to nurture European power.[76]

As indicated above in the context of *Jihad*, the theory that the Empire of Islam was built around the power of the sword is not reflective of a complete picture. Contrary to commonly held views, the successes of Muslim rulers during this initial phase as well as in subsequent centuries were based on a culmination of factors, vital amongst these being the promise of religious tolerance and a more egalitarian and fairer society.

The promise of tolerance did not presuppose equality and non-discrimination for all individuals regardless of gender, religious differences or race. Nor was tolerance shown towards all religions and minorities. Amongst non-Muslims crucial distinctions were made between *ahal al-kitab* (the Peoples of the Book) and the pagans (the non-believers).[77] Christian and Jewish minorities, as *ahal al-kitab*, were accorded the political status of *dhimmis*.[78] Their existence was tolerated in return for their submission and loyalty to the Muslims and a commitment to pay a special capitulation tax, *jizya*. While the *dhimmis* were allowed to follow their own rules on matters of personal status, the ultimate determinant of this status was the Muslim State, which also excluded them from positions of authority and government.[79] In explaining the relationship of Muslims with polytheists, under the rubric of 'the Jihad against Polytheists' Khadduri makes the following observations:

No compromise is permitted with those who fail to believe in God, they have either to accept Islam or fight . . . All the jurists, perhaps without exception, assert that polytheism and Islam cannot exist together; the polytheists, who enjoin other gods with Allah, must choose between war or Islam. The definition of a polytheist, however, has not been precisely given by any jurist. They exclude not only Scripturaries (who believe in Allah though not in His Apostle) but also Magians (Zoroastrians) whose belief in Allah is obscure, but they had some sort of a book. Polytheism seems to have been confined narrowly to paganism, with no implied concept of a supreme deity.[80]

---

[76] G Eaton, *Islam and the Destiny of Man* (Cambridge, Islamic Text Society, 1994) at 29.

[77] AE Mayer, *Islam and Human Rights: Tradition and Politics* 2nd edn (Boulder, Col, Westview Press, 1995) 127.

[78] See B Ye'or, *The Dhimmi: Jews and Christians Under Islam* (London and Toronto, Associated University Press, 1985); Y Courbage and P Fargues, *Christians and Jews Under Islam* (London, I B Tauris, 1997).

[79] DE Azrt, 'The Role of Compulsion in Islamic Conversion: Jihad, Dhimma and Rida' (2002) 8 *Buffalo Human Rights Law Review* 15, at 27.

[80] Khadduri, n 37 above, at 75.

It would appear that in strict doctrinal terms there was a particular dearth of tolerance for pagan or polytheist minorities. Their choices were limited: to embrace Islam or perish.[81] In practice, however, as Khadduri himself acknowledges, there was a huge amount of vagueness as to those who were excluded from the description of polytheists. Furthermore, the show of tolerance towards the *ahal al-kitab* was not infrequently extended to the pagans; this was particularly the case when the Muslims began to interact with other ancient traditions such as Hinduism.[82] The treatment which non-Muslim minorities received varied depending on the ruler in question, the strength of the empire and its geography. Some regimes were more repressive and intolerant than others.

Whilst in the light of modern developments in international law the system described above appears discriminatory, judged by the standards of the time it was hugely impressive: it promised a much greater measure of tolerance than was being practised by the Christian West. According to one authority:

> Although, like Christianity, Islam was an aggressively universalist religion, it also displayed far more tolerance to followers of other faiths, and particularly Jews and Christians who, like followers of Islam were considered to be 'Peoples of the Book'. Jewish and Christian Communities were, therefore, permitted a large degree of freedom in both religious and civil affairs . . .[83]

It also remains the case that the practices of the Prophet Muhammad, and subsequently those of the Muslim rulers, which now form part of the wider code of Islamic law, seriously defy the 'Western images of Muslim conquerors presenting the conquered Peoples with the choice of conversion to Islam or the sword.'[84] To the contrary, 'conquered Christians and Jews were allowed to persist in their beliefs because Islamic law opposes compelled conversions'.[85] Commenting on the facts as they prevailed during the expansion of Islam, Eaton makes the remark that:

> [t]he rapidity with which Islam spread across the known world of the seventh century was strange enough, but stranger still is the fact that no rivers flowed with blood, no fields were enriched with the corpses of the vanquished. As warriors the Arabs might have been no better than other of their kind who had ravaged and slaughtered across the peopled lands but, unlike these others, they were on a leash. There were no massacres, no rapes, no cities burned. These men

---

[81] According to Azrt, 'The other class of non-Muslims who were not dhimmis were slaves, the fate of polytheists and idolaters who had been captured as prisoners of war rather than slain in or after battle. They had the choice only of slavery, conversion to Islam or death; no special communal contract allowed them to quietly or even humbly practice their religion' n 79 above, at 27.

[82] Mayer, n 77 above, at 127.

[83] MD Evans, *Religious Liberty and International Law in Europe* (Cambridge, Cambridge University Press, 1997) at 59.

[84] Mayer, n 77 above, at 126.

[85] *Ibid*, at 126–7.

feared God to a degree scarcely imaginable in our time and were in awe of His all-seeking presence, aware of it in the wind and the trees, behind every rock and in every valley. Even in these strange lands there was no place in which they could hide from this presence, and while vast distances beckoned them ever onwards they trod softly on the earth, as they had been commanded to do. There had never been a conquest like this.[86]

In view of these considerations it would be convincing to argue that the *dhimmis*, the *ahal al-kitab*, in fact enjoyed a better status under the jurisdiction of Islam in comparison to religious minorities within a Christian State.[87] The contention certainly appears to carry considerable weight of authority during the zenith of the Ottoman and Moghul rule.

The Ottoman rule, for several centuries, retained a vast empire with adherents of various religions.[88] While religious minorities were not always treated with tolerance, the Ottomans did experiment with a special mechanism for the granting of autonomy through the *Millet* system—a system which allowed various religious minorities to enjoy a generous measure of autonomy, in social, civil and religious affairs.[89] Van Dyke's comment is a valid one when, analysing the *Millet* system, he notes: 'it was an application of the right of Self-Determination in advance of Woodrow Wilson.'[90] The Ottomans also continued the Islamic practice of granting capitulations to Christians and other westerners. The capitulations provided a degree of autonomy and self-government, including an exercise of civil and criminal jurisdiction over other co-nationals.[91]

While the interaction between the Christian West and the Muslim Ottoman Turks has been considered by international lawyers, scant attention has been paid to another Muslim Turkish dynasty—the Moghuls, whose rule over much of the Indian Sub-Continent lasted for more than 300 years. The Islamic influence provided elements of similarity in the

---

[86] Eaton, n 76 above, at 29–30.

[87] 'Despite incidents of discrimination and mistreatment of non-Muslims, it is fair to say that the Muslim World, when judged by the standards of the day, generally showed far greater tolerance and humanity in its treatment of religious minorities than did the Christian West. In particular, the treatment of the Jewish minority in Muslim societies stands out as fair and enlightened when compared with the dismal record of Christian European persecution of Jews over the centuries'. Mayer, n 77 above, at 127–8 (footnotes omitted).

[88] H Inalcik, *The Ottoman Empire: the Classical Age 1300–1600* (London, Phoenix, 1994); P Mansfield, *The Ottoman Empire and Its Successor* (London, Macmillan, 1973); J McCarthy, *The Ottoman Peoples and the End of Empire* (London, Hodder and Stoughton, 2000).

[89] JA Laponce, *The Protection of Minorities* (Berkeley and Los Angeles, University of California Press 1960) 84–5.

[90] VV Dyke, *Human Rights, Ethnicity and Discrimination* (Westport, Conn and London, Greenwood Press, 1985) 74; '[w]hile the [Millet] system was hardly based on any recognition of "human rights", its application is most compatible with the philosophy of human rights' J Packer, 'The Protection of Ethnic and Linguistic Minorities in Europe' in J Packer and K Myntti (eds), *The Protection of Ethnic and Linguistic Minorities in Europe* (Turku/Åbo, Åbo Akademi, Institute for Human Rights, Åbo Akademi University, 1993) at 42.

[91] Evans, n 83 above, at 60.

approaches of the two empires towards their non-Muslim minorities, though there were also serious differences. Islam had reached the Indian Sub-Continent as early as 711 AD when Muhammad-Bin-Qasim, an Arab, invaded Sindh and paved the way for a succession of Muslim invasions of India. However, it was not until the beginning of the thirteenth century that the first Muslim empire (the Sultanate of Delhi) was established by Qutbudin Aibak.[92] The prospect of Muslim rule nevertheless remained uncertain for a considerable period during the fourteenth and fifteenth centuries in the face of strong indigenous revivalist movements. Muslim control of Northern India, however, was established with the victories of Babur, a Chaghtai-Turk who laid the foundations of the Moghul empire in India in 1526.

Unlike the position in Europe, in the Indian Sub-Continent, Islam was not confronted by monotheistic religions such as Judaism and Christianity, but was met by the ancient Hindu and Buddhist traditions—a fact felt most prominently by the Moghul emperors. The antiquity of the traditions, the existent diversities of the region and the need to placate and retain the support of influential sections of all religious communities were features strongly influential in the formulation of more conciliatory and accommodating policies by the Moghuls. In addition there was also a distinct ideological factor apparent in the approach adopted by a number of Moghul emperors. Professor Alexandrowicz makes the valuable point that:

> [t]he ideology of the Moghuls deviated significantly from that of the Ottoman Empire, as well as from the traditions of pre-Moghul Islamic rulers in India who had been under the political or religious over lordship of the Caliphs (at first effective, then nominal). The reign of the Moghul Emperors Akbar, Jehangir and Shajahan witnessed the victory of a secular policy in inter-group relations in India, no doubt under Hindu influence and in conditions of decline of the *Jihad* ideology.[93]

This secularist policy was most vividly represented during the reign of Emperor Akbar (1556–1605) whose own faith in Islam has been subject to suspicion and doubt.[94] A number of his ordinances and practices provide remarkable examples of religious tolerance and non-discrimination. Marriages between Hindus and Muslims were deemed lawful without the Hindus having to renounce their faith. Many Hindus, in particular Rajputs, were promoted to high office and became active agents in the administration of the country. In deference to the religious sentiments of the Hindus, the slaughter of cows was prohibited, a law which was rigor-

---

[92] S Wolpert, *A New History of India* (Oxford, Oxford University Press, 1989) at 109.

[93] CH Alexandrowicz, 'Kautilyan Principles and the Law of Nations' (1965–66) 41 *British Yearbook of International Law* 301, at 313.

[94] See E Maclagan, *The Jesuits and the Great Mogul* (New York, Octagon Books, 1972); B Gascoigne, *The Great Moghuls* (London, Cape, 1991).

ously enforced.[95] In 1564, the Emperor abolished the pilgrimage tax formerly imposed on Hindus. Notwithstanding opposition from his own quarters, a year later he also abolished the much despised *jizya* hitherto levied from non-Muslim subjects. He followed this by enunciating the principle of *Sulaakins*—universal tolerance and an undertaking to respect the rights of all Peoples, irrespective of religion or creed.[96]

These policies and practices of Emperor Akbar appear remarkable in the context of an era where intolerance and religious extremism were the order of the day: the contrast with the position in Europe would be striking. These virtuous policies of religious non-discrimination must nonetheless be seen in the light of overall circumstances prevailing within the Moghul Empire. The system of governance was dictatorial, repressive and barbarous; tolerance was accorded to religious and linguistic minorities so long as the established order was not challenged. Persian remained the Court language and there exists substantial evidence of rampant discrimination based on ethnic and racial origin even amongst Muslims themselves. Even the show of tolerance exhibited during the reigns of Akbar and Shah Jahan came to a halt under Emperor Alamgir and subsequent Moghul Emperors. The decline of the Empire was symbolised through its increasing intolerance towards minorities, an increase in incompetence accompanied by a rising wave of internal opposition and interest of European powers—a state of affairs not dissimilar to the Ottoman Turks during the period of their decline. The loss of Muslim Empire in India at the hands of the British was to further escalate the problem of religious identity within the Indian Sub-Continent. Embittered at the loss of power, and reduced to a socio-political as well as a numerical minority, throughout the nineteenth century, the Muslims continued to make claims of a distinct identity and self-governance. These claims were ultimately to feature prominently in demands for an independent homeland for the Muslims of the Indian Sub-Continent.

IDEOLOGY OF TOLERANCE AND MODERN STATE PRACTICES

The articulation of principles and practices of modern States on delicate issues of freedom of religion and rights of religious minorities need to be analysed in the light of divergences of interpretation. Whilst having adopted an egalitarian interpretation of the *Sharia's* position on the scope of rights of religious minorities and freedom of religion, earlier sections have nevertheless indicated differences of opinion and have noted the strains that exist in the comprehension of these concepts. Anxiety, tensions

---

[95] SM Ikram, *Muslim Civilization in India* (New York, Columbia University Press, 1969) 144.
[96] *Ibid*, at 172.

and lack of consistency have also characterised the practices of a number of Islamic States.

State practices and juristic opinion that finds modern human rights provisions such as Article 18 of the Universal Declaration on Human Rights[97] and Articles 18[98] and 27[99] of the International Covenant on Civil and Political Rights compatible with the *Sharia* emphasise an egalitarian and broad interpretation of Islamic values.[100] The contemporary differences in interpretation of the *Sharia*, and its compatibility with contemporary norms of international human rights, can be established through a survey of the practices of Islamic States.

An interesting example is provided by the contrasting positions adopted at the time of the drafting of the Universal Declaration of Human Rights. A number of Islamic States were actively involved in the preparation and drafting of the Declaration. Muslim representatives, such as Fereydoun Hoveida of Iran, served on the drafting committee of the Declaration, alongside the French Professor Rene Cassin.[101] Similarly, Pakistan, a State carved out of Colonial India specifically for protecting the identity and interests of Muslims, actively took part in the preparation of the Declaration with the view that '[i]t was imperative that the peoples of

[97] Article 18 provides: Everyone has the right to freedom of thought, conscience and religion; this right includes freedom to change his religion or belief, and freedom, either alone or in community with others and in public or private, to manifest his religion or belief in teaching, practice, worship and observance. See the Universal Declaration on Human Rights (adopted 10 December 1948) GA Res 217A(III), UN Doc A/810 at 71 (1948).

[98] According to Article 18(1) of the Covenant: Everyone shall have the right to freedom of thought, conscience and religion. This right shall include freedom to have or to adopt a religion or belief of his choice, and freedom, either individually or in community with others and in public or private, to manifest his religion or belief in worship, observance, practice and teaching. The International Covenant on Civil and Political Rights 1966 (adopted 16 December 1966, entered into force 23 March 1976) 999 UNTS 171, UKTS 6 (1977), Cmnd 6702, 6 ILM (1967) 368.

[99] This article, the so called 'minority rights article', provides: In those States in which ethnic, religious or linguistic minorities exist, persons belonging to such minorities shall not be denied the right, in community with the other members of their group, to enjoy their own culture, to profess and practise their own religion, or to use their own language. Article 27 of the International Covenant on Civil and Political Rights (1966) 999 UNTS 171, UKTS 6 (1977), Cmnd 6702, (1967) 61 *American Journal of International Law* 870. For useful analysis on the rights of minorities under Article 27 see F Capotorti, *Special Rapporteur: Study on the Rights of Persons Belonging to Ethnic, Religious and Linguistic Minorities*, (1978) United Nations Sales No E78XIVI reprinted New York, United Nations Centre for Human Rights, United Nations Sales (1991) No E91XIV2, at 26. C Tomuschat, 'Protection of Minorities under Article 27 of the International Covenant on Civil and Political Rights' (1983) *Völkerrecht als Rechtsordnung, Internationale Gerichtsbarkeit, Menschenrechte, Festschrift für Herman Mosler*, 949; LB Sohn, 'The Rights of Minorities' in L Henkin (ed), *The International Bill of Rights: The Covenant on Civil and Political Rights* (New York, Columbia University Press, 1981) 270–89; P Thornberry, *International Law and the Rights of Minorities* (Oxford, Clarendon Press, 1991) 141–248; J Rehman, *The Weaknesses in the International Protection of Minority Rights* (The Hague, Kluwer Law International, 2000) 165–202.

[100] See S Mahmassani, *Arkan Huquq-al-Insan* (Beirut, Dar-'ilmli'-Malayin, 1979) 260–4; SM Haider (ed), *Islamic Concept of Human Rights* (Lahore, Book House, 1978).

[101] Mayer, n 77 above, at 11.

the World should recognise the existence of a code of civilised behaviour which would apply not only in international relations but also in domestic affairs'.[102] On the other hand, the *travaux préparatoires* of the Declaration reveal that Article 18 provisions, particularly the clause relating to the 'freedom to change religion or belief', generated considerable debate and disagreement amongst the Islamic States. The provision allowing the freedom to change religion or belief had been initiated by Lebanon, a State which during the '1940s and 1950s was an oasis of toleration, where large Christian, Muslim and Druze communities coexisted in a pluralistic society'.[103] There was, however, an interesting confrontation between two States, both attempting to justify their position on the basis of Islamic law.[104]

The Saudi Arabian representative, Mr Al-Barudy, objected to the terminology as proposed in Article 18 of the Declaration on the basis inter alia of its incompatibility with the ordinances of Islam. In opposition to the Saudi Arabian position, the Pakistani representative, Muhammad Zafarullah Khan, relied upon the *Qur'anic* verse which notes 'let he who chooses to believe, believe and he who chooses to disbelieve, disbelieve' and went on to argue that:

[t]he Moslem religion was a missionary religion: it strove to persuade men to change their faith and alter their ways of living, so as to follow the faith and way of living it preached, but it recognised the same right of conversion for other religions as for itself.[105]

Pakistan found no discord between the provisions of the Declaration and the ordinances of Islam.[106] The Declaration was subsequently

[102] Pakistan's Representative Begum Ikram-ullah, GAOR 3rd Session, Part I, third Committee, 90th meeting, 1 October 1948, 37.

[103] Mayer, n 77 above, at 142.

[104] See J Kelsay, 'Saudi-Arabia, Pakistan and the Universal Declaration on Human Rights' in D Little *et al* (eds), *Human Rights and Conflict of Cultures: Western and Islamic Perspectives on Religious Liberty* (Columbia, University of South Carolina Press, 1988) 33–52; BG Tahzib, *Freedom of Religion or Belief: Ensuring Effective International Legal Protection* (The Hague, Martinus Nijhoff Publishers, 1996) 72–4. On the sensitive question of apostasy in Islamic law and its compatibility with modern human rights law see AA An-Nai'm, 'The Islamic Law of Apostasy and its Modern Applicability: A Case from the Sudan' (1986) 16 *Religion* 197.

[105] UN Doc A/PV. 182, 890.

[106] During the preparation of the Convention on the Prevention and Punishment of the Crime of Genocide (1948) Pakistan had put a particular emphasis on the cultural contributions of religious groups and communities within the States and had also proposed an article according to which 'genocide also [meant] . . . acts committed with the intent to destroy the religion or culture of a religious, racial or national group: (i) Systematic conversions from one religion to another by means of or by threats of violence (ii) Systematic destruction or desecration of places and objects of religious worship and desecration and destruction of objects of cultural value'. The lack of such a provision included in the text of the Convention proved a major disappointment to the Pakistani delegation. In the plenary session, Pakistan's representative Begum Ikram-ullah said, ' . . . it must be realised that very often a people did not differ from its neighbours by its racial characteristics but by its spiritual heritage. To deprive a human group of its separate culture could thus destroy its individuality as completely as physical

adopted with the consent of all Islamic States, except for Saudi Arabia.[107]

Notwithstanding the explicit provisions of Article 18 within the Universal Declaration, allowing for the right to change religion or belief, the existence of any such freedom or right in general international law has been cast into doubt by the opposition of a number of Islamic States. Many of these States, while purporting to follow the *Sharia*, differ in their position. Some challenge the legitimacy of the freedom to change religion and base their arguments upon its incompatibility with apostasy rules within Islam, while others acknowledge the existence of such a freedom but are reluctant to forcefully assert their position. As a consequence of opposition from certain Islamic States it proved impossible to incorporate the express provision to authorise the freedom to change religion or belief in all of the subsequent international instruments.

Muslim States have not been able to establish a consensual view on the meaning and content of freedom of religion within the Islamic jurisprudence. The substantial disparities and ambivalence in approach become evident through a survey of the practices and instruments adopted by Islamic States. Reservations (and Declarations) are frequently put in place which make specific human rights norms subject to their compatibility with the *Sharia*. These reservations (and Declarations) are not followed by an elaboration as to the exact position of the *Sharia* on that particular subject. Human rights obligations are also frequently drafted in an imprecise manner, which allows for a variety of interpretations. The Universal Islamic Declaration on Human Rights (1981)[108]—a document prepared by a number of Islamic States including Egypt, Pakistan and Saudi Arabia under the auspices of the Islamic Council (a private London-based organisation, working in conjunction with the Muslim World League, an international non-governmental organisation)—provides such an example. In its English version the article on Rights of Minorities provides that:

annihilation. Moreover, those guilty of the crime of mass extermination committed that crime because the existence of a community endowed with a separate cultural life was intolerable to them. In other words physical genocide was only the means, the end was the destruction of a peoples spiritual individuality'. GAOR 3rd Session, Part I, 178th meeting, 9 December 1948, 817. This commitment was made evident in Pakistan's bilateral treaty with India in 1950 whereby both States undertook to 'ensure the Minorities . . . complete equality of citizenship, irrespective of religion . . . freedom of occupation, speech and worship . . .' Agreement between India and Pakistan Concerning Minorities (1950) 131 UNTS (1950) para (a). Freedom of religion and support for the religious minorities was strongly advocated by Pakistan during the drafting stages of ICCPR. Article 27 of the ICCPR was treated as 'the most important in the entire Covenant' A/C3/SR1104, 14 November 1961, para 15.

[107] The Declaration was adopted on 10 December 1948 with forty-eight votes in favour, none against and eight abstentions. In addition to Saudi Arabia, South Africa and the Soviet Block States abstained from voting. See AH Robertson and JG Merrills, *Human Rights in the World: An Introduction to the Study of the International Protection of Human Rights* (Manchester, Manchester University Press, 1996) 28.

[108] For an analysis of the Declaration see Mayer, n 77 above, at 22.

(a) The Quranic principle, 'There is no Compulsion in Religion' shall govern the religious rights of non-Muslim minorities.

(b) In a Muslim country, religious minorities shall have the choice to be governed in respect of their civil and personal matters by Islamic law or by their own laws.[109]

The aforementioned provisions are not explicit as to whether these principles are to be applied to all non-Muslims or are limited to the *ahal al-kitab*.[110] Neither do they articulate the substantive rights which non-Muslim minorities have within an Islamic State. There are also significant differences between the English and the Arabic versions, suggesting the possibility of the divergent views of the drafters of the Declaration.

CONCLUSIONS

This chapter has highlighted the significant contributions of the *Sharia* and the *Siyar* in developing law of nations—contributions which are often overlooked amidst the 'Eurocentric' vision of international law. It is remarkable to note the contributions of the *Sharia* and *Siyar* in developing the norms of international commerce, business and trade. Similarly, Islamic practices reflect considerable attention towards forging inter-State relationships. Dispute resolution mechanisms were advanced through such techniques as *tahkím* and mediation. Furthermore, Islamic States actively encouraged diplomatic contacts and liaison. This study shall, in due course, examine the efforts of *Siyar* for promoting international diplomatic law. Having assessed the extraordinary foresight and vision of political leaders and jurists in the early Islamic period, it is significantly disappointing to note the current state of stagnation prevalent in the contemporary Muslim world. The initial historic vision of *Ijtihad* appears to be absent from current Muslim leadership.

The chapter has also examined the scope and meaning of controversial concepts. The enquiry reveals that the term *Jihad* has attracted a range of differing interpretations. Western scholarship, as well as some Muslim jurists, perceives *Jihad* as a weapon of aggression, an instrument of occupation and violence. In reality, as has been demonstrated, such a narrow interpretation is erroneous; it is neither supported by an examination of the principal sources of the *Sharia*, nor is it endorsed by modern Islamic State practices. It would appear that the original message of Islam is one of peace and reconciliation—a message which was frequently overridden by the extreme exigencies of violent circumstances. Expanding upon this original message of Islam, Mahmassani makes the pertinent observation that:

---

[109] Article X (Rights of Minorities).
[110] Mayer, n 77 above, at 131–3.

the original and only reliable texts of Islam expressly advocate [the view] that Islam favours peace as a fundamental basis of its legal framework. These texts regulated war only in the exceptional cases in which it was deemed lawful . . . The word 'peace' and its derivatives are cited in more than one hundred verses of the Koran, while the word 'war' and its derivative verb are mentioned in only six verses.[111]

In so far as the subject of freedom of religion and rights of religious minorities is concerned, there remain significant inconsistencies in the practices of Islamic States. It is contended that these inconsistencies and divisions are only partly a result of differing interpretations of classical Islamic laws. Other, 'extra-legal factors' such as cultural, traditional and customary norms probably have a significant role in the adoption of rules regarding minority rights.[112] The present analysis has established the presence of serious possibilities of compatibility between the *Sharia* and international human rights law. While jurists and juridical treaties have only a limited role in law-making, the underlying message from this study is one of rapprochement and conciliation between the *Sharia* and modern laws of nations.

---

[111] Mahmassani, n 4 above, at 242.
[112] SS Ali and J Rehman, 'Freedom of Religion versus Equality in International Human Rights Law: Conflicting Norms or Hierarchical Human Rights (A Case Study of Pakistan)' (2003) 21 *Nordic Journal of Human Rights* 404.

3

Conceptualising Terrorism in the International Legal Order

INTRODUCTION

THERE IS NO doubt that in the post 11 September 2001 world, international terrorism poses the most substantial threat to
international legal order. Terrorism is recognised as a crime under
international law engendering serious violations of individual and collective group rights.[1] Having said that, as this study elaborates, there is no
established definition as to the meaning and scope of terrorism. The ambi-
guity in definition has been used by a number of States to deny their
Peoples legitimate rights such as freedom of expression and religion, and
collective group rights, particularly the right to self-determination.[2]

International law remains a difficult medium to address the subject of
terrorism. There are a range of difficulties and complexities. There is firstly

---

[1] See R Higgins and M Flory (eds), *Terrorism and International Law* (London, Routledge,
1997); MC Bassiouni (ed), *Legal Responses to Terrorism: US Procedural Aspects* (Dordrecht,
Martinus Nijhoff Publishers, 1988); Y Alexander (ed), *International Terrorism: Political and
Legal Documents* (Dordrecht, Martinus Nijhoff Publishers, 1992); Y Alexander (ed),
International Terrorism: National, Regional and Global Perspectives (New York, Praeger, 1976);
J Lodge (ed), *Terrorism: A Challenge to the State* (Oxford, Martin Robertson, 1981); J Lambert,
Terrorism and Hostages in International Law: A Commentary on the Hostages Convention 1979
(Cambridge, Grotius Publishers, 1990); L Freedman *et al*, *Terrorism and International Order*
(London, Routledge and Kegan Paul, 1986); A Cassese, *Terrorism, Politics and Law: The Achille
Lauro Affair* (Cambridge, Polity Press, 1989); Report by the International Bar Association's
Task Force on International Terrorism, *International Terrorism: Legal Challenges and Responses*
(Ardsley NY, Transnational Publishers, 2003).

[2] See M Pomerance, *Self-Determination in Law and Practice: The New Doctrine in the United
Nations* (The Hague, Martinus Nijhoff Publishers, 1982); A Rigo-Sureda, *The Evolution of the
Right of Self-Determination: A Study of United Nations Practice* (Leiden, Sijthoff, 1973); FL Kirgis
Jr, 'The Degrees of Self-Determination in the United Nations Era' (1994) 88 *American Journal
of International Law* 304; P Thornberry, 'Self-Determination, Minorities, Human Rights:
A Review of International Instruments' (1989) 38 *International & Comparative Law Quarterly*
867; H Hannum, *Autonomy, Sovereignty and Self-Determination: The Accommodation of Conflict-
ing Rights* (Philadelphia, University of Pennsylvania Press, 1990) at 33; Y Blum, 'Reflections
on the Changing Concept of Self-Determination' (1975) 10 *Israel Law Review* 509; R Emerson,
'Self-Determination' (1971) 65 *American Journal of International Law* 459; M Koskenniemi,
'National Self-Determination Today: Problems of Legal Theory and Practice' (1994) 43
International & Comparative Law Quarterly 241.

the complex and thorny area of definition. In defining terrorism perceptions vary in differentiating a terrorist from a freedom fighter. Secondly,
there is the problematic area of assessing the meaning and scope of the so-
called 'political offences'—should individuals who have committed acts
of violence be exempted from prosecution or extradition because their
actions are purportedly based on political motivations?[3] Thirdly, there is
the difficulty of identifying perpetrators of the crime of terrorism—should
the focus of international concern be individuals and other non-State
organisations, or should attention to be directed towards State-sponsored
terrorism? If States are implicated in terrorism, how can international laws
be made more effective? In the existing global order, while in principle all
States are sovereign and equal, some are more sovereign and equal than
others.[4] It is the accountability of the most powerful States which presents
international law with its most difficult test. Finally, there is the subject of
remedies for victims of terrorism. As this study explores, in a fragmented
and incoherent system that deals with international terrorism, victims of
this crime have frequently been denied access to national and international tribunals to claim their rights.[5] In common with other instances,
it is often nationals from the powerful States whose governments can
extract forms of compensation. The Afghanistan and Iraq crises confirm
that there is very little in the hands of those who suffer from the powerful
and the mighty.

---

[3] See CL Blakesley, 'Terrorism, Law and our Constitutional Order' (1989) 60 *University of
Colorado Law Review* 471 at 514; LC Green, 'Terrorism, the Extradition of Terrorists and the
"Political Offence" Defence' (1988) 31 *German Yearbook of International Law* 337; CC Joyner,
'Suppression of Terrorism on the High Seas: The 1988 IMO Convention on the Safety of
Maritime Navigation' (1989) 19 *Israel Yearbook of Human Rights* 343 at 361; M Garcia-Mora,
'The Nature of Political Offenses: A Knotty Problem of Extradition Law' (1962) 48 *Virginia
Law Review* 1226; D Thompson, 'The Evolution of the Political Offense Exception in an Age of
Modern Political Violence' (1983) 9 *Yale Journal of World Public Order* 315; O Lagodny, 'The
European Convention on the Suppression of Terrorism: A Substantial Step to Combat
Terrorism' (1989) 60 *University of Colorado Law Review* 583, at 583.

[4] See R Falk, 'The Iran Hostage Crisis: Easy Answers and Hard Questions' (1980) 74
American Journal of International Law 411.

[5] Professor Dinstein correctly points out that 'the principal obstacle on the path of efforts
to suppress international terrorism is that too many countries display a double standard in
their approach to the problem. While concerned about acts of terrorism directly affecting
their own interests (or those of their close allies) they demonstrate a marked degree of *insou-
ciance* to the predicament of others. In the aggregate, the international community seems to
lack the political will to take concerted action against terrorists of all stripes. As a result, terrorists frequently manage to get away with murder in the literal meaning of the phrase'.
Y Dinstein, 'Terrorism as an International Crime' (1989) 19 *Israel Yearbook of Human Rights* 55
at 56.

THE DEFINITIONAL ISSUES[6]

In his celebrated essay Professor Baxter expresses his doubts about energising efforts to define terrorism. He notes,

> [w]e have cause to regret that a legal concept of 'terrorism' was ever inflicted upon us. The term is imprecise; it is ambiguous; and above all, it serves no operative legal purpose.[7]

Definitional issues have generated substantial complications in formulating international legal standards. The term 'terrorism' is probably the most difficult to define within general international law. Explanation for this difficulty includes varied perceptions over the characterisation of terrorist acts, purpose and motivation behind such acts and the varying identity of the perpetrator. Indeed the issue has been so controversial that divisions have emerged not only in the proposed definitions but more fundamentally as to whether it is worthwhile attempting to define such an elusive concept.[8] The effort to reach an agreement on issues of definition is confronted with complications.[9] One immediate question relates to identifying the 'terrorists'. In any ideological and political conflict, is it possible to objectively distinguish between a terrorist and a freedom fighter? In contemporary politics, our perceptions of acts of violence conducted by such groups as the Palestinians, the Kashmiris, the Tamil Tigers and Northern Irish Republicans is variable.[10] There is a great measure of truth in the well-known cliché that 'One man's terrorist is another man's

---

[6] See G Levitt, 'Is "Terrorism" Worth Defining?' (1986) 13 *Ohio Northern University Law Review* 97; JF Murphy, 'Defining International Terrorism: A Way Out of the Quagmire' (1989) 19 *Israel Yearbook of Human Rights* 13; JF Murphy, 'The Future of Multilateralism and Efforts to Combat International Terrorism' (1986) 25 *The Columbia Journal of Transnational Law* 35; LC Green, 'Terrorism and Armed Conflict: The Plea and the Verdict' (1989) 19 *Israel Yearbook of Human Rights* 131.

[7] R Baxter, 'A Sceptical Look at the Concept of Terrorism' (1974) 7 *Akorn Law Review* 380, at 380.

[8] As Professor Bassiouni makes the point, 'there is . . . no internationally agreed upon methodology for the identification and appraisal of what is commonly referred to as "terrorism"; including: causes, strategies, goals and outcomes of the conduct in question and those who perpetuate it. There is also no international consensus as to the appropriate reactive strategies of states and the international community, their values, goals and outcomes. All of this makes it difficult to identify what is sought to be prevented and controlled, why and how. As a result, the pervasive and indiscriminate use of the often politically convenient label of "terrorism" continues to mislead this field of inquiry'. MC Bassiouni, 'A Policy-Oriented Inquiry into the Different Forms and Manifestations of "International Terrorism"' in MC Bassiouni (ed), n 1 above, at xvi.

[9] R Higgins, 'The General International Law of Terrorism' in R Higgins and M Flory (eds), n 1 above, 13–29 at 14.

[10] H McCoubrey, *International Humanitarian Law* (Aldershot, Ashgate, 1997) at 258.

freedom fighter'.[11] It is also the case that views and values of whether a particular individual or entity is pursuing terrorists acts are subject to political persuasion and nationalistic sentiments. Saddam Hussein, Usama Bin Laden, and the Taliban were all at one stage hailed as friends: The United States and its allies regarded them as freedom fighters engaged in a *just war*.[12]

In addition, there is the complexity of finding agreement in relation to the entities which could conduct terrorist acts. In this context there has remained a major ideological conflict between the developing States, many of whom represent the Islamic bloc, on the one hand, and the developed world on the other. While the developing and Islamic States have emphasised State terrorism largely in the context of racial oppression and colonial regimes, the developed world has concerned itself with individual acts of terrorism.[13] In the post-colonial, post Cold War era, a number of Islamic States such as Libya, Iran, the Sudan and Iraq have protested against what they believe to be American sponsored 'State-terrorism'. An example could be found in the position adopted by Iraq. In its letter dated 26 December 2001, the *Charge d'Affaires* of the Permanent Mission of Iraq to the United Nations addressed the Chairman of the Security Council Committee established pursuant to Resolution 1373 (2001) concerning Counter-terrorism. The letter noted:

> Iraq is the foremost victim of terrorism, including State terrorism. Its leaders, officials and citizens have been exposed to many terrorist kidnapping attempts and its cities and villages have been the target of terrorist acts committed by terrorists who slip across borders—terrorists that receive patronage, training, finance and armament within a framework of State terrorism ie terrorism carried out by States themselves. One such State is the United States of America which openly spends tens of millions of dollars on troops of mercenaries to carry out terrorist operations against Iraq pursuant to what is referred to as the 'Iraq Liberation Act'.[14]

[11] See E Rosand, 'Security Council Resolution 1373, the Counter-Terrorism Committee, and the Fight Against Terrorism' (2003) 97 *American Journal of International Law* 333, at 334; CM Bassiouni, 'Foreword: Assessing "Terrorism" into the New Millennium' (2000) 12 *De Paul Business Law Journal* 1, at 1.

[12] PA Thomas 'September 11th and Good Governance' (2002) 53 *Northern Ireland Legal Quarterly* 366 at 385–6.

[13] Levitt correctly points out that: 'governments that have a strong political stake in the promotion of "national liberation movements" are loath to subscribe to a definition of terrorism that would criminalise broad areas of conduct habitually resorted to by such groups; and on the other end of the spectrum, governments against which these groups' violent activities are directed are obviously reluctant to subscribe to a definition that would criminalise their own use of force in response to such activities or otherwise'. Levitt, n 6 above, at 109; Report by the International Bar Association's Task Force on International Terrorism, n 1 above, at 3.

[14] Letter dated 26 December 2001, the *Charge d'Affaires* of the Permanent Mission of Iraq to the United Nations addressed to the Chairman of the Security Council Committee established pursuant to Resolution 1373 (2001) Concerning Counter-terrorism, para 1. <http://ods-dds-ny.un.org/doc/UNDOC/GEN/N01/723/00/PDF/N0172300.pdf? OpenElement > (3 October 2004).

An objective approach demands that every malicious action (assassinations, killings, bombings, hostage-taking and hijacking) be categorised as a terrorist activity.[15] The motive, characteristics and underlying causes of any such actions must not provide a justification. On the other hand, depending on one's moral and political views many of these actions have been justified or condoned.[16] Analysing statistically, the developing and Islamic world has a forceful argument to make. State-sponsored terrorism is far more devastating in its impact than individual acts of terrorism. This is particularly the case where State-terrorism is generated by militarily powerful States. According to one estimate, the twentieth century witnessed 70 million casualties of State-sponsored terrorism as opposed to 100,000 deaths which were caused by individual non-governmental acts of terrorism.[17]

The debate provoked as a consequence of disagreements over definition has exercised the minds and views of many lawyers, politicians and parliamentary draftsmen. According to one academic, between 1936 and 1981, no less than 109 definitions of terrorism were advanced.[18] One of the earliest and prominent definitions advanced was through the 1937 Convention for the Prevention and Punishment of Terrorism.[19] According to Article 1(2) of this Convention:

> In the present Convention, the expression 'acts of terrorism' means criminal acts directed against a State intended or calculated to create a state of terror in the minds of particular persons, or a group of persons or the general public.

For the provisions of this Convention to be operative an act had to come within the ambit of the aforementioned definition. The action had to be directed against a State party and the concerned activity had to involve one of the enumerated actions in Articles 2 and 3 of the Convention, namely 'any wilful act causing death or grievous bodily harm or loss of liberty' to specified category of public officials, 'wilful destruction of, or damage to, public property' or 'any wilful act calculated to endanger the lives of members of the public'.

As it turned out, neither the definition nor the 1937 Convention could be adopted.[20] Despite this abortive attempt, renewed efforts were made in

[15] R Higgins, 'The General International Law of Terrorism' in R Higgins and M Flory (eds), n 1 above, 13–29 at 14.

[16] See for example the suicide bombings in Palestine, and the official Israeli policy of killing leaders of the Palestinian paramilitary factions and killing of those Palestinians deemed to be 'terrorists'. On the Palestinian issue see below, chapter 7.

[17] MC Bassiouni, *International Terrorism: Multilateral Conventions (1937–2001)* (Ardsley NY, Transnational Publishers, 2001) 46.

[18] W Laqueur, 'Reflections on Terrorism' (1986) 65 *Foreign Affairs* 86, at 88.

[19] The Convention for the Prevention and Punishment of Terrorism, 16 November 1937, 19 League of Nations Official Journal (1938) 23 reprinted 27 UN GAOR, Annex I, Agenda Item No 92, UN Doc A/C.6/418 (1972). This convention was signed by twenty-four States, although only India ratified it.

[20] See A Cassese, 'The International Community's "Legal" Response to Terrorism' (1989) 38 *International & Comparative Law Quarterly* 589, 591.

the 1950s and 1960s to formulate a consensus definition of international terrorism. During 1972 the United States presented a Draft Convention for the Prevention and Punishment of Certain Acts of International Terrorism.[21] The text of the draft provided for offences of 'international significance'. These were defined as those committed with intent to damage the interests of or obtain concessions from a State or an international organisation under certain enumerated transnational circumstances, consisting of unlawfully killing, causing serious bodily harm, or kidnapping another person (including attempts and complicity in such acts).[22] These actions should have been 'committed neither by nor against a member of the armed forces of a State in the course of military hostilities'.[23]

The 1972 US Draft Convention, like the 1937 Convention, failed to gain the approval of the international community. The United Nations General Assembly, however, established an Ad Hoc Committee on International Terrorism to 'consider the observations of States [and] submit its report with recommendations for possible co-operation for the speedy elimination of the problem . . . to the General Assembly'.[24] A Sub-Committee of the Ad Hoc Committee was set up and within the deliberations of the Sub-Committee the following definition of 'international terrorism' was advanced:

> Acts of violence and other repressive acts by colonial, racist and alien regimes against peoples struggling for their liberation . . .
>
> Tolerating or assisting by a State the organization of the remnants of fascist or mercenary groups whose terrorist activity is directed against other sovereign countries;
>
> Acts of violence committed by individuals or groups of individuals which endanger or take innocent human lives or jeopardise fundamental freedoms. This should not affect the inalienable right to self-determination and independence of all peoples under colonial and racist regimes and other forms of alien domination and the legitimacy of their struggle . . .;
>
> Acts of violence committed by individuals or groups of individuals for private gain, the effects of which are not confined to one State.[25]

There are striking differences between the 1972 and 1937 definitions in their dealings with the issue of terrorism. Having been subsumed within the right of self-determination, the concern for the Sub-Committee is primarily about racist and alien regimes. The Sub-Committee created a number of exceptions for those pursing a right to self-determination. Within

---

[21] United States Draft Convention for the Prevention of Certain Acts of International Terrorism, UN Doc A/C.6/L.850 (1972) reprinted in (1972) 67 Dep't State Bull 431.

[22] Article 1.

[23] *Ibid.*

[24] See GA Res 3034 (XXVII) 1972, 27 UN GAOR Supp (No 30) at 119, UN Doc A/RES/3034, paras 9, 10.

[25] 28 UN GAOR Supp (1973).

this definition, the issue of intent, according to one commentator, 'has been turned on its head':[26] private gain rather than political motives present the key-determining factor. Within the overall agenda of the United Nations, the right to self-determination was of peremptory value. As we shall examine shortly, in addition to definitional issues, exceptions based around this right have impinged upon the drafting of substantive treaties such as the Hostage-taking Convention (1979).

RECENT DEVELOPMENTS ON DEFINITIONAL ISSUES

As subsequent sections shall analyse, since the end of the Cold War, a greater consensus has emerged over the necessity to prevent all forms of political violence and terrorism. The General Assembly as well as the Security Council has addressed the issue of terrorism on several occasions.[27] In its Resolution 52/210, the General Assembly established an Ad Hoc Committee 'to elaborate an international convention for the suppression of terrorist bombings and, subsequently, an international convention for the suppression of acts of nuclear terrorism, to supplement related existing international instruments, and thereafter to address means of further developing a comprehensive legal framework of conventions dealing with international terrorism'.[28] The mandate for the Ad Hoc Committee has been renewed annually by the General Assembly. Under the terms of the current mandate as provided by General Assembly Resolution 58/81 (adopted on 9 December 2003) the Committee is required to continue its work towards inter alia drafting a convention on terrorism.[29] A working-group of the Committee considered in 2000 a draft convention proposed by India.[30] However, in actual practice not much headway has been made in producing the substantive provisions of the treaty. The Committee has struggled with the definitional, substantive and procedural issues. According to a recent draft, the Convention would inter alia define terrorism, require States to criminalise terrorism, establish jurisdictional principles and affirms the principle of *aut dedere aut judicare*.[31] During its

[26] See below, chapters 4–7.
[27] Levitt, n 6 above, at 100.
[28] See General Assembly Resolution No 51/210 of 17 December 1996, UN Doc A/RES/51/210; M Halberstam, 'The Evolution of the United Nations Position on Terrorism: From Exempting National Liberation Movements to Criminalizing Terrorism Whenever and Wherever and by Whom Committed' (2003) 41 *The Columbia Journal of Transnational Law* 573 at 579.
[29] General Assembly Resolution No 51/210 of 17 December 1996, UN Doc A/RES/51/210 <http://www.un.org/law/terrorism/> (1 October 2004).
[30] See General Assembly, *Draft Comprehensive Convention on International Terrorism: Working Document Submitted by India* (28 August 2000) UN Doc A/C.6/55/1.
[31] See Report of the Ad Hoc Committee established by General Assembly Resolution 51/210 Dec 17, 1996, Sixth Session (28 January–1 February 2002) UN Doc A/57/37.

Fifty-Sixth Session the working-group produced the following definition of terrorism:

> According to Article 2 (1) a person commits an offence within the meaning of this Convention if that person, by any means, unlawfully and intentionally, causes:
>
> (a) Death or serious bodily injury to any person, or:
> (b) Serious damage to public or private property, including a place of public use, a State or government facility, a public transportation system, an infrastructure facility or the environment; or
> (c) Damage to property, places, facilities or systems referred to in paragraph 1(b) of this article, resulting or likely to result in major economic loss,
>
> when the purpose of the conduct, by its nature or context, is to intimidate a population, or to compel a Government or an international organization to do so or abstain from doing any act.[32]

The definition renders as a criminal offence, making serious and credible threats to commit offences (as stated in Article 1), organising or directing others to commit such offences or contributing to these offences.[33] The draft bans a wide range of criminal behaviour and prohibits any exceptions regardless of 'political, philosophical, ideological, racial, ethnic [or] religious considerations'[34] that might have been the motivating factor. There is also an explicit rejection of the application of the 'political offence exception' for the purposes of extradition.[35] Notwithstanding the commendable features in the draft Convention, it remains in draft form. A recipe for future disagreements has already been evident with the Malaysian proposal (submitted on behalf of the OIC) seeking exemptions for 'Peoples' struggling against armed occupation and foreign aggression.[36] While the Committee continues its efforts, the prospects for a fully acceptable definition as well as achieving consensus in the main body of any such treaty are remote.[37]

In the aftermath of the tragic events of 11 September 2001, the Security Council adopted a landmark resolution, Resolution 1373. The Resolution

---

[32] Measures to Eliminate Terrorism: Report of the Working Group Fifty-Sixth Session, 29 October 2001, UN Doc A/C.6/56/L.9, annex I.9. Text available at: <http://ods-dds-ny.un.org/doc/UNDOC/GEN/N02/248/17/PDF/N0224817.pdf?OpenElement> (15 March 2004); also see Report by the International Bar Association's Task Force on International Terrorism, n 1 above, at 2–3.

[33] *Ibid*, Article 2(2)(3)(4).

[34] *Ibid*, Article 5.

[35] *Ibid*, Article 14.

[36] See SP Subedi, 'The UN Response to International Terrorism in the Aftermath of the Terrorist Attacks in America and the Problem of the Definition of Terrorism in International Law' (2002) 4 *International Law Forum du droit International* 159, at 163.

[37] See J Trahan, 'Terrorism Conventions: Existing Gaps and Different Approaches' (2002) 8 *New England Journal of International and Comparative Law Annual* 215, at 232.

deliberately avoided the thorny issue of defining 'terrorism'.[38] Instead of faltering over the subject of definition, the text of the Resolution addresses key areas for prevention of terrorism and the punishment of terrorists. It also sets up a compulsory implementation mechanism through State reporting, the reports to be monitored by the newly established CTC.

This deliberate avoidance of the issue of definition of terrorism has been a regular feature of modern international law. As this study examines, while a number of documents and binding instruments have been adopted, they deal only with specific aspects of the crime of terrorism— thus international treaties have been formulated in areas of inter alia aircraft hijacking,[39] unlawful acts against the safety of civil aviation,[40] marine terrorism,[41] hostage-taking,[42] and theft of nuclear materials.[43]

REVIEW OF COMPARATIVE REGIONAL PERSPECTIVES ON TERRORISM

A survey of the regional instruments provides an array of definitions of terrorism. These definitions vary, depending upon ideological, social and geo-political views. The Arab Convention on the Suppression of Terrorism (1998)[44] established a definition of terrorism. In elaborating on the concept, 'terrorism' is regarded as:

[38] B Zagaris, 'Financial Aspects of the War on Terror: The Merging of the Counter-Terrorism and Anti-Money Laundering Regimes' (2002) 34 *Law and Policy International Business* (2002) 45, at 76.

[39] See the Convention on Offences and Certain Other Acts Committed on Board Aircraft 1963 (adopted on 14 September 1963, entered into force 4 December 1969) 704 UNTS 219; the Convention for the Suppression of Unlawful Seizure of Aircraft, 1970 (adopted on 16 December 1970, entered into force 14 October 1971) 860 UNTS 105.

[40] See Convention for the Suppression of Unlawful Acts against the Safety of Civil Aviation 1971 (adopted on 23 September 1971, entered into force 26 January 1973) 974 UNTS 177; (1971) 10 ILM 1151.

[41] See the Convention for the Suppression of Unlawful Acts against the Safety of Maritime Navigation 1988 (adopted on 10 March 1988, entered into force 1 March 1992) (1988) 27 ILM 668; the Protocol for the Suppression of Unlawful Acts against the Safety of Fixed Platforms Located on the Continental Shelf 1988 (adopted on 10 March 1988, entered into force 1 March 1992) (1988) 27 ILM 685.

[42] See the Convention on the Prevention and Punishment of Crimes against Internationally Protected Persons, including Diplomatic Agents, 1973 (adopted on 14 December 1973, entered into force 20 February 1977) 1035 UNTS 167; International Convention against the Taking of Hostages 34 UN GAOR Supp (No 39) at 23, UN Doc A/34/39 1979 (adopted on 17 December 1979, entered into force 3 June 1980) (1979) 18 ILM 1456.

[43] See Convention on the Physical Protection of Nuclear Materials 1979 (adopted on 26 October 1979, entered into force 8 February 1987) (1979) 18 ILM 1419.

[44] Arab Convention on the Suppression of Terrorism, signed at a meeting held at the General Secretariat of the League of Arab States in Cairo on 22 April 1998. Deposited with the Secretary-General of the League of Arab States (unofficial translation from Arabic by the United Nations English translation service) text available at <http://www.al-bab.com/arab/docs/league/terrorism98.htm> (4 October 2004).

> Any act or threat of violence, whatever its motives or purposes, that occurs in the advancement of an individual or collective criminal agenda and seeking to sow panic among people, causing fear by harming them, or placing their lives, liberty or security in danger, or seeking to cause damage to the environment or to public or private installations or property or to occupying or seizing them, or seeking to jeopardize a national resources.[45]

The main Council of Europe treaty dealing with terrorism, the European Convention on the Suppression of Terrorism (1977), does not contain a definition of terrorism.[46] Instead, Article 1 lists the offences each of which, for the purposes of extradition, shall not be regarded as a political offence, or as an offence connected with a political offence, or as an offence inspired by political motives. These offences concern Aerial terrorism as expressed in the Hague Convention (1970) and the Montreal Convention (1971), offences against internationally protected persons, hostage-taking and terrorist bombings.[47] Attempts to commit any of these offences are also recognised as constituting 'non-political' acts.[48]

It thus modifies the consequences of existing extradition agreements and arrangements as regards evaluation of the nature of these offences. While the Convention eliminates the possibility for the requested State of invoking the political nature of the offence in order to oppose an extradition request, there are provisions in Article 13(1) whereby ratifying States could enter into reservations and refuse extradition as regards offences mentioned in Article 1. The provisions of Article 1 and the apparent inability to rely upon certain offences as 'political offences' are exceptional features; they have been the object of praise and commendation by legal scholars.[49] This does not, however, create an obligation to extradite, as the Convention is not an extradition treaty as such. The legal basis for extradition remains the extradition treaty, arrangement or the relevant law concerned.

Unlike the Council of Europe, the European Union does not have a specific treaty targeting international or regional terrorism. However, in June 2002 the EU adopted a Framework Decision on Terrorism, which includes a common definition of terrorist offences and serious criminal sanctions, and aims at promoting extradition and information-exchanging procedures across Europe.[50] Article 1 defines 'terrorist offences' as:

---

[45]   *Ibid*, Article 1(2).
[46]   See the European Convention on the Suppression of Terrorism 1977 (adopted on 27 January 1977, entered into force 4 August 1978) ETS No 90, 15 ILM 1272.
[47]   See Article 1(1–5).
[48]   *Ibid*, Article 1(6).
[49]   Cassese, n 20 above, at 594.
[50]   Council Framework Decision of 13 June 2002 on Combating Terrorism, OJ L 164, 22/06/2002 P.0003–0007; text available at <http://www.juris.u-szeged.hu/tanszekek/bunteto/egyeb/pdf/2002475jha.pdf> (4 October 2004).

[. . .] intentional acts referred to as below in points (a) to (i) as defined as offences under national law, which, given their nature or context, may seriously damage a country or an international organisation where committed with the aim of:

— seriously intimidating a population, or
— unduly compelling a Government or international organisations to perform or abstain from performing any act, or
— seriously destabilising or destroying the fundamental political, constitutional, economic or social structures of a country or an international organisation, shall be deemed to be terrorist offences:

(a) attacks upon a person's life which may cause death;
(b) attacks upon the physical integrity of a person;
(c) kidnapping or hostage taking;
(d) causing extensive destruction to a Government or public facility, a transport system, an infrastructure facility, including an information system, a fixed platform located on the continental shelf, a public place or private property likely to endanger human life or result in major economic loss;
(e) seizure of aircraft, ship or other means of public or goods transport;
(f) manufacture, possession, acquisition, transport, supply or use of weapons, explosives or of nuclear, biological or chemical weapons, as well as research into and development of, biological and chemical weapons;
(g) release of dangerous substances, or causing fires, floods or explosions the effect of which is to endanger human life;
(h) interfering with or disrupting the supply of water, power or any other fundamental natural resources the effect of which is to endanger human life;
(i) threatening to commit any of the acts listed in (a) to (h).[51]

The Organisation of African Unity (now the African Union) adopted the Convention on the Prevention and Combating of Terrorism at its 35th Ordinary Session of the Assembly of Heads of State and Government in 1999, in Algiers.[52] The Convention provides a detailed definition of a 'terrorist act'. According to Article 1(3):

(a) any act which is a violation of the criminal laws of a State Party and which may endanger the life, physical integrity or freedom of, or cause serious injury or death to, any person, any number or group of persons or causes or may cause damage to public or private property, natural resources, environmental or cultural heritage and is calculated or intended to:

---

[51] *Ibid*, Article 1.
[52] OAU Convention on the Prevention and Combating of Terrorism (adopted at Algiers on 14 July 1999 and deposited with the General Secretariat of the Organization of African Unity) <http://untreaty.un.org/English/Terrorism.asp> (14 August 2004). Despite the adoption of the Convention, the African States still have to overcome handicaps, generated by lack of means and capabilities to combat terrorism; few African States have these means at their disposal. See *Press Note Meeting of African Union Member States on the Prevention and Combating of Terrorism* (New York, Mission of Algeria to UN, 26 August 2002).

(i)   intimidate, put in fear, force, coerce or induce any government, body, institution, the general public or any segment thereof, to do or abstain from doing any act, or to adopt or abandon a particular standpoint, or to act according to certain principles; or

(ii)   disrupt any public service, the delivery of any essential service to the public or to create a public emergency; or

(iii) create general insurrection in a State;

(b)   any promotion, sponsoring, contribution to, command, aid, incitement, encouragement, attempt, threat, conspiracy, organising, or procurement of any person, with the intent to commit any acts referred to in paragraph (a) (i) to (iii).

The South Asian Association for Regional Cooperation (SAARC) has also addressed the subject of international and regional terrorism. The SAARC Regional Convention on the Suppression of Terrorism takes a broad approach to definitional issues.[53] Article 1 lists a number of international treaties and offences which are deemed terrorist acts. The treaties listed include the Convention for the Suppression of Unlawful Seizure of Aircraft (1970); Convention for the Suppression of Unlawful Acts against the Safety of Civil Aviation (1971); and Convention on the Prevention and Punishment of Crimes against Internationally Protected Persons, including Diplomatic Agents (1973). Furthermore according to the provisions of Article I(d) a terrorist offence includes '[a]n offence within the scope of any Convention to which SAARC Member States concerned are parties and which obliges the parties to prosecute or grant extradition'.

The wide ambit of the definition of terrorism is exemplified by the incorporation of violations against the public order leading to violence against individuals and property. The offences include murder, manslaughter, serious bodily harm, kidnapping, hostage-taking and offences relating to firearms, weapons, explosives and dangerous substances when used as a means to perpetuate indiscriminate violence resulting in death or serious damage to human lives or property. There is further discretion provided to States to expand the scope of terrorists acts, by recognising other serious violent offences and denying these the status of political offences.[54]

This overview of definitions from comparative regional instruments provides interesting perspectives on the debate. A critical review of these instruments, however, reveals the breadth of expansive approaches. This breadth of scope allows a range of terrorist activities to be covered. Having said that, there are provisions which allow Member States undue discretion in curbing dissent and political opposition. This feature is evident in the

---

[53] SAARC Regional Convention on Suppression of Terrorism 1987 (signed at Kathmandu on 4 November 1987, entered into force 22 August 1988). The treaty is deposited with the Secretary-General of the South Asian Association for Regional Cooperation. <http://untreaty.un.org/English/Terrorism.asp.> (14 August 2004); also see chapter 7, below.

[54] See Article II.

OAU and the Arab League Conventions. The OAU Convention includes within its ambit 'acts . . . calculated or intended to create general insurrection in a State'. Similarly, the Arab League Convention regards terrorists as those who 'sow panic among people, causing fear by harming them . . . or seeking to cause damage to the environment or to public or private installations or property or to occupying or seizing them, or seeking to jeopardize national resources'. These definitions are echoed in the domestic legislation of Member States.[55] It is this element of discretion and authorisation to deploy subjective assessment which is dangerous for civil liberties and protection of individual and group rights.

EXAMINING THE SUBSTANCE OF TERRORISM IN THE DEVELOPMENT OF INTERNATIONAL LAW

Terrorism is a crime of antiquity.[56] As a phenomenon as old as human history, terrorism and acts of violence are stamped upon every chronicle of human endeavour. It has, for centuries, been an instrument deployed against the weak and the inarticulate. Human history is littered with examples where terrorism was accompanied by gross violations of human rights including torture and genocide. Amongst these one could mention the horrifying massacres resulting from the Assyrian warfare during the seventh and eight centuries BC, and the Roman obliteration of the city of Carthage and all its inhabitants.[57] Certain religious ideologies, and the wars that were conducted to further those ideologies bore the mark of terrorism and intolerance.[58]

Terrorism is not merely a historical fashion, but has been readily used in modern times. Indeed, the term 'terror' itself was associated with the

[55] The Algerian penal code, for example, includes within its definition of terrorism 'harm[ing] the environment, means of communication or means of transport'. Article 1 of Decree No 93–03, reproduced in article 87 bis of Ordinance No 95.11 of 25 February 1995 amending and supplementing Ordinance No 66.156 of 8 June 1966 enacting the Penal Code. Text provided in the Report submitted by Algeria to the Security Council Committee established pursuant to resolution 1373 (2001) S/2002/972 at 6.

[56] See W Laqueur and Y Alexander (eds), *The Terrorism Reader: A Historical Anthology* (New York, New American Library, Penguin, 1987); J Rehman, *The Weaknesses in the International Protection of Minority Rights* (The Hague, Kluwer Law International, 2000) 51–75.

[57] L Kuper, *Genocide: Its Political Use in the Twentieth Century* (New Haven and London, Yale University Press, 1981) 11–18; J Porter (ed), *Genocide and Human Rights: A Global Anthology* (Washington, DC, University Press of America, 1982); L Kuper, *The Prevention of Genocide* (New Haven, Yale University Press, 1985); L Kuper, *International Action Against Genocide* (London, Minority Rights Group, 1984); H Fein (ed), *Genocide Watch* (New Haven and London, Yale University Press, 1992).

[58] Kuper, *Genocide: Its Political Use in the Twentieth Century*, n 57 above, at 12–14; See Special Rapporteur B Whitaker, *Revised and Updated Report on the Question of the Prevention and Punishment of the Crime of Genocide* UN Doc E/CN.4/Sub.2/1985/6B, 6–7.

Jacobin 'Reign of Terror' in the aftermath of the French Revolution.[59] The Jacobin 'Reign of Terror' resulted in 17,000 official executions, with several thousand deaths and disappearances.[60] The First World War was also the consequence of an international act of terrorism—the assassination of Archduke Franz Ferdinand on 28 June 1914 by the Serbians.[61] In the course of the next hundred and fifty years, the expression was broadened to include 'anyone who attempts to further his views by a system of coercive intimidation; especially applied to members of one of the extreme revolutionary societies in Russia'.[62] During the twentieth century, the rise of nationalism, totalitarian ideologies such as Nazism and Stalinism and the upsurge of racial, religious and linguistic extremism were accompanied by terrorism. It is undeniably the case that the essence of colonialism was violence, intimidation and terrorism of indigenous Peoples.[63] In the aftermath of the Second World War, State-sponsored terrorism was deployed to resist granting the right of self-determination to many of the oppressed nations and Peoples.[64] Colonisation provided a de facto lawful mechanism to violate human dignity, to terrorise indigenous Peoples into submission and humiliation. The terrorism of colonialism produced a backlash. Terrorism was often met with counter-terrorism; whilst the colonisers used terror as an instrument to maintain their hold over their overseas territories, the indigenous Peoples and their national liberation movements resorted to terrorism and political violence as a means to gain emancipation and independence.[65] In their effort to rid themselves of what they perceived as alien, foreign and unlawful domination, resistance movements were formed. Many of the so-called 'national liberation movements' such as the Algerian Liberation Movement (FLN),[66] African National Congress (South Africa),[67] Irish Republican Army (Ireland),[68]

---

[59]   Murphy, n 6 above, at 14; Cassese, n 1 above, at 1.

[60]   Lambert, n 1 above, at 15; E Moxon-Browne, 'Terrorism in France' in J Lodge (ed), *The Threat of Terrorism* (Brighton, Wheatsheaf Books, 1988) 213–28, at 213.

[61]   Dinstein, n 5 above, at 56.

[62]   Cited in Green, n 3 above, at 337.

[63]   See S Qureshi, 'Political Violence in the South Asian Subcontinent' in Y Alexander (ed), n 1 above, at 151–93; see also the Reports of the sessions of the Working Group on Indigenous Populations and the Working Group on Minorities; Porter, n 57 above, at 16; Kuper, *International Action Against Genocide*, n 57, at 15.

[64]   OY Elagab, *International Law Documents Relating to Terrorism* (London, Cavendish, 1995) at iv.

[65]   For a useful analysis see Minority Rights Group (ed), *World Directory of Minorities* (London, Minority Rights Group, 1997).

[66]   See L Kuper, *The Pity of it All: Polarisation of Racial and Ethnic Relations* (Minneapolis, University of Minnesota Press, 1977).

[67]   See S Dubow, *The African National Congress* (Stroud, Sutton, 2000); W Beinart and S Dubow (eds), *Segregation And Apartheid in Twentieth-Century South Africa* (London, Routledge, 1995).

[68]   See H Patterson, *The Politics of Illusion: A Political History of the IRA* (London, Serif, 1997); MLR Smith, *Fighting for Ireland?: The Military Strategy of the Irish Republican Movement* (London, Routledge, 1995).

Indian National Congress and Muslim League (British India) have at one point been deemed terrorist organisations.[69]

The subject of terrorism became a matter of serious contention between States with overseas colonies on the one hand and the newly independent and communist States on the other. Even long after the decolonisation period, the legacies of colonial times often render the subject an unpalatable one. There is a substantial relationship with the right to self-determination for such groups or Peoples as the Palestinians.[70] In this context it needs to be noted that Usama Bin Laden, the prime suspect for the attack on the World Trade Center on 11 September 2001, has repeatedly emphasised the right of self-determination for the Palestinian people as a prerequisite for world peace and security.[71] Another particularly controversial area is the right of the Kashmiri Muslims to self-determination, the conflict between India and Pakistan over the territory of Kashmir already having produced three wars.[72]

INTERNATIONAL EFFORTS TO FORMULATE LEGAL PRINCIPLES PROHIBITING ALL FORMS OF TERRORISM

The War Years and International Friction

International law suffers from an absence of centralised judicial organs, and executive agencies with effective enforcement powers. These limitations have resulted in substantial difficulties in the detection as well as punishment of terrorists. International terrorism was debated by the third (Brussels) International Conference for the Unification of Penal Law held on 26–30 June 1930.[73] At the same time efforts were made by the League of Nations to formulate a binding instrument on international terrorism. Following the assassination of King Alexander of Yugoslavia and Mr Louis Barthou, Foreign Minister of the French Republic in Marseilles in October 1934, the League of Nations drafted a Convention for the

---

[69] P Hardy, *The Muslims of British India* (London, Cambridge University Press, 1972); BR Tomlinson, *The Indian National Congress and the Raj, 1929–1942: The Penultimate Phase* (London, Macmillan, 1976); A Jalal, *The Sole Spokesman: Jinnah, the Muslim League, and the Demand for Pakistan* (Cambridge, Cambridge University Press, 1985).

[70] On the complication generated by the definition of 'Peoples' and 'indigenous Peoples' see J Rehman, 'Minority Rights in International Law: Raising the Conceptual Issues' (1998) 72 *Australian Law Journal* 615.

[71] For further examination see below, chapter 7.

[72] For further consideration see J Rehman, 'Reviewing the Right of Self-Determination: Lessons from the Experience of the Indian Sub-Continent' (2000) 29 *Anglo American Law Review* 454.

[73] H. Labayle, 'Droit international et lutte contre le terrorisme' (1986) 32 *Annuaire français de droit international* 114.

Prevention and Punishment of Terrorism.[74] A number of positive features were contained in this treaty. We have already assessed the various facets of the definition of terrorism as pronounced by the Convention. In addition, the treaty obliged States parties to prevent and punish acts of terrorism. It imposed criminal sanctions for such acts as attacks on the lives and physical integrity of Heads of State and other public officials, destruction of public property and acts calculated to endanger the lives of members of the public.[75] States were also to be under an obligation to institute criminal sanctions for terrorist acts as defined in the Convention. It also recognised the principle of *aut dedere aut judicare*. Despite these many notable aspects, the Convention failed to become operative. A prominent feature (which discouraged further ratifications) was the broad definition accorded to terrorism. The Convention remained ineffective, having received one ratification, that from British India.[76] In any event the forces of aggression and terrorism emerged in Europe; the Second World War heralded the demise of the League of Nations, along with its convention on terrorism.

After the Second World War, further efforts were made to produce a consolidated instrument dealing with terrorism. However, the first two decades of the United Nations period were taken up by a range of issues within which the subject of terrorism formed only an incidental part. The Draft Code on Offences Against the Peace and Security of Mankind as prepared by the International Law Commission in 1954 dealt primarily with the principles enshrined in the Charter of the Nuremberg Tribunal and with the Judgment of the Tribunal.[77] Article 2(6) however defines an offence against the peace and security of mankind as:

> the undertaking or encouragement by the authorities of a State of terrorist activities in another State, or the toleration by the authorities of a State of organised activities calculated to carry out terrorist acts in another State.

Further progress on completion of the code was hampered inter alia by disagreements over the definition of aggression. The General Assembly then turned its attention to the subject of the definition of aggression, an issue that was only resolved through the General Assembly Resolution on the Definition of Aggression (1974).[78] Article 3(g) of the Resolution includes in its explanation of acts of aggression:

[74] The Convention for the Prevention and Punishment of Terrorism, 16 November 1937, 19 League of Nations Official Journal (1938) 23 reprinted 27 UN GAOR, Annex I, Agenda Item No 92, UN Doc A/C.6/418 (1972).

[75] Article 2.

[76] Cassese, n 20 above, at 591.

[77] See UN GAOR Supp (No 9) at 11–12; UN Doc A/2693 (1972). Text available at <http://www.un.org/law/ilc/texts/offences.htm> (5 October 2004).

[78] GA Res 3314 (XXIX) 14 December 1974, GAOR 29th Sess, Supp 31, 142; (1975) 69 *American Journal of International Law* 480.

[t]he sending by or on behalf of a State of armed bands, groups, irregulars or mercenaries, which carry out acts of armed force against another State of such gravity as to amount to the acts listed . . . , or its substantial involvement therein.

There was however a provision which exempted national liberation movements in their struggle for self-determination.[79] Such caveats, although a feature of this Resolution (and a number of subsequent UN General Assembly Resolutions), have added considerable uncertainty as regards the condemnation of terrorist activities. In 1979 the General Assembly passed its Resolution 34/145 which condemned all acts of terrorism.[80] At the same time, the Resolution also condemned

the continuation of repressive and terrorist acts by colonial, racist and alien regimes in denying people their legitimate right to self-determination and independence and other human rights and fundamental freedoms.[81]

The title and the text of the Resolution also confirm that the focus of the Resolution is upon the

underlying causes of those forms of Terrorism and Acts of violence which lie in Misery, Frustration, Grievance and Despair and which Cause Some people to Sacrifice Human Lives including their own in an Attempt to Effect Radical Changes.[82]

The same emphasis on underlying causes is made in General Assembly Resolutions 36/109 (1981)[83] and 40/61 (1985).[84]

An examination of the workings of the United Nations General Assembly reflects fundamental divisions between the Islamic world on the one hand and the developed world on the other. The debates within the United Nations General Assembly have represented these divisions. The developed world has insisted on the absolute prohibition of terrorism regardless of motives and underlying causes. The Islamic States, along

---

[79] Article 7 of the Resolution provides, 'Nothing in this Definition, and in particular Article 3, could in any way prejudice the right to self-determination, freedom and independence, as derived from the Charter, of Peoples forcibly deprived of that right and referred to in the Declaration on Principles of International Law concerning Friendly Relations and Cooperation among States in accordance with the Charter of the United Nations, particularly Peoples under colonial and racist regimes or other forms of alien domination; nor the right of these peoples to struggle to that end and to seek and receive support, in accordance with the principles of the Charter and in conformity with the above-mentioned Declaration'.

[80] Measures to Prevent International Terrorism which Endangers or Takes Innocent Human Lives or Jeopardizes Fundamental Freedoms, and Study of the Underlying Causes of those forms of Terrorism and Acts of Violence which Lie in Misery, Frustration, Grievance and Despair and which Cause Some People to Sacrifice Human Lives including their own in an Attempt to Effect Radical Changes'. UN GA Res 34/145 (1979) 105th Plenary Meeting 17 December 1979.

[81] *Ibid*, para 4.

[82] *Ibid*.

[83] UN GA Res, 36/109, 1981 (10 December 1981).

[84] UN GA Res, 40/61, 1985 (9 December 1985).

with other developing States, have remained suspicious of this approach, claiming that underlying causes of terrorism need to provide the determining factors and that national liberation movements must be allowed to resort to every conceivable means to free themselves from colonial or racist regimes. This conflict has been so severe as to seriously jeopardise any progress in devising international mechanisms to deal with terrorism.

The Islamic States, most of which came into existence after struggles of national liberation, have consistently supported colonised peoples' right to armed resistance and self-determination. As shall be discussed in subsequent chapters, these States have consistently supported the right to self-determination. Thus, speaking in the Sixth Legal Committee, the representative of Yemen noted that he 'resolutely defend[ed]' the position of national liberation movements to achieve their ends by 'all necessary means'.[85] Similarly, according to the representative of the State of Oman, it was wrong to condemn those fighting for self-determination: instead they should be admired and their struggles valued.[86] After the Munich incident (resulting in the deaths of 11 Israeli athletes in September 1972 at the Munich Olympics) the issue of terrorism was considered by the General Assembly and led to the submission of a 'Draft Convention for the Prevention and Punishment of Certain Acts of Terrorism'.[87] The Islamic and Arab States, in expressing their concerns within the United Nations, took the position that terrorism might be used a US-Israeli pretext to deny peoples their legitimate right to self-determination.

This commitment towards the right to self-determination under foreign and alien occupation has been visible in the proposals advanced by the OIC to the draft Convention on Terrorism. Under the proposals advanced by the OIC, the Convention would not be applicable 'during an armed conflict, including in situations of foreign occupation'.[88] Reference to 'foreign occupation' is a sensitive one, as it likely to be used as an Arab-Islamic response to the occupation of Iraq by the US and its allied States. In general, the issue of terrorism is heavily tied to the right of the Palestinian people to self-determination.[89] The Palestinian Liberation Organisation (PLO), as the representative organisation of the Palestinians has countenanced claims of individual violence on the basis that the Palestinian people have the right to self-determination and to act in self-defence against the aggressive and unjustified State violence perpetuated by Israel.

---

[85] UN GAOR, 31st Sess C6 (63 mtg) para 1 UN Doc A/C.6/SR.1370 (1972).
[86] UN GAOR, 27 Sess C6 (1370th mtg) para 46 UN Doc A/C.6/SR.1370 (1972).
[87] UN Doc A/C6/L850 reprinted in (1972) 11 ILM 1382–7. See chapter 4.
[88] See Report of the Ad Hoc Committee Established by General Assembly Resolution 51/210 of 17 December 1996, UN GAOR, 6th Sess, 26th mtg, at 1 UN Doc A/57/37 (2002), Annex IV, 2 at 17; Halberstam, n 28 above, 573 at 581.
[89] Lambert, n 1 above, at 33–4.

Advancing this hypothesis, the PLO representative made the following stark comments in the Security Council in 1986: '[t]he acts of violence by the freedom-fighters against the alien forces of occupation should never be confused with acts of terrorism'.[90] The insistence of the OIC upon the exclusion of acts committed 'during an armed conflict, including in situations of foreign occupation' from the definition of terrorism has been cited as a major hurdle in the drafting of a comprehensive terrorism convention.[91] This ideology has been a continuous theme in the Resolutions and debates of the OIC. During its 9th Summit, in passing the landmark Doha Declaration, the OIC affirmed that:

> a clear separation must be made between terrorism, on the one hand, and people's struggle for national liberation including the struggle of the Palestinian people and the elimination of foreign occupation and colonial hegemony as well as for regaining the right to self-determination, on the other hand.

Impact of the East-West Détente

The ending of the Cold War and a thaw in East-West relations brought about a significant change in the policies of the former communist States. Many of these States have embraced general norms of international law and have also renounced sponsorship of terrorist activities. In addition, over the years there has been a considerable shift in the general position. This changing position can be attributed to a variety of reasons. Firstly, with the independence of a vast majority of former European colonies the basis for supporting national liberation movements has diminished. The case for liberation movements is confined to the struggle against pariah States such as Israel. Secondly, and perhaps more significantly, the new States which emerged from the rubble of decolonisation have themselves been challenged by secessionist movements represented by various groups. Amongst these groups one could cite the Tamil Tigers, the Sudanese Peoples Liberation Army and the Kashmiri Mujaheedaen.[92] These groups adopted similar tactics hitherto used against the nationalists seeking independent Statehood from European colonisers. Many of the new States, while emphasising the principle of territorial integrity, have treated these secessionist organisations as terrorist groups. Increasingly, these organisations have targeted diplomatic personnel and there have been instances of hijacking of national aircrafts owned by developing States. The emergence of common concerns has led to a fluidity in the position of many Islamic States of Asia and Africa.

---

[90] See Cassese, n 1 above, at 79.
[91] See Trahan, n 37 above, at 231.
[92] For consideration of these and other cases see Minority Rights Group, n 65 above.

Signs of a common concern over terrorism were already emerging in the 1970s. According to the Declaration on Principles of International Law Concerning Friendly Relations and Co-operation Amongst States in Accordance with the Charter of the United Nations (1970):[93]

> Every State has the duty to refrain from organising, instigating, assisting or participating in acts of civil strife or terrorist acts in another State or acquiescing in organised activities within its territory directed towards the commission of such acts, when the acts referred to in the present paragraph involve a threat or use of force.

In 1979, the Ad Hoc Committee on Terrorism, a committee formed pursuant to General Assembly Resolution 3034,[94] recommended inter alia that the General Assembly condemn attacks of terrorists, take note of the underlying causes contained in the Committee's reports and work towards elimination of terrorism in compliance with their obligations under international law, refrain from organising, instigating, assisting or participating in terrorist acts in other States and allowing their territory to be used for such acts, and take all possible measures to co-operate with each other to combat international terrorism.

The General Assembly adopted these recommendations, although, as noted in an earlier section, at the behest of the developing and Muslim world these recommendations were tempered by the terminology of 'underlying causes' and the 'right to self-determination'. Further progress was made in 1985 when the UN General Assembly adopted a Resolution in which it urged States to take measures towards the 'speedy and final elimination of the problem of international terrorism'.[95] The Assembly also took the position that it

> [u]nequivocally condemns, as criminal, all acts, methods and practices of terrorism wherever and by whomever committed, including those which jeopardise friendly relations among States and their security [and] deplores the loss of innocent human lives which result from such acts of terrorism.[96]

A distinctive feature of the Resolution is that after a protracted debate of fifteen years, for the first time in the United Nations, this Resolution associates the term 'criminal' with terrorism.[97] Another Resolution (based the 1985 Resolution) condemning terrorism was adopted by the General

---

[93] GA Res 2625 (XXV) 1970 (24 October 1970).
[94] See Report of the Sixth Committee, UN GAOR A/8969 (1972) at 5.
[95] GA Res 40/61 1985 (9 December 1985) para 5.
[96] *Ibid*, paras 1 and 2.
[97] C Van den Wyngaert, 'The Political Offence Exception to Extradition: How to Plug the "Terrorists Loophole" without Departing from Fundamental Human Rights' (1989) 19 *Israel Yearbook of Human Rights* 297 at 297; Cassese, n 20 above, at 605.

Assembly in 1987.[98] In 1994, the General Assembly adopted a Resolution entitled 'Declaration on Measures to Eliminate International Terrorism'.[99] Peace, security and restraint on use of force represent the basis of the Declaration. In condemning terrorism the Declaration also calls upon States to refrain from organising, instigating, assisting or participating in terrorist activities and from acquiescing in or encouraging activities within their territories directed towards the commission of any such acts. In the aftermath of 11 September 2001, there was unequivocal condemnation of international terrorism from all States. The commitment to combat terrorism is also evident in the operations of the Security Council. As this study will examine, the Security Council has adopted a robust approach towards combating international terror. While the politics behind these Security Council measures are the subject of apprehension, the Council has nevertheless utilised its powers in adopting a series of measures against several States including Libya, the Sudan and Iraq.

The most effective international steps undertaken by the Security Council have been under the auspices of Resolution 1373. Passed on 28 September 2001, the Resolution has duly been heralded as 'the cornerstone of the United Nations' counter terrorism effort'.[100] Under the mandate of Chapter VII, the Resolution declares international terrorism a threat to 'international peace and security'. The Resolution requires States inter alia to take all necessary steps to prevent acts of terrorism, prevent the movement of terrorists and to undertake all necessary measures for criminal investigations or proceedings for those engaged in terrorist acts. The Resolution has an unprecedented focus on financial aspects of terrorism, a subject examined elsewhere in this book.[101] In accordance with rule 28 of its provisional rules, the Council also established a Committee, the so-called 'Counter-Terrorism Committee '. The Committee consists of all the members of the Council, and monitors the implementation of Resolution 1373. All States were initially required to report to the Committee within ninety days of the adoption of Resolution 1373. The overwhelming compliance of all States with the reporting obligations represents an obvious reflection of the support for the Security Council's measures, including full co-operation with the Counter-Terrorism Committee. This compliance

---

[98] GA Res 42/159 7 December 1987. Writing in 1989, Lambert made the following useful points: '[T]he change in language in the most recent General Assembly Resolutions must be seen as some progress towards a universal consensus that acts of terrorism are not to be tolerated regardless of the cause. It must also be recognised, however, that the General Assembly continues to send out somewhat mixed signals regarding the issue of national liberation movements'. Lambert, n 1 above, at 44; also see Cassese, n 20 above, at 605.

[99] See UN GAOR Forty Ninth session, 84th Plenary Meeting, Supp No 49, at 303. UN Doc A/Res/49/60, 1994 (9 December 1994).

[100] See Rosand, n 11 above, at 334.

[101] See below, chapter 6.

with the reporting deadlines as set out by the Committee also reveals a willingness to follow international guidelines at an inter-governmental level.

It is noticeable that the General Assembly, throughout its existence, has been active in its condemnation of global terrorism. Such activism and unified views on the subject represents a positive development. At the same time it is important to recognise the fact that a significant reason for such activism is that General Assembly Resolutions are not legally binding per se; ambiguous terminology can be deployed to represent a show of unanimity in condemning terrorism.[102] The situation would be radically different if States were required to subscribe to any internationally binding agreement on global terrorism. The old differences and suspicions are certain to resurface.

DEALING WITH SPECIFIC TERRORIST ACTIVITIES

In the light of substantial disagreements over the definition, nature and scope of terrorism, the international community has been unable to formulate a single consolidated instrument dealing with terrorism.[103] Progress has, however, been made in a number of related areas. A range of treaties have been created under the auspices of the United Nations and regional organisations. In addition, the International Civil Aviation Organisation (ICAO) and the International Maritime Organisation (IMO) have been successful in sponsoring conventions dealing with aerial and maritime terrorism respectively. There are currently more than seventeen conventions and protocols dealing with various aspects of terrorism. These include the Convention on the Prevention and Punishment of Crimes against Internationally Protected Persons, including Diplomatic Agents, adopted by the General Assembly of the United Nations (1973),[104] the International Convention against the Taking of Hostages, adopted by the General Assembly of the United Nations (1979),[105] the International Convention for the Suppression of Terrorist Bombings, adopted by the General Assembly of the United Nations on 15 December 1997 (opened for

---

[102] On the value of General Assembly Resolutions see B Sloan, 'General Assembly Resolutions Revisited: Forty Years After' (1987) 58 *British Yearbook of International Law* 39; SA Bleicher, 'The Legal Significance of Re-Citation of General Assembly Resolutions' (1969) 63 *American Journal of International Law* 444; B Cheng, 'United Nations Resolutions on Outer Space: "Instant" International Customary Law?' (1965) 5 *Indian Journal of International Law* 23.

[103] See R Higgins, 'The General International Law of Terrorism' in R Higgins and M Flory (eds), n 1 above, 13–29 at 14.

[104] 1035 UNTS 167; (1974) 13 ILM 41. See below, chapter 4.

[105] 1316 UNTS 205; (1979) 18 ILM 1460. See below, chapter 4.

signature 12 January 1998),[106] the International Convention for the Suppression of the Financing of Terrorism, adopted by the General Assembly of the United Nations on 9 December 1999,[107] the Convention on Offences and Certain Other Acts Committed on Board Aircraft (1963),[108] the Convention for the Suppression of Unlawful Seizure of Aircraft, signed at the Hague (1970),[109] the Convention for the Suppression of Unlawful Acts against the Safety of Civil Aviation (1971),[110] the Convention on the Physical Protection of Nuclear Material (1980),[111] the Protocol on the Suppression of Unlawful Acts of Violence at Airports Serving International Civil Aviation, supplementary to the Convention for the Suppression of Unlawful Acts against the Safety of Civil Aviation, signed at Montreal on 24 February 1988,[112] the Convention for the Suppression of Unlawful Acts against the Safety of Maritime Navigation (1988),[113] the Protocol for the Suppression of Unlawful Acts against the Safety of Fixed Platforms Located on the Continental Shelf, (March 1988),[114] and the Convention on the Marking of Plastic Explosives for the Purpose of Detection (1991).[115] As we have already seen, there are also a number of regional conventions on terrorism. These include the Arab Convention on the Suppression of Terrorism (1998),[116] the Convention of the Organisation of the Islamic Conference on Combating International Terrorism (1999),[117] the European Convention on the Suppression of Terrorism, concluded at Strasbourg on 27 January 1977,[118] the OAS Convention to Prevent and Punish Acts of Terrorism Taking the Form of Crimes against Persons and Related Extortion that are of International Significance (1971),[119] the OAU Convention on the Prevention and Combating of Terrorism, adopted at Algiers on 14 July

[106] Doc A/Res/52/164; depository notification C.N.801.2001.TREATIES–9 of 12 October 2001.

[107] Resolution A/Res/54/109; depository notifications C.N.327.2000.TREATIES–12 of 30 May 2000. See below, chapter 6.

[108] (1963) 2 ILM 1042.

[109] (1971) 10 ILM 133. See below, chapter 5.

[110] UNTS No 14118 vol 974, at 178.

[111] Opened for Signature on 3 March 1980 (adopted on 26 October 1979, entered into force 8 February 1987) (1979) 18 ILM 1419.

[112] (1988) 27 ILM 627.

[113] *Ibid*, at 668. See below, chapter 5.

[114] For the text of the Protocol see <http://www.unodc.org/unodc/en/terrorism_convention_platforms.html> (19 September 2004). For further analysis see below, chapter 5.

[115] For the text of the Convention see <http://www.unodc.org/unodc/terrorism_convention_plastic_explosives.html> (22 September 2004).

[116] Arab Convention on the Suppression of Terrorism, signed at a meeting held at the General Secretariat of the League of Arab States in Cairo on 22 April 1998 (deposited with the Secretary-General of the League of Arab States).

[117] For analysis of the treaty see below, chapter 7.

[118] (1978) 15 ILM 1272.

[119] (1978) 10 ILM 255.

1999,[120] the SAARC Regional Convention on Suppression of Terrorism (1987),[121] and the Treaty on Co-operation among States Members of the Commonwealth of Independent States in Combating Terrorism (1999).[122] Furthermore, a range of non-binding international instruments has been adopted.

The present study presents an analysis of a number of the aforementioned conventions with their special emphasis on the role and position of Islamic States. It must, however, be noted that there are a range of additional international instruments (or provisions within international instruments) which deal with terrorist activities. These include the Universal Postal Union Convention and the Postal Parcels Agreement banning the posting of explosives, flammable or other dangerous substances in the mail,[123] the Convention on the Prohibition of the Development, Production, Stockpiling and Use of Chemical Weapons and on their Destruction,[124] and the Convention on the Prohibition of the Development, Production, Stockpiling of Bacteriological and Toxin Weapons and on their Destruction,[125] making it illegal for any State to use or allow using chemical or biological weapons. The issue of international terrorism, as this study will consider, is closely tied to humanitarian and human rights issues. Facets of human rights law are examined in subsequent chapters. It is, however, worth making reference to the humanitarian law treaties which prohibit and condemn terrorism during armed conflict. The 1907 Hague Regulations,[126] the four 1949 Geneva Conventions,[127] and the 1977

---

[120] OAU Convention on the Prevention and Combating of Terrorism, adopted at Algiers on 14 July 1999 (deposited with the General Secretariat of the Organization of African Unity).

[121] For text of the Convention see <http://untreaty.un.org/English/Terrorism/Conv18.pdf> (1 September 2003).

[122] Treaty on Co-operation Among States Members of the Commonwealth of Independent States in Combating Terrorism, done at Minsk on 4 June 1999 (deposited with the Secretariat of the Commonwealth of Independent States).

[123] See the Constitution of the Universal Postal Union, open for signature 10 July 1964; Additional Protocol to the Constitution of the Universal Postal Union of 10 July 1964, Article 29 (1)(e) opened for signature 14 November 1969, 810 UNTS 69; Second Additional Protocol to the Constitution of the Universal Postal Union of 10 July 1964, opened for signature 5 July 1974; Third Additional Protocol to the Constitution of the Universal Postal Union of 10 July 1964, opened for signature 28 July, 1984; Fourth Additional Protocol to the Constitution of the Universal Postal Union of 10 July 1964, opened for signature 14 December 1989; Fifth Additional Protocol to the Constitution of the Universal Postal Union of 10 July 1964 opened for signature 14 September 1994; Universal Postal Union Postal Parcels Agreement, Article 19(a)(v) opened for signature 14 September 1994.

[124] Convention on the Prohibition of the Development, Production, Stockpiling and Use of Chemical Weapons and on their Destruction, opened for signature 13 January 1993; 32 ILM 800.

[125] Convention on the Prohibition of the Development, Production and Stockpiling of Bacteriological and Toxin Weapons and on their Destruction, opened for signature 10 April, (1972) 1015 UNTS 163. See B Kellman, 'Biological Terrorism: Legal Measures for Preventing Catastrophe' (2001) 24 *Harvard Journal of Law and Public Policy* 417.

[126] (1910) UKTS 9, Cmnd 5030.

[127] (1950) 75 UNTS 31–83; (1958) 39 UKTS, Cmnd 550.

Protocols[128] have clauses aimed at protecting civilians from acts of terror.[129] Their application is not confined to international wars, but also applies to internal armed conflicts.[130]

CONCLUSIONS

Terrorism, as this chapter has explored, presents a grave threat to international law. It is also likely to seriously jeopardise relations between States, and the communities residing within those States. The tensions and stresses involved in dealing with terrorism are partly due to the conceptual difficulties encountered in grappling with the subject. International law has devised a range of instruments, including international and regional treaties, to deal with the subject of terrorism. The United Nations General Assembly is currently attempting to draft a comprehensive treaty which would provide a definition. However, as our analysis has revealed, there are significant obstacles. As an elusive and slippery concept, attempts to provide a definition of 'terrorism' are likely to be unsuccessful.

Many concepts and legal institutions have survived in the absence of specification and meticulousness. An inability to define legal concepts with precision is not necessarily synonymous with a questionable existence, although it is likely to affect their viability. The present study recommends and endorses a piecemeal approach for dealing with terrorist offences. A range of treaties dealing with various facets of terrorism has come into operation—the challenge facing the international community is their application and enforcement. A further, more taxing exercise is to balance the concerns of terrorism with the protection of civil liberties. The United Nations Policy Working Group makes the following points of profound significance:

The protection and promotion of human rights under the rule of law is essential in the prevention of terrorism. First, terrorism often thrives in environments in which human rights are violated. Terrorists may exploit human rights violations to gain support for their cause. Second, it must be understood clearly that terrorism itself is a violation of human rights. Terrorist acts that take life violate the right to life set forth in article 6 of the International Covenant on Civil and Political Rights. Third, it must also be understood that international law requires observance of basic human rights standards in the struggle against terrorism.[131]

---

[128] (1977) 19 Misc (1977), Cmnd 6927.
[129] Cassese, n 20 above, at 592.
[130] *Ibid*, at 592.
[131] Report of the Policy Working Group on the United Nations and Terrorism A/57/273 (S/2002/875) para 26.

States have and continue to apply such strategies as internment, expulsion orders, and deportations.[132] There is even the debate over legitimising forms of torture were it to prevent acts similar in nature to 11 September 2001. There remains a substantial risk of violation of human rights and civil liberties. Several States, including the United States, Turkey, the United Kingdom, China and Pakistan, have put in place draconian laws which jeopardise civil rights in the name of the 'war on terrorism'.

---

[132] A Vercher, *Terrorism in Europe: An International Comparative Legal Analysis* (Oxford, Clarendon Press, 1992).

4

Hostage-Taking in International Law and Terrorism against 'Internationally Protected Persons'

INTRODUCTION

HOSTAGE-TAKING OF civilians and violence against internationally protected persons represent horrific forms of international terrorism.[1] There are similarities in both actions, a position emphasised by Elagab when he says that hostage-taking 'usually overlaps with crimes which are the subject of one or more international accords such as those involving . . . diplomats'.[2] The Convention on the Prevention and Punishment of Crimes against Internationally Protected Persons acknowledges this overlap through incorporation of crimes of 'kidnapping or other attacks upon the person or liberty of an internationally protected person'.[3] The nexus between hostage-taking and crimes against internationally protected persons is also emphasised by other international instruments such as the European Convention on the Suppression of Terrorism.[4] As this chapter will examine, internationally

---

[1] See J Lambert, *Terrorism and Hostages in International Law: A Commentary on the Hostages Convention 1979* (Cambridge, Grotius Publishers, 1990); E Young, 'The Development of the Law of Diplomatic Relations' (1964) 40 *British Yearbook of International Law* 141; L Dembinski, *The Modern Law of Diplomacy: External Mission of States and International Organizations* (Dordrecht, Martinus Nijhoff Publishers, 1988); OY Elagab, *International Law Documents Relating to Terrorism* (London, Cavendish, 1995) 517–99; R Rosenstock, 'International Convention against the Taking of Hostages: Another International Community Step Against Terrorism' (1980) 9 *Journal of International Law and Policy* 169; E Chadwick, *Self-determination, Terrorism and the International Humanitarian Law of Armed Conflict* (The Hague, Martinus Nijhoff Publishers, 1996); JG Sullivan (ed), *Embassies Under Siege: Personal Accounts by Diplomats on the Front Line* (Washington, DC, Brassey's, 1995).

[2] Elagab, n 1 above, at 517. A similar stance is taken by I Bantekas and S Nash, *International Criminal Law* 2nd edn (London, Cavendish, 2003) at 30.

[3] Article 2, Convention on the Prevention and Punishment of the Crime against Internationally Protected Persons, Including Diplomatic Agents adopted by the General Assembly of the United Nations (1973) 1035 UNTS 167; (1974) 13 ILM 41.

[4] European Convention on the Suppression of Terrorism (adopted 27 January 1977, entered into force 4 August 1978) ETS No 090. <http://conventions.coe.int/Treaty/EN/Treaties/Html/090.htm> (21 September 2004).

protected persons remain particularly vulnerable to kidnapping and being taken hostage. At the same time, however, there is a specialist regime in place to prevent violations committed against internationally protected persons. Internationally protected persons require not only physical protection of their individual person, there is also the necessity of ensuring inviolability of their operations.

Within Islamic law there are serious recriminations for maltreatment of internationally protected persons. Diplomatic immunity and inviolability of their missions remain distinguishing features of *Sharia*, dating back to the time of Prophet Muhammad.[5] There exists a general prohibition on the taking of hostages. It would appear that the classical position sanctions certain exceptions. It has, for instance, been suggested that:

> [u]nder the traditional system of Islamic international criminal law, like the system of international law, hostages might be taken if the taking of the hostages is stated in an agreement for the purpose of implementing its provisions.[6]

However, it is never permissible under the *Sharia* to maltreat, abuse or kill hostages. Muhammad Hamidullah in a detailed examination has listed nineteen practices expressly prohibited by Islamic law—these include the abuse and maltreatment of prisoners and hostages.[7]

In the context of modern international law, there are elements of strains or equivocacy within modern Islamic State practices. While denouncing hostage-taking and embracing the provisions of the hostage-taking Convention, as reflected in the *travaux préparatoires* of the treaty, Islamic States nevertheless remain determined to create exceptions for national liberation movements in their fight against alien or colonial occupation, including hostage-taking of their colonial oppressors. The present chapter reviews the perspective of Islamic States on the subject of hostage-taking and the rights of internationally protected persons.

HOSTAGE-TAKING: DENIAL OF FUNDAMENTAL HUMAN RIGHTS AND THE BREACH OF PEREMPTORY NORMS OF INTERNATIONAL LAW

The right to liberty and freedom of movement documents itself in the primordial annals of history. In the modern age of human rights, unlawful and arbitrary detentions constitute fundamental violations of human

---

[5] MC Bassiouni, 'Protection of Diplomats under Islamic Law' (1980) 74 *American Journal of International Law* 609 at 610.

[6] F Malekian, *The Concept of Islamic International Criminal Law: A Comparative Study* (London, Graham & Trotman, 1994) at 114.

[7] M Hamidullah, *Muslim Conduct of State: Being a Treatise on Siyar, that is Islamic Notion of Public International Law, Consisting of the Laws of Peace, War and Neutrality, Together with precedents from Orthodox Practices and Precedent by a Historical and General Introduction* (Lahore, Sh Muhammad Ashraf, 1977) 205–8.

rights—arguably breaches of the norm of *jus cogens*.[8] The human rights dimension of the right to liberty and freedom of movement has been a pervasive theme in the jurisprudence of international law, although as our discussion highlights, specific instruments targeting the criminality of hostage-taking are of more recent origin.

The symbolic admittance of the crime of hostage-taking in the armoury of international criminal law dates back to the indictments in the Nuremberg Trials for acts of hostage-taking. The prohibition on hostage-taking during armed conflicts, as shall be examined shortly, is also incorporated in international humanitarian law.[9] The wholesale denunciation of hostage-taking as a crime in international law is, however, a product of the United Nations General Assembly's Convention against the Taking of Hostages. The adopting treaty was the culmination of four years of effort on the part of United Nations.[10] The conclusion of the Convention was surrounded by a range of incidents including the Munich killings of 1972,[11] the kidnappings of German businessmen in and outside of the Federal Republic of Germany,[12] the Entebbe raid[13] and the taking of American hostages in Iran.[14]

The treaty—itself a product of laborious compromises—is laced with references to human rights, appealing to humanitarian norms and laws. The preamble recognises that

> everyone has the right to life, liberty and security of person, as set out in the Universal Declaration of Human Rights and the International Covenant on Civil and Political Rights.[15]

Hostage-taking is an 'offence of grave concern' to the international community, and it is of immediate urgency to prevent, prosecute and

---

[8] See eg *United States Diplomatic and Consular Staff in Tehran (United States of America v Iran)*, Judgment 24 May 1980, [1980] ICJ Reports 3, where the International Court notes, 'wrongfully to deprive human beings of their freedom and to subject them to physical constraint in conditions of hardship is in itself manifestly incompatible with the fundamental principles enunciated in the Universal Declaration of Human Rights' (para 91). Also see NS Rodley, 'Human Rights and Humanitarian Intervention: The Case Law of the World Court' (1989) 38 *International & Comparative Law Quarterly* 321 at 326.

[9] See below.

[10] See Rosenstock, n 1 above, at 173.

[11] *Ibid*, at 173.

[12] *Ibid*, at 169.

[13] For further consideration see LC Green, 'Rescue at Entebbe—Legal Aspects' (1976) 6 *Israel Yearbook on Human Rights* 312; MN Shaw, 'Some Legal Aspects of the Entebbe Incident' (1978) 1 *Jewish Law Annual* 232; DJ Harris, *Cases and Materials on International Law* 5th edn (London, Sweet & Maxwell, 1998) 909–11.

[14] *United States Diplomatic and Consular Staff in Tehran Case (United States of America v Iran)* [1980] ICJ Reports 3; Harris, n 13 above, at 358–62; L Gross, 'The Case Concerning United States Diplomatic and Consular Staff in Tehran: Phase of Provisional Measures' (1980) 74 *American Journal of International Law* 395; K Gryzbowski, 'The Regime of Diplomacy and the Tehran Hostages' (1981) 30 *International & Comparative Law Quarterly* 42.

[15] Preamble to the Convention.

punish all acts of taking of hostages.[16] The text of the treaty regards hostage-taking inter alia as seizure, detention, or threats to kill or harm individuals with an objective of compelling third parties to undertake or abstain from particular actions.[17] In this definition of hostage-taking, the human rights dimension of preserving individual liberty and the right not to be exploited is well articulated.

The humanitarian frame of reference is reflected in the obligations on the State party in possession of the hostages. The undertaking is to engage in all appropriate measures inter alia to secure their release and facilitate their departure.[18] In instances where an object comes into the custody of a State party, there is an obligation on the State party to restore it either to the hostage or to an appropriate third party as the case may be.[19] Within this obligation of securing the release of hostages, there is an absence of direction as to the means most appropriate to deal with such situations. The element of subjectivity has allowed powerful States to flex their muscles. The use of force, against hostage-takers, even in a State's own territory has sometimes been counter-productive, harming the intended benificiaries.[20]

In addition to a commitment on the part of States to attempt to secure the release of hostages, there is an obligation to co-operate in the prevention of hostage-taking acts.[21] According to Article 4, States parties are required to co-operate in the prevention of the offences by

taking all practicable measures . . . including measures to prohibit in their territories illegal activities of persons, groups or organisations that encourage, instigate, organise, or engage in the perpetration of acts of taking of hostages

within and outside of their territories, including banning of activities targeted at organising or planning to engage in the activity of hostage-taking. The responsibility of undertaking all practical measures to prevent hostage-taking represents the core of the conventional obligations. There is, however, no specificity as to the means to be adopted in complying with these obligations. As the current 'war on terrorism' confirms, States relish the opportunity of deploying their subjective standards. This award of a *carte blanche* to the governments (both in the western and in the Islamic world) is troubling for advocates of human rights.[22]

---

[16] Preamble to the Convention.

[17] Article 1.

[18] Article 3(1).

[19] Article 3(2).

[20] Examples of such use of force could be found in the Pan American Hijacking in Pakistan in September 1986. In order to secure the release of the hostages, Pakistani Commandos forced their way into the plane. Fifteen passengers were killed, although the hostage-takers were captured. Lambert, n 1 above, at 208.

[21] Article 3(1).

[22] See Report by the International Bar Association's Task Force on International Terrorism, *International Terrorism: Legal Challenges and Responses* (Ardsley NY, Transnational Publishers, 2003) 29–89.

While there is a duty to make hostage-taking actions offences within domestic laws and to ascribe appropriate sentences, there are also requirements designed to ensure fairness in trials. Requests for extradition are to be refused if the requested State has substantial grounds for believing:

(a) that the request for extradition for an offence set forth in article 1 has been made for the purpose of prosecuting or punishing a person on account of his race, religion, nationality, ethnic origin or political opinion; or

(b) that the person's position may be prejudiced:

   (i) for any of the reasons mentioned in subparagraph (a) of this paragraph, or

   (ii) for the reason that communication with him by the appropriate authorities of the State entitled to exercise rights of protection cannot be effected.[23]

ISLAMIC PERSPECTIVES ON THE CONVENTION

The Right to Self-Determination, Hostage-taking and the National Liberation Movements[24]

The right to self-determination is enshrined in the United Nations Charter,[25] in the International Covenants on Human Rights,[26] the Declaration on the Granting of Independence to Colonial Countries and the Declaration on Principles on Friendly Relations and Co-operation among States.[27] Self-determination is now regarded a norm of *jus cogens*[28] although there remains substantial controversy in relation to its substance and content. More specifically there is debate as to entities entitled to this right and whether the right exists in the post-colonial era. Islamic States, whilst being great proponents of the right to self-determination, have

---

[23] Article 9(1).

[24] WD Verwey, 'The International Hostages Convention and the National Liberation Movements' (1981) 75 *American Journal of International Law* 69.

[25] See Article 1 and 55 of the Charter of the United Nations 1945; Charter of the United Nations (signed 26 June 1945, entered into force 24 October 1945) 59 Stat 1031, TS 993, 3 Bevans 1153, UNTS xvi (892 UNTS 119), UKTS (1946) 67.

[26] The Common Article 1 of the International Covenant on Civil and Political Rights (ICCPR) 1966 and the International Covenant on Economic, Social and Cultural Rights (ICE-SCR) 1966; ICCPR (adopted 16 December 1966, entered into force 23 March 1976) GA Res 2200 (XXI) 99 UNTS 171; ICESCR (adopted 16 December 1966, entered into force 3 January 1976) GA Res 2200 (XXI) 993 UNTS 3. Amongst Regional Instruments, the right to Self-Determination is contained in the African Charter on Human and People's Rights 1981 (adopted 27 June 27 1981, entered into force 21 October 1986) OAU Doc CAB/LEG/67/3 rev 5, (1982) 21 ILM 58, Article 20.

[27] See GA Res 1514 (XV) 1960 and GA Res 2625 (XXV) 1970.

[28] MN Shaw, *Title to Territory in Africa: International Legal Issues* (Oxford, Oxford University Press, 1986) at 91; H Gros-Espeil, Special Rapporteur, *Implementation of United Nations Resolutions Relating to the Right of Peoples under Colonial and Alien Domination to Self-Determination*, Study for the Sub-Commission on Prevention of Discrimination and Protection of Minorities, (1977) UN Doc E/CN.4/Sub.2/390, 17–19.

given the right a distinct interpretation.[29] One aspect of this interpretation treats self-determination as being synonymous with independent Statehood.[30] Once independent Statehood is achieved, self-determination is only evident in norms of sovereign equality and non-interference in internal political and economic structures. After independence no further secessionist claims are acceptable, regardless of whether they were based on denial of civil and political rights or economic discrimination. The emphasis on prohibition of secessionist claims has remained particularly strong amongst Islamic States. A number of Member States of the OIC, including Nigeria, Somalia, Pakistan, Indonesia and the Sudan, have faced substantial challenges from dissident groups claiming a right to self-determination. During the 1960s, Nigeria was on the brink of disintegration,[31] and Bangladesh until recently represented the only successful post-colonial secessionist State.[32]

The second aspect of self-determination has been the prioritisation of the right to economic self-determination and the advocacy of permanent sovereignty over natural resources.[33] The *travaux préparatoires* of the human rights covenants confirm that a number of Islamic States, particularly Afghanistan and Saudi Arabia, were at the forefront of incorporating the right to economic self-determination and of permanent sovereignty over natural resources within the two human rights covenants.[34] These rights are now firmly entrenched in Article 1 of both covenants.[35] Although the discussion on the various aspects of self-determination has been long and convoluted, as the present chapter illustrates, the subject nonetheless has had a significant relationship with the crime of hostage-taking.

The lengthy and protracted debate feeds into the third and critical aspect of self-determination, which so nearly stalled the progress of the

---

[29] See A Rigo-Sureda, *The Evolution of the Right of Self-Determination* (Sijthof, Leiden, 1973); A Cassese, *Self-Determination of Peoples: A Legal Reappraisal* (Cambridge, Cambridge University Press, 1995).

[30] R Emerson, 'Self-Determination' (1971) 65 *American Journal of International Law* 459; J Rehman, 'Reviewing the Right of Self-Determination: Lessons from the Experience of the Indian Sub-Continent' (2000) 29 *Anglo-American Law Review* 454.

[31] SK Panter-Brick, 'The Right to Self-Determination: Its Application to Nigeria' (1968) 44 *International Affairs* 254.

[32] See J Rehman, *The Weaknesses in the International Protection of Minority Rights* (The Hague, Kluwer Law International, 2000).

[33] O Schachter, *International Law in Theory and Practice* (Dordrecht, Martinus Nijhoff Publishers, 1991) 301–5.

[34] See GAOR, 3rd Committee, 10th Session, 638th meeting, 70.

[35] Article 1 inter alia provides that: All Peoples have the right of self-determination. By virtue of that right they freely . . . pursue their economic . . . development. All Peoples may, for their own ends, freely dispose of their natural wealth and resources without prejudice to any obligations arising out of international economic co-operation, based upon the principle of mutual benefit, and international law. In no case may a people be deprived of its own means of subsistence. .

Hostage-Taking Convention. There has been an insistence on the part of the Islamic world on the application of an exclusive regime for national liberation movements in their struggle for self-determination. The preamble to the Hostages Convention and its body accords prominence to the right to self-determination. The preamble reaffirms

> the principle of equal rights and self-determination of peoples as enshrined in the Charter of the United Nations and the Declaration on Principles of International Law concerning Friendly Relations and Co-operation among States.[36]

However, hortatory overtures and congratulatory comments were in themselves inadequate. The objective of the Islamic and non-aligned States was to campaign for distinct rights for the national liberation movements fighting colonial and racist regimes. According to this hypothesis, the justification inherent in their cause provided sanctity to actions conducted by national liberation movements, including taking hostage those who had usurped their rights. Thus in the context of the historical struggles of colonised and oppressed peoples, it was insufficient to merely examine cases where individuals were subjected to detention and being taken hostage. A pragmatic approach necessitated a broader definition which also included the seizure or detention of masses under colonial, racist or foreign domination.[37]

During the drafting of the Convention, Islamic States in coalition with other developing countries demanded exceptions for the peoples struggling for liberation. Acts conducted by national liberation movements were distinct and could not be categorised as ordinary criminal activities. Thus, the Syrian representative made the comment that 'acts perpetrated by criminals under ordinary law could not be placed on equal footing with the struggle of national liberation movements which, by their objectives, were entirely different.'[38] In reiterating this agenda, the delegate of Iran made an emphatic claim that:

> [t]he Convention must not in any way impair the exercise of the legitimate right to self-determination and independence of all peoples, and especially those struggling against colonialism, alien domination, racial discrimination and apartheid. Safeguards, in a form to be determined by the Ad Hoc Committee should be devised for that purpose.[39]

---

[36] Preamble to the International Convention against the Taking of Hostages.
[37] See Working Paper submitted by the Libyan Arab Jamahirya UN Doc A/AC.188/L.9, in 1977 Report of the Ad Hoc Committee on the Drafting of an International Convention Against the taking of Hostages 32 UN GAOR Supp (No 39) 106–10; UN Doc A/32/39 (1977).
[38] See Third Report of the Hostages Committee, 14 (para 55).
[39] UN Doc A/32/39 at 41.

The indigenous nationalists movements epitomised struggles for liberation which were just, legitimate and needed the support of the
international community. The *bellum justum* doctrine had now been
refashioned to support those fighting racist regimes and alien and foreign
oppression.[40] Thus, as the argument proceeded, the Convention was
inapplicable 'against national liberation movements which took their
oppressors hostage in the course of a struggle against a colonial government or a racist foreign regime'.[41] According to the delegate of Tanzania,
the draft Convention, as a prerequisite, needs to:

> Recognise the legitimacy of the struggle of national liberation movements and
> the inalienable right of freedom fighters to take up arms to fight their oppres-
> sors. The oppressed peoples and colonial peoples who were held in perpetual
> bondage could not be stopped from taking their oppressors hostage, if that
> became inevitable.[42]

Further support was provided by the delegates of Tanzania and Lesotho,
later joined by the representatives of Algeria, Egypt, Guinea, Libya and
Nigeria. Their proposal was that:

> For the purposes of this Convention, the term 'taking of hostages' shall not
> include any act or acts carried out in the process of national liberation against
> colonial rule, racist and foreign regimes, by liberation movements recognised by
> the United Nations or regional organisations.[43]

A number of Islamic States argued vigorously that national liberation
movements should be exempt from the provisions of the Convention
when action was being taken against colonial and racist regimes. Such a
proposition provoked opposition and concern amongst both the developed world and the remnants of the colonial world. The representative of
Yemen noted:

> either there would be an internationally accepted convention against the taking
> of hostages which did not apply to acts carried by recognised national liberation
> movements in the course of their struggle, or there would be no convention at
> all.[44]

---

[40] Verwey, n 24 above, at 73.

[41] UN Doc A/32/39 at 58 (per the delegate of Tanzania). These sentiments were echoed by
the delegate of Algeria in the second session of the Ad Hoc Committee where he observed
that 'firstly, it should be stipulated that the Convention did not apply to national resistance
movements' UN Doc A/33/39 at 25 (1978).

[42] UN Doc A/32/39 and 35.

[43] UN Doc A/AC.188/L.5 in First Report of the Hostages Committee, at 111.

[44] See First Report of the Hostages Committee, at 83–4 (para 5).

International Humanitarian Laws and the Applicability of Geneva Conventions to Hostage-Taking

There is significant documented evidence of the contributions of Islamic States in refining the laws of war.[45] As one commentator has aptly noted, 'Islamic representatives played important roles in reshaping international humanitarian law to deal with the realities of post-colonial conflict'.[46] This stance, particularly in relation to defending national liberation movements, was motivated because of the considerable engagement of the Islamic world in hostilities, including the Arab-Israeli conflict which broke out in 1948, the Suez crisis of 1956, the Indo-Pakistan conflict over Kashmir, and the Algerian war of independence against the French, during which the French refused to accord due recognition to Algerian belligerents. Thus:

> Islamic participants—both States and non-State entities (most notably the Palestinian Liberation Organisation (PLO))—played an important role in formulating Article 1 of Additional Protocol to the Geneva Conventions, which extended the protections of [International Humanitarian Law] to those fighting colonial domination, foreign occupation or racist regimes. Article 1 (and even the presence of non-State entities) represented a fundamental shift in humanitarian law, beyond the statist model upon which it had long been predicated. This radical shift was, in many ways, the direct product of pressure from Islamic players.[47]

Earlier sections have assessed the campaigns conducted by the Islamic States to retain an exclusive position for the national liberation movements. A specific element of this campaign has been to extract concessions during times of armed conflict. International humanitarian law, as epitomised by the four Geneva Conventions and two additional protocols, already contains prohibitions on hostage-taking.[48] Regarding

---

[45] J Cockayne, 'Islam and International Humanitarian Law: From a Clash to a Conservation Between Civilizations' (2002) 84 *International Review of the Red Cross* 597; H McCoubrey, *International Humanitarian Law: Modern Developments in the Limitation of Warfare* 2nd edn (Aldershot, Ashgate, 1998) 12–14; K Bennoune '"As-Salamu 'Alaykum?": Humanitarian Law in Islamic Jurisprudence' Joint AALS, American Society of Comparative Law and Law and Society Association, 2004 (Annual Meeting) <http://www.aals.org/am2004/islamiclaw/international.htm>.

[46] Cockayne, n 45 above, at 597.

[47] *Ibid*, at p 614 (footnotes omitted).

[48] See Geneva Convention I for the Amelioration of the Condition of the Wounded and the Sick in Armed Forces in the Field (adopted 12 August 1949, entered into force 21 October 1950) TIAS No 3362, 6 UST 3114; Geneva Convention II for the Amelioration of the Condition of the Wounded, Sick and Shipwrecked of Armed Forces at Sea (adopted 12 August 1949, entered into force 21 October 1950) TIAS No 3363, 6 UST 3217, 75 UNTS 35; Geneva Convention III Relative to the Treatment of Prisoners of War (adopted 12 August 1949, entered into force 21 October 1950) TIAS No 3364, 6 UST 3316; Convention IV Relative to the Protection of Civilian Persons in Time of War (adopted 12 August 1949, entered into force 21 October 1950) TIAS No 3365, 6 UST 3516, 75 UNTS 287. During its fourth session, the Geneva Diplomatic Conference on the Reaffirmation and Development of International Humanitarian Law Applicable to Armed Conflicts adopted on 8 June 1977 the

'non-international armed conflicts', the four Geneva Conventions contain a Common Article 3 that prohibits the taking of hostages. The Article provides:

> In the case of armed conflict not of an international character occurring in the territory of one of the High Contracting Parties, each Party to the conflict shall be bound to apply, as a minimum, the following provisions:

> 1.   Persons taking no active part in the hostilities, including members of armed forces who have laid down their arms and those placed hors de combat by sickness, wounds, detention, or any other cause, shall in all circumstances be treated humanely, without any adverse distinction founded on race, colour, religion or faith, sex, birth or wealth, or any other similar criteria.

> To this end, the following acts are and shall remain prohibited at any time and in any place whatsoever with respect to the above-mentioned persons:

> (a) Violence to life and person, in particular murder of all kinds, mutilation, cruel treatment and torture;

> (b) Taking of hostages;

> (c) Outrages upon personal dignity, in particular humiliating and degrading treatment;

> (d) The passing of sentences and the carrying out of executions without previous judgment pronounced by a regularly constituted court, affording all the judicial guarantees which are recognized as indispensable by civilized peoples.

The provisions are further strengthened by Convention IV, Article 34, whereby during 'international armed conflicts' the taking of hostages is prohibited.

While the relevance of self-determination with hostage-taking does not become immediately apparent, the preparatory phases of the Hostage-Taking Convention witnessed major divisions precisely on the relationship between these two issues. As the subsequent discussion reveals, Islamic and other non-aligned States insisted on a specialist regime applicable to national liberation movements during times of peace and armed conflict. These States were determined that the campaigns by NLMs, and their actions during times of armed conflict, were recognised as distinct and did not come under the overall umbrella of the Hostages Convention. This exclusivity for national liberation movements during armed conflicts would bar the application of the Hostages Convention. Explaining the situation, Verwey makes the point that:

Protocol Additional to the Geneva Conventions of 12 August 1949, and Relating to the Protection of Victims of International Armed Conflicts (Protocol I) (adopted 8 June 1977, entered into force 7 December 1979) (1978) 72 *American Journal of International Law* 457; and the Protocol Additional to the Geneva Conventions of 12 August 1949, and Relating to the Protection of Victims of Non-International Armed Conflicts (Protocol II) (adopted 8 June 1977, entered into force 7 December 1978) (1978) 72 *American Journal of International Law* 502. The above treaties are available at the website of Office of the High Commissioner for Human Rights <http://www.unhchr.ch/html/intlinst.htm> (26 September 2004).

[t]he pivot of the compromise was the agreement that [Article 12] on the scope of the Convention would refer to the law of armed conflict embodied in the Geneva Red Cross Conventions and Additional Protocols thereto in such a way as to preclude the conclusion that the Hostages Convention would supersede the law of Geneva.[49]

The First Additional Protocol adopted in 1977 enabled national liberation movements to be recognised as parties to 'international armed conflict'.[50] The point of this furore was, as the Algerian representative argued:

not to codify the law of war or to redefine, in a separate convention, the require-ments relating to the taking of hostages contained in the Additional Protocol of 1977 . . . As parties to international armed conflicts, national liberation move-ments were subject to the law of war, which in essence prohibited acts of hostage-taking.[51]

The Algerian delegate was correct, in that hostage-taking was prohibited by the so-called 'Geneva law'. International humanitarian law is, however, not comprehensive so that, for instance, the Common Article 3 of the four Geneva Conventions in dealing with 'non-international armed conflicts' does not cover hostage-taking of those members of armed forces who continue to take part in hostilities. There are other lacunae in the law which could be best exploited by national liberation movements. Thus in relation to:

Sick, wounded or shipwrecked members of armed forces who are in the power of the enemy as POW's, the enemy might well consider compelling a third party (for instance, a third state whose nationals belong to the same religion or tribe as the POW's in question) to perform a particular act by threatening to kill the POW's if it does not. As far as the law is concerned, it is not at all certain that the prohibition of killing POW's *ipso facto* entails a prohibition of the *threat* to kill them, let alone a prohibition of compulsion of a third party by a threat to them.[52]

Convention IV, in its application to international armed conflict, declares the taking of hostages to constitute 'grave breaches' leading to an *aut dedere aut judicare* obligation. Taking into account the restriction in the applicability of Convention IV only in so far as civilian populations is concerned:

[o]ne could very well conclude, therefore, that the obligation to prosecute or extradite hostage takers under the Geneva Conventions only applies to cases of hostage taking of those civilian persons protected under the terms of Convention IV during an international armed conflict.[53]

---

[49] Verwey, n 24 above, at 77.
[50] Article 1(4) Protocol 1.
[51] UN Doc A/33/39 at 66 (the delegate of Algeria).
[52] Verwey, n 24 above, at 80.
[53] *Ibid*, at 83–4 (emphasis added).

The final product reflects a compromise: the Hostages Convention is inapplicable to national liberation movements during armed conflicts. Article 12 provides that:

> ... the present Convention shall not apply to an act of hostage-taking committed in the course of armed conflicts as defined in the Geneva Convention of 1949 and the Protocols thereto, including armed conflicts mentioned in article 1, paragraph 4, of Additional Protocol I of 1977, in which peoples are fighting against colonial domination and allied occupation and against racist regimes in the exercise of their right of self-determination, as enshrined in the Charter of the United Nations and the Declaration on Principles of International Law concerning Friendly Relations and Co-operation among States in accordance with the Charter of the United Nations.

Furthermore, according to Article 13:

> This Convention shall not apply where the offence is committed within a single State, the hostage and the alleged offender are nationals of that State and the alleged offender is found in the territory of that State.

The objective of the 'package deal'[54] as reflected in Articles 12 and 13 of the Convention was to ensure a consensus. However, in reaching this consensus, numerous weaknesses are exposed. Firstly, in real terms, it is not always straightforward to establish a recognised legal status of a particular group—the current situation in Iraq reflects a tragic situation whereby, notwithstanding a highly questionable occupation of the country, the US military continues to regard the opposition as terrorists, militants or insurgents. Secondly, identification of an armed conflict could have substantial implications for such issues as the application of the Hostage-Taking Convention and the responsibility of the parties for extradition.

Despite its imperfections and 'not [being] usually considered as part of international humanitarian law and not [having been] drafted in the context of armed conflict',[55] the Hostages Convention retains an indelible image in the developments of international humanitarian law. The Statute of the Permanent International Criminal Court acknowledges hostage-taking as a war crime; the definition of hostage-taking is based upon the one established by the 1979 Convention.

Jurisdictional Approaches and Limitations in Extradition Proceedings

The Convention provides a range of jurisdictional grounds including *lex loci*,[56] place of registration of aircrafts and ships, where the offence is

---

[54] Chadwick, n 1 above, at 107.
[55] RS Lee (ed), *The International Criminal Court: Elements of Crimes and Rules of Procedure and Evidence* (Ardsley NY, Transnational Publishers, 2001).
[56] Article 5(1)(a).

committed,[57] nationality of the offender,[58] nationality of the hostage,[59] or the presence of the offender in its territory.[60] It is significant that one of the jurisdictional grounds relates to stateless persons who are habitually resident within a State. The relevant portions of Article 5(1)(b) read:

> Each State Party shall take such measures as may be necessary to establish its jurisdiction over any of the offences as set forth in article 1 . . . by those stateless persons who have their habitual residence in its territory.

This provision was introduced at the behest of Arab States, who were concerned that stateless persons might be tried by a State unsympathetic to their cause.[61] The obvious example and the one which spurred the Arab States into action is that of the millions of Palestinian stateless individuals spread across many Arab States.[62] Further references are made to stateless persons in subsequent provisions of the treaty.[63] In common with other treaties dealing with terrorism, the Convention affirms the principle of *aut dedere aut judicare*. The application of this principle means that in cases where the alleged offender is found in the territory of a State party, that State is under an obligation to extradite him or to submit his case before competent national authorities.[64] Following this principle, an attempt is made to ensure the trial of offenders. The Convention provides various assurances for ensuring a fair trial to the alleged offender. Question marks have been raised about the commitment of Arab/Islamic States in applying the *aut dedere aut judicare* provision. There are allegations that Islamic States lack objectivity and seriousness of purpose in the trial of Palestinians.[65] Accusations were for instance advanced against Egypt in the trial of hostage-takers of the *Achille Lauro*.[66]

The issue of fairness in trial is addressed by the discrimination clause provided in Article 9. According to this Article, States are obliged to refuse

---

[57] *Ibid.*
[58] Article 5(1)(b).
[59] Article 5(1)(a).
[60] Article 5(2).
[61] Article 5(1)(b).
[62] On the issue of Palestinian Statelessness and refugeeism and its causes see below, chapter 7.
[63] See eg Article 6.
[64] Article 8(1).
[65] '. . . in the past, Arab terrorists who have succeeded in diverting aircrafts to Syria and Algeria have been rewarded while their captive passengers have been detained'. In a subsequent paper, the same author notes, 'members of the Arab bloc have often harbored accused perpetrators of unlawful acts against American and Israeli aircraft'. A Abramovsky, 'Multilateral Convention for the Suppression of Unlawful Seizure and Interference with Aircraft Part I: The Hague Convention' (1974) 13 *The Columbia Journal of Transnational Law* 381 at 383; also see A Abramovsky, 'Multilateral Convention for the Suppression of Unlawful Seizure and Interference with Aircraft Part II: The Montreal Convention' (1975) 14 *The Columbia Journal of Transnational Law* 268 at 300.
[66] See MD Larsen, 'The Achille Lauro Incident and the Permissible Use of Force' (1987) 9 *Loyola of Los Angeles Journal of International and Comparative Law* 481.

extradition if there are substantial grounds for suspecting that extradition is being sought on the basis of race, religion, ethnic origin and political opinion and that the alleged offender may be discriminated against on any of the aforesaid grounds, or that he is not allowed to communicate with the State entitled to exercise diplomatic protection. These provisions were included at the behest of Jordan, an Islamic State and a member of the OIC. In its original form the Jordanian proposal read as follows:

> No contracting State shall extradite an alleged offender if that State has substantial grounds for believing:
>
> (a) that the request for extradition for an offence set forth in article 1 has been made for the purpose of prosecuting or punishing a person on account of his race, religion, nationality or political opinion;
> (b) that that person's position may be prejudiced for any of these reasons;
> (c) that the appropriate authorities of the State of which he is a national, or if he is a Stateless person, the appropriate authorities of the State which he requests and which is willing to protect his rights, cannot communicate with him to protect his rights in the requesting State.[67]

The concern on the part of the Jordanian representative was that this particular treaty may be used as a tool for 'an international manhunt' and that all individuals, even the 'wrongdoers . . . had a right to human dignity'.[68] In further advancing his position, the Jordanian delegate noted:

> [I]n a bilateral extradition treaty between neighbouring friendly States, there would normally be provisions to safeguard the rights of persons claimed. A Convention that might have the effect of exposing persons to different legal systems should have similar if not more safeguards.[69]

The Islamic and Arab States supported the Jordanian position. Explaining the various perspectives, Lambert notes:

> At one end of the spectrum were the Arab countries, along with some other developing States, which strongly supported the Jordanian proposal. The Syrian representative, for example, argued that it was 'essential to ensure a humanitarian spirit', while the Algerian delegate asserted that the Convention must contain a provision which allows for the denial of extradition where there is a danger of an offender being prosecuted or punished as a result of religious or racial discrimination. The delegates of Iraq and Pakistan indicated that they viewed Article 9 as a necessary balance to Article 8. At the other end of the spectrum were States, most notably the Soviet Union and its allies, which were vehemently opposed to inclusion of this type of provision. These States asserted that such a provision would allow parties to avoid their obligations under the

---

[67] See Third Report of the Hostages Committee, p 16, paras 64–6.
[68] UN Doc A/32/39 at 27.
[69] UN GAOR, 34th Sess C6 (12th mtg) p 6, para 22. UN Doc A/C.6/34/SR.12 (1979).

Convention and would undermine the 'principle of inevitability of punishment'.[70]

The provisions of Article 9 were controversial, eventually being agreed 'at the end of three years of difficult negotiations when the text was otherwise substantially agreed upon . . .'.[71] The ultimate comprise, it would appear, was reached on the understanding that the requirements of communications could be satisfied either through the good office of the another State or through an agency such as the International Committee of the Red Cross.[72]

In a trial with an international dimension, one aspect of procedural fairness requires that appropriate bodies and individuals be intimated. Within the Hostage-Taking Convention, it is incumbent upon the State holding trials to inform the Secretary-General of the United Nations of the outcome of the proceedings. The Secretary-General of the United Nations is in turn required to pass on information to the relevant States, international organisations, and other interested parties. The provision, although not contained in earlier drafts of the treaty, was inserted in the final stages of the deliberations at the behest of Nigeria.[73]

Article 14 reiterates a fundamental principle of international law. It affirms the prohibition of any violations of territorial integrity or political independence of a State in contravention of the provisions of the United Nations Charter. Islamic States also had an input into the drafting of what emerged as Article 14. The original Article proposed inter alia by Tanzania, Algeria, Libya and Egypt read: 'States shall not resort to the threat or use of force against the sovereignty, territorial integrity or independence of other States as means of rescuing hostages.'[74]

Such a provision was clearly motivated by a determination to prevent a repeat of the Entebbe Affair. The aim was to declare that for the future such aggressive and war-like operations were deemed illegal. The Syrian representative had argued that:

> Nothing in the Convention can be construed as justifying in any manner the threat or use of force or any interference whatsoever against the sovereignty, independence or territorial integrity of peoples and States, under the pretext of rescuing or freeing hostages.[75]

---

[70] First Report of the Hostages Committee, at 36, para 31.

[71] M Halberstam, 'Terrorist Acts Against and On Board Ships' (1989) 19 *Israel Yearbook of Human Rights* 331 at 338.

[72] *Ibid*, at 338.

[73] See Third Report of the Hostages Committee, at 14, para 55.

[74] UN Doc A/AC.188/L.7 in the First Report of the Hostages Committee 111.

[75] UN Doc A/AC.188/L.11 in First Report of the Hostages Committee 112. Comments of the Syrian Representative *ibid* at 84, para 6.

Another example of this situation was to take place with the United States' attempts to rescue its diplomats from Iran, an issue which shall be examined in further detail in this chapter.

INTERNATIONALLY PROTECTED PERSONS AND INTERNATIONAL LAW[76]

Diplomacy and the art of treating diplomats and emissaries have been major preoccupations of international relations.[77] The value of ensuring a safe environment for foreign diplomats and emissaries was recognised by pre-modern societies as a cardinal principal of governance, a point reiterated by the Vienna Convention on Diplomatic Relations (1961).[78] The Preamble to the Convention notes: 'peoples of all nations from ancient times have recognized the status of diplomatic agents.'[79] Many of the historic concepts have now crystallised into 'hard' law through international treaties including the Vienna Convention on Diplomatic Relations (1961),[80] the Vienna Convention on Consular Relations (1963),[81] and the New York Convention on the Prevention and Punishment of Crimes against Internationally Protected Persons (1973).

International law accords special protection to a range of individuals, institutions and to movable and immovable property. Diplomats, consular staff and other emissaries, the so-called 'internationally protected persons', are however particularly vulnerable. Their physical location and the nature of their engagements renders them exposed to actions of unscrupulous and unprincipled administrations.[82] More frequently, they

[76] CL Rozakis, 'Terrorism and the Internationally Protected Persons in the light of ILC Draft Article' (1974) 23 *International & Comparative Law Quarterly* 32; S Mahmoudi, 'Some Remarks on Diplomatic Immunity from Criminal Jurisdiction' in S Mahmoudi *et al* (eds), *Festskrift Till Lars Hjerner: Studies in International Law* (Stockholm, Norstedt, 1990) 327–61; M Hardy, *Modern Diplomatic Law* (Manchester, Manchester University Press, 1968); LS Frey and ML Frey, *The History of Diplomatic Immunity* (Columbus, Ohio State University Press, 1999); B Sen, *A Diplomat's Handbook of International Law and Practice* 3rd edn (Dordrecht, Martinus Nijhoff Publishers, 1988); MN Shaw, *International Law* 5th edn (Cambridge, Cambridge University Press, 2003) 668–93.

[77] See works cited in n 76 above. Dembinski, n 1 above; Elagab, n 1 above; D Elgavish, 'Did Diplomatic Immunity Exist in the Ancient Near East?' (2000) 2 *Journal of the History of International Law* 73; G Mattingly, *Renaissance Diplomacy* (New York, Dover Publications, 1988).

[78] (1965) 19 UKTS; Cmnd 2565; 500 UNTS 95; (1961) 55 *American Journal of International Law* 1064. See Shaw, n 76 above, at 669–75.

[79] See Preamble to the Convention.

[80] Vienna Convention on Diplomatic Relations (adopted 18 April 1961, entered into force 24 April 1964) 1965 UKTS 19; Cmnd 2565; 500 UNTS 95; (1961) 55 *American Journal of International Law* 1064.

[81] Vienna Convention on Consular Relations (adopted 24 April 1963, entered into force 19 March 1967) 1035 UNTS 167; (1974) 13 ILM 41.

[82] See below, the *Iran Hostages Crises*. Also note the detentions of western diplomatic staff by Saddam Hussein's regime in the aftermath of first Gulf war (1990–91). See BK Bodine, 'Saddam's Siege of Embassy Kuwait: A Personal Journal' in JG Sullivan (ed), n 1 above, at 113–31.

are targeted by terrorist organisations, the properties and assets of their States being primary objects of destruction and devastation. As the assassination of Sergio Vieira de Mello, the United Nations envoy in Iraq, affirms, targeting internationally protected persons not only undermines the structures and systems of governance but can provide substantial publicity to the operations of terrorist networks.[83] Iraq, under the current political environment remains a highly volatile State with a lack of security for all, including internationally protected persons. That said, it is also the case that the threat to internationally protected persons has escalated into a major global concern. International criminal law has made responses, although they are limited and in practice largely ineffectual. The principal instrument in the armoury of international criminal law is the New York Convention on the Prevention and Punishment of Crimes against Internationally Protected Persons, the provisions of which will be examined in detail below. The focus of the present study is upon analysing the salient features of the Islamic diplomatic laws. In conducting such an exercise, the analysis brings out the contributions which the *Sharia* has made towards developing modern norms of diplomatic protection. A further and final objective of this assessment is to raise principal points of concern emanating from specific modern Islamic practices.

THE NEW YORK CONVENTION AND INTERNATIONALLY PROTECTED PERSONS

Since the ending of the Second World War, crimes against internationally protected persons have developed into a major global concern.[84] According to one study, during 1946–1980, there were no fewer than 186 attacks either against diplomats or against diplomatic missions themselves; 44 deaths occurred in the process.[85] A proliferation of incidents led the international community to adopt binding instruments condemning and criminalising hostage-taking in all its forms. One unfortunate example of the violation of the rights of internationally protected persons was the murder of the ambassador of Yugoslavia in Stockholm in April 1971.[86]

---

[83] Top UN Envoy Killed in Baghdad Blast' BBC News 20 August 2003 <http://news.bbc.co.uk/1/hi/world/middle_east/3165737.stm> (21 August 2003).

[84] See Data of Attacks on Internationally Protected Persons provided in NK Hevener (ed), *Diplomacy in a Dangerous World: Protection for Diplomats under International Law* (Boulder and London, Westview Press, 1986) 67–71; JF Murphy, 'The Future of Multilateralism and Efforts to Combat International Terrorism' (1986) 25 *The Columbia Journal of Transnational Law* 35 at 46; J Brown, 'Diplomatic Immunity: State Practice under the Vienna Convention on Diplomatic Relations' (1988) 37 *International & Comparative Law Quarterly* 53.

[85] Dembinski, n 1 above, at 167.

[86] See the Pavelic Papers, 'Miro Baresic's Deportation from Sweden' (December 1987) <http://www.pavelicpapers.com/documents/baresic/mb0002.htm> (10 September 2004).

A further, more publicised instance was hostage-taking in Vienna during 1975 whereby terrorists seized 60 OPEC ministers.[87]

Amidst this cycle of violence the United Nations was involved in taking legislative measures to counter attacks on internationally protected persons. In April 1971, the representative of the Netherlands had requested the President of the United Nations Security Council for a binding instrument to overcome existing gaps in international law. This proposal was transmitted to the ILC.[88] The ILC put the question of the protection of the inviolability of diplomats on its agenda for the 1972 session and proceeded to draft articles pertaining to this matter. Simultaneously a working group was established which drew up and presented twelve draft articles to the ILC during the same session.[89] The drafts were discussed, and amendments were submitted by the ILC to the General Assembly's Sixth (Legal) Committee. While there were concerns over some issues, the draft on the whole was well received.

In 1973, the General Assembly adopted by consensus Resolution 3166 (XXVIII) attached to which is the Convention on the Prevention and Punishment of Crimes against Internationally Protected Persons, including Diplomatic Agents (1973).[90] This Convention (also known as the New York Convention) represents the most far-reaching global instrument dealing with crimes committed against Internationally Protected Persons. It has, in the words of Dembinski, three primary functions:

> a) to make sure that every person committing or participating in a crime covered by the Convention will be tried or extradited and will not remain unpunished; b) to dissuade in this way possible offenders from committing these crimes and finally, c) to secure a minimum of international co-operation in preventing them.[91]

The New York Convention protects certain categories of persons from the offences of murder, kidnapping or other attacks upon their official premises, private accommodation and means of transportation. Attempts to commit any such acts are also categorised as offences.[92] Similarly according to Article 2, actions as accomplices and participants are deemed criminal offences.[93] In detailing the category of internationally protected persons, Article 1 provides that for the purposes of this Convention:

---

[87] See 'Suspect in OPEC Hostage-taking Arrested' 15 October 1999 <http://www.ict.org.il/spotlight/det.cfm?id=340>; 'Repentant German Terrorist Given Nine-year Sentence' 15 February 2001 <http://www.ict.org.il/spotlight/det.cfm?id=566> (20 April 2004); B Davies, *Terrorism: Inside a World Phenomenon* (London, Virgin Books, 2003) 103–6.

[88] Dembinski, n 1 above, at 13.

[89] *Ibid*, at 13.

[90] Adopted 14 December 1973, entered into force 20 February 1977; 1035 UNTS 167; (1974) 13 ILM 41.

[91] Dembinski, n 1 above, at 167–8.

[92] Article 2(1)(d).

[93] Article 2(1)(e).

1 'Internationally Protected Person' means

    (a) a Head of State, including any member of a collegial body performing the function of a Head of State under the constitution of the State concerned, a Head of Government or a Minister for Foreign Affairs, whenever any such person is in a foreign State, as well as members of his family who accompany him;

    (b) any representative or official of a State or any official or other agent of an international organization of an intergovernmental character who, at the time when and in the place where a crime against him, his official premises, his private accommodation or his means of transport is committed, is entitled pursuant to international law to special protection from any attack on his person, freedom or dignity, as well as members of his family forming part of his household.

States are required to co-operate with one another in the prevention of crimes against internationally protected persons. Efforts to prevent such crimes entail 'exchange of information and co-ordinating the taking of administrative and other [appropriate] measures'[94] as well as taking 'all practicable measure to prevent preparations in their respective territories for the commission of those crimes within or outside their territories'.[95] The jurisdiction of the State is established when crimes are committed against internationally protected persons either in its territory, on board a ship or aircraft registered in that State or when the offender is one of its nationals.[96] The State is under an obligation to take all necessary steps to establish its jurisdiction if it fails to extradite the individual to another State, thereby confirming the principle *aut dedere aut judicare*.[97] Aspects of this principle are further elaborated through Articles 6 and Articles 7. According to Article 6, parties are required to take appropriate measures to ensure the presence of the alleged offender either to stand trial or to be extradited. These measures are to be reported through the Secretary-General of United Nations to the State where the offence is committed,[98] to the State(s) of which the alleged offender is a national, or, in the case of a stateless person, the State where he is permanently resident,[99] State or States where the internationally protected person is either a national or on whose behalf he was executing his functions,[100] and all other concerned States and international organisations.[101]

---

[94] Article 4(b).
[95] Article 4(a).
[96] Article 3(1).
[97] Article 3(2).
[98] Article 6(1)(a).
[99] Article 6(1)(a).
[100] Article 6(1)(c).
[101] Article 6(1)(d)(e).

Article 7 addresses the core of the obligations enshrined in *aut dedere aut judicare*. It notes that:

> [t]he State Party in whose territory the alleged offender is present shall, if it does not extradite him, submit, without exception whatsoever and without undue delay, the case to its competent authorities for the purpose of prosecution, through proceedings in accordance with the laws of that State.

Article 8 in dealing with extradition matters adopts a broad approach. According to Article 8(1), to the extent to which offences in the Convention are not contained in any extradition treaty, State parties are required to include them as extraditable offences. Furthermore, according to Article 8(2) and 8(3) the present treaty provides a sufficient basis for extradition to take place. For the purposes of extradition, the crimes provided for in the Convention are to be treated as not only in the place in which they occurred but also in the territories of the States required to establish their jurisdiction.

The Convention maintains a focus on the rights of internationally protected persons, although at the same time there is also a concern for preserving the fundamental rights of the alleged offender. Article 9 provides that 'any person regarding whom proceedings are being instituted . . . shall be guaranteed fair treatment at all stages of stages of the proceedings'. The value of this Article goes well beyond ensuring the human rights of the alleged offender to represent an indispensable counterbalancing factor to the increased powers that State parties acquire by the provisions against 'alleged Offenders'.[102]

A commitment to uphold the fundamental rights of the accused is further reinforced through the course of trials, during which State parties undertake to afford each other full assistance and co-operation with criminal proceedings, including the supply of evidence at their disposal necessary for the proceedings.[103] Disputes arising from the Convention are subject to arbitration and settlement by the International Court of Justice.[104]

So far as the Convention on the Prevention and Punishment of Crimes against Internationally Protected Persons is concerned, while a number of Islamic States have made declarations or entered reservations, these relate principally to two issues. The first concerns the unacceptability of Islamic States being bound by the provisions of Article 13(1), which provides the ICJ with jurisdiction to settle a dispute at the behest of one of the parties to the dispute. The reservations to the jurisdiction of the ICJ are widespread not only in relation to the present Convention, but also in other international treaties. This is particularly the case with some of the leading

---

[102] Rozakis, n 76 above, at 61.
[103] Article 10(1).
[104] Article 13(1).

human rights treaties.[105] There are no peculiarly ideological bases for entering a reservation. States are reluctant to subject themselves to the automatic jurisdiction of an international tribunal or court, without providing a specific consent. Algeria, Iraq, Kuwait, Pakistan, the Syrian Arab Republic, Tunisia and Yemen have all made reservations to Article 13(1). The second set of reservations are, however, based on ideological grounds. Iraq, Jordan, Kuwait, the Syrian Arab Republic and Yemen have made declarations stating that their accession to the Convention does not signify recognition of the State of Israel.

ISLAMIC PERSPECTIVES ON THE PROTECTION OF DIPLOMATS

Islamic diplomatic law remains a firmly established part of the *Sharia* and *Siyar*. Furthermore, and as noted earlier, Islamic practices contributed to the overall growth of the subject in general international law.[106] Under Islamic law, diplomats are accorded protection and immunities, including protection from arrest and detention. There are references to the security and well-being of diplomats in the primary as well as secondary sources of Islamic law.[107] In our earlier analysis, the Islamic concept of *amân* was examined.[108] The application of *amân* to foreign diplomats and emissaries has meant guarantees of their complete physical and personal protection. The pledge of *amân* is legally enforceable, its violations are rendered impermissible. The *Qur'an* places a mandatory injunction on Islamic States to secure the personal safety and well-being of diplomats and their families. In his analysis of the *Qur'an*, Professor Bassiouni makes the following observations:

> The Koran in *Surat al Naml* (27:23–44) supports that proposition in its description of the exchanges of envoys between the prophet Sulaiman (Solomon) (992–952 BC) and Bilqis, Queen of Sheba. Bilqis is described as having sent a delegation bearing gifts to Sulaiman, who considered it an insult (an attempt to bribe him). Sulaiman rejected the gifts and sent the delegation back. In the same *Surat*, it is stated (by Bilqis):
>
> > But I am going to send him a present, and wait to see with what answer my ambassadors return. [27:35]

---

[105] See B Clark, 'The Vienna Convention Reservations Regime and the Convention on Discrimination against Women' (1991) 85 *American Journal of International Law* 281. Also see RJ Cook, 'Reservations to the Convention on the Elimination of All forms of Discrimination against Women' (1990) 30 *Virginia Journal of International Law* 643; WA Schabas, 'Reservations to the United Nations Convention on the Rights of the Child' (1996) 18 *Human Rights Quarterly* 472.

[106] Chapter 2 above.

[107] MC Bassiouni, 'Protection of Diplomats under Islamic Law' (1980) 74 *American Journal of International Law* 609 at 610.

[108] Chapter 2 above.

[the response of Sulaiman]

> Go back to them, and be sure we shall come to them with such haste as they will never be able to meet: we shall expel them from there in disgrace, and they will feel humiliated. [27:37]

These verses clearly indicate that emissaries were contemplated as the ordinary means of diplomatic communications between Muslim and non Muslim heads of state, and that the emissaries were immune from the wrath of the host state and were not held responsible for the acts or messages sent by their head of state. Thus, even when Sulaiman was offended, he did nothing against the emissaries but send them back whence they came. There is therefore a dual Koranic mandate that no Muslim state may transgress: protection must be granted to envoys, and expulsion is the only sanction to be taken against them.[109]

The *Qur'anic* injunctions are further strengthened by the *Sunna* of Muhammad. After the conquest of Mecca and the establishment of the first Muslim State:

> deputations received by the Prophet . . . enjoyed not only immunity but also preferred treatment, which applied to the envoys and their staff and servants. They were not to be molested, mistreated, imprisoned or killed. Envoys also had freedom of religion, as is demonstrated by the delegation of Christians of Najran who held their services in a mosque. . . in fact, so great was the Prophet's belief in the immunity of envoys that during that period when Abu-Ra'fi, the emissary of Quraish, wanted to convert to Islam, the Prophet admonished him:

> > I do not go back on my word and I do not detain envoys [you are an ambassador]. You must, therefore, go back and if you still feel in your heart as strongly about Islam as you do now, come back [as a Muslim].[110]

There is further compelling evidence of the respect and dignity to be accorded to diplomats within Islamic law. In bringing forth this evidence, Zawati relies upon the Prophet's *Hadith*. He writes:

> To enable them to exercise their duties and functions, diplomatic agents enjoy full personal immunity under Islamic international law. They are not to be killed, maltreated or arrested even if they are convicted or have a criminal record. The prophet Muhammad granted these privileges and immunities to diplomatic envoys in his lifetime. Two incidents are on record: first, the prophet granted immunity to Ibn al-Nawwāha and Ibn Āthāl, the emissaries of Musaylama—the liar—, in spite of their extremely rude behaviour towards him. The Prophet said: 'I swear by *Allāh* that if emissaries were not immune from killing, I would have ordered you to be beheaded'. Second, the Prophet treated kindly Wahshī, the ambassador of the people of al-Tāif, who had murdered Hamza, the Prophet's uncle at the battle of Uhud. The Prophet's generous

---

[109] Bassiouni, n 107 above, at 610–11 (footnotes omitted).
[110] *Ibid*, at 611–12 (footnotes omitted).

treatment convinced him to embrace Islam. Moreover, Islamic law accorded *droit de chapelle* to diplomatic agents. The Prophet allowed a delegation from the Christian of Najran to hold their service in his mosque. In addition to the above privileges, the property of diplomatic agents is exempt from customs duties and other taxes during their stay in *dar-al-Islam*.[111]

ARTICULATION OF THE RIGHTS OF INTERNATIONALLY PROTECTED PERSONS UNDER ISLAMIC LAW

The array of examples both from the Holy book, *Qur'an* and the *Sunna* of the Prophet Muhammed is impressive. However, in order to satisfy the requirements of legal analysis, these broad principles require further specification. They also need to be placed in the context of the physical practices emergent from the Islamic world. Islamic criminal law proscribes three types of offences: *Hudood*, *Qisas* and *Tazir*. Penal sanctions are fixed for the *Hudood* and *Qisas*.[112] By contrast, the punishment for *Tazir* is discretionary. Espionage, as an offence is not categorised either as a *Hudd* or *Qisas* offence.[113] As a discretionary offence, the *Tazir*, detention for espionage is unlawful. As already noted, under Islamic law diplomats and their families are given immunity from the jurisdiction of host States. Diplomats are not to be targeted or prosecuted for any acts of breaches committed by their own States. It is equally impermissible to detain or arrest diplomats or to take them as hostages. As the *Sunna* of Prophet Muhammad establishes in his treatment of the Christians of Najran, foreign emissaries are to enjoy freedom of religion. Even if proven, under Islamic law, the most serious penalty for diplomats engaged in espionage would be a declaration of *persona non grata* expulsion.[114] Hostage-taking or the detention of diplomats or other consular staff breaches Islamic criminal law. In their existing treaty manifestations, Islamic States are therefore de minimus obliged to accord these guarantees provided under classical Islamic laws. These aforementioned protections accorded to diplomats and emissaries which now form part of customary international law, are also restated in the primary conventions on diplomatic immunities. The Vienna Convention on diplomatic Relations (1961) secures a number of these rights, including:

---

[111] See HM Zawati, *Is Jihād a Just War? War, Peace, and Human Rights Under Islamic and Public International Law* (Lewiston, NY, Edwin Mellen Press, 2001) 79–80.

[112] G Benmelha, 'Ta'azir Crimes' in MC Bassiouni (ed), *The Islamic Criminal Justice System* (London, Oceana Publications, 1982) 211–25, at 212.

[113] Bassiouni, n 107 above, at 623.

[114] *Ibid*, at 625.

— the inviolability of the person of the diplomatic agent (Article 29)
— the inviolability of the private residence of the diplomatic and protection as the premises of the mission (Article 30(1))
— broad immunities from civil and criminal jurisdiction (except for specific personalised cases) (Article 31)
— exemptions from social security, direct taxation of the receiving State (Articles 33, 34 and 35)
— Immunities to Consular Officers and employees for acts conducted in the course of their official duties (Articles 41 and 43 of the 1963 Convention)

The practices of Islamic States have in general been exemplary, though there have unfortunately been some black spots; the principal case being the detention of US nationals by the Iranian authorities. The charge of espionage even if proven to be valid as a *Tazir* offence is insufficient to justify arrest and detention.

As mentioned earlier, the most significant and problematic case relates to the detention and hostage-taking of US diplomats and other Consular staff in Iran in the aftermath of the Iranian revolution of 1979. The incident produced considerable tensions between the two countries, litigation before the World Court and was ultimately resolved through a political settlement.[115] The case has a long and protracted history emanating from the successful revolution in Iran, the triumphant return of the Iranian spiritual leader Ayatollah Khomeini and the admission of the Shah of Iran into the US, ostensibly for the purpose of medical treatment.[116] During the autumn and winter of 1978, there were visible signs of hostility towards the existing regime of the Shah of Iran. By December 1978, there was general unrest, with escalation in anti-western, particularly anti-American sentiment.

On 16 January 1979, the Shah left Iran. The arrival of Ayatollah Khomeini on 1 February marked the beginning of revolution in Iran. During February 1979, a group of armed Iranian revolutionaries seized the US embassy in Tehran. However, on this occasion, the Iranian officials acted robustly and control of the compound was handed back to the US authorities. Furthermore, assurances were provided by the new Iranian regime against a repeat of the incident. Notwithstanding these assurances, on 4 November 1979 several hundred Iranian students along with other protesters stormed the US Embassy in Tehran and took control of the premises by force. US consulates in other parts of Iran were also occupied. The demonstrators took control of premises, seized control of the archives

---

[115] Gross, n 14 above, at 395; K Gryzbowski, n 14 above, at 42; TM Franck and D Niedermeyer, 'Accommodating Terrorism: An Offence against the Law of Nations' (1989) 19 *Israel Yearbook of Human Rights* 99 at 105–6.

[116] For an analysis see N Mangård, 'The Hostage Crisis, The Algiers Accords, and the Iran-United States Claims Tribunal' in S Mahmoudi *et al* (eds), *Festskrift Till Lars Hjerner: Studies in International Law* (Stockholm, Norstedt, 1990) 363–418.

and documents and arrested dozens of US nationals and others present on the premises. In all, fifty-two US nationals were held hostage, fifty of whom were diplomatic and consular staff. The initial act on the US Embassy could not be attributed to Iran since the perpetrators were not agents of the State. However, there was a subsequent approval of these acts by the religious leader, Ayatollah Khomeini accompanied by a tacit approval and commendation of these actions by the State. In a decree issued on 17 November 1979, the Ayatollah took the view that:

> [the American Embassy] was a 'centre of espionage and conspiracy' and that 'those people who hatched plots against our Islamic movement in that place do not enjoy international diplomatic respect'.[117]

With this blessing and approval of the de facto head of the State, the decision to attack and keep the American Embassy under occupation became an act of the State.[118] The militants therefore became agents of the Iranian government, with Iran having international legal responsibility for this action.

On 29 November 1979, the International Court of Justice was approached by the US through a multilateral application under Article 40 of the Statute of the Court and Article 38 of the Rules of the Court seeking provisional measures under Articles 41 and 81 of the Statute of the Court.[119] The application required the Court inter alia to declare that the Iranian action in taking the diplomats hostage violated international law and to order the immediate release of the hostages. While the Iranian government never officially appeared in the case, in a letter submitted to the Court on 9 December 1979 it took the position that the issue related to the sovereignty of Iran and that the 'Court cannot and should not take cognizance of the case'.[120] Indeed the Iranian government claimed that the subject matter for the Court was not justiciable and involved the application and interpretation of treaties.[121] Instead there were a string of issues attached to what was essentially a political conflict.

According to the Iranian regime, the United States had continually interfered in its affairs for over 25 years, resulting in the exploitation of Iran and its peoples.[122] While not stated in the letter to the Court, Iran also demanded the extradition of the Shah to Iran to face prosecution for his alleged crimes. These factors, according to the Iranian government, when combined, justified its action of detaining the US diplomats.

---

[117] *United States Diplomatic and Consular Staff in Tehran Case (US v Iran)* [1980] ICJ Rep 3, para 73.

[118] *Ibid.*

[119] *Case Concerning United States Diplomatic and Consular Staff in Tehran (United States of America v Iran) Request for the Indication of Provisional Measures* [1979] ICJ Rep 7.

[120] *Ibid*, para 8 (the text of the letter can be found in the Order of the Court; para 1 of the letter).

[121] *Ibid*, para 3 of the letter.

[122] *Ibid*, para 2 of the letter.

The ICJ promptly rejected all of the arguments advanced by the Iranian government, declaring that detentions of internationally protected persons were a violation of international law. As provisional measures, the Court unanimously made the order that Iran should immediately restore the premises of the US Embassy and consulate to the possession of the United States authorities.[123] The order required the release of all US nationals who had been held hostage,[124] with complete diplomatic and consular protection being immediately restored.[125] Finally the Court required the Iranian government to refrain from any attempts at holding trials of any of the diplomatic and consular staff.[126]

In the absence of any effective response from the Iranian authorities to the Court's interim order, and while further proceedings were pending, the US government undertook a number of measures including a covert military rescue mission to release the hostages. The rescue missions failed due to technical reasons. In its judgment of 24 May 1980, the Court went on to pronounce a number of issues including whether Iran had violated international treaties, inter alia, the 1961 and 1963 Vienna Conventions on Diplomatic and Consular Relations. In finding Iran in breach of the provisions of 1961 and 1963 Conventions, the Court took the approach that:

> for its own conduct [Iran] was in conflict with its international obligations. By a number of provisions of the Vienna Conventions of 1961 and 1963, Iran was placed under the most categorical obligations, as a receiving State, to take appropriate steps to ensure the protection of the United States Embassy and Consulates, their staff, their archives, their means of communication and the freedom of movement of the members of their staff . . . In the view of the Court, the obligations of the Iranian Government here in question are not merely contractual obligations established by the Vienna Conventions of 1961 and 1963, but also obligations under general international law. The facts . . . establish to the satisfaction of the Court that on 4 November 1979 the Iranian Government failed altogether to take any 'appropriate steps' to protect the premises, staff and archives of the United States' mission against attack by the militants, and to take any steps either to prevent this attack or to stop it before it reached its completion. They also show that on 5 November 1979 the Iranian Government similarly failed to take appropriate steps for the protection of the United States Consulates at Tabriz and Shiraz . . .This inaction . . . constituted a clear and serious violation of Iran's obligations to the United States under the provisions of Article 22, paragraph 2, and Articles 24, 25, 26, 27 and 29 of the 1961 Vienna Convention on Diplomatic Relations and Articles 5 and 36 of the 1963 Vienna Convention on Consular Relations. Similarly, with respect to the attacks of the Consulates of Tabriz and Shiraz, the inaction of the Iranian authorities entailed

---

[123]   *Ibid*, 47(I)A(i).
[124]   *Ibid*, 47(I)A(ii).
[125]   *Ibid*, 47(I)A(iii).
[126]   *Ibid*, para 12.

clear and serious breaches of its obligations under the provisions of several further articles of the 1963 Convention on Consular Relations.[127]

The Court went on to comment that:

[t]he frequency with which at the present time the principle of international law governing diplomatic and consular relations are set at naught by individuals or groups of individuals is already deplorable. But this case is unique and of particular gravity because here it is not only private individuals or groups of individuals that have disregarded and set at naught the inviolability of a foreign embassy, but the government of the receiving State itself . . . Such event cannot fail to undermine the edifice of law carefully constructed by mankind over a period of centuries, the maintenance of which is vital for the security and well-being of the complex international community of the present day, to which it is more essential than ever that the rules developed to ensure the ordered progress of relations between its members should be constantly and scrupulously respected.[128]

The Court's admonition was not directed only at Iran and its agents. It was also critical of the military intervention by the United States in Iran, especially at a time when it was in the course of preparing a judgment adjudicating upon the claim of the United States. The US action, in the words of the Court, undermined respect for judicial processes. The hostages were released in January 1981 through a settlement between the United States and Iranian governments.[129]

THE *SHARIA* AND HOSTAGE-TAKING OF INTERNATIONALLY PROTECTED PERSONS: COMMENTS ON THE *US DIPLOMATIC AND CONSULAR STAFF IN TEHRAN* CASE

Taken at face value, the pronouncements of the ICJ are consonant with the ordinances of *Sharia*. There is thus, as such, no critical conflict involving religious doctrines or ideology. The purported defences advanced by the Iranian regime were based not on Islamic principles but on national, political and economic grievances; there was a sense of unfairness, injustice and exploitation perpetuated by successive United States governments. The advancement of *Sharia* and *Siyar* was therefore not relevant to the Iranian claims. Indeed the robust defences presented by the Iranian authorities were a reaction against the accusation of its deviation from the path both of international law and the *Sharia*.

---

[127] *United States Diplomatic and Consular Staff in Tehran Case (US v Iran)* [1980] ICJ Rep 3, paras 61–7.

[128] *Ibid*, para 92.

[129] For an analysis see N Mangård, 'The Hostage Crisis, The Algiers Accords, and the Iran-United States Claims Tribunal' in S Mahmoudi *et al* (eds), n 116 above, 363–418.

The Khomeini regime can surely be labelled as outcasts and violators of both temporal and religious law: there is no doubting this fact. While the matter appears to be straightforward, the reality however is far more complex. The principal aggravation for the Iranian regime was what it perceived as the 'shameless exploitation'[130] of its country. Iran's complaint related to the abuse and continual interference in its domestic affairs by successive US administrations for over a quarter of a century: the use of embassies as spy-nests, and the active engagement of embassy personnel in the formation and training of SAVAK, the secret police which carried out harrowing atrocities against the Iranian people. There was also the Iranian demand for the return of the Shah to face trial for alleged atrocities. Reza shah Pehalvi had gone to the United States ostensibly on health grounds, and the US government actively protected him in exile, as it had done when he was the head of the State of Iran. There were no extradition treaties between Iran and the US to facilitate the possible return of the Shah. The Carter administration found in this a perfectly well-grounded defence. Even in the absence of any legal obstacles, as has been pointed out, it is nearly impossible that the US government had agreed to extradite the Shah to Iran.

In the wider scheme of things, one has to assess the fairness of a legal system. As a corrective instrument, Law is meant to inject objectivity and impartiality in the societal fabric. However, if the Law itself is crooked and arbitrary then its application produces hugely disturbing consequences. The arbitrariness and one-sidedness of the Law raise serious fundamental concerns. As Richard Falk aptly points out:

> Why should the rules protecting diplomatic immunity be so much clearer than the rules protecting a weak country against intervention? Or why should 'asylum' be available to a cruel tyrant associated with the massive commission of state crimes, including torture, arbitrary execution, and economic plunder? What kind of international law is it that protects foreign police and torture specialists by conferring upon them the status of 'diplomats'? . . . What we find then is both a proimperial and progovernmental bias built into modern international law. This double bias is a natural consequence of the fact that states dominate the global scene and some states dominate others. Whether such a framework is adequate or not is one of the deeper, unexamined issues posed by the Iranian crisis. Khomeini clearly rejects this bias: 'What kind of law is this? It permits the US Government to exploit and colonise peoples all over the world for decades. But it does not allow the extradition of an individual who has staged great massacres. Can you call it law?'[131]

---

[130] Para 2 of the Iranian letter.
[131] R Falk, 'The Iran Hostage Crisis: Easy Answers and Hard Questions' (1980) 74 *American Journal of International Law* 411 at 412–13 (citing Ayatollah Khomeine at 413); also see NK Hevener, 'Reflection on the Interpretation of the Law of Diplomatic Protection' in NK Hevener (ed), n 84 above, 45–64.

As noted earlier, the Iranian government claimed as 'shameless' the historical exploitation of the country by the United States. The judgments of the International Court of Justice establish that the Iranian authorities acted in violation of international conventions relating to diplomatic and consular relations. There is also a consensus amongst Islamic jurists that Iran violated the established principles of the *Sharia* and *Siyar*.[132] In the context of a revolution, inspired at least initially by a nationalistic movement, it is important to recognise that religious sentiment was ultimately abused. Neither the Islamic faith nor *Sharia* authorise the detention of diplomats. Reviewing the case from an Islamic legal perspective, Bassiouni notes:

> [t]he use of diplomats as 'hostages' to secure the return of a person wanted for prosecution find no support in Islamic law . . . even when offending diplomats were concerned, according to the Sunna and thereafter Ali's practice the most that was done was to expel them. Otherwise they were held inviolate and not personally accountable for the acts of their governments. The very idea of holding diplomats 'hostage' to accomplish a political objective is contrary to Islam.[133]

One of the primary reasons advanced by the Khomeini government for detaining the US diplomats was their alleged espionage. An analysis of the *Sharia* and *Siyar* affirms that modern diplomatic law is in conformity with Islamic laws on the subject. Treatment of the diplomats as hostages was therefore not only a breach of the New York Convention, but also of the *Siyar* principles, the *Qur'anic* injunctions and the *Sunna* of Prophet Muhammad.

In its action of taking over the diplomatic premises, the Iranian regime breached the Vienna Convention on Diplomatic Relations (1961) to which Iran is a party. According to Article 22(1): 'the premises of the mission shall be inviolable. The agents of the receiving State may not enter them, except with the consent of the head of the mission.' Article 29 notes that:

> [t]he person of a diplomatic agent shall be inviolable. He shall not be liable to any form of arrest or detention. The receiving State shall treat him with due respect and shall take all appropriate steps to prevent any attack on his person, freedom or dignity.

Again the most severe action that is permissible is stated in Article 9(1), according to which:

---

[132] H Moinuddin, *The Charter of the Islamic Conference and Legal Framework of Economic Cooperation Among its Member States: A Study of the Charter, the General Agreement for Economic, Technical and Commercial Co-operation and the Agreement for Promotion, Protection and Guarantee of Investments Among Member States of the OIC* (Oxford, Clarendon Press, 1987) 111 (footnotes omitted); Bassiouni, n 107 above, at 620.

[133] Bassiouni, n 107 above, at 620.

[t]he receiving State may at any time and without having to explain its decision, notify the sending State that the head of the mission or any member of the diplomatic staff of the mission is *persona non grata* or that any other member of the staff of the mission is not acceptable. In any such case, the sending State shall, as appropriate, either recall the person concerned or terminate his functions with the mission. A person may be declared *non grata* or not acceptable before arriving in the territory of the receiving State.

ABUSE OF IMMUNITY BY INTERNATIONALLY
PROTECTED PERSONS[134]

We have already seen that the principle of inviolability of internationally protected persons is firmly established in Islamic diplomatic law. While the inviolability of diplomats forms the fundamental norm, there are nevertheless substantial questions concerning the abuse of immunity by diplomats. In this regard, a number of cases have emerged from the Islamic world. As noted above, Article 22 of the Vienna Convention on Diplomatic Relations 1961 provides for the absolute inviolability of premises of the diplomatic mission. This appears to provide an absolute rule, with arguably no exceptions attached to it.[135] Could issues of national security provide a defence to breaches of the provisions of Article 22? This subject was dealt with during the Iraq/Pakistan saga of 1973.[136] In February 1973 a container en route to the Iraqi Embassy in Islamabad was accidentally damaged. The damage exposed a large quantity of arms in the container. Upon this discovery, the Iraqi Ambassador in Islamabad was summoned by the Pakistan Ministry of Foreign Affairs. He was informed that arms were being smuggled onto the premises, where they were being stored. Notwithstanding the refusal of the Iraqi Ambassador to authorise a search, a raid was carried out by the Pakistani authorities in his presence. A huge consignment of arms was found stored in crates. This included 59 containers filled with explosives, arms and ammunition ready

---

[134] JC Barker, *The Abuse of Diplomatic Privileges and Immunities: A Necessary Evil* (Aldershot, Dartmouth, 1996); R Higgins, 'The Abuse of Diplomatic Privileges and Immunities: Recent United Kingdom Experience' (1985) 79 *American Journal of International Law* 641; R Higgins, *Problems and Process: International Law and How We Use It* (Oxford, Clarendon Press, 1994) 86–90; S Zappalà, 'Do Heads of State in Office Enjoy Immunity from Jurisdiction for International Crimes: The Ghaddafi Case Before the *French Cours de Cassation*' (2001) 12 *European Journal of International Law* 595; PR Ghandhi and JC Barker, 'The Pinochet Judgment: Analysis and Implications' (2000) 40 *Indian Journal of International Law* 657.

[135] Article 22 (1) provides: The premises of the mission shall be inviolable. The agents of the receiving State may not enter them, except with the consent of the head of the mission. See 767 *Third Avenue Associates v Permanent Mission of the Republic of Zaire to the United Nations* (1993) 988 F 2d 295; 99 ILR 194; AD McNair, *International Law Opinions: Selected and Annotated* Vol 1 (Cambridge, Cambridge University Press, 1956) 85; Shaw, n 76 above, at 671.

[136] See R Khan, *The American Papers: Secret and Confidential India-Pakistan-Bangladesh Documents 1965–1973* (Karachi, Oxford University Press, 1999).

to be sent to support the armed insurrection by Baluch separatists. Pakistan made official protests to Iraq, declared the Iraqi Ambassador and an attaché *persona non grata* and recalled its own ambassador. Pakistan's forcible entry was prima facie in breach of Article 22 of the Convention, although it is clear that Iraq had initially violated the provisions of Article 41(3), which prohibit the use of the premises in any manner incompatible with the provisions of the Convention.[137] It is arguable that in instances where there was a substantial risk to national security, this raid and search of premises was justified. It probably is the case that in the current environment, a substantial risk of terrorism may provide a necessary basis for premises to be searched in a diplomatic mission.

Another case, which continues to be the subject of debate, involved the Libyan diplomatic mission (also known as the Libyan Peoples' Mission).[138] In 1984, a demonstration was held outside the Libyan diplomatic mission, the Libyan Peoples' Bureau, in London by the opponents of Colonel Ghaddafi. At the same time a pro-Ghaddafi demonstration was held, with the two groups being separated by police through barricades. During the demonstrations by the anti-Ghaddafi protestors shots were fired from the Libyan mission, killing a woman police officer and injuring at least a dozen protestors. As a consequence, the UK government severed its relations with Libya. In accordance with the provisions of the Vienna Convention, the Libyan diplomats and other occupants of the Bureau were declared *persona non grata* and required to leave the United Kingdom.[139] The mission building was evacuated and searched (in the presence of Saudi Arabian observers) and arms found.[140] Upon departure from the Bureau, the diplomatic bags of individuals were not opened and searched.[141]

According to the provisions of Article 27, State parties undertake to provide free communication for the mission for official purposes,[142] and all official correspondence of the mission shall be inviolable.[143] The

---

[137] Dembinski, n 1 above, at 194; Shaw, n 76 above, at 672.

[138] Higgins, 'The Abuse' n 134 above, at 643–5; Barker, n 134 above, at 1–4; 'Fletcher probe police visit Libya' BBC News (UK Edition) 25 March 2004 <http://news.bbc.co.uk/1/hi/england/london/3567431.stm> (20 September 2004).

[139] Barker, n 134 above, at 3.

[140] See the Memorandum by the Foreign and Commonwealth Office, Foreign Affairs Committee Report, 5; Harris, n 13 above, at 353; Barker, n 134 above, at 4.

[141] *Ibid*, at 4.

[142] According to Article 27(1), '[t]he receiving State shall permit and protect free communication on the part of the mission for all official purposes. In communicating with the Government and the other missions and consulates of the sending State, wherever situated, the mission may employ all appropriate means, including diplomatic couriers and messages in code or cipher. However, the mission may install and use a wireless transmitter only with the consent of the receiving State'.

[143] Article 27(2) provides that '[t]he official correspondence of the mission shall be inviolable. Official correspondence means all correspondence relating to the mission and its functions'.

sacrosanct nature of 'the diplomatic bag' is well established. According to Article 27(3) the diplomatic bag is not to be opened or detained. Materials within the diplomatic bag 'must bear visible external marks of their character and may contain only diplomatic documents or articles intended for official use'.[144] While the principle appears absolute, could there be instances where the inviolability of 'the diplomatic bag' may be compromised? Various approaches have been adopted, and indeed certain States have expressly advanced reservations to Article 27(4). Libya has entered a reservation to the provision, declaring its right to open a diplomatic bag in the presence of an official representative of the relevant diplomatic mission. Failure to receive permission to open the diplomatic bag from the sending State would result in its being returned. Other Islamic States, namely Saudi Arabia and Kuwait, have entered similar reservations. Bahrain has also made a reservation to Article 27(3) which would also permit the opening of the bag in limited circumstances.[145] In addition, there are number of cases emergent from the Islamic world which have tested this issue. In the *Dikko incident* (1984), a former Nigerian governmental minister was kidnapped and an attempt was made to smuggle him from the United Kingdom to Nigeria.[146] He was drugged, then placed in a crate ready for shipment to Nigeria where he was to face trial for criminal offences. Although the shipment crate was labelled 'diplomatic baggage' there were no 'visible external marks' as required by Article 27(4) of the Vienna Convention in order for it be assigned the status of a diplomatic bag. There was thus no breach of the Article when customs officers opened it.[147] According to the UK foreign office, in the present instance, even if there had been a sealed bag, the overriding obligation to preserve and protect human life would have justified the opening of the bag. Following the incident two Nigerian diplomats were expelled and one person (who was unsuccessful in claiming immunity) was sentenced to twelve years of imprisonment.[148] In an earlier incident in 1964, an Israeli diplomatic agent was drugged, bound and gagged and found in a box, which was sealed as a diplomatic bag. The bag was ready to be smuggled from the Egyptian Embassy in Rome when the Italian official intercepted the bag. The First Secretary at the Egyptian Embassy was declared *persona non grata*. The First Secretary along with two other officials were expelled as a consequence.[149]

---

[144] Article 27(4).
[145] Shaw, n 76 above, at 677.
[146] See the Foreign Affairs Committee Report, at xxxiii–xxxiv. A Akinsanya, 'The Dikko Affair and Anglo-Nigerian Relations' (1985) 34 *International & Comparative Law Quarterly* 602.
[147] Barker, n 134 above, at 4–5.
[148] Harris, n 13 above, at 355.
[149] See *Keesings Contemporary Archives*, at 20580; Harris, n 13 above, at 355–6; Shaw, n 76 above, at 676.

CONCLUSIONS

The present chapter has reviewed the two most widely practised forms of terrorist act—hostage-taking of private individuals and violence against internationally protected persons. The international community of States has responded to these actions through its characteristic approach of devising international standards. These international standards are reflected in the New York Convention on the Prevention and Punishment of Crimes against Internationally Protected Persons (1973), the Vienna Convention on Diplomatic Relations (1961) and the Vienna Convention on Consular Relations. In its assessment of the protection of diplomats and emissaries, this study has highlighted the remarkable degree of respect endowed on such agents by classical Islamic law. The *Sharia* accords absolute protection of diplomatic staff; the detention and misuse of US Consular staff was therefore in absolute violation of the tenets of *Sharia* and *Siyar*.

As regards the prohibition of hostage-taking, the principal instrument is the 1979 Hostages Convention. The present research has established the significant role of Islamic States in the drafting of the provisions and the eventual adoption of the treaty. Islamic States, however, also have had a distinct vision relating to national liberation movements and the rights of peoples to self-determination. They have been the staunchest supporters of national liberation movements, even claiming exemptions of application for these movements. They have, in the words of the Libyan representative, claimed that the term 'taking of hostages':

> [I]s the seizure or detention, not only of a person or persons, but also of masses under colonial, racist or foreign domination, in a way that threatens him or them with death or severe injury or deprives them of their fundamental freedoms.[150]

With the demise of colonial and racist regimes, the Libyan proposal may in contemporary terms appear superfluous, a piece of political rhetoric. There is, however, considerable slipperiness in the term 'colonialism and foreign domination'. The unauthorised occupation of Iraq, without a basis or precedent in international law, can be castigated as the modern post-colonial example of 'alien and foreign domination'. It may well come to pass that the struggles of the Iraqis are eventually recognised as legitimate: a protracted and prolonged occupation by the United States forces, it is anticipated, will constitute occupation by an alien and foreign power.

---

[150] See Working Paper submitted by the Libyan Arab Jamahirya UN Doc A/AC.188/L.9, in 1977 Report of the Ad Hoc Committee on the Drafting of an International Convention Against the taking of Hostages 32 UN GAOR Supp (No 39) 106–10; UN Doc A/32/39 (1977).

5

Aerial and Maritime Terrorism[1]

INTRODUCTION

11 SEPTEMBER 2001 evokes horrific memories of destruction and devastation and can be classed as the ultimate act of terrorism. Whilst the locus of this most profound tragedy has been the United States, aerial terrorism represents a global concern. Firmly entrenched in the category of crimes against humanity, aerial terrorism includes:

> hijacking aircraft[s], firing heat-seeking missiles at aircraft[s], bombing aircraft[s], or airport lounges, gunning down passengers at airports and more recently turning aircrafts into guided missiles aimed at financial and governmental institutions.[2]

Hijacking and sabotage of aeroplanes is a relatively recent phenomenon with instances of hijacking reaching noticeable proportions in the latter half of the twentieth century. Maritime terrorism, by contrast, has groundings in antiquity. Piracy, although a distinct offence, bears relationship with violence and terrorism on board ships.

Recent acts of terrorism have raised concerns about the safety of travel by air and by sea. It is unfortunate that allegations have been advanced

---

[1] See A Cassese, *Terrorism, Politics and Law: The Achille Lauro Affair* (Cambridge, Polity Press, 1989); E McWhinney, *Aerial Piracy and International Terrorism: The Illegal Diversion of Aircraft and International Law* 2nd rev edn (Dordrecht, Matinus Nijhoff Publishers, 1987); E McWhinney, *The Illegal Diversion of Aircraft and International Law* (Leyden, Sijthoff, 1975); SK Agrawala, *Aircraft Hijacking and International Law* (Bombay, NM Tripathi Private Limited, 1973); PS Dempsey, 'Aviation Security: The Role of Law in the War Against Terrorism' (2003) 41 *The Columbia Journal of Transnational Law* 649; AE Evans, 'Aircraft Hijacking: Its Causes and Cure' (1969) 63 *American Journal of International Law* 695; AE Evans, 'Aircraft Hijacking: What is Being Done' (1973) 67 *American Journal of International Law* 641; C Emanuelli, 'Legal Aspects of Aerial Terrorism: The Piecemeal vs. the Comprehensive Approach' (1975) 10 *Journal of International Law and Economics* 503; D Fiorita, 'Aviation Security: Have All the Questions Been Answered' (1995) 20 *Annals Air Space Law* 69; GP McGinley, 'The Achille Lauro Affair—Implications for International Law' (1985) 52 *Tennessee Law Review* 691; BA Lee, 'The Legal Ramifications of Hijacking Airplanes' (1964) *American Bar Association* 1034; S Shubber, 'Is Hijacking of Aircraft Piracy in International Law?' (1968–1969) 43 *British Yearbook of International Law* 193; GF FitzGerald, 'Development of International Legal Rules for the Repression of the Unlawful Seizure of Aircraft' (1969) 7 *Canadian Yearbook of International Law* 269.

[2] Dempsey, n 1 above, at 651.

against a number of Islamic States for their involvement in aerial and maritime terrorism. The scars of the humiliation inflicted by the nineteen terrorists of 11 September on the Islamic world remain visible.

This chapter assess the validity of claims made by critics of Islamic States. In its examination of the international treaties on aerial and maritime terrorism, the research confirms the significant involvement and interest of Islamic States. There are difficulties of implementation, and it would appear that violence and terrorist activities have been conducted by non-State actors. There is also the duplicity and exploitation of a global order, which perpetuates existing inequities.

AERIAL TERRORISM

> The greatest threat posed to . . . civil aviation today is its increasing unsafety. It is so ironical that whereas the operational hazards and natural barriers to safe, efficient and reliable civil aviation have been, more or less, overcome through progress in science and technology, the hazards created by man himself remain unconquered and are rather on the increase.[3]

Notwithstanding its limited history there have been numerous instances of aerial terrorism.[4] During the Second World War, the Axis forces used aircrafts to be crashed into buildings resulting in tragic, civilian casualties. After the Second World War, civilian aircrafts became a particular terrorist target. According to one estimate, between 1949 and 1985 there were nearly 800 incidents of hijacking with over a 60 per cent success rate.[5] During this period 87 bombing incidents involving aircrafts led to the deaths of 1539 individuals.[6] Since 1985 there has been a rise in hijackings as well as the number of attacks on aeroplanes during the 1990s. In 2000, 24 instances of hijacking took place with 42 cases of interferences with civil aviation.[7] During 2001–2003, the level of interferences has remained static. Notwithstanding the gravity of offences, no single set of motives can be identified as the cause of aerial terrorism.[8] Hijacking of planes has been undertaken by those fleeing communist or dictatorial and oppressive

---

[3] Agrawala, n 1 above, at 13.

[4] According to Dempsey, the first recorded instance of aerial hijacking took place in 1931 with Peruvian revolutionaries commandeering a Ford Tri-Motor. Dempsey, n 1 above, at 654.

[5] JL Rhee, 'Rational and Constitutional Approaches to Airline Safety in the Face of Terrorist Threats' (2000) 49 *DePaul Law Review* 847, at p 847.

[6] *Ibid.*

[7] Dempsey, n 1 above, at 644–5.

[8] RIR Abeyratne, 'Hijacking and the Tehran Incident—A World in Crisis' (1985) 10 *Air Law* 120, at 123.

regimes.[9] Sometimes such acts have been conducted by those of an unsound mind. At other times, financial gain has been the driving force behind aerial hijacking; these hijackers are so-called 'sky bandits'.[10]

In a spate of hijackings that took place in the US during the late 1960s, a prominent feature was that hijackings were conducted principally by individuals with criminal records, military deserters, or those with family or personal difficulties. Such aerial hijacking was therefore largely undertaken for personal reasons as opposed to ideological motives.[11] The last quarter of the twentieth century, however, witnessed significant changes not only in the nature of aerial piracy also in hijackers' psychological motivations.[12] The largest and perhaps most disconcerting group of aerial hijackers are those committing this offence for ideological or political motivations. The nineteen hijackers involved in the 11 September incidents formed part of this last category.

COMBATING AERIAL TERRORISM

Although the past century has witnessed horrific acts of hijacking and sabotage, efforts to combat such deeds have only been piecemeal. The first practical response to this form of terrorism was conducted through the adoption of the Convention on Offences and Certain Other Acts committed on Board Aircraft, signed in Tokyo on 14 September 1963.[13] The Convention was adopted under the auspices of ICAO. The treaty deals principally with crimes committed on board civilian aircrafts. The primary purpose of the Tokyo Convention is to protect the safety of the aircraft and of the persons or property thereon and to maintain good order and discipline on board.[14] The Convention authorises the aircraft commander, crew members and passengers to take reasonable actions in order to

---

[9] Such incidents of aerial hijacking, although rare, still take place, for example the hijacking of the Arina airliner in January 2000. Upon making a landing at London's Stansted Airport, the hijackers made a claim for political asylum—<http://news.bbc.co.uk/1/hi/world/south_asia/633658.stm> (30 April 2004); See BBC Analysis, 'Who are the Hijackers?' 7 January 2004 (20 September 2004); 'Straw Makes Decision on Afghan Hostages' Guardian Unlimited <http://www.guardian.co.uk/stansted/article/0%2C2763%2C191509%2C00.html> (30 April 2004).

[10] McWhinney, n 1 above, at 10.

[11] On the US position see J Rogers, 'Bombs, Borders and Boarding: Combating International Terrorism at US Airports and the Fourth Amendment' (1997) 20 *Suffolk Transnational Law Review* 501; S Manning, 'The United States Response to International Air Safety' (1996) 61 *Journal of Air Law and Commerce* 505.

[12] Evans, 'Aircraft Hijacking: Its Causes and Cure', n 1 above, at 697.

[13] Adopted 14 September 1963, entered into force 4 December 1969 (1963) 2 ILM 1042.

[14] Text of the treaty can be found <http://untreaty.un.org/English/Terrorism/Conv1.pdf > (1 October 2004).

protect the safety of the aircraft, or of persons or property therein.[15] The focus of the Convention is not upon hijacking, but deals more generally with crimes in the air. The offence of hijacking was added as an afterthought; it was incorporated only to prevent a further protocol on the subject.[16]

The Convention nevertheless establishes a number of jurisdictional rules dealing with aerial hijacking. The State of registration has the principal jurisdiction to try offences committed on board the aircraft.[17] However, additional grounds of jurisdiction exist inter alia in cases of the territory of the State where the offence has effect,[18] where the offence has been committed by or against a national or permanent resident of such State[19] or where the offence is against the security of such State.[20] The Convention addresses the issue of unlawful seizure in Article 11. According to this Article, an unlawful seizure or other unlawful control of the aircraft is an offence and State parties are obliged to take 'all appropriate measures' to take control of the aircraft.[21] In the event of an unlawful seizure or hijacking the State party where the aircraft lands is required to allow passengers and crew to continue their journey and to return the aircraft and its cargo to those entitled to its lawful possession.[22]

For the purposes of extradition, Article 16 of the Convention provides that offences committed on board the aircraft shall be treated as if they are committed not only in the place where they occurred but also in the territory of the registering State. Other provisions of the Convention concern such matters as taking offenders into custody, restoring control of the aircraft to the commander and the continuation of the aircraft's journey.[23] The Convention represents an important development in international efforts to combat aerial terrorism. For the first time, it provides for formal international control over crimes committed by hijackers. At the same time

---

[15] Article 6(1)(2).

[16] Demsey, n 1 above, at 663; '[the Convention] was not at all specifically aimed at aircraft hijacking. There was not even a mention in the draft of hijacking as a separate category until 1962. Clauses were added relating to hijacking only to forestall the need for a separate protocol. It was (erroneously) thought that hijacking involved criminal activity of a kind which would anyway come under the Convention. The Convention does not provide for the manner in which a hijacker should be dealt with, but only seeks to alleviate the consequences of an unlawful seizure for the passenger, the crew and the aircraft, by calling upon the State of landing to permit them to continue their journey as soon as practicable (Article 11).' Agrawala, n 1 above, at 14.

[17] See D Freestone, 'International Cooperation against Terrorism and the Development of International Law Principles of Jurisdiction' in R Higgins and M Flory (eds), *Terrorism and International law* (London, Routledge, 1997) 43–67, at 49.

[18] Article 4(a).

[19] Article 4(b).

[20] Article 4(c).

[21] Article 11(1).

[22] Article 11(2).

[23] Articles 6–15.

there are a number of shortcomings in the treaty. It does not define or list any offences which States parties are required to suppress. As noted earlier, the inclusion of the offence of hijacking was incidental to a more general attempt to deal with crime on board aircrafts.[24] There is no restatement declaring hijacking as an international crime. There are similarly no obligations regarding the extradition or prosecution of offenders.[25]

In a resolution adopted during the Sixteenth Session of ICAO (in 1968), the limitations of the Tokyo Convention were highlighted. A request was made to the Council for the adoption of a more comprehensive treaty, leading to the drafting and adoption of the Hague Convention for the Suppression of Unlawful Seizure of Aircraft 1970. The 1970 treaty is the first convention to pronounce aircraft hijacking as an international offence, with a viable policy of enforcement procedures.[26] According to the Convention an offence is committed when any person:

> who on board an aircraft in flight . . . unlawfully, by force or threat thereof, or by any other form of intimidation, seizes, or exercises control of that aircraft; or is an accomplice of a person who performs or attempts to perform any such act . . .[27]

The complications arising out of such terminologies as 'unlawfulness', being 'on board', 'unlawful force' and 'intimidation, seizure and control of aircraft' have been explored by commentators.[28] According to Article 2, parties are obliged to make offences under the Convention punishable in their national legal systems by severe penalties. There is, however, no description of the nature of penalties to be awarded. The absence of minimum penalties provided in the Convention is, according to one scholar:

> one of the notable concessions that the proponents of strong action against hijacking were forced to make in pursuit of the elusive goal of a unanimous role in favour of the Convention as a whole.[29]

Article 3 accords a definition to aircraft being in flight. According to this definition the aircraft is in flight from the moment all its external doors are closed following embarkation.[30] The aircraft remains in flight until the time its external doors are opened for disembarkation.[31] In instances of forced landing, the flight is considered to be continuing until control is assumed by competent authorities.[32] Article 3 also contains a rather anom-

---

[24] Agrawala, n 1 above, at 13.
[25] Dempsey, n 1 above, at 665.
[26] *Ibid*, at 666.
[27] Article 1(a)(b).
[28] S Shubber, 'Aircraft Hijacking under the Hague Convention 1970—A New Regime' (1973) 22 *International & Comparative Law Quarterly* 687, at 691.
[29] McWhinney, *Aerial Piracy*, n 1 above, at 42.
[30] Article 3(1).
[31] *Ibid*.
[32] *Ibid*.

alous provision whereby the Convention is restricted in its application to the place of take-off or place of actual landing of the aircraft on board which the offence is committed outside of the State where the aircraft was registered.[33] This provision, it is contended, is unduly restrictive, excluding instances of domestic hijacking.

Jurisdiction to conduct trials is granted inter alia to the State where the aircraft is registered, to the State where the aircraft lands, an offence having been committed with the alleged offender still on board[34] and to the State of the place of business or residence of the lessee in case of leases without crew.[35] Article 6 provides further details of circumstances where the offender or alleged offender is apprehended in a contracting State. In these circumstances the contracting State is required to take him into custody for such time as is necessary to enable any proceedings to be instituted against him.[36] The State is also required to carry out preliminary investigations[37] and to communicate without delay to the nearest appropriate representative of the State of which he is a national.[38] There is also an obligation upon the State having custody of the alleged offender to notify immediately to the State where the aircraft was registered, the State of nationality of the detained person, and any other relevant parties as it considers appropriate.[39]

Article 8 regards the offences contained in this Convention as extraditable and deemed to be included in any extradition treaty existing between contracting States. An undertaking is provided by contracting States to include the offences contained in the present treaty in every extradition treaty.[40] A contracting State may treat the present treaty as a sufficient basis for extradition.[41] If the offender is not extradited, the State party where the offender is found is under an obligation (regardless of whether the offence was committed in its territory) to submit the case to competent authorities for the purpose of prosecution.[42] Article 7 therefore establishes the obligation *aut dedere aut judicare*. It needs to be reiterated that the obligation is not an undertaking to prosecute the individual but to submit his case to the authorities for the prosecution. In case of offences conducted under this treaty, State parties are required to take appropriate measure to restore control of the aircraft.[43] Where an offence does take

---

[33] Article 4(1)(a).
[34] Article 4(1)(b).
[35] Article 4(1)(c).
[36] Article 6(1).
[37] Article 6(2).
[38] Article 6(3).
[39] Article 6(4).
[40] Article 8(1).
[41] Article 8(2).
[42] Article 7.
[43] Article 9(1).

place, the contracting State in which the aircraft or its passengers are found has an obligation to facilitate the continuation of the journey of the passengers and crew and to return the aircraft to its lawful owners or possessors.[44]

The Convention obliges parties to allow one another judicial assistance in criminal proceedings brought in respect of the offence.[45] It also requires States parties to report to the Council of ICAO any relevant information in their possession regarding the circumstances of the offence, the action taken in relation to the offender or alleged offender and particularly the results of any extradition or legal proceedings.[46] The Hague Convention has a number of positive features. In the words of Dempsey, the Convention:

> acted as a deterrent because prosecution of extradition became mandatory; therefore few States became available as safe havens. In addition, it likely narrowed the gap between the number of attempted hijackings and the number of unsuccessful hijackings. Finally it enhanced international law regarding the prosecution and imposition of penalties upon hijackers.[47]

DEALING WITH AERIAL SABOTAGE

Whilst both the 1963 and 1970 Conventions deal with offences committed aboard aircrafts, the subject of aerial sabotage was left to be addressed by the Convention for the Suppression of Unlawful Acts against the Safety of Civil Aviation adopted in Montreal in 1971. At this point there was concern that while incidents of aircraft hijacking were decreasing, there was an alarming increase in acts of sabotage.[48] The precursor to this Convention was the extra-ordinary session of the ICAO Assembly in June 1970 in Montreal. During this session, a recommendation was made to draft a treaty covering inter alia acts of sabotage through bombing on board aircrafts and on ground installations. According to Article 1 of the Convention, a person commits an offence if he unlawfully and intentionally:

> performs an act of violence against a person on board an aircraft in flight if that act is likely to endanger its safety; destroys an aircraft or causes it to damage; places or causes to be placed on an aircraft in service a device or substance which is likely to destroy that aircraft or to cause damage to it which renders it incapable of flight or endangers its safety destroys or damages air navigation facilities or interferes with their operation, if any such act is likely to endanger

---

[44] Article 9(2).
[45] Article 10.
[46] Article 11.
[47] Dempsey, n 1 above, at 668.
[48] *Ibid*, at 669.

the safety of aircraft in flight or communicates information which he knows to be false, thereby endangering the safety of aircraft in flight.

Article 1 also makes it an offence to attempt to commit the aforementioned offences.[49] Since the adoption of the Convention, a number of issues have arisen involving nationals from Islamic State parties.[50] The Lockerbie bombing in which two Libyan nationals were implicated represented a significant violation of Article 1. Similarly, the hijackers of the aeroplanes on 11 September, all of whom were nationals of Islamic States, breached the provisions of Article 1.[51] The Montreal Convention provides for jurisdictional principles which are similar to the Hague Convention.[52] Through its various provisions, the Convention deals with such issues as custody,[53] prosecution and extradition of the alleged offender.[54] The Convention, like the earlier Hague and Tokyo Conventions, does not apply to aircraft used in military, customs or police services. Neither does it apply to a purely domestic, non-international situation.[55] As in the case of the 1970 Hague Convention, this is a troubling feature of the Convention and has evoked considerable criticism. Commenting on this unsatisfactory limitation, and examining this provision, Trahan notes:

[I]n the context of September 11—because the hijacked aircrafts departed from and were intended to land within the United States—if the aircrafts were registered in the United States, the Montreal Convention would not apply to any alleged offender found in the United States. This is probably not problematic regarding the crimes committed on September 11 because, even without convention obligations, the United States would undertake the obligations imposed under the Montreal Convention, such as taking into custody any alleged perpetrators found in the United States, investigating the crime, and commencing prosecutions.

This exclusion could be problematic, however, if a country does not take such prosecution obligations as seriously. For instance, had the event occurred in Syria or Libya and the aircraft been registered in those countries, even though both countries are parties to the Montreal Convention, none of the Montreal Convention obligations to prosecute the perpetrators would apply. Thus, the exclusions built into the conventions pertaining to acts occurring within a single state arguably should be reconsidered. Given the increasingly global reach of

---

[49] Article 1(2).

[50] JA Frank, 'A Return to Lockerbie and the Montreal Convention in the Wake of September 11th Terrorist Attacks: Ramifications of Past Security Council and the International Court of Justice' (2002) 30 *Denver Journal of International Law and Policy* 532.

[51] According to the information currently available of the nineteen hijackers, fifteen had Saudi Nationality, one with Egyptian nationality, one with Lebanese nationality while two held United Arab Emirates passports. <http://www.cia.gov/cia/public_affairs/speeches/2002/dci_testimony_06182002/DCI_18_June_testimony_new.pdf.> (15 April 2004).

[52] Article 5.

[53] Article 6.

[54] Article 8.

[55] Article 4(2)(3).

terrorist organizations, terrorists acts occurring within a single state may have broad ramifications, and all states arguably have an interest in having convention obligations apply and seeing terrorists active within a single state prosecuted.[56]

Article 5(1) attempts to provide a wide basis of jurisdiction, approaching the threshold of universal jurisdiction. The Convention follows the principle of *aut dedere aut judicare*, although, as has been noted by commentators in the light of the Lockerbie cases, the principle remains ineffective where State complicity is arguably in support of the alleged terrorists themselves.[57] In accordance with Article 7 of the Convention, in instances where a State has in its custody an individual accused of a terrorist act, the requested State must either extradite that individual to the requesting State or submit the case to its competent authorities for the purpose of prosecution in accordance with the law of that State. In addition, Article 8 provides that in the absence of bi-lateral agreements signatory States may treat the Convention as a legal basis for extradition. Since in the Lockerbie cases, no extradition treaties existed between Libya and the US or Libya and the UK, Libya was therefore able to claim justification in refusing extradition. There is no requirement or obligation for extradition within general international law.

A further treaty, the Protocol on the Suppression of Unlawful Acts of Violence at Airports Serving International Civil Aviation, supplementary to the Convention for the Suppression of Unlawful Acts Against the Safety of Civil Aviation, Montreal, was adopted in February 1988.[58] The Protocol was a response to the bombings in Frankfurt, Tokyo, Rome and Munich during the 1980s.[59] While this instrument provides further legal safeguards for airports, tragic attacks have continued to occur and the impact of the Protocol is yet to be realised fully.[60] The Protocol is geared towards dealing with acts of violence which endanger or are likely to endanger the safety of persons at airports serving international civil aviation or which jeopardise the safe operations of such airports. The 1988 Protocol adds to the definition of offences as provided in Article 1 of the Montreal Convention, thereby providing for the punishment of any person who unlawfully commits an act of violence against a person at an airport

---

[56] See J Trahan, 'Terrorism Conventions: Existing Gaps and Different Approaches' (2002) 8 *New England International and Comparative Law Annual* 215, at p 227–8.

[57] Frank, n 50 above, at 536.

[58] Protocol on the Suppression of Unlawful Acts of Violence at Airports Serving International Civil Aviation, supplementary to the Convention for the Suppression of Unlawful Acts Against the Safety of Civil Aviation, Montreal, 24 February 1988.

[59] Dempsey, n 1 above, at 686.

[60] See 'Troops "in control" of Sri Lanka Airport' (25 July 2001) CNN.com <http://www.cnn.com/2001/WORLD/asiapcf/south/07/24/srilanka.airport.attack/> (22 September 2004).

serving international civil aviation which causes or is likely to cause death or serious injury by any device, substance or weapon. The jurisdictional issues are addressed in Article III, which also affirms the principle of *aut dedere aut judicare*.

ISLAMIC TREATY RATIFICATIONS ON AERIAL TERRORISM

In their official practices, Islamic States have maintained a huge commitment to comprehensively ban aerial piracy and aerial terrorism. This commitment is evident from the large-scale ratifications of international treaties that deal with aerial terrorism. As noted earlier, the Tokyo Convention was the earliest instrument concerned with offences committed on board aircrafts. Considerable interest was shown by Islamic States in the treaty even at a time when many States remained largely disinterested. All Islamic States have ratified this Convention. A number of declarations and reservations have been made by these States, although they do not relate to the substantive provisions of the Convention. Algeria, Bahrain, Egypt, Oman, the Syrian Arab Republic and Tunisia have reserved their position in relation to Article 24(1), which relates to settlement of disputes. Article 24(1) provides:

> [a]ny dispute between two or more Contracting States concerning the interpretation or application of this Convention which cannot be settled through negotiation, shall, at the request of one of them, be submitted to arbitration. If within six months from the date of the request for arbitration the Parties are unable to agree on the organisation of the arbitration, any one of those Parties may refer the dispute to the International Court of Justice by request in conformity with the Statute of the Court.

This provision is not an unusual one, and by the same account the reservations made also follow the pattern followed in international treaties. The kingdom of Morocco has, for instance, without making a specific reservation to Article 24(1), asserted the necessity of unanimous consent of the parties concerned prior to proceedings being brought before the International Court of Justice. A further set of reservations has been advanced by Middle Eastern Islamic States. Despite having entered into treaties to which Israel is a party, Bahrain, Iraq, Morocco, Oman and the United Arab Emirates have stated their non-recognition of Israel as a State in general international law or the existence of any diplomatic relations with it.

The Convention for the Suppression of Unlawful Seizure of Aircraft, signed in The Hague on 16 December 1970, depicts a consistent pattern of State practice in so far as the behaviour of Islamic countries is concerned. The reservations relate principally to the non-recognition of Israel and non-acceptance of relations with it. Reservations to that effect have been placed by Kuwait, Libyan Arab Jamahiriya, Oman, Saudi Arabia and the United Arab Emirates. The other reservation placed by Islamic States relates to the referral of disputes to the International Court of Justice.[61] A similar trend is reflected in so far as reservations to the Convention for the Suppression of Unlawful Acts against the Safety of Civil Aviation (1971) are concerned. Kuwait's reservations to the Convention concern the non-recognition of Israel and having diplomatic relations with it, as do Saudi Arabia's and the United Arab Emirates'. Afghanistan, Algeria, Bahrain, Indonesia, Morocco, Oman, Qatar, Saudi Arabia and Tunisia have placed reservations allowing for the automatic jurisdiction of the International Court of Justice under Article 14(1) of the Convention. Article 14 of the Convention, as our subsequent examination reveals, was indeed to be of pivotal importance in the Lockerbie incident. Libya, in its attempt to resolve the matter, had invoked Article 14(1) of the Convention appealing to the International Court of Justice. Such an action, according to the Libyan government, represented its efforts to uphold international rule of law. Although the US and the UK were opposed to involving the ICJ, Libya received support and acclaim from the OIC and the League of Arab States as well as from various Islamic States including Sudan, Iraq, Mauritania, Yemen, Morocco, and Iraq.[62]

One innovative reservation to the Convention was placed by the State of Cameroon. Cameroon gained independence on 1 January 1960, and has been at the forefront in opposing racist and colonial regimes. In its reservatory note, it claimed that:

> [I]n accordance with the provisions of the Convention of 23 September 1971, for the Suppression of Unlawful Acts directed against the Security of Civil Aviation, the Government of the United Republic of Cameroon declares that in view of the fact that it does not have any relations with South Africa and Portugal, it has no obligations towards these two countries with regard to the implementation of the stipulations of the Convention.

This reservation has, no doubt, been rendered obsolete due to the political and constitutional changes within South Africa and Portugal. There a number of Afro-Caribbean States parties. These are Burkino Faso, Chad, Comoros, Gambia, Guinea, Guniea-Bissau, Guyana, Libyan Arab Jamahiriaya, Mali, Mauritania, Morocco, Niger, Nigeria, Senegal, Sierra Leone, Sudan, Suriname, Togo, and Uganda.

The Protocol on the Suppression of Unlawful Acts of Violence at Airports Serving International Civil Aviation, Supplementary to the Convention for the Suppression of Unlawful Acts against the Safety of Civil Aviation signed at Montreal on 28 February 1988 has attracted

---

[61] Note the reservations made by Algeria and Libyan Arab Jamhiriya.
[62] F Beveridge, 'The Lockerbie Affair' (1992) 41 *International & Comparative Law Quarterly* 907, at 910.

significant approval from Islamic States. There is a large body of consensus over the principles enshrined in the treaty, with only two reservations being advanced to the non-procedural aspects. Kuwait reiterated its opposition to the existence and recognition of Israel as a State, whereas the Syrian Arab Republic has reserved its position in relation to Article 14(1) of the Convention which relates to the powers of the International Court of Justice upon adjudication of disputes.

INCIDENTS OF CONFLICT AND ISLAMIC STATES

11 September 2001 represents the most horrific incident committed against civil aviation. The vile acts of the hijackers resulted in 2,972 deaths, with financial losses running into the billions.[63] As has been examined elsewhere in this study, the long-term consequences of 9/11 have been phenomenal.[64] The scars of the tragedy are writ large on the psyche of the American public. This incident has also created 'Islamophobia', with Muslim minorities in many parts of the world having to face increasing hostility and prejudices.[65] 11 September evoked absolute condemnation from all Islamic States individually as well as from the organisations that represent Islamic interests.[66] There is nevertheless the stigma that all the hijackers originated from the Arabic speaking world; the finger of suspicion is strongly directed at al-Qaeda, an organisation purportedly representing the interests of oppressed Muslims. Members of al-Qaeda had been protected by the Taliban, a militant group of Islamic clergy who had seized power in Afghanistan. Subsequent investigations into the 9/11 plot have revealed that there was clandestine financial and material support given by Arabs to individual members of al-Qaeda.

Other than the Taliban, the 11 September inquiries have thus far stopped short of directly implicating Islamic governments.[67] On previous occasions relating to aerial sabotage and bombings, Islamic States are alleged to have been involved. Israel's raid in Entebbe in July 1976, in Israel's own contention was a consequence of the violation of its rights by

---

[63] See JNB Frank and J Rehman, 'Assessing the Legality of the Attacks by the International Coalition against Terrorism against Al-Qaeda and Taliban in Afghanistan: An Inquiry into the Self-Defence Argument under Article 51 of the United Nations Charter' (2003) 67 *Journal of Criminal Law* 415.

[64] See below, chapter 7.

[65] See below, chapter 8.

[66] See below, chapter 7.

[67] See <http://www.pm.gov.uk/files/pdf/culpability_document.pdf> (1 October 2004); also see <http://image.guardian.co.uk/sysfiles/Guardian/documents/2001/11/14/Culpability_document.pdf> (18 June 2002) Unclassified Version of Director of Central Intelligence George J Tenet's Testimony before the Joint Inquiry into Terrorist Attacks Against the United States (22 July 2004).

Uganda.[68] Israel sent two aircraft to rescue its nationals who had been held hostage in a hijacked aircraft and were being held in Uganda. The intervention resulted in the rescue of Israeli nationals, although at a significant cost. Over twenty-five people are estimated to have been killed, including at least twenty Ugandan soldiers, all of the hijackers and three hostages. The reality of the situation, however, is that military intervention in Ugandan territory was a violation of international law and breached the ban on the use of force as provided in the United Nations Charter. In June 1985, a Trans-World Airlines Flight 847 was hijacked shortly after take-off from Athens Airport. In this case the Greek government traded the terrorists for the return of Greek nationals on board. It is arguable that both Greece (where the offence took place) and Lebanon (the State of the nationality of the hijackers) did not follow the provisions of the Tokyo, the Hague and the Montreal Conventions.[69]

In terms of the direct culpability of State actors, the Lockerbie incident probably provided the most disturbing feature in the relationship between Islamic and western States. The incident has had profound implications both for international law as well as for developing norms for combating terrorism.[70] The most problematic aspect of the saga has been the alleged involvement of Libya in terrorist activities.[71] On 21 December 1988, Pan American Flight 103 exploded over the Scottish border town of Lockerbie en route to New York. All 259 persons on board were killed, as were 11 residents of Lockerbie. On 19 September 1989, a French airliner Union de transport aériens (UTA) Flight 772 exploded over Niger, killing 171 passengers and its crew. In both acts of terrorism, evidence was brought forward by the United States, the United Kingdom and France alleging involvement of the Libyan government.

JUDICIOUSNESS AND APPROACHES TO ACCOUNTABILITY

The impatience and the urgency on the part of the United States to resort to the use of force against al-Qaeda and the Taliban in the aftermath of 9/11 reflect a paucity of faith in international legal institutions. A judicious

---

[68] For commentaries on the incident see LC Green, 'Rescue at Entebbe—Legal Aspects' (1976) 6 *International Yearbook on Human Rights* 312; MN Shaw, 'Some Legal Aspects of the Entebbe Incident' (1978) 1 *Jewish Law Annual* 232.

[69] See Dempsey, n 1 above, at 726.

[70] The Convention on the Marking of Plastic Explosives was adopted as a consequence of the Lockerbie tragedy. See Trahan, n 56 above, at 223.

[71] See SE Evans, 'The Lockerbie Incident Cases: Libyan-Sponsored Terrorism, Judicial Review and the Political Question Doctrine' (1994) 18 *Maryland Journal of International Law and Trade* 21; A Klip and M Mackarel, 'The Lockerbie Trial—A Court in the Netherlands' (1999) 70 *Revue international de droit penale* 777; R Black, 'Analysis: The Lockerbie Disaster' (1999) 3 *Edinburgh Law Review* 85.

approach towards trials of the alleged perpetrators of the crimes of 9/11 was not considered practical or relevant. Both the United Nations General Assembly and Security Council condemned the events of 11 September 2001. In its Resolution of 12 September, the Security Council condemned the terrorist acts, stating that they were a threat to international peace and security.[72] The Council called upon all States to urgently work together to bring to justice the perpetrators, organisers and sponsors of terrorist attacks. A further resolution, Resolution 1373, was adopted on 28 September 2001 requiring States inter alia to adopt and implement the existing international legal instruments on terrorism, to suppress the financing of terrorism and freezing of funds for terrorist actions. The Security Council placed onerous legal obligations on States.[73] It had reiterated and reaffirmed the right to self-defence under international law, though there was no authorisation to use force in Afghanistan.[74] By then, however, the die had been cast. Plans had firmly been put in place to start an unrelenting military campaign against the Taliban and al-Qaeda. This action was taken despite the attempted mediation of individual Islamic States and the OIC to obtain the custody of Usama Bin Laden from the Taliban.[75] The bombing campaign was initiated despite the knowledge that there was a risk of huge collateral damage; innocent Afghans who had for years suffered at the hands of the Russians, the war-lords, the *Mujaheedians*, and subsequently the Taliban had to pay the ultimate price. As was predictable, it has not been possible to capture Usama Bin Laden.

[72] S/RES/1368 Adopted by the Security Council at its 4370th meeting.

[73] See below, chapter 6.

[74] See M Byers, 'Terrorism, the Use of Force and International Law after 11 September' (2002) 51 *International & Comparative Law Quarterly* 401; SD Murphy, 'Contemporary Practice of the United States Relating to International Law' (2002) 96 *American Journal of International Law* 237, at 244; D Brown, 'Use of Force against Terrorism after September 11th: State Responsibility, Self-defense and Other Responses' 11 (2003) *Cardozo Journal of International and Comparative Law* 1, at 18.

[75] See AA An-Nai'm, 'Upholding International Legality Against Islamic and American Jihad' in K Booth and T Dunne (eds), *Worlds in Collision: Terror and the Future of Global Order* (London, Palgrave, 2002) 162–72, at 169. Even in the presence of overwhelming and unequivocal evidence against al-Qaeda, there would still remain the question of the imputablity of terrorist acts upon the Afghan State and the Taliban government. Substantial doubts have been raised as regards the role of Afghanistan and the Taliban in authorising the terrorist acts of 11 September 2001; it appears to be the established legal position that in the absence of firm evidence against the Taliban for aiding and supporting the attacks on the United States, the bombing of Afghanistan was unlawful under general international law. On this particular issue, the International Bar Association's task force observe that '[a] strict interpretation of the UN Charter suggests that whilst it might be permissible for a State to take defensive action against groups mounting ongoing attacks, taking military action against another state which is not directly participating in attacks perpetuated by terrorist based within its borders would be impermissible'. Report by the International Bar Association's Task Force on International Terrorism, *International Terrorism: Legal Challenges and Responses* (Ardsley NY, Transnational Publishers, 2003) at 23; JJ Paust, 'Use of Armed Force against Terrorists in Afghanistan, Iraq, and Beyond' (2002) 35 *Cornell International Law Journal* 533 at 557.

A number of cases have been brought against 'Muslim terrorists' within the United States domestic courts—the success in dealing with terrorism has been inadequate and partial. The United States has domestically also engaged with individual cases of 'Islamic terrorists'; their successes have been limited and partial.[76]

While the international community waits for an appropriate and impartial judicial involvement with those alleged to have committed the 9/11 massacres, this review needs to assess the role of law in previous aerial disasters. A manipulation of political institutions and the use of power to extract a favourable outcome is evident from an inspection of two aerial incidents: the Lockerbie incident, which has been high on the legal and political agenda, and the other equally tragic though less well publicised incident of 3 July 1998.[77] The dispute was caused by the destruction of an Iranian aircraft, Iran Air Airbus A-300 (IR flight 655) by two surface-to-air missiles launched from the *USS Vincennes*, a guided-missile cruiser with the United States Forces stationed in the Middle East. At the time of the impact, the Airliner, while within Iranian airspace was conducting a regularly scheduled flight and had 290 passengers on board. The incident was raised in the United Nations. The Security Council, while expressing concern and distress, remained dormant as far as matters of accountability were concerned.[78] There was no remorse or guilt evident in the US response: the finger of blame was pointed at the Airliner and the course it took, instead of those who had launched the missiles.[79] The Iranian government raised the issue initially before the International Civil Aviation Organisation and subsequently before the International Court of Justice, alleging inter alia violations of the Chicago Convention (1944) and the Montreal Convention (1971) by the United States. In its pleadings before the International Court of Justice, the Iranian government sought a declaration alleging violations of Articles 1, 3 and 10(1) of the Montreal Convention.[80] The government also sought compensation from the United States for the:

---

[76] PD Trooboff, 'Aircraft Piracy, Federal Jurisdiction, Non-Resident Aliens on Foreign Soil' (1989) 83 *American Journal of International Law* 94.

[77] See DK Linnan, 'Iran Air Flight 655 and Beyond: Free Passage, Mistaken Self-Defense, and State Responsibility' (1991) 16 *The Yale Journal of International Law* 245; YM Ibrahim, 'As Iran Mourns, Khomeini Calls for "War" on US' *New York Times* 5 July 1988 at A9.

[78] See SC Res 616 (1988). Resolution adopted 20 July 1988. For an examination of the facts of the case see (1989) 28 ILM 896.

[79] See MR Gordon, 'Questions Persist on Airbus Disaster: Why Did Airliner Ignore Warnings? Why was Ship unaware of Schedule?' *New York Times* 5 July 1988 at A8; also see *Newsweek Magazine*, 13 July 1992 (for criticisms of Captain Will Rogers).

[80] See *Aerial Incident of 3 July 1988* (*Islamic Republic of Iran v United States of America*) [1989] ICJ Reports 132.

injuries suffered by the Islamic Republic and the bereaved families as a result of these violations, including additional financial losses which Iran Air and the bereaved families have suffered for the disruption of their activities.[81]

The cases were withdrawn, never having reached a point of adjudication on its merits. In February 1996 both Iran and the US notified the Court that their governments had agreed to discontinue the case as a consequence of an agreement.[82]

In so far as the accusations against Libya were concerned, the Libyan government had denied any involvement in the bombing of either the Pan American flight or the UTA flight. The United Kingdom and United States governments formally requested the extradition of two Libyan officials, Abdel Basset Al-Megrahi and Al-Amin Khalifa Fhimah, and on 14 November 1991 provided the Libyan government with indictments of charges. Warrants of arrest were also issued by Scottish courts against the aforementioned individuals. The French government made formal requests for the extradition of the individuals involved in the bombing of the UTA airliner.[83]

The refusal of the Libyan government to extradite the named individuals was unacceptable to the United States, United Kingdom and French governments. Unilateral sanctions were imposed by the United States upon Libya.[84] The three permanent members of the Security Council, adamant about gaining custody of the individuals, invoked the powers of the Council. In the face of such intransigence, on 18 January 1992, Libya took steps to request arbitration as provided for in the Montreal Convention which would determine the obligations of the parties under the Convention. Article 14(1) of the Convention provides as follows:

> Any dispute between two or more Contracting States concerning the interpretation or application of this Convention which cannot be settled through negotiation, shall, at the request of one of them, be submitted to arbitration. If within six months from the date of the request for arbitration the Parties are unable to agree on the organization of the arbitration, any one of those Parties may refer the dispute to the International Court of Justice by request in conformity with the Statute of the Court.

---

[81] See *Application Instituting Proceedings, Aerial Incident of 3 July 1988 (Islamic Republic of Iran v United States of America)* filed in the Registry of the Court 17 May 1989 (1989) 28 ILM 842 at 10 (para IV C). Text available at <http://www.icj-cij.org/icjwww/icases/iirus/iirus_ipleadings/iirus_iapplication_19890517.pdf > (22 April 2004).

[82] See *Case concerning the Aerial Incident of 3 July 1988, Islamic Republic of Iran v United States of America,* 22 February 1996, General List No 79 <http://212.153.43.18/icjwww/icases/iirus/iirus_iorders/irus_iorder_19960222.pdf> (1 July 2004).

[83] Beveridge, n 62 above, at 907.

[84] These sanctions were to be further reinforced through the Iran-Libya Sanctions Act 1996, 50 USCS 1701. See HR REP No 104–523 (II) at 9 (1996) USCCAN 1311, 1312.

Instead of responding to the Libyan advances, the three permanent members relied upon the political agency of the Security Council. The Council passed three resolutions. In its Resolution SC 731, the Council noted its concern about the persistence of acts of international terrorism in which States are directly involved in illegal activities against civil aviation.[85] It also noted with concern the outcome of the investigation into the Lockerbie explosion that implicated officials from the Libyan government. The Resolution requested Libya to comply with the US, UK and French requests for action as regards Pan American Flight 103 and Union de transport aériens Flight 772. The Resolution provides inter alia that the Council:

> Strongly deplores the fact that the Libyan Government has not yet responded effectively to the above requests to cooperate fully in establishing responsibility for the terrorist acts referred to above against Pan American flight 103 and Union de transports aériens flight 772.[86]

> Urges the Libyan Government immediately to provide a full and effective response to those requests so as to contribute to the elimination of international terrorism.[87]

In its characterisation of the situation, and requiring Libya to pay compensation, the Resolution is prejudicial to any legal adjudication of the matter.[88] Resolution 731 does not explicitly express the mandate for its adoption by the Security Council. The assumption therefore is that in strictly legal terms it does not carry the mandatory obligations of the Resolutions adopted under Chapter VII. Furthermore, Libya did not accept the allegations made against the two individuals named by the US and UK. On 3 March 1992, prior to the expiry of the six-month notice period, Libya appealed to the ICJ invoking Article 14 of the Montreal Convention.[89] Libya's arguments in the pleadings were inter alia that while the dispute concerned the provisions of the Montreal Convention, the US was failing to comply with the arbitration provisions, as established by the Convention. Libya also requested an order of provisional measures to protect its rights under international law.

Under the terms of the Montreal Convention, Libya was obliged either to try the individuals or extradite the accused individuals.[90] Libya contended that it was prosecuting the two named persons in accordance with the provisions of the Convention. Libya also contended that it was relying upon Article 14, according to which any dispute over interpretation and

---

[85] SC Res 731 (21 January 1992). Text available at <http://ods-dds-ny.un.org/doc/RESOLUTION/GEN/NR0/010/90/IMG/NR001090.pdf?OpenElement> (30 April 2004).

[86] *Ibid,* para 2.

[87] *Ibid,* para 3.

[88] Beveridge, n 62 above, at 911.

[89] *Ibid,* at 908.

[90] See Article 7 of the Convention.

application of the Convention that could not be settled by negotiation should be submitted to arbitration. Three explanations have been provided for such a course of action:

First, Libya was concerned that to surrender Al-Megrahi and Fhimah would be tantamount to admitting guilt, a proposition the Libyan government was probably unwilling to face. Second, the refusal to surrender the men and the following application to the ICJ were attempts to stall the prosecution and the sanctions. Finally, according to Libya, it could not surrender Al-Megrahi and Fhimah because Libyan domestic law prohibits the extradition of nationals.[91]

In order to pre-empt any orders made by the Court, the Security Council, spurred on by the United States and the United Kingdom, passed another resolution, Resolution 748, on 31 March 1992. In this resolution passed under Chapter VII, the Council demanded that Libya immediately comply with obligations set out in Resolution 731 and cease and desist from all forms of terrorist acts.[92] Security Council Resolution 748 placed punitive sanctions against Libya, which were to remain in place until full compliance had been achieved. These sanctions resulted in the following measures:

— Refusal of permission of flights to and from Libya;
— Prohibition of the supply of any aircraft components, servicing of aircraft, certification of Libyan aircraft, certification of airworthiness for Libyan aircrafts, the payment of new claims against existing insurance contracts for the Libyan aircrafts;
— Prohibition of any provision of arms and related materials;
— Prohibition of the provision of any technical advice, assistance or training relating to manufacture, maintenance or the use of items;
— Withdrawal of officials in Libya advising on military strategies;
— Significant reductions in the numbers of staff in Libyan diplomatic missions;
— Shutting down of offices of the Libyan Arab Airline; and
— Taking all steps by States to deny or to expel those Libyans who have been denied entry to or expelled from other States because of involvement in terrorist activities.

Security Council Resolution 748 was punitive in its nature and draconian in its effects. The measures adopted by the Council were also overriding of established treaty obligations on inter alia diplomatic relations.[93] It raised considerable tensions in the Council and was adopted

---

[91] Evans, n 71 above, at 42 (footnotes omitted); also see S Zappalà, 'Do Heads of State in Office Enjoy Immunity from Jurisdiction for International Crimes: The Ghaddafi Case Before the *French Cours de Cassation*' (2001) 12 *European Journal of International Law* 595, at 610.

[92] SC Res 748 (31 March 1992) <http://www.geocities.com/CapitolHill/5260/748.html> (30 April 2004).

[93] See MN Shaw, *International Law* 5th edn (Cambridge, Cambridge University Press, 2003) at 670.

with an abstention of five members, including China, a permanent member. The abstaining States had considerable misgivings about the imposition of sanctions, particularly at a time when the matter was awaiting consideration by the International Court. The Resolution had significant implications both on the relationship of the Security Council with the International Court of Justice and upon the subsequent order that was handed down by the World Court. In terms of the characterisation of terrorism as a threat to international peace and security, the Resolution represented a significant new development.[94]

On 14 April 1992, the Court voted by a majority of 11 to 5 against indicating provisional measures. The Court was heavily influenced by Resolution 748. It made the observation that under Article 25 of the Charter, all States including Libya were under an obligation to carry out the decisions of the Security Council. Security Council Resolution 748 was binding upon Libya and a cumulative effect of Article 25 and Chapter VII Resolutions led to their superseding of the provisions of the Montreal Convention.[95] The Court also took the view that the indication of provisional measures was likely to restrict the scope of the application and effect of Resolution 748. The judgment of the Court raised dissent and was problematic. A majority of the judges took the position that had it not been for Resolution 748, Libya could not be regarded as being at fault.[96]

The sanctions that were imposed by Resolution 748 came into operation on 15 April 1992. A further Security Council Resolution, Resolution 883, was passed on 11 November 1993.[97] This Resolution, which took effect on 1 December 1993, placed further bans on the sales of Libyan equipment for refining and exporting petroleum, placed a freeze on Libyan financial assets overseas and restricted Libyan diplomatic missions, blocked Libya's national airlines and restricted the maintenance of its airfields. Libya's protestations at what it considered an unjust imposition of power by the Security Council continued until 1998. During this period, Libya defended its position by placing reliance on its own constitution which restricts extradition of its nationals. It also argued that a trial either in the United Kingdom or in the United States would not be fair because of the pre-existing bias against the accused and prejudicial media coverage.[98]

Interaction with judicial institutions did, in the end, take place. While the ICJ had in 1992 voted against the Libyan application for granting

---

[94] Beveridge, n 62 above, at 912.

[95] See [1992] ICJ Reports 3; A Aust, 'Lockerbie: The Other Case' (2000) 49 *International & Comparative Law Quarterly* 278, at p 282.

[96] *Libya v UK; Libya v US Question of Interpretation and Application of the 1971 Montreal Convention Arising from the Aerial Incident at Lockerbie, Order of 14 April 1992* [1992] ICJ Reports 3.

[97] (11 Nov 1993) SC Res 883.

[98] See I Bantekas and S Nash, *International Criminal Law* 2nd edn (London, Cavendish, 2003) at 409.

provisional measures, it nevertheless allowed the case to advance to a hearing of preliminary objections.[99] Both the US and the UK challenged Libya's assertion that a justicable dispute existed as provided for in the provisions of the Montreal Convention. In dismissing the preliminary objections, the Court found that a substantive dispute existed between the parties over the interpretation of Article 14(1) as well as Articles 5–8 of the Montreal Convention.[100] In the determination of the merits of the case, the Court was faced with the question as to whether the SC Resolutions passed under Chapter VII were amenable to judicial review.[101]

Libya, exhausted by years of sanctions, wilted and agreed to have trials of the two accused in a third—neutral—State. The US and UK governments, frustrated by the Libyan intransigence, the large-scale and on-going flouting of the provisions of the sanctions and under pressure from the relatives of the deceased, agreed to trials being conducted in the Netherlands. In a letter dated 24 August 1998, the US and UK governments submitted to the United Nations Secretary-General a proposal for conducting trials of the two suspected Libyans before a Scottish Court in the Netherlands.[102]

In 1998, the United Kingdom and the Netherlands reached an agreement whereby the latter agreed to hold in its territory trials of the two Libyans accused of complicity in the Lockerbie bombing.[103] The agreement came into force on 8 January 1999. The end of the apparent deadlock proved a welcome relief to the Security Council, which in a resolution passed on 27 August 1999, required all States to co-operate with the arrangement.[104] A significant feature in allowing for the trials to be conducted in the Netherlands was the official endorsement accorded to the agreement by the League of Arab States, the OAU and the OIC. During the years 1994–1997, several communications were advanced, in particular by the OIC, forwarding the idea of trial in the Netherlands and the resolution of the Lockerbie dispute.[105]

---

[99] *Questions of Interpretation and Application of the 1971 Montreal Convention arising from the Aerial Incident at Lockerbie, Libyan Arab Jimahuriya v United Kingdom Judgment* [1998] ICJ Reports 9; *Libyan Arab Jimahuriya v USA* [1988] ICJ Reports 115.

[100] Paras 25–9.

[101] Beveridge, n 62 above, at 658; E Zubel, 'The Lockerbie Controversy: Tension Between the International Court of Justice and the Security Council' (1999) 5 *Annual Survey of International and Comparative Law* 259.

[102] See Letter dated 24 August 1998 from the Acting Permanent Representatives of the United Kingdom of Great Britain and Northern Ireland and the United States of America to the United Nations addressed to the Secretary-General. UN Doc S/1998/795 (1998).

[103] *Agreement between the Netherlands and the United Kingdom Concerning a Scottish Trial in the Netherlands* (1999) 38 ILM 926.

[104] SC Res 1192 (27 August 1999).

[105] Aust, n 95 above, at 284.

The mechanics of the agreement itself were unique in a number of respects. The court, although based in the Netherlands, applied Scots laws in issues regarding the accused, the alleged offender, investigation and pre-trial procedures. However, contrary to Scots law, a trial by jury was not to be conducted. Dutch law was applicable in other respects. The terms of the agreement provided that the Court had wide-ranging powers including significant competence in day-to-day operational matters, and exchange of Letters of Understanding with the Dutch Ministry of Justice. The Netherlands government undertook to allow the entry and protection of witnesses and international observers.

The well-publicised trial of the two accused commenced on 3 May 2000, concluding on 31 January 2001. In delivering its judgment, the Court convicted one of the accused, Al-Megrahi, of the offence of murder in respect of the bombing of the Pan American Flight.[106] The judgment, although detailed in its exposition of evidence and accumulation of fact, did not analyse significant points of law.[107] Notwithstanding large circumstantial evidence against Al-Megrahi, the Court took the view that it established the culpability of the accused beyond reasonable doubt. Al-Megrahi was sentenced to life imprisonment. He appealed against the conviction, which was based on the treatment by the trial court of the evidence that was presented against him and the submissions that were made by the defence. The Appeal Court of High Court of Justifier however turned down his appeal with the case having been officially closed.[108] After considerably protracted negotiations, an agreement was reached between the governments of the US, the UK, Libya and the legal representatives of the relatives of the deceased. The contentious aspects in reaching the agreement had been the level of compensation to be paid by the Libyan government, the level of the withdrawal of sanctions and the acknowledgement of the Libyan government's nuclear and biological weapons programmes.[109]

---

[106] See *Her Majesty's Advocate v Megrahi, No 1475/99*, slip op (High Ct Judiciary at Camp Zeist Jan 31, 2001), reprinted in (2001) 40 ILM 582.

[107] See Bantekas and Nash, n 98 above, at 409.

[108] *Al-Megrahi v HM Advocate*, Opinion in Appeal against Conviction, 14 March 2002 (Appeal No: C104/01).

[109] SR Weisman, 'US will Keep Penalties Against Libya: Officials Say' *New York Times*, 14 August 2003 <http://www.nytimes.com/2003/08/15/international/middleeast/15DIPL.html> (15 April 2004). In the final settlement, the Libyan government agreed to pay each member of the family US $10 million. From this amount, US $4 million was to be paid at the termination of the US sanctions and the outstanding $2 million after the removal of Libya from the US list of State-sponsored terrorism. See SD Murphy 'Contemporary Practice of the United States Relating to International Law: Settlement of Dispute—Libyan Payment to Families of Pan Am Flight 103 Victims' (2003) 97 *American Journal of International Law* 987.

ACCOUNTABILITY FOR TERRORIST OFFENCES

The preceding discussion has established the limits that are placed on judicial legal mechanisms, in efforts to establish accountability and liability for terrorist related offences. As noted earlier, efforts to assign responsibility through judicial mechanisms for the crimes of 11 September have yet to bear fruitful results. The resort to the Security Council and use of political expediency to bomb Afghanistan was a regrettable though not unexpected response of the United States. On previous occasions, the United States has given short shrift to the World Court and other legal mechanisms. Reliance has instead been placed on the executive powers of the Security Council. In the Lockerbie crisis the role of the Security Council was tested by Libya's invocation of the provisions of the Montreal Convention before the ICJ. The Court was asked to review the powers of the Council when exercising jurisdiction under Chapter VII. The response of the Court was feeble, though in the dynamics of power-politics perfectly understandable. As one commentator has appropriately noted:

> ... the *Lockerbie* [case] not only posed the question of the substantive limits to the Security Council's powers, but also crucially involved the issue whether the ICJ has jurisdiction to decide on the legality of the Council's acts. Libya openly challenged the legality of the Security Council's embargo resolutions in *Lockerbie* ... To date the ICJ has been successful in avoiding a straightforward answer to these questions, but it has implicitly exercised some degree of judicial review in some cases by not calling into question, but rather confirming the legality of, acts of the Security Council.[110]

The ultimate outcome of the Lockerbie case, although limited, was nonetheless not unexpected. Once the trials of the two Libyans accused of the bombing were conducted through a mutual agreement between the parties, the parties moved towards a political settlement. As a consequence of the agreement notified to the World Court in September 2003, the case was withdrawn from its docket.[111] The Court was once again spared having to deal with difficult and stressful questions about the balance between legal and political institutions.

---

[110] A Reinisch, 'Developing Human Rights and Humanitarian Law Accountability of the Security Council for the Imposition of Economic Sanctions' (2001) 95 *American Journal of International Law* 851, at 865.

[111] See *Case Concerning Questions of Interpretation and Application of the 1971 Montreal Convention Arising from the Aerial Incident at Lockerbie (Libyan Arab Jamahiriya v United States of America)*, 10 September 2003, General List No 89 <http://212.153.43.18/icjwww/idocket/ilus/ilusorder/ilus_iorder_20030910.PDF> (30 April 2004); also see D Marcella, 'Passport to Justice: Internationalizing the Political Question Doctrine for Application in the World Court' (1999) 40 *Harvard International Law Journal* 81.

MARITIME TERRORISM

Maritime Terrorism and International Law

Under general international law, the crime of piracy has a universal juris-diction allowing any State to prosecute the offenders.[112] The 1958 Convention on the High Seas and the 1982 UN Convention on Law of the Sea list piracy as an offence. Piracy is defined as any of the following acts:

(a) any illegal acts of violence or detention, or any act of depredation, commit-ted for private ends by the crew or the passengers of a private ship or a private aircraft, and directed:

(i) on the high seas, against another ship or aircraft, or against persons or property on board such ship or aircraft;
(ii) against a ship, aircraft, persons or property in a place outside the juris-diction of any State;

(b) any act of voluntary participation in the operation of a ship or of an aircraft with knowledge of facts making it a pirate ship or aircraft;

(c) any act of inciting or of intentionally facilitating an act described in sub-paragraph (a) or (b).[113]

Piracy entails acts of violence against a ship or crew members on board a ship and thus shares significant similarities with maritime terrorism. In reliance upon this, commentators have advocated the application of a common regime for the two offences. However, there are significant dif-ferences. Firstly, piracy requires actions to achieve 'private ends'. Terrorists, by contrast, rely upon political motivations. It is thus highly debatable as to whether the actions of pirates could be regarded as being motivated by political considerations. Secondly, and more problematic, is the 'two-ship' requirement. In circumstances when passengers or their crew use violence on board a ship without outside assistance, it is difficult to satisfy the 'two-ship' requirement.

Although the threat from maritime terrorism has remained real and immediate, international agencies have failed to engage with the subject meaningfully. There has been a scarcity of attention paid to maritime ter-rorism in the provisions of the Conventions: the 1958 Convention on the High Seas and the Law of the Sea Convention contain no special clauses

---

[112] See Article 101 of the Law of the Sea Convention (1982); MN Shaw, *International Law* 5th edn (Cambridge, Cambridge University Press, 2003) at 549–50; OY Elagab, *International Law Documents Relating to Terrorism* (London, Cavendish, 1995) 465.

[113] Article 101 of the UN Convention on the Law of the Sea 1982 UN Doc A/CONF. 62/122 (opened for signature 10 December 1992); See Article 15, Law of the Sea Convention 1958, 29 April 1958, 450 UNTS 82.

regarding terrorism.[114] While a number of instances of maritime terrorism have taken place, it was only the impact of *Achille Lauro* which led to a noticeable international response. The *Achille Lauro* incident also prompted the international community to take concrete action as regards formulating binding standards for protection of ships from terrorists. For the purposes of the present examination, the *Achille Lauro* hijacking is significant for a variety of reasons.[115] There have however been additional acts of terrorism such as the attack on the *USS Cole*. The terrorist attack killed seventeen and injured thirty-nine US soldiers during a fuel stop at the Yemenese port of Eden on 12 October 2000. A further terrorist attack took place in October 2002, when a small fishing vessel packed with explosive materials collided with a French tanker off the coast of Yemen. The resulting explosion and oil spillage into the sea caused grave damage to the environment and marine life.[116]

THE *ACHILLE LAURO* INCIDENT AND ISLAMIC STATE PRACTICES

Four men belonging to the Palestinian Liberation Front, a section of the PLO, hijacked an Italian registered transatlantic liner on 7 October 1985. The hijacking took place when the ship was in international waters, ten nautical miles from the coast of Egypt. At the time of the hijacking the ship was carrying 201 passengers of various nationalities, including 14 Americans and 6 British citizens.[117] Upon taking control of the liner, the hijackers demanded the release of 50 Palestinian prisoners from Israeli prisons. They forced the pilot to direct the ship firstly towards the Syrian port of Tartus. Upon the refusal of the Syrians to allow the ship to dock, the hijackers diverted the ship to Libya. However, the Libyan authorities not only refused to allow the ship to rest in its harbour but also joined

---

[114] See JSC Mellor, 'Missing the Boat: The Legal and Practical Problems of the Prevention of Maritime Terrorism' (2002) 18 *American University International Law Review* 341 at 377.

[115] For detailed consideration of the incident see J McCredie, 'Contemporary Uses of Force against Terrorism: The United States Response to Achille Lauro—Question of Jurisdiction and its Exercise' (1986) 16 *Georgia Journal of Comparative and International Law* 435; MD Larsen, 'The Achille Lauro Incident and the Permissible Use of Force' (1987) 9 *Loyola of Los Angeles Journal of International and Comparative Law* 481; M Halbertsam, 'Terrorism on the High Seas: The Achille Lauro, Piracy, and the IMO Convention on Maritime Safety' (1988) 82 *American Journal of International Law* 269; JJ Paust, 'Extradition and United States Prosecution of Achille Lauro Hostage-Takers: Navigating the Hazards' (1987) 20 *Vanderbilt Journal of Transnational Law* 235; GV Gooding, 'Fighting Terrorism in the 1980s: The Interception of the Achille Lauro Hijackers' (1987) 12 *Yale Journal of International Law* 158; J-P Pancracio, 'L'affaire de L'Achille Lauro et le droit international' (1985) 31 *Annuarie français de droit international* 219.

[116] J Romero, 'Prevention of Maritime Terrorism: The Container Security' (2003) 4 *Chicago Journal of International Law* 597, 598.

[117] Larsen, n 115 above, at 481.

other States in condemning the hijacking.[118] There was also explicit condemnation of the hijacking by the leader of the PLO, Yassar Arafat.
Incensed at the behaviour of Arab States, the hijackers killed a Jewish
American citizen, Leon Klinghoffer. His killing was particularly abhorrent
and revolting since he was elderly and bound to a wheelchair. In the
meantime, an emissary of PLO (Abul Abbas) had arrived in Cairo, Egypt
and communicated with the terrorists. The terrorists forced the ship to
move to Port Said in Egypt, where it cast anchor on 9 October. It was at this
stage that the Egyptian government drafted an arrangement whereby the
hijackers were to be allowed 'safe passage' and handed over to the
Palestinian authorities for any proceedings against them. The Egyptian,
Italian and German governments agreed on this arrangement of safe
passage for the hijackers, although no such agreement was forthcoming
from the United States or British governments.

Upon landing at Port Said, the Egyptians took charge of the four hijackers. The hijackers, along with two representatives (from the PLO, who had
negotiated with the hijackers) were placed on an aircraft bound for
Tunis.[119] The plane never reached Tunis, since the Tunisian authorities
refused landing permission. The plane then attempted to land in Greece,
an attempt that was also unsuccessful because of the Greek government's
refusal to allow the plane to land. The plane then turned back towards
Cairo, but was intercepted by United States fighter aircraft, and forced to
land at the NATO base of Sigonella in Sicily (Italy).[120] The Italian government resisted claims from the Reagan administration to allow the hijackers to be transported to the United States. The Egyptian Boeing carrying
the hijackers was surrounded by Italian soldiers. The Italian assertion was
a valid one since the crimes, although committed in international waters,
took place in an Italian registered vessel. The hijackers were therefore
taken into custody by the Italian administration. At the same time, it was
agreed to allow the two Palestinian negotiators and the crew of the
Egyptian Boeing to return to Egypt. The US made further efforts, albeit
unsuccessful, to obtain custody of the Palestinian negotiators. The terrorists were tried in Italian courts, the trials being held in the Italian Court of
Assizes in Genoa. During the trials, only five out of the fifteen accused
(three hijackers and two of their accomplices) appeared before the court.
The fourth hijacker, being a 17 year old, appeared before a juvenile court.
The three adult terrorists were awarded life sentences, whereas the juvenile terrorist was given a sentence of sixteen years and three months. On
10 May 1988 the Court of Cassation in Italy reconfirmed all the sentences.

---

[118] Cassese, n 1 above, at 29–31.
[119] *Ibid*, at 37.
[120] Larsen, n 115 above, at 482.

EXAMINING THE LEGITIMACY OF THE US USE OF FORCE

The use of force by the United States in the aftermath of the *Achille Lauro* affair generated considerable criticisms. The US intercepted the Egyptian airliner carrying the hijackers, forcing it to land in Italy. There were efforts to forcibly remove the hijackers for trial in the United States. In reviewing this case, the right to self-defence cannot form the basis of the US claim. The US had not been under attack, existing or imminent, nor is it logical to suggest that the interception of the Egyptian airliner was necessary and proportionate in the circumstances.[121] The action of the United States has been justified as legitimate usage of reprisals. It is argued that since Egypt had failed to comply with *aut dedere aut judicare* as provided for in the Hostages Convention, and the United States had been affected by the actions of the hijackers, the forcible interception of the Egyptian airliner was justified.[122] This position is untenable since reprisals can no longer be justified as a legitimate expression of use of force. It is unfortunate that the United States has consistently resorted to the use of force instead of invoking legal and judicial mechanisms.

In the light of the aforementioned observations, it is not surprising that leading international lawyers have criticised the role of the United States in the *Achille Lauro* incident. Commenting on this case, Professor Cassese writes:

> The United States preferred violence to law, leaving behind an unfortunate legacy that has polluted international law and aggravated political and diplomatic relations between states. By setting a dangerous precedent (sooner or later, other states could follow this example) and by trampling on the sovereign rights of two allies, the Americans allowed their emotions to prevail over reason, with negative consequences for all the states involved in the affair.[123]

THE ADOPTION OF THE CONVENTION

Subsequent to *Achille Lauro* saga, the Convention for the Suppression of Unlawful Acts against the Safety of Maritime Navigation was adopted in Rome during March 1988. As was indicated earlier, Egypt, along with Italy and Austria, were the initial sponsors for the drafting of the Convention. In order to shorten what would otherwise be a long and complex process, the Council of the IMO established an Adhoc Preparatory Committee which was to be open to all States with the 'mandate to prepare, on a priority basis, a draft Convention for the suppression of Unlawful Acts

---

[121] *Ibid*, at 484–5.
[122] *Ibid*, at 487–96 .
[123] Cassese, n 1 above, at 80–1.

against the Safety of Maritime Navigation'. The meetings of the Preparatory Committee took place in March and May 1987 in London and Rome respectively. A final text was approved in a conference held in Rome in March 1988.

Amongst the innovative features of the Convention there is within the definition of terrorist offences the inclusion of murder as a separate crime. Although exceptional, when compared to the Convention for the Suppression of Unlawful Seizure of Aircraft (the Hague Convention) and Convention for the Suppression of Unlawful Acts against the Safety of Civil Aviation (the Montreal Convention) the Convention regards murder as a distinct offence. As Halberstam points out, prior to the adoption of the Maritime Convention, it was only the Convention on Internationally Protected Persons which made it an offence to kill or injure a person.[124] This inclusion, as was considered earlier, was prompted directly by the murder of Leo Klinghoffer on board the *Achille Lauro*.[125] Having said that, in order for injury or murder to be established as an offence under the Convention, the act of injury or murder must be in connection with the commission or attempted commission of the acts as stated in Article 1(a) to (f) of the treaty. This Convention has many positive features. It represents the first substantial attempt by the international community to deal with maritime terrorism. The Convention defines a 'ship' as 'a vessel of any type whatsoever not permanently attached to the sea-bed'.[126] The Convention does not cover ships used in military, customs or police service.[127]

According to Article 3(1) of the Convention, any person commits an offence if he unlawfully and intentionally seizes or exercises control over a ship by force or threat thereof or any other form of intimidation; or performs an act of violence against a person on board a ship if that act is likely to endanger the safe navigation of that ship; or destroys a ship or causes damage to a ship or its cargo which is likely to endanger the safe navigation of that ship; or places or causes to be placed on a ship, by any means whatsoever, a device or substance which is likely to destroy that ship, or cause damage to that ship or its cargo or which endangers or is likely to endanger the safe navigation of that ship; or destroys or seriously damages maritime navigational facilities or seriously interferes with their operation, if any such act is likely to endanger the safe navigation of a ship; or communicates information which he knows to be false, thereby endangering the safe navigation of a ship; or injures or kills any person, in connection with the commission or the attempted commission of any of the offences set forth in subparagraphs (a) to (f).

---

[124] Halberstam, n 115 above, at 294.
[125] M Halbertsam, 'Terrorist Acts Against and on Board Ships' (1989) 19 *Israel Yearbook of Human Rights* 331 at 333.
[126] Article 1.
[127] Article 2.

The jurisdictional basis for the Convention is extensive and covers territorial as well as high seas.[128] Equally, Article 4 provides that the treaty is applicable to ships navigating or scheduled to navigate into, through or from waters beyond the outer limit of the territorial sea of a single State, or the lateral limits of its territorial sea with adjacent States, or when the alleged offender is found in the territory of a State party.

According to Article 6 of the Convention, each State party is obliged to take the necessary measures to establish jurisdiction over the offence when it is committed against or on board a ship flying its flag at the time of the offence, when the offence took place in its territory; by a national of that State or where its nationals have been targeted; where the offence is committed by a stateless person habitually resident in its territory; or where the offence has been committed to compel the State to do or to abstain from taking a particular course of action. Upon obtaining the custody of an alleged offender, the State where the alleged offender has been found remains under an obligation to ensure that all necessary arrangements for criminal proceedings or extradition are instituted.[129] These provisions are further strengthened by the *aut dedere aut judicare* obligations as stated in Article 10(1) of the Convention.

HUMAN RIGHTS CONCERNS

When reviewing the provisions of the Maritime Terrorism Convention, a prominent feature is the relevance of human rights law to the prevention and suppression of terrorist acts. The preamble to the Convention makes reference to the right to life, liberty and security of persons as enunciated in the International Bill of Rights. It condemns terrorism as a violation of fundamental human rights and points to situations arising out of colonialism, racism and those 'involving mass and flagrant violations of human rights. . .'. The text of the Convention also shows significant concern for human rights. As noted above, the drafting and adoption of the treaty was influenced by the callous murder of a civilian. The Convention also attempts to protect the rights of the alleged offender. According to Article 10(2):

> Any person regarding whom proceedings are being carried out in connection with any of the offences set forth in article 3 shall be guaranteed fair treatment at all stages of the proceedings, including enjoyment of all the rights and guarantees provided for such proceedings by the law of the State in the territory of which he is present.

---

[128] Article 4.
[129] Article 7(1).

While endorsing the values of human rights, an arguably positive feature of the convention is that it does not per se provide exemptions on the basis of the 'political offence' exception. This approach needs to be applauded since, as we have already examined in our conceptual survey, 'political offence' exceptions can forestall all meaningful efforts towards accountability of individuals involved in terrorist acts.[130] We have noted in an earlier chapter the complicated issues raised with the defence of 'political offences'. The 1988 Maritime Convention provides that these acts 'shall be deemed to be included as extraditable offences'[131] in cases where an extradition treaty exists between States, thereby implying that these acts cannot be subject to the 'political offence' exemption.[132] The absence of an extradition treaty means that any extradition is 'subject to the . . . conditions provided for by the law of the requested State'.[133] This discretionary approach towards the domestic constitutional system, however, retains the risk of States not responding to extradition requests, instead relying upon exemptions such as the 'political offence' clauses.[134]

Within the Convention, a number of articles are dedicated to the prevention of acts of maritime terrorism. According to Article 13, States parties are required to exchange information and are obliged to co-operate in the prevention of offences by undertaking all practical measures to prevent preparations for the commission of offences within or outside of their territory. The obligation to provide and exchange all relevant information is reiterated in Articles 14 and 15 of the treaty.

At the time of approving the Convention in March 1988, a Protocol was also adopted. This Protocol addresses acts committed against 'fixed platforms', fixed platforms being defined as an artificial island, installation or structure permanently attached to the sea-bed for the purpose of exploration or exploitation of resources or for other economic purposes. The offences under the Protocol are almost identical to those under the Rome Convention, differing only in so far as is necessary to take into account the differences between ships and such platforms.[135] Despite the many positive features of the Convention and the Protocol on Maritime Terrorism, a number of weaknesses have been pointed out. These instruments do not deal with State-terrorism. Nor do they provide for universal jurisdiction, the absence of which is likely to generate problems where either the State is not a party to the treaty or the offence is committed by a

---

[130] See above, chapter 3.
[131] Article 11(1).
[132] A Cassese, 'The International Community's "Legal" Response to Terrorism' (1989) 38 *International & Comparative Law Quarterly* 589, at 594.
[133] Article 11(2)(3).
[134] Cassese, n 132 above, at 594.
[135] Article 2.

national belonging to the State not party to the treaty.[136] Furthermore, in instances where States have become parties, the Convention and the Protocol place no obligation to search for alleged terrorists. Commenting on this lacuna in the Convention, Cassese makes the valid point that:

> the [1988 Convention] imposes no specific obligation to search for suspects believed to be present in the territory of a State party. As regards arrest, the Convention merely requires a State to arrest suspects 'upon being satisfied that the circumstances so warrant' and 'in accordance with its law'. In this it repeats the language used in a number of earlier treaties, the 1970 Hague Convention, the 1971 Montreal Convention and the 1973 and the 1979 New York Conventions. States are thus left a large measure of discretion to decline to arrest suspects for reasons more 'political' than 'evidential'.[137]

ISLAMIC STATES' INVOLVEMENT WITH THE MARITIME CONVENTION

The geographical proximity and the vast coastline endowed to the Islamic world necessitate a compulsive interest in maritime affairs. Islamic States have been at the forefront of developing maritime laws and laws of the sea. Repulsion and criticism of acts of piracy and maritime terrorism are therefore a natural response from the Islamic world. As examined earlier, the seizure of *Achille Lauro* was condemned unequivocally by all Islamic States. While the hijackers formed a disparate segment of the PLO, the act itself was unauthorised and was censured by Yassar Arafat, the head of the PLO. After the tragedy, the subject as well as the incident was considered extensively both by the United Nations General Assembly[138] and the International Maritime Organisation.[139] During the Fifty-seventh Session of the International Maritime Organisation Council in June 1986, Egypt, alongside Austria and Italy, advanced the proposal of drafting a specific convention dealing with maritime terrorism.[140]

The *travaux préparatoires* of the drafting stages of the Convention reflect a considerable imprint of the advocacy by Islamic States. A number of Arab States were anxious to ensure greater accountability for acts of maritime terrorism. Both Kuwait and Saudi Arabia advanced ambitious proposals expanding the ambit of liability. According to the Kuwaiti proposal, individuals were to be held accountable quite regardless of whether they were acting on behalf of their governments. The Kuwaiti proposal

---

[136] CC Joyner, 'Suppression of Terrorism on the High Seas: The 1988 IMO Convention on the Safety of Maritime Navigation' (1989) 19 *Israel Yearbook of Human Rights* 343 at 365.

[137] See Cassese, n 132 above, at 595–6 (footnotes omitted).

[138] UN GA Res 40/61, 40 UN GAOR Supp No 53, UN Doc A/40/53 (1986).

[139] IMO Doc C57/25, 1 October 1985.

[140] See IMO Doc C57/DWP.1, para 25(a)(2) (12 November 1986).

called for an amendment to Article 3 incorporating liability for an individual 'whether acting on his own initiative or on behalf of a government'. If approved, the revised Article would have read as follows: '[a]ny person, whether acting on his own initiative or on behalf of a government, commits an offence if that person unlawfully and intentionally . . . commits any of the prohibited actions'.[141] The primary objective of the proposal as elaborated by the Kuwait delegate was to ensure the applicability of the Convention to persons who have committed an offence albeit on behalf of their governments. The proposal, according to the Kuwaiti representative, did not alter matters of State responsibility but was only intended to strengthen individual personal liability.[142] This proposal remained contested as many delegates considered it superfluous. Individual liability was already expressly contained in the provisions of the Convention. Instead the concern was that an additional reference to the State may discourage ratifications, and it was ultimately left out.

Further radical proposals were advanced by the Saudi delegation which were aimed at expanding the scope of liability to individuals as well as governments.[143] The Saudi delegate suggested that in conferring responsibility the revised Article 3 should read, 'Any ordinary person or *government* commits an offence . . .' An additional proposal from the Saudis noted that, 'States whose naval forces . . . committed any of the offences shall' inform the Secretary-General of the 'measures taken to put an immediate end to such offence'. These proposals, however, proved to be controversial and were likely to ignite the debate about the criminal liability of States. In the end, these proved unacceptable to the delegates.[144] Lamenting the exclusion of the Kuwaiti and Saudi proposals on State liability, Professor Joyner makes the observation that:

> The Convention defines an impermissible offence as one being committed by natural persons. It fails to treat offences that might be perpetrated by governments, ie State-sponsored terrorism. An argument can be made that the Convention would have been improved—though the negotiations undoubtedly would have been more protracted—if the provision had been made for State parties to take concerted legal sanctions against governments that support unlawful activities.[145]

Islamic States were also at the forefront of restricting the extradition of individuals whose State of nationality did not have formal diplomatic relations with the State requesting such extradition. In an earlier chapter, we noted the success of Jordan in having such a provision incorporated in

---

[141] See IMO Doc PCUA 2/5, 2 June 1987, at 12, para 65.
[142] *Ibid*, at 13 (para 68).
[143] See IMO Doc PCUA 1/3, 3 (26 February 1987).
[144] *Ibid*, Article 12.
[145] Joyner, n 136 above, at 365.

the Hostages Convention.[146] These efforts were primarily designed to prevent Arab nationals being extradited to Israel, with which Arab States have refrained to have diplomatic relations. The Kuwaiti attempt in the Maritime Convention to have similar provisions incorporated, however, failed. Kuwait, in its efforts to have its submission approved, had suggested that these provisions reflected customary international law or norms of *jus cogens*, submissions which were ultimately rejected.[147]

CONCLUSIONS

Aerial and maritime terrorism represent substantial threats to civilised societies. Notwithstanding the tragedy of 11 September and the more recent threats to civil aviation, the pressures on air transportation are enormous. Aerial travel has become a virtual necessity in the twenty-first century. Although the international community has adopted a range of instruments, our examination has exposed substantial defects in the substantive provisions as well in compliance with the relevant treaties. One significant shortcoming is the requirement that the aircraft must have been intercepted in international territorial jurisdiction for the treaty regulations to be applicable. With the enormous growth in domestic air travel, the ambit of 'terrorism' must necessarily be expanded to apply in such instances. A further procedural problem is one of lack of full compliance with *aut dedere aut judicare* requirements; there is strength in the argument that some States have appeared less than fully committed in the application of this principle. In order to ensure that the perpetrators of international terrorism are brought to justice, it is incumbent upon States themselves to conduct proper investigations, extradite individuals or submit cases for prosecution. A final point relates to the operational difficulties in the dispute settlement mechanisms contained in the aerial terrorism treaties. As the Lockerbie incident confirms, States—certainly those with political leverage—have been keen to sideline the arbitration and judicial mechanism contained in the treaties. These States, instead of keeping faith with judicial settlements provisions provided in the treaties, have relied upon the Security Council to coerce the other party into submission. Such an approach is problematic; not only does it bring the Council into a conflicting position with the legal mechanisms, it is also an endorsement for political views of the powerful States to prevail over legal considerations.

Maritime terrorism, in contrast to acts of sabotage against civilian airliners, has received rather limited attention. The Maritime Convention and

---

[146] See Article 9(1)(b)(ii) Hostages Convention.
[147] Halbertsam, above n 125, at 338–9.

the Protocol attached to it were a response to the seizure of the *Achille Lauro* and the tragic murder of one of its passengers. The Convention and the Protocol have established a number of useful principles in dealing with maritime terrorism. That said, the Convention has been considered problematic for 'its reactive, as opposed to preventative nature'.[148] For States such as the United States, maritime terrorism is a real, unfortunate prospect. With a coastline of 88,633 miles, and over 350 seaports providing nearly 75 per cent of United States national trade, its vulnerability to terrorism remains obvious. Furthermore, there is little in the Convention that would prevent a tragedy similar to 9/11 taking place on a large-scale cruise-liner.

[148] Mellor, above n 114, at 384.

6

Financing of International Terrorism

INTRODUCTION

FINANCING OF INTERNATIONAL terrorism raises problematic and troubling issues. Modern day terrorists are reliant upon finances, which depending on the scope of their offences can reach astronomical proportions. At the same time, as the events of 11 September demonstrate, grave acts of terror can be conducted without having to rely upon huge caches of funds and materials. While dependence upon at least some material and financial support remains critical for conducting successful operations, the detection of financial avenues through which terrorism is supported poses greater complexities. Terrorists are likely to have the means and ability to utilise myriad options to exploit financial markets and institutions to support their own ends. As one commentator notes:

> [t]he synchronized suicide attacks of September 11, 2001, highlighted the critical role financial and logistical support networks play in the operations of international terrorist organisations. The Challenge in tackling these networks, however, is that they are entrenched, sophisticated, and often shrouded in a veil of legitimacy (such as operating under the camouflage of purportedly charitable and humanitarian activity).[1]

With both State and non-State actors involved in committing offences, terrorism can be supported by financial dealings of private agents, banks and other monetary institutions. The scrutiny of funds raised through donations, charities,[2] charitable trusts,[3] smuggling, drug trafficking[4] and

---

[1] M Levitt, 'Iraq, US and the War or Terror: Stemming the Flow of Terrorist Financing: Practical and Conceptual Challenges' (2003) 27 *The Fletcher Forum of World Affairs* 59 at 60.

[2] See GA Res 51/210 adopted 17 December 1996, para 3(f).

[3] See UK Charities Commission, Iran Aid (10 December 2001) available at: <www. charity-commission.gov.uk/investigations/inquiryreports/iran.asap> (20 March 2004). In accordance with Sections 15 and 16 of the Terrorism Act 2000, the UK authorities are required to criminalise fund-raising and use and possession of funds directed for terrorist purposes; CP Walker, *Blackstone's Guide to Anti-Terrorism Legislation* (Oxford, Oxford University Press, 2002) 68–74.

[4] S Leader and D Wiencek, 'Drug Money: The Fuel for Global Terrorism' (2000) 12 *Jane's Intelligence Review* 49; AP Schmid, 'The Links Between Transnational Organized Crimes and Terrorist Crimes' (1996) 2 *Transnational Organised Crime* 40.

money laundering[5] present considerable challenges to domestic as well as international financial institutions.[6] Individual States have attempted to curb the international financing of terrorism through sanctions or other coercive measures, although often with insignificant success.[7]

The present chapter examines the work of the United Nations and its agencies in combating the financing of international terrorists. Although critical to the investigation, the narrow focus of the study does not allow an assessment of the work of such key organisations as the World Bank, the International Monetary Fund,[8] the International Organisation of Securities Commission,[9] the regional organisations and G–20.[10] Similarly the new stringent laws introduced by the US[11] and the UK[12] will be assessed only in so far as they impinge upon the Muslim Diaspora. In pursuit of this study's overall purpose, the chapter does however provide an

---

[5] See Financial Action Task Force [FATF] Report on Money Laundering Typologies (2000–2001), Doc FATF-XII, at 19–20 (1 February 2001).

[6] I Bantekas, 'The International Law of Terrorist Financing' (2003) 97 *American Journal of International Law* 315 at 316.

[7] See above, chapters 4 and 5. On the background of international economic sanctions see BE Carter, *International Economic Sanctions: Improving the Haphazard US Legal Regime* (Cambridge, Cambridge University Press, 1988); GC Hufbauer *et al*, *Economic Sanctions Reconsidered: History and Current Policy* (Washington, DC, Institute for International Economics, 1985).

[8] See Report by the International Bar Association's Task Force on International Terrorism, *International Terrorism: Legal Challenges and Responses* (Ardsley, NY, Transnational Publishers, 2003) 123–4.

[9] See S Chenumolu, 'Revamping International Securities Law to Break the Financial Infrastructure of Global Terrorism' (2003) 31 *The Georgia Journal of International and Comparative Law* 385.

[10] The organisation, which consists of nineteen States, the European Union, the International Monetary Fund and the World Bank, reviews global policy with the objective of providing international financial stability. See G20 Finance Ministers and Central Bank Governors, available at <http:www.g20.org. org/news/003-e.html> (17 November 2001). See B Zagaris, 'G20 Nations Agree to Freeze Terrorist Assets and IMF will Provide Technical Aid' (2002) 18 *International Enforcement Law Reports* 29.

[11] See the provisions of the Uniting and Strengthening America by Providing Appropriate Tools Required to Intercept and Obstruct Terrorism Act of 2001, Pub L No 107–56, 115 Stat, 272 [USA Patriot Act of 2001]. Title III of the Act provides details of the role of the financial institutions in the fight against terrorism (International Money Laundering Abatement and Financial Anti-Terrorism Act of 2001, Pub L No 107–56, at III). These institutions are protected from civil liability in case they reveal details of suspicious transactions (*Ibid*, tit III S 351). The USA Patriot Act also enhances the government's powers to freeze Assets and in some cases its extra-territorial jurisdiction (S 317(2)(3)) and S 311). The Act also expands the existing laws relating to the curbing of money-laundering (See Money Laundering: Anti-Terrorism Legislation Enacted Containing Money Laundering Provisions, 33 Sec Reg & L Rep 1532 (2001). Through the application of Presidential Executive Order 13224, seventy-nine financial accounts were frozen during the period between 11 September and 6 December 2001. Bantekas, n 6 above, at 329; B Zagaris, 'Financial Aspects of the War on Terror: The Merging of the Counter-Terrorism and Anti-Money Laundering Regimes' (2002) 34 *Law and Policy International Business* 45.

[12] See J Rehman, 'International Terrorism and Muslim Minorities in Europe: Islamophobia after 9/11 (2005) 3 *European Yearbook of Minority Issues* 217.

insight into Islamic financial and economic institutions. After 11 September 2001, Islamic financial institutions have come under increasing scrutiny and criticism and it is important to assess the validity of these criticisms.

THE UNITED NATIONS AND ATTEMPTS TO CURB FINANCING OF INTERNATIONAL TERRORISM

Operations of the General Assembly, the World Court and the Security Council

The events of 11 September 2001 highlighted the debate surrounding the financing of terrorism. Even prior to the attacks in the US, the international community was conscious of the relevance of finances in perpetuating acts of terrorism.[13] In our earlier analysis we alluded to the General Assembly Resolution adopted in 1994, in which the Assembly referred to the conventional methods of the financing of international terrorism which included drug trafficking, unlawful arms trading, money laundering, and smuggling of nuclear materials.[14] A further resolution, Resolution 51/210, was adopted by the General Assembly in 1996, which required States to take steps through their constitutional and administrative frameworks to stop the funding of terrorist organisations. The Resolution prohibits terrorist funding through all possible means including charitable contributions, drug dealing, racketeering, and the movement of capital funds.[15] In a further Resolution, the General Assembly emphasised the significance of preventing and prohibiting the financing of terrorism; it urged Member States to adopt its earlier Resolution 51/210.[16] The major achievement of the General Assembly was, however, the adoption of the International Convention for the Suppression of the Financing of Terrorism in 1999. The various facets of the Convention are of enormous potential in terms of the efforts to suppress international and regional terrorism.

---

[13] See S Chenumolu, n 9 above, at 385.

[14] See UN GAOR 49th Sess 84th Plen Mtg Supp No 49, at 303 (UN Doc A/Res/49/60 (1994)). See chapter 3 above.

[15] See Measures to Eliminate International Terrorism, UN GAOR, 51st Sess UN Doc A/RES/51/210 (1996), paras 3 and 5.

[16] The Assembly '[Reiterated] its call upon all States to adopt further measures in accordance with the relevant provisions of international law, including international standards of human rights, to prevent terrorism and to strengthen international cooperation in combating terrorism and to that end, to consider in particular the implementation of the measures set out in paragraphs 3(a) to (f) of its resolution 51/210'; and the Assembly '[Reiterated] its call upon States to refrain from financing, encouraging, providing training for or otherwise supporting terrorist activities'. Measures to Eliminate Terrorism, UN GAOR, 53rd Session A/RES/53/108 (1998).

In general international law, financing of terrorism per se has historically not been addressed as a specific cause to trigger the right to self-
defence. Although no firm principles have yet been established, the
concern with financiers of terrorism is becoming evident in the jurisprudence on the use of force. The World Court referred to the subject in the
Nicaragua case.[17] In this case, the Court, by a majority of twelve votes to
three, decided that:

> the United States of America, by training, arming, equipping, financing and
> supplying the *Contra* forces or otherwise encouraging, supporting and aiding
> military and paramilitary activities in and against Nicaragua, has acted, against
> the Republic of Nicaragua, in breach of its obligations under customary inter-
> national law not to intervene in the affairs of another State.[18]

In common with the General Assembly, the Security Council has addressed
the subject of financing terrorism in a number of its resolutions. As has been
examined in our analysis of aerial terrorism, the Council passed various resolutions against Libya for its support of terrorism. These sanctions were
placed against Libya for its apparent support of international terrorism,
including financial and material support of the terrorists.[19] In 1996, the
Council called upon Sudan to desist from supporting or assisting those terrorists attempting to assassinate the Egyptian President during his visit to
Ethiopia.[20] There was a heavy condemnation by the Council of terrorism in
the aftermath of the bombing of the US embassies in Kenya and Tanzania.[21]
The Security Council required all States to desist from providing support to
terrorist organisations. The Council also addressed the issue of acquiescence of the Taliban government in allowing Bin Laden and al-Qaeda to
operate in Afghanistan in its Resolution 1214. Through Resolution 1267, the
Security Council established a committee with the task of collating a list of
Taliban entities, including those which were owned or controlled, indirectly
or directly, by the Taliban.[22] In its Resolution 1269, the Council specifically
referred to 'terrorist financing', acknowledging the role of the State in shel-
tering, financing, funding, and a failure to adopt preventative mechanisms
for the engagement of terrorist organisations.[23]

---

[17] See *Nicaragua Case (Merits)* [1986] ICJ Reports 14.
[18] *Ibid*, para 292(3). Judges Oda, Schwebel and Sir Robert Jennings dissented. For
commentaries see TD Gill, 'The Law of Armed Attack in the *Nicaragua* Case' (1988) 1 *Hague
Yearbook of International Law* 30; JL Hargrove, 'The Nicaragua Judgment and the Future of the
Law of Force and Self-defence' (1987) 81 *American Journal of International Law* 135; RStJ
MacDonald, 'The Nicaragua Case: New Answers to Old Questions?' (1986) 24 *Canadian Year
Book of International Law* 127.
[19] SC Res 748 (31 March 1992) <http://www.geocities.com/CapitolHill/5260/ 748.html>
(30 April 2004). Also see provision of Security Council SC Res 883 (11 Nov 1993). See above,
chapter 5.
[20] SC Res 1054 (26 April 1996).
[21] *Ibid*.
[22] SC Res 1267, para 4(b) (15 October 1999).
[23] SC Res 1269 (19 October 1999).

In a subsequent Resolution, Resolution 1333, the Council demanded that the Taliban:

> cease the provision of sanctuary and training for international terrorists and their organisations, take appropriate and effective measures to ensure that the territory under its control is not used for terrorist installations and camps, or for the preparation or organisation of terrorist acts against other States or their citizens, and cooperate with international efforts to bring indicted terrorists to justice.[24]

In the post 11 September 2001 era, the allied campaign against the Taliban under the auspices of Security Council Resolutions 1368 and 1373 has allowed the financing of terrorism to be established as a separate cause of action.[25] Security Council Resolution 1373, in particular, has had a profound role to play in scrutinising the financing of international terrorism.[26] Within Resolution 1373, the focus on the prevention of financing of terrorism has been so sharp that it has sometimes been mistakenly regarded as being exclusively directed at financial aspects of terrorism.[27] With a mandate established under Chapter VII, the Council decided that all States shall prevent and suppress financing of all forms of terrorist acts.[28] States, under this Resolution, are required to criminalise the deliberate provision or collection of funds with the intention or knowledge that they are to be used for any terrorist purposes.[29] States are also required to immediately freeze the assets of persons engaged in terrorist acts.[30] States are also to adopt and implement the existing international instruments (including ratification of the International Convention for the Suppression of the Financing of Terrorism) and in so doing undertake to carry out all possible efforts to suppress the recruitment of new members by terrorist organisations and eliminate their weapons supply.[31]

States are under an obligation to deny safe haven to those who finance terrorists, and to bring to justice all those engaged in the financing of terrorism.[32] The Resolution requires States to offer one another assistance for criminal investigation and proceedings related to the financing or support of terrorist acts.[33] States are to prevent the movement of terrorists or their groups by effective border controls. The Council also determined that States shall intensify and accelerate the exchange of information regarding

---

[24] SC Res 1333 para 1 (19 December 2000).
[25] Bantekas, n 6 above, at 317.
[26] *Ibid.*
[27] See E Rosand, 'Security Council Resolution 1373, the Counter-Terrorism Committee, and the Fight Against Terrorism' (2003) 97 *American Journal of International Law* 333, at 334.
[28] SC Res 1373 para 1(a) (28 September 2001).
[29] *Ibid*, para 1(b).
[30] *Ibid*, para 1(c).
[31] *Ibid*, para 3(a)–(g).
[32] *Ibid*, para 2(c).
[33] *Ibid*, para 2(f).

terrorist actions or movements; forged or falsified documents; traffic in arms and sensitive materials; use of communications and technologies by terrorist groups; and the threat posed by the possession of weapons of mass destruction.[34] In addition, States are required to exchange information and co-operate to prevent and suppress terrorist acts and to take action against the perpetrators of such crimes.[35] The Council, pursuant to Chapter VII of the UN Charter, established the Counter-terrorism Committee. All States were required to submit initial reports on the steps they had taken to implement the provisions of the Resolution to the Committee within 90 days of the Resolution being adopted (28 September 2001). The reporting procedures, as set out in this Resolution, have on the whole proved to be a success. Furthermore, the information emerging out of these reports has been particularly revealing in ascertaining Islamic State practices in prohibiting the financing of international terrorism.[36] Subsequent resolutions of the Security Council have affirmed both the substantive principles as well as the implementation mechanisms installed in Resolution 1373.[37]

COMBATING FINANCING OF TERRORISM: THE INTERNATIONAL CONVENTION FOR THE SUPPRESSION OF THE FINANCING OF TERRORISM (1999)

Obligation to Establish Financing of Terrorism Offences under Domestic Law

With increasing concerns centred around the role of finances, the Convention represents the first concerted effort to curb the financing of terrorist activities. As indicated earlier, prior to the adoption of this treaty, the General Assembly had already condemned the financing of terrorism in a number of its resolutions. The preamble to this Convention makes reference to the 1994 and 1996 General Assembly Resolutions. According to the Convention, a person commits an offence if by any means directly or indirectly, unlawfully or wilfully he provides or collects funds with the intention that these should be used or in the knowledge that they are to be used, in full or in part, in order to carry out:

---

[34] *Ibid*, para 3(a).
[35] *Ibid*, para 3(b).
[36] For a review of the work of the Counter Terrorism Committee see <http://www.un. org/Docs/sc/committees/1373/> (22 September 2004); MN Shaw, *International Law* 5th edn (Cambridge, Cambridge University Press, 2003) at 1051–2.
[37] See SC Res 1390 (adopted 16 January 2002); SC Res 1452 (adopted 20 December 2002).

[a]ny of the offences established under instruments listed in the Annex to the Convention;[38]

or

[a]ny other act intended to cause death or serious bodily injury to a civilian or to any other person taking an active part in a situation of armed conflict when the purpose of such an action is that of intimidating a population, or compelling a government or an international organisation to do or to abstain from doing any act.[39]

In order for the provisions listed in Annex A to be operative, the relevant State party needs to have ratified the treaty in question. Since the nine conventions contained in the Annex do not cover the whole range of terrorist offences, it was felt necessary to fill that lacuna by including what is, in effect, an additional definition of terrorism.[40] The purpose of the latter clause is to enlarge the scope of the Convention to include the myriad forms of terrorism. However, the twin-track definition leads to the rather odd result that acts of financing covered by the mini-definition will be an offence under the Convention, even though many of the substantive acts themselves will not be offences under the other conventions.[41] Those actively engaged in financing terrorism, those conspiring, aiding, or abetting such activities also commit criminal offences.[42] State parties are

---

[38] The instruments presently listed in Annex A are as follows:

Convention for the Suppression of Unlawful Seizure of Aircraft (1970);
Convention for the Suppression of Unlawful Acts against the Safety of Civil Aviation (1971);
Convention on the Prevention and Punishment of Crimes against Internationally Protected Persons, including Diplomatic Agents (1973);
International Convention against the Taking of Hostages (1979);
Convention on the Physical Protection of Nuclear Material (1980);
Protocol for the Suppression of Unlawful Acts of Violence at Airports Serving International Civil Aviation, supplementary to the Convention for the Suppression of Unlawful Acts against the Safety of Civil Aviation (1988);
Convention for the Suppression of Unlawful Acts against the Safety of Maritime Navigation (1988);
Protocol for the Suppression of Unlawful Acts against the Safety of Fixed Platforms located on the Continental Shelf (1988);
International Convention for the Suppression of Terrorist Bombings (1997).

Article 2(2) provides that, on depositing its instrument of ratification, acceptance, approval or accession, a State Party which is not a party to a treaty listed in the Annex may declare that, in the application of this Convention to the State Party, the treaty shall be deemed not to be included in the Annex. The declaration shall cease to have effect as soon as the treaty enters into force for the State Party, which shall notify the depositary of this fact.

Similarly, the declaration can also be made in the unlikely event that a Party to the Convention ceases to be bound to any of the nine conventions.

[39] Article 2(1) and (2).

[40] This additional definition is provided by Article 2(1)(b).

[41] See *Implementation Kits for the International Counter-Terrorism Conventions* (London, Commonwealth Secretariat, 2002) 270. Website: <http://www.un.org/unodc/terrorism_documents.html> (30 July 2004).

[42] See *Washington Report* by the United Nations Association of the United States of America (UNA—USA) 27 April 2002; website: <http://www.unausa.org/newindex.asp?place> <http://www.unausa.org/policy/> News ActionAlerts/info/dc042202.asp (15 March 2004).

therefore obliged to establish offences of attempting to commit, participate in, organise, direct, or contribute to the commission of financial terrorism.[43] The Convention makes clear that such offences can be committed both by natural persons and by legal persons.[44]

It is for the first time in the UN international counter-terrorism conventions that the scope of the treaty is extended to legal persons. According to Article 5 of the Convention, an obligation is imposed upon States parties to hold legal persons liable 'when a person responsible for the management or control of that legal entity has, in that capacity, committed' an offence as stated in Article 2 of the Convention.[45]

While the Convention requires intention or knowledge that terrorism is being financed, it is not necessary to prove that the funds were actually used to carry out a specific financing offence.[46] This provision, although patently sensible, could in practice create difficulties in establishing proof that a specific sum of money was used to finance a particular terrorist offence, or even category of offences. As subsequent discussion reveals, in a number of cases, religious, national or charitable institutions could perform acts which in part support forms of terrorism or aggression.

The Convention preserves the principle of State sovereignty as the provisions of Article 3 restrict the application of the Convention to offences where there is an international element, for example, where the offender or victim is a non-national of the territorial State or there are other extra-territorial factors for seeking jurisdiction. This particular aspect has been highlighted by Trahan as potentially problematic.[47]

As noted above, Article 5 extends, for the first time in terrorism related instruments, to legal as well as natural persons. Liability is dependent on a person 'responsible for the management or control' of the entity having 'in that capacity' committed a financing offence. The provisions require that liable entities must be subject to 'effective, proportionate and dissuasive criminal, civil or administrative sanctions . . . includ[ing] monetary sanctions'.[48] Article 6 requires that such offences cannot be justified by considerations of a political, philosophical, ideological, racial, ethnic, religious or other similar nature; these explicit considerations seem to be designed to prevent the courts taking into account the motives of offenders when passing sentence.

---

[43] Article 2(2).
[44] Articles 2(1), 5.
[45] Article 5(1).
[46] Article 2(3).
[47] See J Trahan, 'Terrorism Conventions: Existing Gaps and Different Approaches' (2002) 8 *New England Journal of International and Comparative Annual* 215, at 227.
[48] Article 5(3).

Obligation to Establish Jurisdiction, to Detect and Freeze Funds

State parties are required to establish jurisdiction over those offences which are committed in their territory, or on board a vessel flying their flag or an aircraft registered under their laws at the time the offence is committed, or by their nationals.[49] The Convention also allows, but does not oblige, State parties to establish jurisdiction over the offences in a number of other circumstances where there is a connection between the offence, or the offender, and the State party concerned.[50] State parties are obliged to identify, detect and freeze or seize any funds used or allocated for the purpose of committing the offences, as well as the proceeds derived from such offences. Identified funds and proceeds are subject to forfeiture. States are obligated to consider using forfeited funds to compensate victims of the offences set out in the Convention. The Convention requires that these obligations be implemented without prejudice to the rights of third parties acting in good faith.[51] The Convention also requests, but does not oblige, State parties to conclude agreements on sharing with other State parties, on a regular or case-by-case basis, of the funds derived from the above forfeitures.[52]

Obligation to Extradite or Prosecute Alleged Offenders Found in the Territory

The Convention creates obligations on States parties with a view to ensuring the investigation and prosecution of any alleged offender. Parties are required to investigate allegations that a person in their territory has committed a Convention offence and, if the outcome of the investigation so warrants, to take measures to ensure that person's presence for the purpose of prosecution or extradition.[53] A State party in which an alleged offender is present has jurisdiction in respect of the offence, and is obliged to prosecute the alleged offender, unless the alleged offender is extradited.[54] The Convention, therefore, and in common with other terrorism treaties, provides for the application of the principle of *aut dedere aut judicare*.[55]

Article 10(2) provides that, if the law of the requested party requires that extradition of its own nationals can only be done on the condition that the

---

[49] Article 7(1).
[50] Article 7(2).
[51] Article 8(1)(2)(4)(5).
[52] Article 8(3).
[53] Article 9(1)(2).
[54] Article 10(1).
[55] Article 10.

convicted person is returned to serve any sentence imposed, and such condition is agreed by the requesting party, conditional extradition is sufficient to discharge the obligation in Article 10(1). Article 11(1) requires State parties to deem the Convention offences to be included as extraditable offences in extradition treaties they have with other State Parties. State parties further undertake to include such offences in new extradition treaties to be subsequently concluded between them.

Those State parties that do not make extradition conditional on the existence of a treaty, commit to recognise the Convention offences as extraditable offences between themselves, subject to the conditions provided by the law of the State to which the request was made (Article 11(3)). In cases where a State party makes extradition conditional upon the existence of a treaty and another State party requests an extradition when there is no extradition treaty in force, then the Convention may be considered as a legal basis for the extradition (Article 11(2)). The State Party that finally prosecutes the alleged offender must communicate the outcome of the proceedings to the Secretary-General of the United Nations, who will transmit the information to the other State parties.[56]

Obligation to Provide Assistance in the Prosecution of Alleged Offenders

The Convention obliges State parties to co-operate with each other in relation to investigations, extradition and mutual legal assistance concerning the Convention offences, and lays down conditions for such co-operation. In particular, the Convention prevents State parties refusing requests for mutual legal assistance on the ground of bank secrecy, or for extradition or mutual legal assistance on the sole ground that it concerns a fiscal offence or a political offence. It nevertheless preserves the right of State parties to refuse requests for extradition or mutual legal assistance if they have substantial grounds for believing that the request has been made for the purpose of prosecuting or punishing a person on account of that person's race, religion, nationality, ethnic origin or political opinion or that compliance with the request would cause prejudice to that person's position for any of these reasons.[57]

There are instances where a person is in the custody of one State party although his presence is requested by another State party. In such instances, the State party having custody is required to assist in the investigation or prosecution of Convention offences and to allow the transfer if the person freely consents and the competent authorities of both States

---

[56] Article 19.
[57] Articles 12–15.

agree.[58] The State to which the person is transferred is obliged to keep that person in custody, unless the transferring State requests or agrees otherwise, and to return the person to the transferring State's custody without requiring extradition proceedings. The person transferred must receive credit for service of the sentence being served in the transferring State for time spent in the custody of the State to which he was transferred.[59] The transferred person cannot be prosecuted or detained in the territory of the State to which he is transferred in respect of acts or convictions prior to his departure from the territory of the transferring State, unless the transferring State agrees otherwise.

The Convention confirms the rights of a person detained pursuant to the Convention in a foreign country to consular assistance and the right of any State party having a claim to jurisdiction to invite the International Committee of the Red Cross to communicate with and to visit the alleged offender.[60] The Convention also provides for guarantees of fair treatment, including enjoyment of all rights and guarantees in conformity with the law of the State in the territory of which that person is present and applicable provisions of international law, including international human rights law.[61]

Obligation to Co-operate in Preventing Convention Offences

State Parties are obliged to co-operate in the prevention of the Convention offences by taking all practicable measures.[62] Such measures would include inter alia prohibiting illegal activities of persons and organisations that knowingly encourage, instigate, organise or engage in the commission of a Convention offence, and better customer identification procedures for financial institutions. State parties are further obliged to consider supervisory measures for all money-transmission agencies and measures to track cross-border transportation of cash and bearer negotiable instruments. State parties are required to exchange accurate and verified information in accordance with their domestic law and to co-ordinate administrative and other measures to prevent the commission of a Convention offence.[63] In accordance with the provisions of Article 18, special attention needs to be paid to unusual or suspicious transactions. These would include transactions having a complex or unusual pattern or

---

[58] Article 16(1).
[59] Article 16(3).
[60] Article 9(3)(4)(5).
[61] Article 17.
[62] The suggested measures are based on *The Forty Recommendations of the Financial Action Task Force* (FATF) <www.oecd.org/fatf/40Recs_en.htm> (25 September 2004). Although expressed as obligations, they are only obligations to 'co-operate'.
[63] Article 18(1)(2)(3).

those that do not appear to have an economic or lawful purpose.[64] If the beneficiaries are unidentifiable, accounts are not to be opened.[65] Financial institutions are under an obligation to make concerted efforts to identify account owners.[66] If the title of an account is held by a legal entity, then the financial entity must verify its proof of incorporation from a public register or from the customer.[67] Under the Convention, financial institutions are required to report suspicious activities of customers without fear of civil and criminal liability.[68] Actions taken in good faith are therefore a defence and customer confidentiality may be breached without the risk of litigation. Finally, Article 18(4) requests States parties to exchange information through the International Criminal Police Organisation (Interpol).

Savings Clauses and Dispute Settlement

The Convention includes a number of savings clauses to safeguard the sovereignty of State parties and preserves existing provisions of international law. Article 20 obliges State parties to carry out their obligations under the Convention in a manner consistent with the principles of sovereign equality and territorial integrity of States and that of non-intervention in the domestic affairs of other States. Article 3, as noted earlier, provides that the Convention does not apply where the offence has no transnational element, with the exception of the provisions on law enforcement co-operation, judicial assistance and prevention. Article 21 confirms that nothing in the Convention affects other rights, obligations and responsibilities of States and individuals under international law, in particular the purposes and principles of the Charter of the United Nations and international humanitarian law. Article 22 further confirms that nothing in the Convention entitles a State party to undertake in the territory of another State party the exercise of jurisdiction and performance of functions, which are exclusively reserved for the authorities of that other State party by its domestic law. Any dispute arising between two or more State parties to the Convention which cannot be settled through negotiation shall, at the request of one of the States involved in the dispute, be submitted to arbitration. If, within six months, the parties cannot agree on the organisation of the arbitration, any of the State parties involved may refer the dispute to the International Court of Justice.[69] Article 24(2) allows States to

---

[64] Article 18(1)(b).
[65] Article 18(1)(b)(i).
[66] Article 18(1)(b)(ii).
[67] Article 18(1)(b).
[68] Article 18(1)(b)(iii).
[69] Article 24(1).

declare, when they sign or ratify the Convention, that they are not bound by the dispute settlement provision in Article 24(1). The other State parties will consequently not be bound by Article 24(1) with respect to any State party which has made such a reservation. Article 24(3) provides that any State which has made a reservation in accordance with Article 24(2) may at any time withdraw that reservation by notification to the Secretary-General of the United Nations.

Treaty Action

In accordance with Article 26(1), the Convention entered into force on 23 May 2001, which was the thirtieth day following the date of the deposit of the twenty-second instrument of ratification, acceptance, approval or accession with the Secretary-General of the United Nations. For each State ratifying, accepting, approving or acceding to the Convention after the deposit of the twenty-second instrument of ratification, acceptance, approval or accession, the Convention shall enter into force on the thirtieth day after deposit by such State of its instrument of ratification, acceptance, approval or accession.[70] The Convention is open to accession by any State that did not sign it by 31 December 2001.[71] The instrument of accession must be deposited with the UN Secretary-General.[72] A party may denounce the Convention by written notification to the Secretary-General of the United Nations; denunciation shall take effect one year following the date on which notification is received by the Secretary-General of the United Nations.[73]

Article 23 provides for the addition of related treaties to the Annex. According to the article the annex may be amended by the addition of relevant treaties that:

(a) are open to the participation of all States;
(b) have entered into force;
(c) have been ratified by at least twenty-two State parties to the Convention.

After the entry into force of the Convention, any State party may propose such an addition to the UN Secretary General who, if the proposal meets the above conditions, will seek the views of the other State parties. The proposal is adopted after 180 days, unless one third of the State parties object to it within that time. An adopted amendment to the Annex enters into force for all those State parties that deposited an instrument of

[70] Article 26(2).
[71] Article 25(1).
[72] Article 27.
[73] Article 8(1)(2)(4)(5).

ratification relating to the amendment thirty days after twenty-two State parties have ratified the amendment. For each State party ratifying the amendment after the deposit of the twenty-second instrument, the amendment enters into force on the thirtieth day after deposit by such State party of its instrument of ratification.

The Convention is silent on the question of amendment of its terms, apart from the Annex. Consequently, the provisions of Article 40 of the Vienna Convention on the Law of Treaties would apply to amendments.[74] With the exception of the dispute settlement provision in Article 24, the Convention is otherwise silent on the question of reservations to its provisions. As with general amendments to the Convention, the provisions of Section 2 of the Vienna Convention on the Law of Treaties would thus apply to the question of reservations.

Appreciating the Diversity of Islamic Legal and Financial Systems

Islam's relationship with the financing of terrorist acts has been the subject of considerable contemporary debate: an issue, no doubt, augmented by the financial and material support provided by Usama Bin Laden to al-Qaeda. Whilst there are points of reflection and the application of certain Islamic principles require a review, it would be imprudent and wholly unfair to castigate the Muslim faith as supporting terrorism and violence.[75] A mature analysis of the subject highlights both the distinctions of Islamic ideology in financial matters, and the rationale for adopting such differing approaches.[76] Islam is not simply a religion, but aims to provide a complete code of moral, social, political, economic and financial behaviour. The *Sharia* sets out guidelines for banking and finance; it integrates religion with economics.[77] On the face of it, the Islamic position appears to contrast strikingly with global liberal economies which dissociate religion

[74] See the Vienna Convention on the Law of Treaties (1969) (adopted on 22 May 1969, entered into force 27 January 1980) UKTS 58 (1980); Cmnd 7964; 1155 UNTS 331; (1969) 8 ILM 679.

[75] See SP Huntington, *The Clash of Civilizations and the Remaking of World Order* (London, Simon & Schuster, 1996) 263–5.

[76] See H Moinuddin, *The Charter of the Islamic Conference and Legal Framework of Economic Cooperation Among its Member States: A Study of the Charter, the General Agreement for Economic, Technical and Commercial Co-operation and the Agreement for Promotion, Protection and Guarantee of Investments Among Member States of the OIC* (Oxford, Clarendon Press, 1987); A Saeed, *Islamic Banking and Interest: A Study of the Prohibition of Riba and its Contemporary Interpretation* (Leiden, Brill, 1999); SA Meenai, *The Islamic Development Bank: A Case-Study of Islamic Cooperation* (London and New York, Kegan Paul International, 1989); JM Taylor, 'Islamic Banking—The Feasibility of Establishing an Islamic Bank in the United States' (2003) 40 *American Business Law Journal* 385.

[77] See generally G Bilal, 'Islamic Finance: Alternatives to the Western Model' (1999) 23 *Fletcher Forum of World Affairs* 145 at 146; CN Khan, 'Commonwealth of Muslim States' (1963) *Voices of Islam* 41; M Ahmad, 'Umma—The Idea of a Universal Community' (1975) *Islamic Studies* 27.

from business—an ethos and ideology upon which modern financial institutions such as the International Monetary Fund (IMF), the World Bank and the World Trade Organization (WTO) are established. For the critics of the Islamic economic system, a significant point of confusion and concern is the apparent difficulty in applying the Islamic prohibition on *riba* within modern international banking.[78] In their survey of Islamic State practices they also show disquiet over labour and environmental standards, a reluctance to democratise the political and economic systems, an apparent endorsement of human rights violations, and in many cases support of terrorist acts.

In responding to these concerns a number of factors need to be considered. Firstly, from earlier discussion it is clear that the breadth and diversity of the *Sharia* principles have allowed Islamic States not only to accept modern international economic, environmental, labour and human rights regulations, but in a number of instances to advance them to suit the needs of the modern world.[79] An overwhelming majority of Islamic States approve existing human rights standards including international treaties on the rights of women and children. The Convention on the Rights of the Child has been adopted by all Islamic States save for Somalia.[80]

It is also significant that no Islamic State has made reservations to Article 32 of the Convention on the Rights of the Child[81] or to Article 10(3)[82] of the International Covenant on Economic Social and Cultural Rights (1966)[83] provisions which deal with the economic and social

---

[78] See Saeed, n 76 above, at 12–37.
[79] See chapter 2, above.
[80] See the Convention on the Rights of the Child (1989) (adopted 20 November 1989, entered into force 2 September 1990) 1577 UNTS 3, (1992) UKTS 44, Cmnd 1976.
[81] According to Article 32:

   (1) States Parties recognise the right of the child to be protected from economic exploitation and from performing any work that is likely to be hazardous or to interfere with the child's education, or to be harmful to the child's health or physical, mental, spiritual, moral or social development.
   (2) States Parties shall take legislative, administrative, social and educational measures to ensure the implementation of the present article. To this end, and having regard to the relevant provisions of other international instruments, States Parties shall in particular: (a) Provide for a minimum age or minimum ages for admission to employment; (b) Provide for appropriate regulation of the hours and conditions of employment; (c) Provide for appropriate penalties or other sanctions to ensure the effective enforcement of the present article.

[82] According to Article 10(3): The States Parties to the present Covenant recognise that . . . Special measures of protection and assistance should be taken on behalf of all children and young persons without any discrimination for reasons of parentage or other conditions. Children and young persons should be protected from economic and social exploitation. Their employment in work harmful to their morals or health or dangerous to life or likely to hamper their normal development should be punishable by law. States should also set age limits below which the paid employment of child labour should be prohibited and punishable by law.

[83] International Covenant on Economic Social and Cultural Rights (adopted 16 December 1966, entered into force 3 January 1976) 993 UNTS 3; (1977) UKTS 6. See DS Ehrenberg, 'The

exploitation of children. A strong support for the Convention on the Elimination of All Forms of Discrimination against Women is similarly forthcoming.[84] The acceptance of the broad principles of international law and the ratification of treaties is not to suggest that the approaches adopted by Islamic States are identical to those of other States. On the contrary, as the numerous reservations to international treaties confirm, there remains the potential of substantial departure. However, these differences or disagreements are not an unusual feature of general international law. Modern treaty law expressly authorises States to enter reservations, whereas consent and acquiescence is the essence of customary law. In the more specific context of international economic law, regional and international organisations have accepted reservations and exceptions in trading policies, including exceptions on moral or religious grounds.[85] The present study has attempted to challenge any possible nexus between terrorism and the *Shaira* per se. The same argument could be applied in relation to the financing of terrorist acts. Although there are stresses and strains within Islamic ethos whereby on occasions the lines between financial support of Muslim *Ummah* in self-defence and funding acts of violence have become blurred, that does not represent a complete picture. In reality, the essence of Islam is in opposition to both the substantive acts of terrorism and the financing of these actions.

El-Ayouty's point is a valid one:

> co-operation in terrorism is anti-Islamic. The likes of Bin Laden believe that financing terror activities is a worthy contribution to the cause of Islam. But the Koran says, 'spend your wealth for the cause of Allah'. The terrorists also claim that pan-Islamic cooperation in terrorist activities accords with Islam. It is not at all, as Islam specifically prohibits conspiring for criminal activities. The Koran says, 'help ye one another unto righteousness and pious duty. Help not one another unto sin and transgression'. The objective of cooperation between Muslims is to attain the common good and to ward off injustice.[86]

The Prohibition of *Riba* in the Islamic Banking System

The Islamic banking system's prohibition of *riba* evokes considerable controversy. Critics contend that it is impossible for investors and financiers

Labor Link: Applying the International Trading System to Enforce Violations of Forced and Child Labor' (1995) 20 *Yale Journal of International Law* 361.

[84] Convention on the Elimination of All Forms of Discrimination against Women (adopted 18 December 1979, entered into force 3 September 1981) (1982) Misc 1, Cmnd 8444; (1981) 19 ILM 33.

[85] See S Charnovitz, 'The Moral Exception in Trade Policy' (1998) 38 *Virginia Journal of International Law* 689; PM Nichols, 'Trade without Values' (1996) 90 *North Western University Law Review* 658.

[86] See Y El-Ayouty, 'International Terrorism under the Law' (1999) 5 *ILSA Journal of International and Comparative Law* 485, at 490, citing a verse from the *Qur'an* 5: 2.

to operate in the banking and financial world without reliance upon usury. Suggestions have been made about the incompatibility of Islamic laws with modern financial regimes.[87] In this context, the apparent incompatibility between the *Sharia* and the modern banking system is exaggerated. Two significant points—first a jurisprudential one and second a substantive one—need to be noted. Firstly, amongst Islamic jurists substantial disagreements exist as to the precise meaning of *riba* and its applicability within the modern socio-legal environment.[88] Abduallah Saeed summaries these disagreements in the following manner:

> There are two predominant views concerning riba. Many Muslims would contend that the interpretation of riba as provided in [Islamic law] is the proper interpretation and so must be followed. This interpretation implies that any increase charged in a loan transaction over and above the principal is riba. For others, the prohibition of riba is understood as relating to the exploitation of the economically disadvantaged in the community by the relatively affluent. This element of exploitation may or may not actually exist in modern bank interest. These Muslims would argue that the interpretation of riba in [Islamic legal] literature is inadequate and does not take into consideration the moral intent of the prohibition as expounded in, or inferred from, the Quran and Sunna.[89]

The latter view is reinforced by Islamic jurists arguing that the *raison d'être* for the prohibition of *riba* is injustice, as formulated in the *Qur'anic* statement, *'la tažlimuna wa-la tažlumun'* (Do not commit injustice and no injustice will be committed against you).[90] One leading scholar, Muhammed Asad, has argued in favour of business and commercial transactions with interest attached to those transactions. He points out that:

> the opprobrium of riba (in the sense in which this term is used in the Qu'ran and in many sayings of the Prophet) attaches to profits obtained through interest-bearing loans involving an exploitation of the economically weak by the strong and resourceful . . . With this definition in mind, we realise that the question as to what kind of financial transactions fall within this category of riba is, in the

---

[87] For detailed consideration of the subject see Saeed, n 76 above; ND Ray, *Arab Islamic Banking and the Renewal of Islamic Law* (London, Graham and Trotman, 1995); FE Vogel and SL Hayes III, *Islamic Law and Finance: Religion, Risk and Return* (The Hague, Kluwer Law International, 1998); CH Kennedy, 'Judicial Activism and Islamization After Zia: Toward the Prohibition of Riba' in CH Kennedy (ed), *Pakistan: 1992* (Boulder, Col, Westview Press, 1993) 57–74.

[88] HP Glenn, *Legal Traditions of the World: Sustainable Diversity in Law* (Oxford, Oxford University Press, 2000) at 169–70.

[89] Saeed, n 76 above, at 17.

[90] *Ibid.* Concern for welfare and prevention of abuse in the society are justifications provided for the prohibition. Taylor makes the point that '[a]rising out of the Islamic tenet of concern for community flow the anti-abuse concepts applicable in financial affairs. The primary example of this anti-abuse concept is the Qur'anic prohibition of riba' Taylor, n 76 above, at 389; BL Seniawski, 'Note—Riba Today: Social Equity, the Economy and Doing Business under Islamic Law' (2001) 39 *The Columbia Journal of Transnational Law* 701, at 708.

last resort, a moral one, closely connected with the socio-economic motivation underlying the mutual relationship of borrower and lender.[91]

Attached to this jurisprudential feature is the fact that the *Qur'an* (the principal source of the *Sharia*) only regards *riba* as *haram* or forbidden; usury is taken as a purely civil matter, the transaction akin to an unenforceable or invalid contract.[92] Secondly, on the substantive front, an examination of Islamic banking systems confirms that the abolition of interest on loans and investments does not mean an end to all the profit and gains which an investor or lender could legitimately expect. Islamic law has devised detailed mechanisms in the nature of *Mudaraba* and *Musharaka* as an alternative to interest based banking. *Mudaraba* is essentially a contract between two parties, the investor (*rabb al-mal*) and the contractor (the *mudarib*), the objective of the contract being a trade or a joint venture between the parties. In return for the investing capital on the part of the *rabb al-mal*, the *mudarib* contributes his labour and time to the joint venture. It is an essential requirement of the *Mudaraba* agreement that the profit should be shared between the two parties on a pre-agreed proportional basis. Losses, however, are borne only by the investor.[93] The *Musharaka* business venture is similar in nature to *Mudaraba*, although in the case of *Musharaka* all the parties act as partners and investors in the venture. The profits and losses of each of the partners are borne in accordance with their respective investments. Amongst the numerous positive features in the investments based on *Mudaraba* and *Musharaka*, the more apparent ones are the direct and caring involvement of the investor (or the lender), the sharing of responsibilities and a more equitable system of distributing profits and losses. According to a World Bank official:

> Whereas the conventional system focuses primarily on the economic and financial aspects of transactions, the Islamic system places equal emphasis on the ethical, moral, social and religious dimensions, to enhance equality and fairness for the good of society as a whole. The system can be fully appreciated only in the context of Islam's teachings on the work ethics, wealth distribution, social and economic justice and the role of the state.[94]

While recent experimentation by the Islamic Development Bank and by a number of States including Egypt, Saudi Arabia and Pakistan has resulted

---

[91] M Asad, *The Message of the Qur'an* (Gibraltar, Dar al-Andalus, 1984) at 633.

[92] NJ Coulson, *A History of Islamic Law* (Edinburgh, Edinburgh University Press, 1964) 11–12.

[93] Saeed, n 76 above, at 51; AA El-Ashker, *The Islamic Business Enterprise* (London, Wolfboro, NH, Croom Helm, 1987) 75; NA Saleh, *Unlawful Gain and Legitimate Profit in Islamic Law: Riba, Gharar and Islamic Banking* (Cambridge, Cambridge University Press, 1986) 103.

[94] Z Iqbal, 'Islamic Financial Systems' (1997) 34 *Finance and Development* 42, at 42. Also see V Sundararajan *et al*, 'Monetary Operations and Government Debt Management under Islamic Banking' Working Paper of the International Monetary Fund, September 1998, WP/98/144.

in increased administration and costs, the essential principles behind the Islamic banking systems are attractive and compare favourably to the economic policies being pursued by the western world.[95]

Islamic Financial and Charitable Institutions

In the aftermath of the tragic events of 11 September 2001, considerable scepticism has been generated regarding Islamic financial institutions and charitable institutions. Such scepticism strikes at the very core of Islamic values, for this is a religion whose foundational principles rely heavily upon charity, compassion and egalitarianism. Prophet Mohammed, himself a posthumous child (the Prophet's father having died before his birth) as well as an orphan, cherished ideals of supporting the poor and the needy.[96]

Indeed, so strong has been the urge to build an egalitarian and more equal society that Islam prescribes one of its principal tenets—the so called five pillars—the obligation to pay *Zakat*: a tax on wealth. The *Zakat* is payable on a variety of property, including savings and investments, produce, saleable property and precious metals.[97] The tax payments are compulsory and are required from all adults who can afford to pay them. There are frequent references to *Salaat* (prayer) in conjunction with *Zakat* within the *Qur'an*, a feature highlighting the significance of *Zakat*.[98] According to the Holy *Qur'an* there are huge rewards for those who offer *Zakat*. It notes that:

> [t]he case of those who spend their wealth in the cause of Allah is like that of a grain of corn, which grows seven ears, and in each ear there are a hundred grains. Allah multiplies it even more for whomsoever He pleases.[99]

The *Qur'an* also identifies the recipients of the *Zakat*. In addition to the poor and the needy, *Zakat* needs to be distributed to those operating in the cause of Allah, the *Sabil Allah*.[100] The distribution of funds and monies *fi Sabil Allah*, in particular for the propagation of *Jihad*, raises disconcerting

---

[95] The Islamic System 'gives the provider of money a strong incentive to be sure he is doing something sensible with it. What a pity the west's banks did not have that incentive in so many of their lending decisions in the 1970s and 1980s. It also emphasises the sharing of responsibility, by all the users of money. That helps to make the free-market system more open: you might say more democratic'. *The Economist* 6 August 1994 at 10–11.

[96] R Landau, *Islam and the Arabs* (London, George Allen and Unwin Ltd, 1958) 34; CG Weeramantry, *Islamic Jurisprudence: An International Perspective* (London, Macmillan Press, 1988) 3.

[97] MN Siddiqi, *Muslim Economic Thinking: A Survey of Contemporary Literature* (Jeddah, International Centre for Research in Islamic Economics, King Abdul Aziz University, 1981) 61–3. Weeramantry, n 96 above, at 59–60.

[98] See FM Denny, *An Introduction to Islam* (New York, Macmillan Press, 1994) 124–6.

[99] The *Qur'an* (2: 262).

[100] The *Qur'an* (9: 60).

issues, leading to a re-examination of the core values of *Jihad*. As discussed earlier, *Jihad* entails supporting actions in the cause of Allah, including the provision of financial and material support. Examples of such support could be the funding of religious and charitable institutions such as *Madrisas* (religious schools) or the repatriation of Muslim refugees.[101] There are, however, controversial aspects attached to this debate which allow, for example, the financing of armed militia in Chechnya, Palestine and Kashmir.

Historically, Muslims have felt at ease in making contributions to Islamic charities as part of or in addition to the compulsory *Zakat*. Many of the Islamic charities and charitable institutions have traditionally been non-registered: this non-registered status has generated considerable misgivings about their activities. In the aftermath of 11 September 2001, various US and UK based charities were banned and their accounts were frozen. In its report on a London based charity, Iran Aid, the UK Charity Commission established the following findings: misleading promotional literature and high pressure sales techniques; failure to maintain proper accounting records; transfer of the charity's proceeds to a middleman outside the charity's designated target country who was unqualified to handle such amounts; the inability of the trustees to explain why certain funds were missing; and the illegal destruction of records.[102]

The *Hawala* System

In addition to the distinct economic banking systems, Islamic societies have adopted divergent and informal patterns of transfer of financial assets. A modern contemporary strategy of transferring monies is the so-called the *hawala* system. The *hawala* system has a variety of meanings, ranging from 'to change or transform' (Arabic), 'trust' (Hindi), 'transfer of money between two persons through a third person' (non-Arabic Muslim), to 'reference' (Urdu).'[103] The *hawala* banking system has been adopted by many Islamic communities established in the western industrialised world. As an informal though highly reliable means of transfer of cash and other assets, the system often proves to be highly useful (particularly in Europe and North America) for white-collar migrant workers who are unaware of the technicalities of western models of banking. The system of *hawala*, however, remains a subject of suspicion and intrigue;

---

[101] On *Madrisas* see above, chapter 2.
[102] See UK Charities Commission, Iran Aid (10 December 2001) available at <www.charity-commission.gov.uk/investigations/inquiryreports/iran.asap> (17 January 2002).
[103] Comments made by A Lambert, in FN Baldwin Jr, 'Organised Crime, Terrorism, and Money Laundering in the Americas' (2002) 15 *Florida Journal of International Law* 3, at 13.

this is an unfortunate development since the system has great value and is extremely reliable.[104] A number of criticisms have been raised as regards the *hawala* system; some of these are genuine, while others form part of the overall malaise and suspicion generated against the Islamic communities since the events of 11 September 2001. According to Lambert:

> [W]hy all the fuss over hawala banking? As with virtually all financial systems in place today, wherever the opportunity exists, they are hijacked and abused by drug traffickers, corrupt officials, and other major criminals eager to find a way of laundering or moving their ill-gotten gains away from the prying eyes of the authorities and law enforcement. In the case of hawala, there is no require- ment about meeting the requirements of identification, providing information on the source of funds, or record keeping. In recent times, evidence has been obtained to show that the hawala network has been used to funnel money to terrorist groups in the disputed Kashmir valley, as a conduit for funding the 1998 bombings of US embassies in Kenya and Tanzania. According to a Pakistani-based CIA agent, he used the hawala system to funnel money to muja- hadin guerrillas fighting the Soviets in Afghanistan, to launder money for the Cali and Medellin drug cartels from Colombia, to provide finance for the trafficking of humans and obviously to finance the attacks of September 11th.[105]

According to another commentator,

> [s]ubsequent to September 11 events, European and US enforcement authorities targeted numerous alternate remittance, or underground banking systems, known as *hawala*, which operate as unlicensed banks and are used to transfer money around the world with little regulation. Although these networks are used primarily by Muslims to send money to relatives, authorities believe they also serve as vehicles to launder money, traffic in drugs and arms and finance terrorists. The US Federal Bureau of Investigation specifically linked some of these networks to bin Laden, prompting President George W Bush to adopt Executive Order 13,224, by which he ordered the closure of these operations and the financial starvation of terrorist organizations.[106]

9/11 AND IMPLICATIONS FOR ISLAMIC COMMUNITIES AND INSTITUTIONS

A highly disturbing feature is that since 11 September 2001, Islamic organ- isations and individuals have been under scrutiny. In the aftermath of the tragedy in America, the US administration has listed dozens of organisa- tions and individuals allegedly linked to terrorist organisations.[107] These include anti-Israeli groups such as *Hamas*, *Hizbollah* and the *Palestinian*

---

[104] See Report by the International Bar Association's Task Force on International Terrorism, n 8 above, at 119.

[105] Lambert cited in Baldwin, n 103 above, at 14.

[106] Bantekas, n 6 above, at 320; also see Zagaris, n 11 above, at 45.

[107] *Ibid* at 52.

Islamic Jihad (Shaqaqi faction).[108] While the immediate past of all these organisations has been tainted with violence, critics of the US policy condemn the banning of the organisations as part of the pro-Zionist campaign to annihilate the Palestinian cause.

The definition of terrorism and the identification of terrorists have clearly been problematic for Islamic States. There remains a major debate on the position of such organisations as *Anasar-al-Islam, Hizbollah*, and the *Palestinian Islamic Jihad*. The US has recently placed these organisations on its list of proscribed groups, and has required that their financial assets be frozen.[109] On the other hand, many Arab and Islamic States regard *Hizbollah* and the *Palestinian Islamic Jihad* as genuine liberation movements. Amongst the organisations, institutions and agencies whose assets have been frozen are those who have provided invaluable support to Muslims in distress, and there is little concrete evidence that they have supported terrorism. One example is that of the Rabita Trust, a Pakistani charity with the current President of Pakistan, General Prevaiz Musharraft, as one of its members.[110] The Rabita Trust is well known for its contribution to the rehabilitation of Biaharis in Bangladesh.[111] Other examples include Arab multi-national companies such as *Al Barakaat* and *Al Taqwa* with businesses in over forty countries. While the US has accused these two organisations of assisting al-Qaeda (and with the active support of other States have frozen their assets), vehement denials are presented by the directors of these organisations.

The linking of individuals and organisations with al-Qaeda and the freezing of their assets has already been the subject of legal challenges in various jurisdictions.[112] In the United Kingdom, a challenge was brought forward by Mr Yassin Kadi (also known as Yasin al-Qadi) before the High Court in London. His name was included in the list produced by the US and UK governments on 11 October 2001.[113] In the present proceedings

---

[108] See Redesignation of Foreign Terrorist Organisations, Press Statement (Revised) Richard Bulter, Washington DC, US Department of State, 2 October 2003 <http://www.state.gov/r/pa/prs/ps/2003/24851.htm> (30 July 2004).

[109] See Foreign Terrorist Organisations: Designation of Ansar-al-Islam (AI), Redesignation of three others. Press Statement Richard Boucher, Spokesman, Washington DC, US Department of State, 22 March 2004 <http://www.state.gov/r/pa/prs/ps/2004/30649.htm> (2 August 2004).

[110] See 'UK Takes Steps to Freeze More Terrorist Assets' (12 October 2001) <http://www.hm-treasury.gov.uk/newsroom_and_speeches/press/2001/press_110_01.cfm> (30 July 2004); also see A Gillan, 'Funding: Assets of 39 More Individuals and Organisations Are Frozen: Addresses in London on New List' *The Guardian* 13 October 2001 at 5.

[111] See J Rehman and N Roy, 'South-Asia' in Minority Rights Group (ed), *World Directory of Minorities* (London, Minority Rights Group, 1997) 545–7.

[112] See S Schmemann, 'Swedes Take up the Cause of 3 on US Terror List' *New York Times* 26 January 2002 at A9 (describing the stance adopted by Swedish public and government and the unhappiness generated at the freezing of assets of three Somali-born and Swedish Naturalised citizens).

Mr Kadi, a Saudi businessman, has challenged the governments over the seizure and freezing of his assets for his alleged links with al-Qaeda. In his petition, Mr Kadi alleges inter alia that the UK government has breached the provisions of the Human Rights Act 1998 by depriving him of the use and enjoyment of his properties and interfering 'in a most grave and serious' way with his private life.[114] The European Union, through its Terrorism Framework Decision has also engaged in the freezing of assets of individuals and organisations.[115] Actions undertaken in pursuance of these regulations have led to serious objections and lawsuits; they undermine civil liberties and minority rights and clearly generate further risk of Islamophobia.[116] The picture is depressing and reflects the concerns expressed by the International Bar Association's Task Force, when it notes:

> The effect on the right of individuals whose assets are frozen either through specific legislation or inclusion on a list is profound. Therefore it is of particular concern that neither the relevant Security Council resolutions nor the guidelines published by the CTC establish a minimum legal framework regulating the process of asset freezing. In effect, states that introduce these measures often protect the secrecy of the information they possess. The opportunity to challenge the state's action is therefore restricted as persons affected by freezing orders and the like simply have no information as to the basis of the order, and

[113] See 'UK Takes Steps to Freeze More Terrorist Assets' <http://www.hm-treasury.gov.uk/newsroom_and_speeches/press/2001/press_110_01.cfm> (30 July 2004).

[114] 'Saudi Fights Asset Freeze' *The Guardian* 13 November 2001 <http://politics.guardian.co.uk/attacks/story/0,1320,592493,00.html> (22 September 2004); J Burns, 'Court Fight over Frozen Assets' *Financial Times* 9 November 2001 at 4; see also Testimony of Mathew Epstein with Evan Kohlmann Before the House Committee on Financial Services Sub-Committee on Oversight and Investigations 'Progress Since 9/11: The Effectiveness of US Anti-Terrorist Financing Efforts' at <http://financialservices.house.gov/ media/pdf/031103me.pdf> (30 July 2004).

[115] See Council Framework Decision in Combating Terrorism, 13 June 2002, 2002 OJ (L 164); Council Common Position of 27 December 2001 on the Application of Specific Measures to Combat Terrorism, 2001 OJ (L 344) updated subsequently by Council Common Position of May 2, 2002; Council Common position of June 17, 2002, updating Common Position 2001/931/CFSP on the Application of Specific Measures to Combat Terrorism and Repealing Common Position 2002/340/CFSP(2002) OJ (L 160) 32–5; Council Common Position of 28 October 2002, updating Common Position 2001/931/CFSP on the Application of Specific Measures to Combat Terrorism and Repealing Common Position 2002/462/CFSP, 2002 OJ (1.295) 1–4 and by Council Common Position of 12 December Measures to Combat Terrorism and Common Position 2002/931/CFSP on the Application of Specific Measures to Combat Terrorism and Repealing Common Position 2002/847/CFSP 2002 OJ (L 337) 93–6 and Council Regulation (EC) No 2580/2001 on Specific Restrictive Measures directed against Certain Persons and Entities with a View to Combating Terrorism, 2001 OJ (L 344) 70–5 amended by Commission Regulation (EC) No 2580/2001 on Specific Measures Directed Against Certain Persons and Entities with a View to Combating Terrorism, 2003 OJ (L 106), 22–3 and as currently implemented by Council Decision of 12 December, 2002 implementing Article 2(3) of Council Regulation (EC) No 2580/2001 on Specific Restrictive Measures directed against Certain Persons and Entities with a view to Combating Terrorism and repealing Council Decisions 2002/848/EC, 2002 OJ (L 337) 85–6.

[116] See *Aden and Others v Council and Commission* T–306/01 R_1; J Wouters and F Naert, 'The European Union and "September 11"' (2003) 13 *Indiana International and Comparative Law Review* 719, 729.

are thus disadvantaged in any challenge they make to the orders affecting them. Whilst it is accepted that there may be security reasons for failing to provide certain information, this must be balanced by the need of the individuals to protect themselves from such draconian measures . . . The freezing of assets has the potential to irreparably damage financial interests, as well as to stigmatise a person's name and reputation.[117]

CURBING THE FINANCING OF TERRORISM AND ISLAMIC STATE PRACTICES

The significance of the OIC has been highlighted throughout this study. While a focused analysis of the OIC's position, including a detailed examination of its Convention on Combating International Terrorism can be found in a subsequent chapter, some limited references are nevertheless essential in the present context.[118] The OIC has taken a special interest in combating the financing of terrorism. The 1999 Convention on Combating International Terrorism states that 'all forms of international crimes, including illegal trafficking in narcotics and human beings, money laundering, aimed at financing terrorist objectives, shall be considered terrorist crimes'.[119] According to Article 3, Member States are obliged not to 'participate in any form of . . . financing . . . terrorist acts whether directly or indirectly'.[120] Member States are also required to prohibit activities related to the financing of terrorism within their border.[121]

During its consideration of the provisions of 'areas of Islamic cooperation for preventing and combating terrorist crimes',[122] Article 4 requires States parties to 'undertake to promote exchange of information among them as such regarding: activities and crimes committed by terrorist groups . . . [and their] means and sources that provide finance[s] . . .'[123] Member States are also required to share information that may 'contribute to confiscating any . . . funds spent or meant to be spent to commit a terrorist crime.'[124] The Convention therefore provides a fundamental basis for addressing the financing of international terrorism.[125] There is a significant amount of convergence in Islamic financial institutions with those of the western world.[126] In addition to attempts at the multilateral

---

[117] See Report by the International Bar Association's Task Force on International Terrorism, n 8 above, at 126–7.
[118] See chapter 7 below.
[119] Pt I, Article 2(d).
[120] Pt II, Article 3(1).
[121] Pt II, Article 3(A)(1).
[122] *Ibid*, Division II.
[123] Division II, Article 4(1)(a).
[124] *Ibid*, Article 4(4)(b).
[125] See Chenumolu, n 9 above, at 414.

level, individual Islamic States have made considerable endeavours to introduce transparency in financial systems as well as eradicating all forms of international terrorism. The UAE, for example, has called for increasing transparency in financial undertakings and strict compliance with international standards.[127]

In its report on the implementation of Security Council Resolution 1373 (2001) Albania made reference to a number of laws in its Penal Code to combat the financing of terrorism. It referred to Article 287/a of Law No 8733 dated 24 January 2001 'On some amendments in the Law No 7895, dated 27.01.1995 of the Penal Code of the Republic of Albania'.[128] In addition reference was made to Articles 44/2 and 45/3 of Law 8365, dated 02.07.1998 'On the Banks in the Republic of Albania'.[129] The objective of these Penal enactments, according to the Albanian government, is the 'sequestration and confiscation of assets or bank accounts pertaining to a criminal offence as well as any related benefit (Article 30 and 36 of the Penal Code of the Republic of Albania and Article 274 of the Code of Criminal Procedure)'.[130] In its report the Albanian government also noted special measures of freezing bank accounts for up to thirty days of those suspected of money laundering under the Law entitled 'On Prevention of Money Laundering'.[131]

In Algeria, fund-raising activities must be authorised in advance in accordance with Ordinance 77.03 of 19 February 1977. Any breach is punishable by one month to two years of imprisonment.[132] In response to concerns of diversion of funds to terrorist organisations, the Bangladesh government noted that approval of government is:

> mandatory to receive donations from abroad as per foreign Donations (Voluntary activities) Regulation Ordinance, 1978. The existing rules of the country also do not permit to mobilize funds (donations or other similar funds) for making remittances outside the country. There is strict Central Bank supervision to identity and monitor unusual and unwarranted transactions in the individual account. [Furthermore] under the new Money Laundering Act 2002,

---

[126] J-F Seznec, 'Ethics, Islamic Banking and the Global Financial Market' (1999) 23 *Fletcher Forum of World Affairs* 161; HS Shaaban, 'Commercial Transactions in the Middle East: What Law Governs'? (1999) 31 *Law and Policy International Business* 157; HL Stovall, 'Arab Commercial Laws—Into the Future' (2000) 34 *International Law* 839.

[127] Article 8(1)(2)(4)(5).

[128] Report of the Albanian Government on the Implementation of Security Council Resolution 1373 (2001) on Combating Terrorism, S/2001/1309 (13 December 2001) at 3, available at <http://ods-dds-ny.un.org/doc/UNDOC/GEN/N02/206/00/PDF/N0220600.pdf?OpenElement> (11 October 2004).

[129] *Ibid.*

[130] *Ibid.*

[131] *Ibid.*

[132] See Report submitted by Algeria to the Security Council Committee established pursuant to Resolution 1373 (2001) S/2001/1280 (27 December 2001) at 11, available at <http://ods-dds-ny.un.org/doc/UNDOC/GEN/N02/205/90/IMG/N0220590.pdf?OpenElement> (11 October 2004).

steps are underway to instruct all banks and financial institutions to report any suspicious/unusual transactions immediately in a prescribed manner. As per Section 19(4) of the aforementioned Act, if the institutions fail to do so, it may be subjected to a penalty of up to Taka one hundred thousand, with a minimum of Taka ten thousand.[133]

Similar legislative enactments have been promulgated by the Middle Eastern State of Bahrain. Its Decree No 4/2002, promulgated on 29 January 2001, confers wide ranging powers on national authorities to receive reports from institutions it stipulates, including banks and other financial agencies, on any suspicious 'transactions which could possibly be linked to terrorist offences'. The Law defines 'criminal activity' as 'any activity that constitutes a punishable offence in the State of Bahrain or any other country'.[134]

In its submission to the Counter-Terrorism Committee, the government of Qatar reported that a draft bill was being finalised which would render the financing of terrorism a criminal offence. A law on money laundering had already come into operation.[135] This legislation was subsequently approved and promulgated on 16 February 2004 in the form of 'Law No 3 on Counter-Terrorism'.[136] The Law intends to deal comprehensively with all forms of terrorist actions.[137]

In the light of the resurgence of militancy and terrorism within Saudi Arabia, the legislative and constitutional approaches of the Kingdom are of particular relevance. Saudi Arabia, as noted above, is a member of the G–20 States and as part of that organisation has agreed to establish financial and fiscal units that will focus on regulatory measures to report, prevent and punish activities involving the financing of international and regional terrorism. Furthermore, a stricter regime has been put in place for ensuring that charitable donations are not used for illegal and terrorist activities. The relevant regulation was enacted in 1976: it prohibits the col-

---

[133] Supplementary Report submitted by Bangladesh on the implementation of Security Council Committee established pursuant to Resolution 1373 (2001) S/2002/1137 (8 October 2002) at 3–4, available at <http://ods-dds-ny.un.org/doc/UNDOC/GEN/N02/642/72/PDF/N0264272.pdf?OpenElement> (19 October 2004).

[134] Report of the State of Bahrain on the steps it has taken to implement the implementation of Security Council Committee established pursuant to Resolution 1373 (2001) S/2001/1210 (14 December 2001) at 5, available at <http://ods-dds-ny.un.org/doc/UNDOC/GEN/N01/704/79/PDF/N0170479.pdf?OpenElement> (19 October 2004).

[135] Report containing the replies of the State of Qatar to the Questions of the Security Council's Counter Terrorism Committee established pursuant to Resolution 1373 (2001) S/2002/1211 at 3, available at <http://ods-dds-ny.un.org/doc/UNDOC/GEN/N02/225/98/PDF/N0222598.pdf?OpenElement> (21 October 2004).

[136] Report containing the replies of the State of Qatar to the Questions of the Security Council's Counter Terrorism Committee established pursuant to Resolution 1373 (2001) S/2004/179 (10 March 2004) at 4, available at <http://ods-dds-ny.un.org/doc/UNDOC/GEN/N04/266/92/PDF/N0426692.pdf?OpenElement> (21 October 2004).

[137] *Ibid.*

lection of contributions from persons, groups or other entities without a licence from the Ministry of Justice and Social Affairs and without a declaration of purpose and a statement of the manner in which contributions are to be utilised. There is a prohibition on charitable institutions raising funds in a manner which is incompatible with the objectives of the mission of the charity. Overseas transfers of charitable donations and funds must be approved by the higher committee on fund-raising after it ascertains the legitimacy of the purposes for which they are being used.[138]

Pakistan, another Islamic State, has also reported the criminalisation of 'actual, proposed or potential acts of terrorism' under its Anti-Terrorism Act of 1997.[139] The Anti-Terrorism Act provides for the freezing of the accounts of a 'proscribed organisation'.[140] However, the determination and identification of such an organisation, being a sensitive subject, is under the jurisdiction of the federal government. Furthermore, section 110 of the 1997 Act allows an 'authorised officer' to detain only 'cash recovered' that is intended or suspected of being intended for terrorism. In its elaboration of this provision, the government of Pakistan explained that the provisions also authorises seizure of all financial instruments and other valuables that can be cashed and used for criminal purposes. Pakistan also reported the drafting of separate anti-laundering legislation to reinforce the provisions of the 1997 Act.[141]

CONCLUSIONS

Financing of terrorism unfortunately remains a major concern for the international community. Terrorists are reliant upon economic and financial resources, and there are so many variants in which funds can be raised. Terrorists have made use of lawful as well as unlawful criminal means to finance terrorism; the apprehension of funds generated through charities and ostensibly for humanitarian ends has proved particularly difficult to scrutinise. It is also the case that sometimes, differing perceptions of the cause lead States to take diametrically opposed views. The issue of the struggle of the Palestinians is a pertinent example. Israel and

---

[138] Report of the Kingdom of Saudi Arabia submitted pursuant to paragraph 6 of Security Council Resolution 1373 (2001) Concerning Counter-Terrorism S/2001/1294 (27 December 2001) at 4, available at <http://ods-dds-ny.un.org/doc/UNDOC/GEN/N01/722/76/PDF/N0172276.pdf?OpenElement> (21 October 2004); also see Report of the Kingdom of Saudi Arabia submitted pursuant to paragraph 6 of Security Council Resolution 1373 (2001) Concerning Counter-Terrorism S/2003/583 (2 June 2003).

[139] Supplementary Report of Pakistan to the Counter-Terrorism Committee of the Security Council S/2003/307 (12 March 2003) at 3, available at <http://ods-dds-ny.un.org/doc/UNDOC/GEN/N03/280/85/PDF/N0328085.pdf?OpenElement> (22 October 2004).

[140] *Ibid.*

[141] *Ibid.*

its allies may regard any form of financial support for the Palestinian cause as promoting terrorism; in their view any organisation and institution working to finance the Palestinians' struggle for their lawful rights is promoting terrorism. The Islamic community, however, firmly believes in the integrity of the right of self-determination of the people of Palestine. There are many individuals and charitable institutions committed to supporting the Palestinians.

The United Nations has implemented a number of significant initiatives in its efforts to combat the scourge of financing international terrorism. The key international instrument is the 1999 Convention. The Convention has several positive features. However, there are also significant issues as regards the substance and implementation of the treaty. While the terrorist attacks in the US in 2001 and subsequent Security Council resolutions have spurred increasing ratifications of this Convention, it is sobering to acknowledge that prior to 11 September 2001 only four States had ratified the treaty.[142] In its efforts to restrain financial terrorism, the role of the Security Council is possibly of the greatest practical impact. The reporting mechanisms under Security Council Resolution 1373 have thus far had a high rate of compliance. The Resolution has, however, deliberately avoided the thorny issue of defining 'terrorism';[143] the application of this Resolution to organisations such as *Hizbollah* and *Islamic Jihad* raises the spectre of considerable hostility and backlash. While the overall compliance with Security Council Resolution 1373 needs to be applauded, the Counter-Terrorism Committee does not have the power to impose sanctions on non-complying States.[144] Furthermore, the future role of the Committee also remains speculative.

The present chapter has briefly examined the OIC Convention on Terrorism. Notwithstanding the presence of several useful provisions, the role of the Convention in its efforts to eradicate the financing of terrorism has remained limited; the Convention does not present a focus on the financing issues: a comprehensive approach is therefore required to place effective restraints upon financial terrorism.

---

[142] These States were the United Kingdom, Botswana, Sri Lanka and Uzbekistan. FN Baldwin, Jr, 'Organised Crime, Terrorism, and Money Laundering in the Americas' (2002) 15 *Florida Journal of International Law* 3 at 10.

[143] Zagaris, n 11 above, at 76.

[144] Levitt, n 1 above, at 62.

7

The OIC and Approaches to International Terrorism

INTRODUCTION

IN THE CONTEMPORARY debate on terrorism, a number of misconceptions have arisen concerning Islam, the *Sharia*, and the practices of Islamic States. The issue of Islamic identity is not without complexities, a subject examined in an earlier chapter.[1] We have also considered that there are many States who despite having significant ethnic, cultural and religious diversity claim to have an Islamic identity.[2] In the light of this diversity, States purporting to be 'Islamic' have no single unified base. There is a heterogeneous conglomeration of States emerging from all regions of the world.[3] With their diverse political, historical and regional influences, these States have associated themselves with a range of international and intergovernmental organisations. The motive of these organisations frequently differs widely—from the advancement of human rights—to economic co-operation—to strengthening of security and defence. Amidst these varied organisations, as we have already seen, there is however one inter-governmental organisation, the OIC, which has been established with the objective inter alia to 'promote Islamic Solidarity among Member States'. In this regard the OIC can be seen as the mouthpiece of the community of Islamic States. Since its establishment, the OIC has expressed a special commitment to the eradication of all forms of terrorism. The OIC adopted the Convention on Combating International Terrorism[4] and in the aftermath of the attacks on the United States in

---

[1] See chapter 2 above.

[2] *Ibid.*

[3] For useful overviews of the constitutional and legal positions see VV Dyke, *Human Rights, Ethnicity and Discrimination* (Westport, Conn and London, Greenwood Press, 1985); Minority Rights Group (ed), *World Directory of Minorities,* (London, Minority Rights Group, 1997); D Vajpeyi and Y Malik (eds), *Religious and Ethnic Minority Politics in South Asia* (Glenn Dale, Riverdale Company Publishers, 1989).

[4] Adopted at Ouagadougou on 1 July 1999. Deposited with the Secretary-General of the Organisation of the Islamic Conference, Annex to Resolution No: 59/26–P: Convention of the Organisation of the Islamic Conference on Combating International Terrorism (1999), text available at <http://www.oic-un.org/26icfm/c.html> (5 October 2004).

September 2001 has actively campaigned for further initiatives to condemn and combat terrorist acts.

Consideration is given below to the manner in which the OIC has addressed issues of discrimination, violence and international terrorism. The present chapter examines the workings of this organisation, particularly in relation to combating international terrorism. There is a detailed assessment of the legal instruments adopted by the OIC for combating international terrorism.

In the present context it is important to highlight the role and practices of individual States parties to the OIC. The discussion also underlines the tensions and dangers encountered by Islamic States when dealing with particular facets of militancy and extremism: as in the case of Palestine and Kashmir, there is a fine line to be drawn. The Palestinian and Kashmiri groups are often labelled as terrorist. In reality, however, it is the unrelenting persecution and violation of their human rights which has led these disparate peoples and communities to resort to extremism.

TERRORISM, ANTAGONISM AND A LACK OF TRUST AMONGST ISLAMIC STATES

The creation of the OIC has accompanied a considerable history of mistrust and antagonism not only between Muslim and non-Muslim States but also amongst Islamic States themselves. While taking pride in an Islamic heritage, there has been hostility on the basis of nationalism, colour, race, ethnic background and language.[5] The heroes of one Muslim State have been the villains for others.[6] There is an uneasy relationship between Arab and non-Arab States. Even amongst Arab States themselves, there have been differences between conservative States such as Saudi Arabia, Kuwait and Jordan and radical or revolutionary States such

---

[5] A striking example of linguistic dissent and struggle for nationalistic and linguistic autonomy is presented by the case of the Bengalis. On 21 February 1952, the Bengalis initiated a campaign against the imposition of Urdu and the refusal of the (then West Pakistan) authorities to grant equal status to Bangla. This campaign ultimately proved to be the springboard for a mass movement leading to the establishment of an independent Pakistan. See *The Bangladesh Today*, 21 February 1952, at 11. On 17 November 1999, UNESCO in remembrance of this struggle declared 21 February as the International Mother Language Day. In passing a resolution to this effect, UNESCO General Meeting observed: 'Recognising the unprecedented sacrifice made by Bangladesh for the cause of mother language on 21 February 1952, [UNESCO] proposes that 21 February be proclaimed "International Mother Language Day" through out the world to commemorate the martyrs who sacrificed their lives on this very date in 1952' cited by A Mujahidee, 'International Mother Language Day' *The Daily Star* (Dhaka, Bangladesh) 21 February 2004 at 24.

[6] See eg the Bangladesh/Pakistan conflict. See *The Bangladesh Today* (Dhaka, Bangladesh), 21 February 1952 at 8–12.

as Iraq, Syria, Yemen and Libya.[7] Islamic States have engaged in territorial disputes, accompanied by accusations of human rights violations. The eight year Iran-Iraq war (1980–1988) and the invasion of Kuwait by Iraq in August 1990 represent two recent unfortunate examples of territorial disputes that escalated into full scale military interventions with unfortunate violations of international humanitarian and human rights laws.[8] There have been substantial accusations amongst Islamic States of promoting terrorists and insurgencies in neighbouring States. In its report to the Counter-Terrorism Committee, the government of Iraq made the following allegation against Iran:

> Iran grants safe haven to numerous terrorist organisations, such as those known as the Supreme Council for Islamic Revolution in Iraq, the Badr Corps and the Islamic Da'wah Party, which are under the supervision of Iranian military secret agencies and are known to the international community through their terrorist acts both in the Arab world and elsewhere. These are extremist groups whose activity is based on the notion of terrorism (killing, destruction and kidnapping) as a strategy for achieving their ends. The Iranian Government has established these and other organizations on a religious extremist basis known to all. They have carried out dozens of terrorist acts against peace-loving citizens, civilian installations and governmental institutions in Iraq and we have a long record of their heinous crimes.[9]

The peoples of the Islamic world have also suffered at the hands of their rulers, politicians and statesmen. A number of Islamic States have witnessed corruption, nepotism, military rule, and absence of rule of law. Denials of human rights and 'internal self-determination' have generated considerable problems, leading to civil war, ethnic tensions and in some

---

[7] H Moinuddin, *The Charter of the Islamic Conference and Legal Framework of Economic Cooperation Among its Member States: A Study of the Charter, the General Agreement for Economic, Technical and Commercial Co-operation and the Agreement for Promotion, Protection and Guarantee of Investments Among Member States of the OIC* (Oxford, Clarendon Press, 1987) at 70; BBC News UK edition, 'US Court Reveals Libya "Terror" Plot: A plea bargain in a US court has revealed details of an alleged Libyan plot to assassinate Saudi Arabia's de facto leader Crown Prince Abdullah 31 July 2004' <http://news.bbc.co.uk/1/hi/world/americas/3941475.stm> (30 September 2004).

[8] The tragic human rights record of Iraq was ultimately to provide justifications to the US and its allies for invading the country in March 2003. Commenting on the position adopted by Iraq, the late Professor McCoubrey makes the point that '[a] party to armed conflict who casts off significant legal constraints runs the risk of acquiring a "pariah" status in the view of nations, which may compromise neutral political support even from states which might otherwise be disposed to be friendly. The record of Iraq in the 1980–88 Gulf War, including the use of chemical weapons, and in the subsequent 1990–91 Gulf Conflict inflicted much damage upon Iraqi international relations, and played a role in the near-unanimous opposition to Iraq in the latter conflict'. H McCoubrey, *International Humanitarian Law: Modern Developments in the Limitation of Warfare* (Aldershot, Ashgate, 1998) 5.

[9] Responses of the Government of Iraq to the questions raised by the Chairman of the Counter-Terrorism Committee established pursuant to Resolution 1373 (2001) S/2002/943 (19 August 2002) at 9.

cases secessionist movements.[10] In his characterisation of 'violence-prone' Middle Eastern conflicts, Payne focuses almost exclusively on Islamic States of the region. He lists the 'clashes between Syria and Jordan, between Egypt and Libya, between Sudan and Libya, between Algeria and Morocco, and between Somalia and Ethiopia and civil wars in Chad, Oman, Sudan, Iraq, Morocco, Mauritania, and Yemen—not to mention the terrorism that blights the entire region'.[11]

THE ESTABLISHMENT OF THE OIC: REACTING TO EXTERNAL AGGRESSION

Notwithstanding considerable divisions within the Islamic world, there has been a determined effort to resist external aggression and violence. Indeed, this was the driving force behind the establishment of OIC. The Arab-Israeli war (1967) was followed by the tragic arson attack against the Al-Aqsa Mosque on 21 August 1969.[12] In the aftermath of the violent attack on the Al-Aqsa Mosque, the first Islamic Summit Conference was convened. The Conference, which was attended by Heads of State and representatives of twenty-four States as well as the Palestinian Observers, condemned the attack on the Mosque. It called upon Muslim States to promote co-operation and mutual assistance. A series of conferences took place between March 1970 and March 1972, leading to the formulation of a constitution for the organisation and the establishment of the OIC itself.[13]

The objectives and principles of the OIC reflect a determination not only to uphold international law, but also to fight violence and terrorism through peaceful means.[14] The Objectives and Principles of the organisations, according to the Charter, are as follows:

A) Objectives:

The objectives of the Islamic Conference shall be
— to promote Islamic solidarity among Member States;
— to consolidate cooperation among Member States in the economic, social, cultural, scientific and other vital fields of activities, and to carry out consultations among Member States in international organizations;
— to endeavour to eliminate racial segregation, discrimination and to eradicate colonialism in all its forms;

---

[10] R Emerson, 'Self-Determination' (1971) 65 *American Journal of International Law* 459; J Rehman, 'Reviewing the Right of Self-Determination: Lessons from the Indian Experience' (2000) 29 *Anglo-American Law Review* 454.

[11] JL Payne, *Why Nations Arm* (Oxford, Basil Blackwell, 1989) 121.

[12] On the Arab-Israeli war see 'OIC in Brief' <http://www.oic-oci.org/> (27 September 2004).

[13] See Moinuddin, n 7 above.

[14] For the text of the OIC Charter, see 'Charter of the OIC' <http://www.oic-oci.org/> (27 September 2004).

— *to take necessary measures to support international peace and security founded on justice;*

— *to coordinate efforts for the safeguarding of the Holy Places and support of the struggle of the people of Palestine, to help them regain their rights and liberate their land;*

— *to back the struggle of all Muslim peoples with a view to preserving their dignity, independence and national rights;*

— *to create a suitable atmosphere for the promotion of cooperation and understanding among Member States and other countries.*

B) Principles:

The Member States decide and undertake that, in order to realize the objectives mentioned in the previous paragraph, they shall be inspired and guided by the following principles:-

— *total equality between Member States;*

— *respect of the right of self-determination, and non-interference in the domestic affairs of Member States;*

— *respect of the sovereignty, independence and territorial integrity of each Member State;*

— *settlement of any conflict that may arise by peaceful means such as negotiation, mediation, reconciliation or arbitration;*

— *abstention from the threat or use of force against the territorial integrity, national unity or political independence of any Member State.*

A principal objective of the Charter of the OIC is to 'take necessary measures to support international peace and security founded on justice'. This is an important undertaking, re-affirming the commitment of the Member States to uphold international peace and security in accordance with international law. The reference to 'justice' is an unusual one; as an amorphous concept 'justice' or 'just action' could have varied forms of application. The OIC is also committed to eliminating racial segregation and discrimination, and eradicating all forms of colonialism. In the context of the Charter, these are important provisions. It is principally to the credit of the Islamic world that the norm of racial equality has been elevated to an established principle of general international law. All of the members of the OIC have a legacy of direct or indirect colonialism. During the latter part of 1960s and the early 1970s the Islamic world led the charge towards the eradication of all forms of colonialism and apartheid. This was a movement which was instrumental in adopting a series of international instruments for the abolition of racial discrimination and the demolition of colonisation, apartheid and racial oppression. In its Resolution 1510 (XV) of 12 December 1960, the General Assembly condemned all manifestations and practices of racial, religious and national hatred in the political, economic, educational and cultural spheres of the life of society as violations of the Charter of the United Nations and the provisions of the Universal Declaration on Human Rights.[15]

---

[15] GA Res 1510 (XV) Manifestation of Racial and National Hatred (12 December 1960).

In 1962, the General Assembly requested the Economic and Social Council to prepare a draft Declaration and Convention on the Elimination of All Forms of Racial Discrimination. The General Assembly in its Resolution 1904 (XVIII) adopted on 20 November 1963, proclaimed the Declaration on the Elimination of All Forms of Racial Discrimination.[16] Two years later, the United Nations General Assembly adopted with overwhelming support, the Convention on the Elimination of All Forms of Racial Discrimination.[17] The Convention has been approved and ratified by an overwhelming majority of the Member States of the OIC. In 1973, with strong inspirational support from the Islamic States, the General Assembly adopted the Convention on the Suppression and Punishment of the Crime of Apartheid.[18]

This powerful approach on the part of Islamic States has had a tremendous effect on the development of human rights law: if the overall picture is assessed, it is highly persuasive to argue that as a consequence of the pressure exerted by the Islamic and the developing world, the prohibition of racial discrimination is now established as a norm of *jus cogens*. A divergence of opinion exists as to the content of *jus cogens*.[19] Taking a more liberal approach, as Judge Tanaka did in the *South West Africa Case*, it is possible to view the whole human rights regime as having a character of *jus cogens*. He says:

> If we can introduce in the international field a category of law, namely *jus cogens*, recently examined by the International Law Commission, a kind of imperative law which constitutes the contrast to *jus depositivum*, capable of being changed by way of agreement between States, surely the law concerning the protection of human rights may be considered to belong to *jus cogens*.[20]

On the other hand, an overtly generous view on *jus cogens* might stretch the concept to unacceptable limits so as to risk its indelibility, and it is important to bear in mind Professor Brownlie's cautionary remark that '[t]he major distinguishing feature of [the rules of *jus cogens*] is their relative indelibility'.[21] Nonetheless, regardless of the extent to which one

[16] Declaration on the Elimination of All Forms of Racial Discrimination, GA Res 1904 (XVIII) 20 November 1963.

[17] International Convention on the Elimination of All Forms of Racial Discrimination 1965; (1969) UKTS 77; Cmnd 4108; 60 UNTS 195; (1966) 5 ILM 352; adopted on 21 December 1965, entered into force 4 January 1969.

[18] International Convention on the Suppression and Punishment of the Crime of Apartheid Adopted and opened for signature, ratification by GA Res 3068 (XXVIII) (adopted 30 November 1973, entered into force 18 July 1976).

[19] For a consideration of the meaning of *jus cogens* see Articles 53 and 64 of the VCLT (1969); YBILC 1966, vol 247–8; see E Schwelb, 'Some Aspects of International *Jus Cogens* as Formulated by International Law Commission' (1967) 61 *American Journal of International Law* 946; M Whiteman, '*Jus Cogens* in International Law with a Projected List' (1977) 7 *Georgia Journal of International and Comparative Law* 607.

[20] *South West Africa Cases* [1966] ICJ Rep 6, at 298.

[21] I Brownlie, *Principles of Public International Law* 4th edn (Oxford, Clarendon Press, 1990) 513.

is prepared to agree with Judge Tanaka, out of the general category of human rights, prohibition of racial discrimination stands out as a safe candidate for inclusion in the list of *jus cogens*. According to Schwelb:

> [i]f there is a subject matter in the present-day international law which appears to be a successful candidate for regulation by peremptory norms, it is certainly the prohibition of racial discrimination.[22]

Mckean's point is persuasive when he suggests that even on a narrow view 'the principle of equality and non-discrimination are prime candidates for inclusion in the list of *jus cogens*'.[23] He reiterates this view in a more assertive manner, saying that there are good reasons 'for accepting that the principles of equality and non-discrimination, in view of their nature as fundamental constituents of international law of human rights, are part of *jus cogens*'.[24] Dicta in both the *Barcelona Traction Case*[25] and the *Namibia Case*[26] reinforce this assertion. The judgment of the Court in the *Namibia Case* is absolutely clear on the position of international law in relation to non-discrimination. The Court, while condemning the '[o]fficical governmental policy pursued by South Africa to achieve a complete physical separation of races and ethnic groups in separate areas within the territory', took the view that

> [t]hese measures establish limitations, exclusions or restrictions for the members of indigenous population [and that] to establish instead and to enforce, distinction, exclusions, restrictions and limitations exclusively based on grounds of race, colour, descent or national or ethnic origin which constitute a denial of fundamental human rights is a flagrant violation of the purposes and principles of the Charter.[27]

In the *Barcelona Traction Case*, in its description of the basic human rights in 'contemporary international law' the Court refers to 'protection from racial discrimination'.[28] In a similar vein, the Court's position as reflected in cases such as *Western Sahara*[29] and the *East Timor Case*[30] provides a condemnation of denials of the right to racial equality and self-determination.[31]

---

[22] Schwelb, n 19 above, at 956.

[23] W Mckean, *Equality and Discrimination under International Law* (Oxford, Clarendon Press, 1983) at 282.

[24] *Ibid*, at 283.

[25] *Barcelona Traction, Light and Power Co Case (Belgium v Spain)* [1970] ICJ Rep 3.

[26] *Legal Consequences for States of the Continued Presence of South Africa in Namibia (South West Africa) Notwithstanding Security Council Resolution 276* [1971] ICJ Rep 6.

[27] *Ibid*, paras 130 and 131.

[28] See above n 25, 3 (para 33).

[29] *Western Sahara Case* [1975] ICJ Rep 12.

[30] *East Timor Case* [1995] ICJ Rep 90.

[31] See chapter 3 above.

Efforts to eradicate apartheid and racial discrimination have formed part of the overall effort to promote the right of self-determination. The Islamic world in its efforts to abolish apartheid and racial oppression elevated the status of self-determination to a legally binding right with a *jus cogens* character.[32] While obstruction of the right to self-determination was an international crime, all States had to provide every possible form of assistance, including military support in aid of peoples struggling for a legitimate right to self-determination. As this study has examined elsewhere, the parameters of the right to self-determination have never been appropriately defined, nor is there consensus on the meaning of 'self'.[33] There has been considerable debate as to the extent to which the right to self-determination applies outside the colonial context.[34] Regardless of the controversies surrounding the right to self-determination, the Islamic world is unanimous in projecting and affirming the right to self-determination for the people of Palestine.[35] There is also a substantial amount of evidence that Israel, as the oppressor, has been practicing a policy of apartheid and racial discrimination against the Palestinian people—a recent example of such practices is confirmed by the passage of the Nationality and Entry into Israel Law (2003).[36]

Thus amongst the least controversial entities recognised as having the right to self-determination are the Palestinian people; as shall be examined shortly, there are sound reasons for such a universal recognition. It is therefore hardly surprising to notice that the OIC Charter commits itself to 'support the struggle of the people of Palestine, to help them regain their

[32]   On the right to self-determination see chapter 4 above.

[33]   *Ibid.* For a general analysis of this right in international law see H Hannum, *Autonomy, Sovereignty and Self-Determination: The Accommodation of Conflicting Rights* (Philadelphia, University of Pennsylvania Press, 1990) 33; Y Blum, 'Reflections on the Changing Concept of Self-Determination' (1975) 10 *Israel Law Review* 509; R Emerson, 'Self-Determination' (1971) 65 *American Journal of International Law* 459; T Franck, 'Post-Modern Tribalism and the Right to Secession' in C Brölmann, R Lefeber and M Zieck (eds), *Peoples and Minorities in International Law* (Dordrecht, Martinus Nijhoff Publishers, 1993) 3–27; M Pomerance, *Self-determination in Law and Practice: The New Doctrine in the United Nations* (The Hague, Martinus Nijhoff Publishers, 1982); A Rigo-Sureda, *The Evolution of the Right of Self-determination: A study of United Nations Practice* (Leiden, Sijthoff, 1973).

[34]   See J Rehman, 'Reviewing the Right of Self-Determination: Lessons from the Experience of the Indian Sub-Continent' (2000) 29 *Anglo-American Law Review* 454.

[35]   For commentaries see EW Said, *The Politics of Dispossession: the Struggle for Palestinian Self-Determination 1969–1994* (London, Chatto & Windus, 1994); H Cattan, *Palestine and International Law: the Legal Aspects of Arab-Israeli Conflict* (London, Longman, 1973); HB Talal, *Palestinian Self-Determination: A Study of the West Bank and Gaza Strip* (London, Quartet Books, 1981).

[36]   The Law aims to prevent family unification where one spouse is resident in Occupied Palestinian Territories. For implications of this Law on the Palestinians see the joint submission made by Al-Haq, the Palestinian Centre for Human Rights and Adalah to the UN Commission on Human Rights, 60th Session (15 March–23 April 2004) <http://www.pchrgaza.org/Commission/2004/CHR%20Item%206%20-%20Racism.pdf> (1 October 2004).

rights and liberate their land'. Furthermore, in the light of the religious significance of Palestine, and the religious bias of the OIC, the Charter reference to 'coordinated efforts for safeguarding the [Muslim] Holy places' is entirely appropriate and justified.

The principles of the Organisation replicate established principles of international law. These principles include sovereign equality of Member States, respect for territorial integrity and independent Statehood. There is a commitment to resolve disputes through peaceful means and to abstain from threat or use of force contrary to the provisions of the United Nations Charter.[37] In the present context it is pertinent to elaborate upon the reference to the settlement of conflicts through peaceful means. This provision bears similarities to Article 2(3) of the United Nations Charter, according to which Member States are under an obligation to settle their disputes by peaceful means. The necessity of resolving disputes peacefully as opposed to resorting to the use of force or violence is a well-established principle of international law. A number of provisions of the United Nations Charter provide for dispute resolution through peaceful means. These include Articles 33 and 37 of the Charter. According to Article 33(1):

> [t]he parties to any dispute, the continuance of which is likely to endanger the maintenance of international peace and security, shall, first of all, seek a solution by negotiation, enquiry, mediation, conciliation, arbitration, judicial settlement, resort to regional agencies or arrangements, or other peaceful means of their own choice.

The significance accorded to peaceful settlement of disputes within the OIC Charter is highlighted by the provisions relating to the International Islamic Court of Justice. Although the prospects of having an effective International Islamic Court of Justice appear unrealistic at the present time, a draft statute has nevertheless been produced.[38] The aforementioned provisions from the OIC Charter represent substantial commitments to rely upon the rule of law and to resort to judicial and legal mechanisms in resolving disputes; violence and terrorism are not to be tolerated, at least in the official practices of Member States. In addition to Palestine, there are other regions where Muslim interests have been undermined and they have been victims of foreign or alien occupation. Concerns have been raised by the OIC regarding Chechnya, Kashmir and more recently the US occupation of Iraq. These concerns of 'foreign occupation' led the OIC to submit alternative draft proposals to the

---

[37] Principles of OIC.
[38] See I Hussain, *Issues in Pakistan's Foreign Policy: An International Law Perspective* (Lahore, Progressive Publishers, 1988) 90–117.

Convention on Terrorism currently being drafted by the General Assembly's Ad Hoc Committee.[39]

The text of draft Article 18 as proposed by the Member States of the OIC reads as follows:

1 Nothing in this Convention shall affect other rights, obligations and responsibilities of States, peoples and individuals under international law, in particular the purposes and principles of the Charter of the United Nations, and international humanitarian law.

2 The activities of the parties during an armed conflict, including in situations of foreign occupation, as those terms are understood under international humanitarian law, which are governed by that law, are not governed by this Convention.

3 The activities undertaken by the military forces of a State in the exercise of their official duties, inasmuch as they are in conformity with international law, are not governed by this Convention.

4 Nothing in this article condones or makes lawful otherwise unlawful acts, nor precludes prosecution under other laws.[40]

AGGRESSION AND TERRORISM VERSUS THE RIGHT TO SELF-DETERMINATION: CASES OF CRISES

The Kashmiris[41]

The subject of the denial of the right to self-determination of the peoples of Kashmir and Palestine evokes considerable emotions on the part of Muslims; the redress of their grievances has been high on the agenda of Bin Laden and organisations such as al-Qaeda and Jaish-e-Mohammad. It is also the case that continuing violations of the rights of Kashmiris and Palestinians have led to enormous frustration, anger and mushrooming of militant organisations, willing to resort to force to achieve self-determination.

Kashmir has a bitter and painful political history, the roots of the conflict going back to the partition of India in 1947. The main constitutional instrument for determining the future position of the princely States such as

---

[39] See chapter 3 above. GA Res 51/210 of 17 December 1996, UN Doc A/RES/51/210; M Halberstam, 'The Evolution of the United Nations Position on Terrorism: From Exempting National Liberation Movements to Criminalizing Terrorism Whenever and Wherever and by Whom Committed' (2003) 41 *The Columbia Journal of Transnational Law* 573 at 579; also see SP Subedi, 'The UN Response to International Terrorism in the Aftermath of the Terrorist Attacks in America and the Problem of the Definition of Terrorism in International Law' (2002) 4 *International Law Forum du droit international* 159.

[40] See Report of the Ad Hoc Committee Established by GA Res 51/210 of 17 December 1996, GAOR, 57th Session A/57/37, Annex IV (28 January–1 February 2002).

[41] A Lamb, *Kashmir: A Disputed Legacy, 1846–1990* (Hertingfordbury, Roxford Books, 1991); A Azmi, *Kashmir: An Unparalleled Curfew* (Karachi, Panfwain Printing Press, 1990); T Ataöv, *Kashmir and Neighbours: Tale, Terror, Truce* (Aldershot, Ashgate, 2001).

Kashmir was the Indian Independence Act of 1947, section 7(1)(b) of which provided that:

> The suzerainty of His Majesty over the Indian states lapses, and with it, all treaties and agreements in force at the date of the passing of this Act between His Majesty and the rulers of the Indian states, all functions exercisable by His Majesty at the date with respect to Indian states or the rulers thereof and all powers, rights, authority or jurisdiction exercisable by His Majesty at that date in or in relation to Indian states, by treaty, grant usage, sufferance or otherwise.[42]

Notwithstanding the presence of a number of complexities surrounding the issue of succession, the strict legal position appears to be that with the lapse of the agreements made with the British government, sovereignty reverted to the princely States which then had the option of accession to, merger or integration with the Dominions of India or Pakistan. In practice, however, a vast majority of States decided to accede to India or Pakistan before the Indian Independence Act came into force on 15 August 1947.[43] In the case of the State of Jammu and Kashmir the Hindu ruler of a Muslim majority State vacillated in making a decision as to whether to accede to India or Pakistan. Amidst his hesitation and indecisiveness, the law and order situation deteriorated rapidly—Muslims from tribal areas were shocked and aggrieved by stories of atrocities being committed against their fellow Muslims in Kashmir. Thus an 'invasion' by the Azad Kashmir tribal peoples took place, this invasion having been instigated through the 'undoubted tales of horrible cruelties against their co-religionists in Jammu, coupled with heartening news of the insurrection, which first set them on their course of invasion'.[44] Under the pressure of this growing conflict, in October 1947, the ruler of Jammu and Kashmir decided to appeal to India for help and acceded to India. Accession took place on the condition that on the restoration of order a referendum would be held in order for the people to determine their political destiny.[45] Indian troops

---

[42] For the text of the Act see S Mahmood, *Constitutional Foundations of Pakistan* (Lahore, Jang Publishers, 1989) at 31.

[43] See T Poulose, *Succession in International Law: A Study of India, Pakistan, Ceylon and Burma* (New Delhi, Orient Longman, 1974) 30–56.

[44] 'Jammu and Kashmir' *The Daily Telegraph* 12 January 1948 at 8.

[45] On 27 October 1947, Lord Mountbatten, the then Governor-General of India, in accepting the Kashmir Maharaja's offer of accession of the State with India noted as follows: 'In the special circumstances mentioned by your Highness, my Government has decided to accept the accession of Kashmir state to the Dominion of India. In consistence with their policy that, in the case of any state where the issue of accession has been the subject of dispute, the question of accession should be decided in accordance with the wishes of the peoples of the state, it is my Government's wish that, as soon as law and order have been restored in Kashmir and her soil cleared of the invader, the question of the state's accession should be settled by a reference to the people'. Letter of His Highness the Governor-General of India addressed to His Highness the Maharaja of Jammu and Kashmir, 27 October 1947 cited in KS Hasan (ed), *Documents on the Foreign Relations of Pakistan: The Kashmir Question* (Karachi, Institute of International Affairs, 1966) 57–8.

were rushed into the territory and stopped the advance of the tribal army from Pakistan. The Line of Control established as a result of this action became the border between India and Pakistan, and also the line dividing the territory of Jammu and Kashmir between the Indian and Pakistani jurisdictions.

In the meantime, the partition of British India in August 1947 was to produce disastrous consequences not only for the Kashmiris but for the entire population of the Sub-Continent. The incision of India was ill-considered and arbitrary in nature and was to be the largest inter-State migration of the twentieth century. It resulted in the physical extermination of hundreds of thousands of men, women and children and created millions of refugees. Almost a million people were killed during this period; approximately eight million people migrated from India to Pakistan while there was a similar exodus of Hindus and Sikhs from Pakistan to India. In the aftermath of the partition, religious minorities were subjected to discrimination, persecution and genocide. The Muslim Kashmiris became a particular target of a sustained campaign of persecution and violation of fundamental human rights, including their right to self-determination.

Jammu and Kashmir also became a victim of the proxy war between India and Pakistan—the Kashmiri peoples becoming the main victims of this conflict. Notwithstanding the violations of the human rights of Kashmiris, India continues to defy international scrutiny through a reliance upon Article 2(7) of the United Nations—claiming the issue of Kashmir (and violations committed in the region) as a matter exclusively within its domestic jurisdiction.[46]

Despite the protracted nature of the Kashmir conflict, the role of the United Nations has been ineffectual. On 1 January 1948 India took the question of Kashmir before the United Nations Security Council with a formal complaint against Pakistan. India's complaint was lodged under Article 35 of Chapter VI, a Chapter dealing with 'Pacific Settlement of Disputes'. The subject of the complaint soon became entangled with claims of aggression and counter-claims of genocide. The Security Council, in its response adopted two resolutions. In its first Resolution of 17 January 1948, it asked both governments to refrain from aggravating the situation and to apprise the Council of any material changes to the situation.[47] By its second Resolution of 20 January 1948, the Council

---

[46] Article 2(7) of the Charter provides: Nothing contained in the present Charter shall authorise the United Nations to intervene in matters which are essentially within the domestic jurisdiction of any state or shall require the Members to submit such matters to settlement under the present Charter; but this principle shall not prejudice the application of enforcement measures under Chapter VII.

[47] SC Res S/651 (S/651/1948). Resolution adopted at the Two Hundred and Twenty-Ninth meeting of the Security Council, 17 January 1948.

established a Commission (the United Nations Commission for India and Pakistan—UNCIP). UNCIP consisted of three nominated members, one nominated by India and Pakistan each and the third by both States. UNCIP, based on its views and detailed negotiations with the two protagonists, adopted two resolutions.[48] The essence of these resolutions, adopted on 13 August 1948 and 5 January 1949, was the withdrawal of troops, demilitarisation of the region, and the future of the territory to be decided through a free and impartial plebiscite. None of the objectives laid down by UNCIP could however be achieved. India, meanwhile, progressed towards a complete accession of Kashmir, through the use of the Kashmir constituent Assembly.

Despite the conflict being the source of two wars (1947–1949 and 1965), endangering peace and security (most recently in 1999), and encouraging terrorism and fundamentalism, the Security Council has never undertaken binding action under Chapter VII of the UN Charter.[49] On its part India contends that it has satisfied the right to self-determination, through local elections and using the Kashmir constituent Assembly as the ultimate constitutional mouthpiece. India continues to accuse Pakistan of continued military support of the 'Azad Kashmir Army' and of encouraging militancy and terrorism in the region. Pakistan, in turn, lays blame on India for denial of the right of self-determination to the people of Kashmir.[50] The region clearly has been in the grip of militants. In the aftermath of 11 September 2001, the US administration placed various individuals and organisations on the list of terrorist organisations. These included a number of Kashmiri militant organisations, including Jaish-e-Mohammad, a group which has attacked Indian security forces

---

[48] For the text of these Resolutions see SK Sharma and SR Bakshi (eds), *Kashmir and the United Nations* (New Delhi, Anmol Publications, 1995) at 44–8.

[49] For legal analysis of the validity of the Security Council's Resolutions and the role of the Security Council in dispute resolution see SD Bailey, 'The Security Council' in P Alston (ed), *The United Nations and Human Rights: A Critical Appraisal* (Oxford, Clarendon Press, 1992) 304–36; SD Bailey, *Voting in the Security Council* (Bloomington, Ind, Indiana University Press, 1969); SD Bailey, *The Procedure of the UN Security Council* (Oxford, Clarendon Press, 1988); R Higgins, 'The Place of International Law in the Settlement of Disputes by the Security Council' (1970) 64 *American Journal of International Law* 1; RA Brand, 'Security Council Resolutions: When do they Give Rise to Enforceable Legal Rights? The United Nations Charter, the Byrd Amendment and a Self Executing Treaty Analysis' (1976) 9 *Cornell International Law Journal* 298; MC Wood, 'Security Council Working Methods and Procedures: Recent Developments' (1996) 45 *International & Comparative Law Quarterly* 150; B Fassbender, *UN Security Council Reform and the Right of Veto: A Constitutional Perspective* (The Hague, Kluwer Law International, 1998); D Sarooshi, *The United Nations and the Development of Collective Security: The Delegation by the UN Security Council of its chapter VII Powers* (Oxford, Clarendon Press, 1999).

[50] See I Hussain, *Kashmir Dispute: An International Law Perspective* (Islamabad, National Institute of Pakistan Studies, 1998); RG Wirsing, 'Kashmir Conflict: The New Phase' in CH Kennedy (ed), *Pakistan: 1992* (Boulder, Col, Westview Press, 1993) 133–65.

and claimed responsibility for suicide bombing in Srinagar in October 2001.[51]

The lack of enthusiasm of both India and Pakistan to resolve the dispute through peaceful means is also evident in their reticence to approach mechanisms of conflict resolution. Both countries have accepted the compulsory jurisdiction of the Court, although their accompanying declarations are very restrictive in scope. Pakistan's declaration pursuant to Article 36(2) excludes from the jurisdiction of the Court all disputes relating to questions which fall exclusively within the domestic jurisdiction of Pakistan.[52] A similar approach is adopted by India. In its most recent declaration entered on 15 September 1974 India excludes from the jurisdiction of the International Court of Justice, inter alia, those matters which are essentially within its domestic jurisdiction. In order to ensure that no challenges regarding international frontiers with Pakistan and Bangladesh are raised before the World Court, India's declaration excludes the Court's jurisdiction for all disputes with present or previous Commonwealth Member States. Furthermore the Court is denied jurisdiction in disputes 'relating to or connected with facts or situations of hostilities, armed conflicts, individual or collective actions taken in self-defence, resistance to aggression . . .' and disputes with India concerning or relating inter alia to its frontiers or any other matter concerning boundaries.[53] The intention of such a narrow and limited declaration is clearly to forestall efforts to have the Kashmir issue adjudicated by the World Court.

In addition to the United Nations, the subject of the rights of the Kashmiri peoples has frequently been raised by the OIC. In innumerable Resolutions the OIC has campaigned for the protection of their civil and political rights and granting them their inalienable and fundamental right of self-determination.[54] The OIC set up a Kashmiri Contact Group in 1994

---

[51] See Foreign Terrorist Organisations: Designation of Ansar-al-Islam (AI), Re-designation of three others. Press Statement Richard Boucher, Spokesman, Washington, DC, US Department of State, 22 March 2004 <http://www.state.gov/r/pa/prs/ps/2004/30649.htm> (29 September 2004); B Zagaris, 'Financial Aspects of the War on Terror: The Merging of the Counter-Terrorism and Anti-Money Laundering Regimes' (2002) 34 *Law and Policy International Business* 45, 53.

[52] See <http://www.icj-cij.org/icjwww/ibasicdocuments/ibasictext/ibasicdeclarations.ht> for the text of the Declaration (1 October 2004).

[53] For the text of the Declaration see <http://www.icj-cij.org/icjwww/ibasicdocuments/ibasictext/ibasicdeclarations.htm> (1 October 2004).

[54] The OIC has thus far passed three Jammu and Kashmir related Resolutions expressing solidarity with the peoples of Kashmir and reiterating their inalienable right of self-determination. For further details see <http://www.pakistan.gov.pk/foreignaffairs-division/policies/pak-int/pak-org/pak-org.jsp> (1 July 2004). A number of declarations have also been passed. The most recent declaration was adopted during the tenth session of the Islamic Summit Conference Putrajaya, Malaysia, 11–18 October 2003. See OIC 'Declaration on Jammu and Kashmir' <http://www.bernama.com/oicsummit/speechr.php?id=75&cat=BI> (1 October 2004).

with the objective of further canvassing the cause of Kashmiris. The headquarters of the group are in New York. The group, which consists of five members, includes Pakistan, Turkey, Niger, Saudi-Arabia and the OIC's Secretary-General's representative. India and Pakistan have recently entered into a further peace initiative promising resolution to all their outstanding disputes, including Kashmir.[55] In reality, however, there continue to be frequent incidents of extra-judicial killings, arbitrary detentions and torture perpetuated by the Indian security forces. In addition, thousands of people have 'disappeared'—possibly executed without any information as to their whereabouts being given to their families and friends.[56] The cycle of persecution and repression has given rise to militancy amongst Kashmir Muslims. Many of the Muslim Kashmiri groups have without a doubt a history of violence—they have been brutalised at the hands of the Indian army and State authorities. However, with the denial of all avenues to a peaceful dialogue they resort to militancy and extremism.

The Palestinians[57]

The Palestinians have a lot in common with the Kashmiri Muslims. There are many similarities in their historical backgrounds. In both cases, Britain was the imperial power in charge, an imperialism dependent on a policy of 'divide and rule'. In Kashmir as well as in Palestine, religious and nationalist sentiments unleashed irreversible forces of hatred and repulsion; amidst this quagmire Jews and Muslims of Palestine (much like the Hindus, Muslims and Sikhs of Kashmir) found it difficult to accept the possibility of co-existence.

In the case of Palestine, the problem of Jewish immigration in the first half of the twentieth century signalled a major change to the physical geography. Towards the end of the nineteenth century, the Jewish population was no more than 25,000, and they lived amongst the Palestinians, who numbered 550,000.[58] As in the case of Kashmir, Britain

---

[55] S Majumder, 'Analysis: Making Determined Progress' BBC News 6 September 2004 <http://news.bbc.co.uk/1/hi/world/south_asia/3631550.stm> (1 October 2004).

[56] On 'disappearances' in Kashmir see Amnesty International Report <http://web.amnesty.org/library/Index/engASA200021999> (28 September 2004).

[57] There is a significant amount of legal literature on this subject. Note reference made to studies n 35 above; also see I Abu-Lughod (ed), *The Arab-Israeli Confrontation of June 1967: An Arab Perspective* (Ann Arbor, UMI Books on Demand, 1996); W Laqueur, *The Road to War, 1967: The Origins of the Arab-Israel Conflict* (London, Weidenfeld & Nicolson, 1968); A Cassese, *Self-Determination of Peoples: A Legal Reappraisal* (Cambridge, Cambridge University Press, 1995); N Guyatt, *The Absence of Peace: Understanding the Israeli-Palestinian Conflict* (London, Zed Books, 1998); C Bell, *Peace Agreements and Human Rights* (Oxford, Oxford University Press, 2000).

[58] See Guyatt, n 57 above, at 2.

exploited the religious and nationalistic divisions within the local population.[59] In order to gain support of the Arabs in the British war against the Ottomans, Palestinian Arabs were enticed with the prospect of an independent State.[60] Soon thereafter, in 1918, the British Foreign Secretary, Lord Balfour, produced the famous Balfour Declaration promising a 'homeland' for the Jewish people.[61] The Balfour Declaration, the prospect of a Jewish State and the terrible atrocities committed against the Jews in Europe prompted huge Zionist migrations into Palestinian lands. By 1947, the Jewish population in Palestine had swelled to over 600,000.[62]

The terrible annihilation which the Jewish people suffered during the Second World War evoked enormous emotions. However, out of this tragedy emerged the ambitious plot of replacing Palestine with a permanent Jewish homeland—the State of Israel. In the process of creating Israel, terrible violations of human rights were to take place. The newly arrived Jews took over the lands, properties and livelihoods of the native Palestinians. It was ironic that many of the atrocities that had been visited upon innocent Jews by the Nazis were to be repeated by the Jews themselves against the Palestinians. Echoing this sentiment, Guyatt makes the following observations:

> . . . the re-emergence of anti-semitism in parts of Europe was a strong incentive for Jews to migrate, especially after Hitler's consolidation of power in 1933. However, the terrible developments in Europe should not be allowed to obscure the Palestinian perspective on Jewish immigration. The Palestinian people were clearly not to blame for the rise of Hitler, or of his racist agenda. Although some Israelis have tried to implicate Palestinians in the Nazi genocide, it is undeniable that the indigenous population of Palestine played no part whatsoever in the cleansing of Jewish areas of Europe. Instead the Palestinians were faced in the 1930s and the 1940s with the loss of their own lands at the hands of Jewish victims fleeing to Palestine to escape Hitler. In Palestine, there was no just compromise between the Palestinians and the Jewish settlers; instead the sins visited on European Jews were subsequently visited on Palestinians entirely innocent of the initial crimes.[63]

After the end of the Second World War, Britain referred the matter of Palestine's future to the newly established United Nations. The United Nations General Assembly responded through the creation of a United Nations Special Committee on Palestine (UNSCOP) to propose a solution for the territory.[64] UNSCOP could not adopt a unanimous view. A

---

[59] Bell, n 57 above, at 70.
[60] *Ibid.*
[61] *Ibid.*
[62] Guyatt, n 57 above, at 2.
[63] *Ibid*, at 3 (footnote omitted).
[64] Cassese, n 57 above, at 234.

majority recommended partition and the creation of two independent States. In addition, there was to be an internationalised zone consisting of Jerusalem. The minority view, however, was the establishment of a federal union consisting of autonomous Palestinian and Jewish zones.[65] The General Assembly ultimately opted for the partition plan. Through its Resolution 18(II) of 29 November 1947, the General Assembly recommended the creation of three separate entities within the mandated territory: a Jewish State, a Palestinian State and an international zone (consisting of the holy city of Jerusalem) under UN supervision.[66] There was unfortunately a bias in the UN plan which proved a recipe for future disasters. It granted Jews—by then a third of the population of Palestine—56 per cent of the land. Such a plan was unacceptable to the Palestinian people who felt betrayed, cheated and humiliated.[67] Amidst the withdrawal of the British, and an escalation of the conflict, the Zionist leadership announced the setting up of the State of Israel on 14 May 1948. The unacceptability of the proposed partition plan led to a civil war also involving the new State of Israel and its Arab Muslim neighbour States.[68] By the time the hostilities ended in 1949, the State of Israel had made further substantial territorial gains. The conflict also resulted in the creation of tens of thousands of Palestinian refugees, residing in squalor in makeshift camps in the West Bank, Gaza and Jordan.[69]

Further occupation of Palestinian lands was to take place during 1967, a consequence of pre-emptive war imposed by Israel.[70] The 1967 war (the six-day war) brought additional misery and upheavals for the Palestinians. Over 100,000 people were displaced with the Israeli occupation of the Golan Heights and Quneitra region. Around 160,000 refugees from the West Bank along with 15,000 refugees from the Gaza Strip had to escape to East Jordan. They were subsequently to be joined by another quarter of a million Palestinian refugees, formerly residents of the West Bank and the Gaza Strip.[71]

---

[65] *Ibid.*

[66] For the text of the Resolution see Israel Ministry of Foreign Affairs, Future Government of Palestine—General Assembly Resolution 181–II (29 November 1947) <http://www.mfa.gov.il/MFA/Foreign%20Relations/Israels%20Foreign%20Relations%20since%201947/1947-1974/Future%20Government%20of%20Palestine-%20General%20Assembly%20R > (2 October 2004).

[67] Guyatt, n 57 above, at 4–6.

[68] Bell, n 57 above, at 71.

[69] According to Takkenberg, 'some 750,000 Palestinians had fled their homes and were living in make shift refugee camps in the Gaza Strip, the West Bank, Jordan, Lebanon and Syria. Holocaust survivors from Europe's displaced persons camps flocked into Israel and took over the farms and homes of the departed Arabs. The first wave of oriental Jews also came in: For many of them it was like entering the gates of Paradise. For the Palestinians a long misery had begun'. L Takkenberg, *The Status of Palestinian Refugees in International Law* (Oxford, Clarendon Press, 1998) at 13.

[70] See Cassese, n 57 above, at 234.

[71] Takkenberg, n 69 above, at 17–18.

After the ceasefire, Israel occupied the Gaza Strip, the West Bank, East Jerusalem, Sania Desert and the Golan Heights. The Sania Desert was returned to Egypt as a consequence of the agreement at Camp David (September 1978). All other territories have, however, remained in Israeli possession.[72] Notwithstanding substantial international pressure and internal uprising (most recently reflected through an *intifada*) Israel has continued with the policy of occupation of Palestinian lands. In order to consolidate its hold on the illegal occupation, Jewish settlements have been expanded and developed. The Palestinians have been forcibly deprived of all of their fundamental human rights, including their right to existence and that of self-determination. They are excluded from their properties and possessions; dubbed as terrorists they are hounded, persecuted and tortured by the Israeli military on a daily basis. Israel refuses to acknowledge the illegality of its occupation, and there is a continuation of the policy of persecution, repression, extra-judicial killings and physical extermination of the Palestinian Muslims.[73]

In a further effort to encroach on Palestinian lands and to deprive Palestinians of their livelihoods, Israel recently embarked upon the task of building of a wall, the so-called 'security wall'.[74] The construction of this wall has been criticised by the international community, and declared unlawful by an advisory opinion of the International Court of Justice.[75] The international community—with very few exceptions—has also supported the cause of the Palestinians. Amongst numerous of its Resolutions, the United Nations General Assembly has reiterated the Palestinian right to self-determination. The General Assembly Resolution of 10 December 1969 accords recognition to the 'inalienable rights of the Palestinians';[76] the Resolution of 8 December 1970 deems the Palestinians 'entitled to equal rights and self-determination, in accordance with the Charter of the United Nations';[77] and General Assembly Resolution of

[72] Takkenberg, n 69 above, at 17–18.
[73] See O Ben-Naftali and KR Michaeli, 'Justice-Ability: A Critique of the Alleged Non-Justiciability of Israel's Policy of Targeted Killings' (2003) 1 *Journal of International Criminal Justice* 368.
[74] See J Freedland, 'Through the Heart: Israel's 100km 'security barrier' makes life a misery, and a two-state solution a virtual impossibility' *The Guardian* 26 May 2004 at 21; 'Israel's Wall is "Illegal"' *Times* 9 July 2004 at 19.
[75] ICJ Advisory Opinion, *Legal Consequences of the Construction of a Wall in the Occupied Palestinian Territory* <http://www.icj-cij.org/icjwww/idecisions.htm> (3 October 2004).
[76] GA Res 2535(XXIV) 10 December 1969 (United Nations Relief and Works Agency for Palestine Refugees in the Near East) A/RES/2535(XXIV)A–C.
[77] GA Res 2672 (XXV) United Nations Relief and Works Agency for Palestine Refugees in the Near East A/RES/2672 (XXV) A–D (8 December 1970). The General Assembly *Recognising* inter alia, that the problem of the Palestinian Arab refugees has arisen from the denial of their inalienable rights under the Charter of the United Nations and the Universal Declaration of Human Rights,
Recalling its resolution 2535 B (XXIV) of 10 December 1969, in which it reaffirmed the inalienable rights of the people of Palestine,

22 November 1974 reaffirms the Palestinians' right to self-determination.[78] The Security Council of the United Nations has also passed innumerable resolutions requiring Israel to withdraw from occupied territories. In the aftermath of the Israeli-Arab war of 1967, the Security Council passed Resolution 242 demanding a withdrawal of Israeli forces from the lands occupied as a consequence of the war.[79] An additional resolution reiterating withdrawal and termination of all military activities was adopted in 1973.[80] In the 1980s and 1990s the Council passed a series of Resolutions emphasising the unacceptability of acquisition of territory through the use of force.[81] There has also been some progress in developing a peace dialogue through such initiatives as the Camp David, Madrid and Oslo negotiations.[82]

From this discussion, it is obvious that there is no shortage of concern for the plight of the Palestinians. Having said that, in retrospect (and in the light of insensitive and belligerent policies instituted by Israel post 11 September 2001) not much appears to have been achieved. The Israelis have the one unwavering staunch ally—the United States—whose power and influence in this uni-polar world order remains critical. United States foreign policy has been inconsistent, often acting against the interests and aspirations of the Palestinians. Under the current republican regime of President George W Bush the US approach has been particularly disappointing. Notwithstanding consistent and blatant violations of international law by the Israelis, the United States' attitude is one of continued support for Israel. The Palestinians feel particularly aggrieved at the United States' lack of sensitivity for their cause; instead there appears to be an active and sustained campaign of assisting and promoting Israel in its ruthless, unlawful policies of repression and illegal occupation of Palestinian lands.[83]

Bearing in mind the principle of equal rights and self-determination of peoples enshrined in Articles 1 and 55 of the Charter and more recently reaffirmed in the Declaration on Principles of International Law concerning Friendly Relations and Co-operation among States in accordance with the Charter of the United Nations,

1. *Recognizes* that the people of Palestine are entitled to equal rights and self-determination, in accordance with the Charter of the United Nations;
2. *Declares* that full respect for the inalienable rights of the people of Palestine is an indispensable element in the establishment of a just and lasting peace in the Middle East.

[78] Question of Palestine, A/RES/3236 (XXIX), GA Res 22 November 1974.

[79] See SC Res 242 S/RES/242 (22 November 1967).

[80] SC Res 338 S/RES/338 (22 October 1973).

[81] See SC Res 1322 S/RES/1322 (7 October 2000); SC Res 476 S/RES/476 (30 June 1980); SC Res 478 S/RES/478 (20 August 1980); SC Res 672 S/RES/672 (12 October 1990); SC Res 1073 S/RES/1073 (28 September 1996).

[82] For a useful discussion of these initiatives see Bell, n 57 above, at 81–91.

[83] For a recent example of such an action note the United States opposition to Security Council Resolution aimed at preventing the removal of the Palestinian leader, Yasir Arafat. UN Doc S/2003/891 examined by SD Murphy, 'Contemporary Practice of the United States Relating to International Law: International Organization: UN Resolution Demanding

THE OIC AND LEGAL INSTRUMENTS COMBATING
INTERNATIONAL TERRORISM

The OIC has repeatedly taken the position that the subject of international and regional terrorism needs to be reviewed comprehensively. Such a comprehensive review would include examination of substantive issues. Conceptual and definitional problems would also need to be revisited. In its Ninth Summit (in Doha, the State of Qatar during 12–13 November 2000), the final communiqué dealt with the issue of definition of terrorism in the following terms:

> The Conference expressed again its support for the convening of a conference under the aegis of the United Nations to define the concept of terrorism and make a distinction between terrorism and people's struggle for national liberation.[84]

This position had been repeated in the Declaration that emerged from the Ninth Summit, where the OIC took the view that:

> We again condemn all forms and manifestations of terrorism whatever its source as reflected in the unanimous adoption of the Agreement of the Organization of the Islamic Conference on Combating Terrorism, and in the repeated promises for the convening of a World Conference under the auspices of the United Nations to address this phenomenon in an effective manner away from racism and bias and to consider effective ways and means to eradicate it. We reaffirm here that a clear separation must be made between terrorism, on the one hand, and people's struggle for national liberation including the struggle of the Palestinian people and the elimination of foreign occupation and colonial hegemony as well as for regaining the right to self-determination, on the other hand.[85]

The OIC has been at the forefront in its efforts to deal with international, regional and domestic terrorism. The primary instrument in this regard is the Convention of the OIC on Combating International Terrorism. The Convention was adopted at Ouagadougou on 1 July 1999. The preamble to the treaty is of particular significance since it not only condemns terrorism as a violation of *Sharia* principles but also establishes the essential relationship between terrorist acts and breaches of fundamental human rights. The preamble provides inter alia:

---

that Israel not Deport or Threaten Palestinian President' (2004) 98 *American Journal of International Law* 171; also see J Quigley, 'International Law violations by the United States in the Middle East as a factor behind Anti-American Terrorism' (2002) 63 *University of Pittsburgh Law Review* 815.

[84] Ninth OIC Summit, Doha, State of Qatar, 16–17 Sha'ban 1421 H, 13 November 2002 (Final Communiqué).

[85] *Ibid.*

Pursuant to the tenets of the tolerant Islamic *Sharia* which reject all forms of violence and terrorism, and in particular those based on extremism and call for protection of human rights, which provisions are paralleled by the principles and rules of international law founded on cooperation between peoples for the establishment of peace

Abiding by the lofty, moral and religious principles particularly the provisions of the Islamic *Sharia* as well as the human heritage of the Islamic *Ummah* . . .

The preamble goes on to affirm principles of general international law, *inter alia* sovereignty, territorial integrity, political independence and non-intervention in domestic affairs. There is also an important acknowledgement of the right to self-determination and a firm belief that 'terrorism constitutes a gross violation of human rights in particular the right to freedom and security, as well as an obstacle to the free functioning of institutions and socio-economic development, as it aims at destabilizing States'. With such strong preambular condemnation of international terrorism, the text of the treaty provides a detailed definition of terrorism.

Defining Terrorism

We have noted in our earlier analysis the difficulties associated with defining terrorism.[86] In the light of these difficulties, it is positive to find a comprehensive definition of terrorism within the text of an international treaty. The definition is further elaborated by references to additional treaties dealing with the subject. Article 1(2) of the Convention defines terrorism as:

any act of violence or threat thereof notwithstanding its motives or intentions perpetrated to carry out an individual or collective criminal plan with the aim of terrorizing people or threatening to harm them or imperilling their lives, honour, freedoms, security or rights or exposing the environment or any facility or public or private property to hazards or occupying or seizing them, or endangering a national resource, or international facilities, or threatening the stability, territorial integrity, political unity or sovereignty of independent States.

Terrorism is given a very broad meaning. According to the above definition an act is regarded as a terrorist act if its aim is to terrorise people or threaten them with harm. The threat need not be a specific one so long as it endangers lives, honour, rights, freedoms and security of the individuals concerned. Terrorism could also be directed against the State, its stability, territorial integrity, sovereignty and independence. Furthermore, terrorism could be conducted against public as well as private property through seizure or an unacceptable level of damage. Environmental

---

[86] See chapter 3 above.

concerns are at the forefront, a direct consequence of some of the most tragic conflicts entered into by OIC Member States themselves. The eight-year Iran-Iraq war was a travesty so far as environmental issues were concerned. Similarly, deliberate damage was inflicted upon the environment in the aftermath of the Iraqi invasion of Kuwait in August 1990.[87] Substantial damage to the environment and natural resources occurred in Iraq as a consequence of recent United States and allied military intervention. One of the critical subjects which needs to be assessed is the liability of the Coalition forces in the aftermath of the US invasion of March 2003. Significant evidence of widespread abuse of the human, financial, cultural and historical resources of Iraq has now emerged.[88] Under general international law and in international humanitarian law, the occupation forces remain liable for damage and harm inflicted during their occupation.

In its section on definitions, the OIC Convention elaborates on the meaning of 'terrorist crimes'. By this it is meant:

> any crime executed, started or participated in order to realize a terrorist objective in any of the Contracting States or against its nationals, assets or interests or foreign facilities and nationals residing in its territory punishable by its internal law.

There then follows a list of International Conventions which further define the concept of international terrorism. All acts stated in the following Conventions are enshrined as terrorism:

a) Convention on 'Offences and Other Acts Committed on Board Aircrafts' (Tokyo, 14.9.1963).

b) Convention on 'Suppression of Unlawful Seizure of Aircraft' (The Hague, 16.12.1970).

c) Convention on 'Suppression of Unlawful Acts Against the Safety of Civil Aviation' signed at Montreal on 23.9.1971 and its Protocol (Montreal, 10.12.1984).

d) Convention on the 'Prevention and Punishment of Crimes Against Persons Enjoying International Immunity, Including Diplomatic Agents' (New York, 14.12.1973).

e) International Convention Against the Taking of Hostages (New York, 1979).

f) United Nations Law of the Sea Convention of 1982 and its related provisions on piracy at sea.

---

[87] G Plant, *Environmental Protection and the Law of War: A 'Fifth Geneva' Convention on the Protection of the Environment in the Time of Armed Conflict* (London, John Wiley, 1992); see J Rehman, 'Islamic Law and Environmental Regulations: An Analysis of the Rules and Principles contained in the *Sharia* and Modern Muslim States Practices' paper prepared for the University of Tezukayama (Japan), January 2004 (Unpublished, on file with the author).

[88] See 'The "Taguba Report" on Treatment of *Abu Ghraib* Prisoners in Iraq' <http://news.findlaw.com/hdocs/docs/iraq/tagubarpt.html> (30 July 2004); 'The Roots of Torture: The Road to Abu Ghraib Began After 9/11, When Washington Wrote New Rules to Fight a New Kind of War'. *The Newsweek World News* (United States, 24 May 2004).

g) Convention on the 'Physical Protection of Nuclear Material' (Vienna, 1979).

h) Protocol for the Suppression of Unlawful Acts of Violence at Airports Serving International Civil Aviation-Supplementary to the Convention for the Suppression of Unlawful Acts Against the Safety of Civil Aviation (Montreal, 1988).

i) Protocol for the Suppression of Unlawful Acts Against the Safety of Fixed Platforms on the Continental Shelf (Rome, 1988).

j) Convention for the Suppression of Unlawful Acts Against the Safety of Maritime Navigation (Rome, 1988).

k) International Convention for the Suppression of Terrorist Bombings (New York, 1997).

l) Convention on the Marking of Plastic Explosives for the purposes of Detection (Montreal, 1991)

This is a comprehensive list of treaties that exist in the international arena tackling international terrorism. The commitment to eradicate all forms of terrorism remains firm; the clause in Article 2(4) excluding States that have not ratified any of the aforementioned conventions is rendered largely redundant due to a significant ratification of anti-terrorism treaties by Islamic States.

The Convention nevertheless presents a strong affirmation of the right of self-determination. Accordingly, therefore, peoples' struggle against foreign aggression and colonial or racist regimes is not to be considered a terrorist crime. Self-determination is a well-established right in international law, and as we have noted already, one with a *jus cogens* character. Peoples' struggle, including an armed struggle to gain the right to self-determination is not to be regarded as terrorism.[89] The international community remains under an obligation to support peoples struggling for their right to self-determination. There is thus a substantial risk of conflict between a people's struggle for self-determination, which involves an armed uprising and resistance on the one hand, and the complete prohibition of terrorist activities and all forms of violence on the other. This apparently conflicting approach has been regarded as generating 'a great amount of confusion'[90] and has been criticised in various quarters.[91] There is substance in such criticisms. For members of the OIC the struggle for liberation and self-determination is only legitimate when conducted 'in accordance with the principles of international law'.[92] When applied within the domestic context of Member States such provisions reveal

---

[89] Article 2(a).

[90] Report by the International Bar Association's Task Force on International Terrorism, *International Terrorism: Legal Challenges and Responses* (Ardsley NY, Transnational Publishers, 2003) at 2.

[91] *Ibid.*

[92] Article 2(a).

troubling features. Many of the States have inherently undemocratic systems of governance; denials of the 'internal' right of self-determination and negation of rule of law are widespread.[93]

According to established principles within the Convention, an example of the breach of norms of international law would be where aggression is conducted against kings, heads of State, their spouses, or their descendants.[94] Any form of aggression is impermissible against crown princes, vice-presidents or others enjoying diplomatic immunity.[95] Similarly no cause or political motivation can justify murder, robbery of individuals and sabotage or destruction of public property.[96] Furthermore, crimes in the nature of illegal drug trafficking, money laundering and financing of terrorists cannot be condoned, whatever the motives behind such an act.[97]

Fundamentals of Islamic Cooperation for Combating Terrorism

Part II of the Convention, entitled 'Foundations of Islamic Cooperation for Combating Terrorism', addresses a range of issues. There is first and foremost a commitment on the part of State parties not to initiate or participate in the organisation or financing of terrorists acts.[98] There is secondly a commitment to prevent and combat terrorist crimes and to undertake preventative measures. Such measures include barring their territories from being areas of planning and organisation of terrorist acts. States parties undertake to co-operate in combating international terrorism; they are obliged to co-ordinate with other Contracting States, in particular those which suffer from similar and common terrorist acts.[99] Such co-operation can be evidenced in detecting transportation, importing, stockpiling and use of weapons and other means of aggression unless it is intended for a specific purpose. The States parties also undertake to develop and strengthen systems of surveillance, which also entails securing borders and land, sea and air passages to prevent infiltration. There is also a commitment to re-enforce protection, security and safety of diplomatic and consular persons and missions and to protect personnel in international organisations. State parties undertake to promote intelligence activities and co-ordinate them with the intelligence activities of each Contracting State pursuant to their respective intelligence policies, with the view to exposing the objectives of terrorist groups and organisations thwarting

---

[93] See J Rehman, *The Weaknesses in the International Protection of Minority Rights* (Kluwer Law International, The Hague, 2000).

[94] Article 2(c)(1).

[95] Article 2(c)(2)(3).

[96] Article 2(d).

[97] Article 2(a).

[98] Article 3(1).

[99] Article 3(2).

their designs and revealing the extent of their danger to security and stability. States parties also undertake to set up a database to collect and analyse data on terrorist elements and their movements. This database is intended to be regularly monitored and reviewed.[100]

The Convention sets out a commitment to arrest those who have committed terrorist acts. There is an obligation either to submit the case to competent authorities for the purpose of prosecution in national courts or to extradite the individuals concerned in accordance with the rules laid out. This provision is a reaffirmation of the principle of *aut dedere aut judicare*, a fundamental norm of international law relating to terrorism. The State parties also undertake to provide effective protection to individuals working in the field of criminal justice and to witnesses and investigators. There is an obligation to render all necessary assistance to the victims of terrorist acts.[101]

Division II of the treaty provides further details regarding Areas of cooperation. There is an emphasis on exchange of information. Information is to be exchanged on all areas, including activities and crimes committed by:

> terrorist groups, their leaders, their elements, their headquarters, training, means and sources that provide finance and weapons, types of arms, ammunition and explosives utilized as well as other ways and means to attack, kill and destroy.[102]

The co-operation extends to confiscation of arms, weapons, explosives and any other incendiary or terrorist device.[103] Another key element of co-operation is the pledge by Member States to support each other in the investigation of terrorist offences. In the broader picture, there is an undertaking to have an exchange of expertise, to exchange studies and to enhance research on combating terrorist acts.[104] States parties also commit themselves to providing technical assistance and to holding joint sessions. There is to be further co-operation in the field of education, which advances an ideology of tolerance and human values.[105] This is a particularly significant view since it challenges the stereotypical prejudicial vision of Islam as retrogressive and decadent. It provides:

> Promoting information activities and supporting the mass media in order to confront the vicious campaign against Islam, by projecting the true image of tolerance of Islam, and exposing the designs and danger of terrorist groups against the stability and security of Islamic States.[106]

---

[100] Division I, Article 3(A)8.
[101] Division I, Article 3(B)4.
[102] Division II, Article 4(1)(a).
[103] Division II, Article 4(1)(4)(b).
[104] Division II, Article 4(1)(1)—Exchange of Information.
[105] Division II, Article 4(1)(1)—Education and Information Field.
[106] Division II, Article 4(1)(1)—Education and Information Field.

The Convention urges States parties to introduce in their educational curricula lessons of humanity and tolerance. In earlier discussion, we examined the flexibility that is inherent in *Sharia*.[107] In order to adapt to developing norms of social existence, the value of *Ijtihad* was emphasised.[108] The same point and reliance upon *Ijtihad* is relied upon by the Convention when it notes:

> Supporting efforts aimed at keeping abreast of the age by introducing an advanced Islamic thought based on ijtihad by which Islam is distinguished.

The Convention provides for co-operation in the judicial field.[109] While emphasising the significance of extradition, it notes that extradition is not permissible in a range of instances,[110] including situations where the offence is one of a political nature, where the extradition is sought solely for dereliction of military obligations, if the action at the time of the extradition request has elapsed, if there is a tenuous connection of the State requesting extradition, if pardon was granted and included the perpetrators of these crimes, or if the legal system of the requested State does not permit extradition of its nationals.[111]

Section II of the Convention is dedicated to what is termed 'Rogatory Commission'.[112] Article 9 sets out the obligations of States in this respect. It notes:

> Each Contracting State shall request from any other Contracting State to undertake in its territory rogatory action with respect to any judicial procedures concerning an action involving a terrorist crime and in particular:
>
> (1) To hear witnesses and testimonies taken as evidence.
> (2) To communicate legal documents.
> (3) To implement inquiry and detention procedures.
> (4) To undertake on the scene inspection and analyse evidence.
> (5) To obtain necessary evidence or documents or records or their certified copies.

In its efforts to combat terrorism the Convention lays particular emphasis upon exchange of information among Member States, co-operation in the investigation of alleged terrorist acts, exchange of expertise and technical assistance and extradition of offenders. A special emphasis is placed upon judicial co-operation, exchange of evidence, and extradition. The Convention provides for very detailed implementation procedures; indeed some of the provisions of the implementing procedures are so

---

[107] See chapter 2 above.
[108] *Ibid.*
[109] See Chapter II, Section 1, Article 5.
[110] *Ibid.*
[111] See Chapter II, Article 6(3)–(8).
[112] See Section II, Article 9.

detailed that they appear more in the nature of supplementary executive ordinances than the body of the treaty. Chapter I, Part III, Article 23, for example, requires that a detailed and comprehensive extradition request is to be submitted in writing, with the original (or authenticated copy of) the indictment, arrest, order or any other instrument of identical weight.[113] According to Article 24, the judicial authorities in the requesting State may also seek preventative orders subject to the arrival of an extradition request.[114] The maximum duration of preventative detention is sixty days.[115] There are also significant and detailed provisions for protecting witnesses and experts. For a requesting State to secure the presence of witnesses the summons are to include appropriate terms including allowances for travel expenses, accommodation etc.[116] No coercive means are to be used to force the presence of witnesses,[117] nor can they be detained or prosecuted while providing evidence.[118]

Part IV of the treaty deals with final provisions. Article 39 provides that after ratification or accession State parties are required to deposit the instrument with the General Secretariat of the OIC. The Secretariat shall inform all Member States of the details of the deposition. According to Article 40(1) the Convention is to enter into force thirty days after the deposit of the seventh instrument of ratification or accession at the OIC General Secretariat. Article 41 provides that it is impermissible for any State party to make any reservations, explicitly or implicitly to act in conflict with the provisions of the Convention. While it is permissible to withdraw from the Convention, it can operate only when a written request is made to the Secretary General and with a lapse of six months since such a request was made.[119]

THE ROLE OF THE OIC AND ITS MEMBER STATES IN THE AFTERMATH OF 11 SEPTEMBER 2001

In the aftermath of attacks in the United States on 11 September 2001 there was condemnation of terrorist acts by individual Members as well as by the Organisation itself. All Member States expressed their deepest regret and passed condolences to the families of individuals who died on 11 September. This expression of tragedy was without any exceptions or reservations. There was also an urgency to distance Islam and *Sharia* from

---

[113] See Chapter I, Part III, Article 23.
[114] *Ibid*, Article 24.
[115] Article 26.
[116] Article 35.
[117] Article 35.
[118] Article 36(1)(2).
[119] Article 42(1)(2).

the motives of terrorist hijackers. The same sentiments were advanced by the OIC in its final communiqué of the Ninth extra-ordinary Session of the Islamic Conference of Foreign Minster (ICFM), in Doha, Qatar. The conference stressed that:

> such shameful terrorist acts [as those of 11 September 2001] are opposed to the tolerant message of Islam which spurns aggression, calls for peace, co-existence, tolerance and respect among people, highly prizes the dignity of human life and prohibits killing of the innocent. It further rejected any attempts alleging the existence of any connection or relation between the Islamic faith and the terror- ist acts as such are not in the interest of the multilateral efforts to combat terror- ism and further damage relations among peoples of the world. It stressed the need to undertake a joint effort to promote dialogue and create links or contacts between the Islamic world and the west in order to reach mutual understanding and building bridges of confidence between the two civilizations.[120]

The resolve to condemn terrorism in all its forms was apparent in the Kuala Lumpur Declaration on International Terrorism adopted at the extra-ordinary Session of the Islamic Conference of the Foreign Ministers on Terrorism.[121] In this Declaration the Ministers present their response to the 11 September attacks.[122] Invoking Islamic solidarity, they recall the earlier measures that had been adopted by the OIC for combating inter- national terrorism, in particular the OIC Convention on Terrorism, the Code of Conduct for Combating International Terrorism, the Declaration of the Ninth extra-ordinary Session of ICFM and other relevant Resolutions passed by the Conference.[123] In two important provisions the Declaration reaffirms the commitment to 'the principles and true teach- ings of Islam which abhor aggression, value peace, tolerance and respect as well as prohibiting the killing of innocent people'[124] and reject 'any attempt to link Islam and Muslims to terrorism as terrorism has no associ- ation with any religion, civilization or nationality'.[125] There is an absolute and unequivocal condemnation of terrorism in all its manifestations and forms, the Declaration regarding terrorism as a serious threat to inter- national peace and security and a grave violation of human rights.[126]

---

[120] Final Communiqué of the Ninth Extraordinary Session of the Islamic Conference of Foreign Ministers, Doha, Qatar, 10 October 2001.

[121] Declaration on International Terrorism adopted at the extraordinary session of the Islamic Conference of the Foreign Ministers on Terrorism, Kuala Lumpur, adopted 3 April 2002, text available at <http://www.oic-oci.org/english/fm/11_extraordinary/declaration.htm> (12 October 2004).

[122] *Ibid*, Article 1.

[123] *Ibid*, Article 2.

[124] *Ibid*, Article 4.

[125] *Ibid*, Article 5.

[126] *Ibid*, Article 7: We unequivocally condemn acts of international terrorism in all its forms and manifestations, including state terrorism, irrespective of motives, perpetrators and victims as terrorism poses a serious threat to international peace and security and is a grave violation of human rights.

There is also a reiteration of the norms of international law, in particular the support of peoples under colonial, alien and foreign occupation. The Declaration acknowledges the strength and binding nature of all relevant United Nations Security Council Resolutions, in particularly Security Council Resolution 1373.[127] There is also an interest in expediting accession or ratification of relevant international Conventions and Protocols relating to anti-terrorism. The struggle of the Palestinian people for self-determination is commended and members advocate the necessity for an independent Palestinian State to be established. By the same token there is condemnation of Israel for:

> escalating military campaign against the Palestinian people, including the daily brutalization and humiliation of its civilians, resulting in mounting casualties, strangulation of the Palestinian economy, systematic and indiscriminate destruction of houses and residential facilities as well as infrastructure, institutions and structures of the Palestinian National Authority.[128]

There is an urgency on the part of the Foreign Ministers to address the main causes of terrorism. The Declaration pleads against unilateral action against any Islamic country, on the ostensible basis of combating international terrorism. While such a unilateralist approach is seen as contrary to international law, this has been precisely the course adopted by the United States against several Members of the Organisation. The most recent example is the use of military force against Iraq. The Kuala Lumpur Declaration presents a Plan of Action, whereby a thirteen member openended Ministerial Level OIC Committee on International Terrorism is established.[129] The Committee is required to present its recommendations to Member States and to the ICFM for consideration and action. The mandate of the Committee is to create:

> 1 Measures to strengthen OIC cooperation and coordination in combating international terrorism;
> 2 Ways of expediting the implementation of the OIC Code of Conduct and the Convention on Combating International Terrorism;
> 3 Measures in projecting the true image of Islam. These include holding seminars and workshops to promote a better understanding of Islam and its principles;
> 4 Measures in strengthening dialogue and understanding among different civilizations, cultures and faiths, for instance, by building on initiatives such as the United Nations Dialogue Among Civilizations and the OIC-EU Joint Forum on Harmony and Civilization;
> 5 Other measures, as appropriate and in accordance with the Charter of the OIC as well as Summit and ICFM resolutions, in response to developments affecting Muslims and Islam arising from action to combat terrorism.

---

[127] *Ibid*, Plan of Action, Articles 6 and 7.
[128] *Ibid*, Article 12.
[129] *Ibid*, Plan of Action.

CONCLUSIONS

The present chapter has examined the role of the OIC in combating international and regional outbursts of terrorism. In the light of various initiatives undertaken to deal with terrorism, the OIC deserves credit. The Organisation is also to be applauded for its role in condemning and curbing terrorist and sectarian movements that have surfaced within Islamic States. As this chapter has discussed, there is great value in the OIC's Convention on Terrorism. The Convention not only represents a symbolic opposition to acts of terror, many of its provisions are well articulated and in an appropriate environment should provide a workable framework. Notwithstanding these positive and valuable approaches, the Organisation remains deficient in dealing with the dangers of terrorism. This is particularly the case when substantial threats emanate from non-State actors such as al-Qaeda. Our examination has revealed the terrible atrocities that are being visited upon the people of Palestine and Kashmir; such an environment provides a prefect breeding ground for new recruits for al-Qaeda and other radical organisations.

The plethora of institutions that form parts of the OIC appear disjointed and lack co-ordination. There are also considerable practical difficulties attached to the implementation of the Terrorism Convention. The constitutional structures of many of the States that form part of the Organisation represent a significant impediment. In the existing phase of international relations the character of Islamic States is under review. Several of the Islamic regimes have been castigated as supporters of terrorism. There is some validity in accusations and recriminations against a number of governments currently in charge of Islamic States—they regularly invoke the tools of oppression, violence and terrorism to perpetuate their existence. Terrorism features prominently in the denials of their peoples' legitimate rights and negation of the right to 'internal' self-determination. In addition, several regimes have been implicated in the exportation of terrorism overseas, a feature which is highly troubling and problematic.

8

Concluding Observations

POSITIONING ISLAM WITHIN THE CONTEXT OF INTERNATIONAL TERRORISM

ISLAM AND ITS values are a point of contention in the world order that has been constructed after 11 September 2001. There is much debate about the credentials of Islam in the context of terrorism. Critics of Islam continue to regard it as an aggressive, authoritarian religion which sanctions violence and terrorism.[1] Islamic values are also often regarded as violating internationally recognised human rights.[2] There is no denying the fact that there are stresses and strains in the interpretation of any faith, religion or ideology: as a great religion, Islam has been subjected to divergent interpretations. It is also an undeniable and unfortunate reality that many contemporary Islamic States have undemocratic and authoritarian regimes, which perpetuate their existence through fear, violence and terrorism. While it is tragic that independent Statehood for Islamic countries rarely went hand in hand with order and cohesion, the political elite itself has to account for subsequent legal and political instability. Many of these elites continued with the policies of their former European masters.[3] Others, in opposition, turned towards religious ideologies or ethnic and nationalistic loyalties to jostle for power. Islam and imposition of *Sharia* therefore became part of the political rhetoric. The vision of the *Sharia* portrayed by the Taliban in Afghanistan (1996–2003), or by General Zia-ul-Haq in Pakistan (1977–1988) and President Ja'far Nimeiri in Sudan (1969–1985) was self-promotional: it was brutal, unforgiving and did not accord with the egalitarian and humanitarian notion also emanating from classical and modern Islamic

---

[1] See the introductory chapter of this book.

[2] *Ibid.* In particular note the comments made by the Italian Prime Minister Silvio Berlusconi.

[3] See J Rehman and N Roy, 'South Asia' in Minority Rights Group (ed), *World Directory of Minorities* (London, MRG, 1997) 534–69, at 534; P Thornberry, 'Self-Determination, Minorities, Human Rights: A Review of International Instruments' (1989) 38 *International & Comparative Law Quarterly* 867.

jurisprudence.[4] The primary deduction that could be derived from the experiences of Afghanistan, Iran, Pakistan and the Sudan is that schemes of Islamisation have been deployed to perpetuate and prolong undemocratic and arbitrary dictatorial regimes.

Opponents of Islam, as well as the extremist segments within the Islamic community, are likely to interpret *Sharia* as insensitive to modern international law and human rights. The present study has, however, challenged the myopic vision which perceives Islamic values as rigid and stagnated. It has also demonstrated that if understood rationally, the *Sharia* principles are not antithetical to promoting international law and a just legal order. An examination of the sources and content of the *Sharia* reveals a breadth and flexibility which reflects modern values of international law and human rights. It is this flexibility and breadth which has allowed conservative Islamic States such as Pakistan to fully endorse the standards established in the Universal Declaration on Human Rights and the Convention on the Elimination of All Forms of Discrimination against Women.[5]

The Islamic concept of *Jihad* is often erroneously labelled as synonymous with aggressive war and terrorist acts. In its essence, *Jihad* is an expression of endeavour and exertion in the cause of Allah: the principal form of *Jihad*, according to the *Sunna* of the Prophet, being acts of persuasion as opposed to aggression or violence.[6] The modern interpretation of *Jihad* authorising the use of force is limited to exceptional instances of self-defence—this is in consonance with the principles set out in the United Nations Charter.[7]

Islam is not, as some critics would argue, all about wars of aggression. In fact, as has been explored in the course of this work, the *Sharia* and *Siyar* have made monumental contributions to general international law and in establishing peaceful relations amongst nations and communities. Classical as well as modern Islamic legal systems criminalise acts of terrorism—it has been contended forcefully that if the trials of those

---

[4] On the Taliban see A Rashid, *Taliban: Militant Islam, Oil and Fundamentalism in Central Asia* (New Haven and London, Yale University Press, 2000); MJ Gohari, *The Taliban: Ascent to Power* (Karachi, Oxford University Press, 2000); on President Zia-ul-Haq's Islamisation policies and their after-effects see J Rehman, 'Minority Rights and Constitutional Dilemmas of Pakistan' (2001) 19 *Netherlands Quarterly of Human Rights* 417; on Sudan see C Eprile, *Sudan: The Long War* (London, Institute for the Study of Conflict, 1972); G Morrison, *The Southern Sudan and Eritrea: Aspects of Wider African Problems* (London, Minority Rights Group, 1973); AE Mayer, *Islam and Human Rights: Tradition and Politics*, 2nd edn (Boulder, Col, Westview Press, 1995) 156–9.

[5] See J Rehman, 'Accommodating Religious Identities in an Islamic State: International Law, Freedom of Religion and the Rights of Religious Minorities' (2000) 7 *International Journal on Minority and Group Rights* 139; SS Ali and J Rehman, 'Freedom of Religion versus Equality in International Human Rights Law: Conflicting Norms or Hierarchical Human Rights (A Case Study of Pakistan)' (2003) 21 *Nordic Journal of Human Rights* 404.

[6] See chapter 1 above.

[7] See Article 2(4) and Article 51 of the United Nations Charter.

involved in the 11 September attacks were conducted under Islamic laws their outcome would be unlikely to be different from trials held in other domestic or international legal systems.[8]

Modern Islamic States, conscious of the need to build a peaceful co-existence, have unequivocally accepted laws prohibiting the use of force. The commitment to condemn all forms of terrorism was evident in the absolute denunciation of the 11 September attacks.[9] Furthermore, the closest allies of the United States in the so-called 'war on terrorism' are from the Islamic world.

RATIONALISING THE DEBATE ON A CULTURE OF CONFLICT AND THE 'CLASH OF CIVILISATIONS'

In common with other great civilisations, the Islamic world has experienced momentous changes. At its zenith, Islam was the focus of attention and the cradle of human civilisation. The rationale for its dominance and prevalence was that:

> It was the best social and political order the times could offer. It prevailed because everywhere it found politically apathetic people robbed, oppressed, bullied, uneducated, and unorganised and it found selfish and unsound governments out of touch with people. It was the broadest, freshest and cleanest political idea that had yet come into actual activity in the world.[10]

Over time, however, the freshness and creativity behind the original Islamic ideology gave way to factionalism and in-fighting. Islamic legal approaches also faced stagnation—all doors to Ijtihad, it was argued, had been closed.[11] In a state of stagnation, Islamic communities found themselves overpowered and dominated by others who were more strategic, manipulative and powerful. Islamic laws and indigenous systems of governance were further disturbed by the misfortunes of colonialism. Islamic legal systems were removed and replaced by schemes whose objectives pure and simple were exploitation, abuse and subjugation. European colonialism legitimised racial superiority, slavery, ethnic cleansing and genocide.[12] In its historic developments, it has to be conceded that international law sanctified all acts of mass terrorism so

---

[8] See FE Vogal, 'The Trial of Terrorists Under Classical Islamic Law' (2002) 43 *Harvard International Law Journal* 53, at 63–4.

[9] See the final Communiqué of the Ninth Extraordinary Session of the Islamic Conference of Foreign Ministers, Doha, Qatar, 10 October 2001.

[10] HG Wells, *The Outline of History: Being a Plain History of Life and Mankind* (London, Cassell, 1925) at 613–14.

[11] NJ Coulson, *A History of Islamic Law* (Edinburgh, Edinburgh University Press, 1964) at 202.

[12] J Strawson, 'Introduction: In the name of Law' in J Strawson (ed), *Law After Ground Zero* (London, GlassHouse Press, 2002) at xix and xx.

long as these were conduct by 'civilised nations' over colonised indigenous people. The contemporary post-colonial world that emerged in the
aftermath of the Second World War was fashioned in the vision of the
imperialist political elite.[13] New States were carved out in a design hitherto established by the European powers, containing a recipe for future
ethnic and political conflict. More problematic were the schemes and
designs for preserving the global political and legal order. The tool of
western imposition was established through the powers and composition
of the Security Council. This was a body designed to maintain and enforce
international peace and security. A designation of permanent membership
and veto power was introduced to ensure that law or politics could not
adopt a course detrimental to specific interests. It was a legal order in
denial of justice, equity and fairness for all the peoples of the world. The
Islamic world has suffered at the hands of this unfairness of international
law. The Security Council has proved to be least supportive in matters
which mean the most to the Muslim peoples—the role of individual members of the Council, particularly the United States, in support of Israel has
been disappointing and has provoked resentment.

Notwithstanding the blatant and shocking violations of human rights
perpetuated by the State of Israel, there is little condemnation emanating
from the United States or Europe. Palestinians, on the other hand, are
frequently condemned as terrorists. Israel—with complete impunity—
continues to perpetuate practices of racial and religious oppression, extra-
judicial killings, torture, and forcible exclusion of millions of Palestinians
out of their homelands. Palestinians are denied their most fundamental
and inalienable right of self-determination. Nearly half of the Palestinian
population has been forced into refugeeism and statelessness, having to
suffer humiliation on a daily basis: witnessing their families and friends
brutalised and degraded it is little surprise that many resort to extremism
and militancy.[14]

Inherent in the international stance are policies bearing 'double-
standards'. No tangible action has been taken against Israel for its
violations of human rights, development of nuclear arsenal, weapons of
mass of destruction or for its innumerable breaches of United Nations
Security Council Resolutions. Yet, individual members of the Council continued to bomb Iraq intermittently during the 1990s and were eventually
unable to resist its invasion in March 2003 on suspicion that the regime

---

[13] See the discussion on the concept of *uti possidetis* and its implication on the modern State
structures—chapter 1 above.

[14] See chapter 7 above. See in particular examination of the Palestinian issue by N Guyatt,
The Absence of Peace: Understanding the Israeli-Palestinian Conflict (London, Zed Books, 1998);
C Bell, *Peace Agreements and Human Rights* (Oxford, Oxford University Press, 2000);
L Takkenberg, *The Status of Palestinian Refugees in International Law* (Oxford, Clarendon Press,
1998).

was developing weapons of mass destruction in breach of Security Council Resolutions.[15] The build up to the invasion of Iraq also saw a human rights argument advanced by the United States and the United Kingdom. President Saddam Hussein's dictatorial government and Iraq's repression of its ethnic and religious communities were put forward as additional grounds for justifying invasion and removal of the regime. This argument is fallacious in that for decades Saddam Hussein conducted such actions with the knowledge and support of the United States. Furthermore, the promotion and protection of human rights has only been a factor when its suits the political ambitions of powerful States; the worst violators of human rights in the neighbourhood of Iraq continue to be the closest allies and friends of the United States.[16] Indeed this so-called 'war on terrorism' has presented an excuse to dictatorial and autocratic regimes across the globe to repress, ignore and violate fundamental human rights—the world is silent and even appreciative of such actions so long as these regimes continue to purport allegiance to the ambitions of United States foreign policy.[17] Such duplicity, double-standards and selectivity have troubled not only the Muslim communities but also others who retain an objective vision of law and politics. According to a leading international lawyer, Professor Brownlie:

> The issue of selectivity can lead to claims of human rights violations being used as a powerful political weapon. Probably the most egregious example of this is provided by the case of Iraq. The Iraq-Iran War raged for eight years (1980–8). Iran was not the aggressor. During the conflict leading Western powers gave assistance to the Iraqi Government in the form of matrices for chemical weapons (which were used against Iran) and satellite intelligence. The Security Council took no action under Chapter VII of the Charter. In contrast, in the period from 1991 up to the United States attack on Iraq in March 2003, the same State took a strong line on the bad rights record of the Iraqi regime and the attack was

---

[15] For a useful discussion see D McGoldrick, *From '9–11' to the 'Iraq War 2003': International Law in an Age of Complexity* (Oxford, Hart, 2004) 47–86.

[16] Note the criticisms of violations of human rights conducted in the US Middle Eastern allies such as Saudi Arabia and Kuwait. See Amnesty International's Reports for 2004 on Saudi Arabia <http://web.amnesty.org/report2004/sau-summary-eng> (23 September 2004); and Amnesty International's Report for 2004 on Kuwait <http://web.amnesty.org/report2004/kwt-summary-eng> (23 September 2004).

[17] A recent Amnesty International Report reinforces this point when it notes: '[t]he impact of the so called "war on terror" (henceforth "war on terror") on human rights in the Gulf and the Arabian Peninsula has been profound and far reaching. Governments in the region and the US government have treated nationals and residents of the area with a disturbing disregard for the rule of law and fundamental human rights standards. The results have been mass arrests, prolonged detention without charge or trial, incommunicado detention, torture and ill treatment, strict secrecy surrounding the fate and whereabouts of some detainees, and apparent extra-judicial killings. These human rights violations have had profound effects not only on individual victims but also on their relatives and the general human rights situation in the region.' See Amnesty International, 'The Gulf and the Arabian Peninsula: Human rights fall victim to the "War on Terror"' (22 June 2004) AI Index: MDE 04/002/2004 <http://web.amnesty.org/library/Index/ENGMDE040022004?open&of=ENG-USA> (1 October 2004).

justified in public statements in part by reference to human rights factor. Here is revealed a purely cyclical version of human rights, contingent upon collateral political considerations.[18]

This study has taken the view that, more than religious disagreements, it is the economic and political inequalities which have contributed to this so-called 'clash of civilisations'. Beliefs based around religion, culture or values are often used as instruments to perpetuate these economic, political and social inequities. The Muslim populations—disenchanted and disillusioned by their own leaders—are effectively deprived of any political and economic leverage. Their economic and socials needs and requirements are frequently ignored. They suffer from poverty, hopelessness and disenfranchisement. In the growing spiral of violence and economic inequities currently raging in Palestine, Iraq, Chechnya, Afghanistan and other parts of the world, Muslims are likely to be the biggest losers.

It is unfortunate that modern international law itself has perpetuated a vicious and unjust pattern of world governance in which the unscrupulous, powerful and rich States dominate at the expense of all others. As this study has noted, there were precious few tears shed when in 1988 the Iranian Airliner was downed by the United States, killing all 286 passengers on board. Similarly there was little remorse at the bombing of Libya in 1986, the lengthy sanctions imposed on Libya and Iraq, the bombing of Sudan or the recent missile attack killing six Yemeni individuals in 2002.[19] There are tens of thousands of Afghanis who have become victims of allied bombings since October 2001. Like the victims of 11 September 2001, they too are innocent of any crime, and yet there is no pain felt for them, there are no services held for them, there are no memorials in their honour. Furthermore, as shall be examined in the next section, hundreds of civilians continue to languish in the United States base of Guantánamo, denied their fundamental rights. There is also the war in Iraq, which defies both reason and international law and yet is being justified and pursued with intensity.[20] In the wider scheme of things, it is the grievances and frustrations of these marginalised Muslim communities that are likely to fuel the clash of civilisations.

[18] I Brownlie, *Principles of Public International Law* 6th edn (Oxford, Oxford University Press, 2003) at 557.

[19] See C Downes, '"Targeted Killings" in an Age of Terror: The Legality of the Yemen Strike' (2004) 9 *Journal of Conflict and Security Law*, 277; J Quigley, 'International Law Violations by the United States in the Middle East as a Factor behind Anti-American Terrorism' (2002) 63 *University of Pittsburgh Law Review* 815.

[20] The verdict of Kofi Annan, the United Nations Secretary-General, represents the position in so far as the United Nations Organisation and the Charter is concerned. He notes, 'I have indicated it [ie the invasion of Iraq] was not in conformity with the UN charter from our point of view, from the charter point of view, it was illegal.' BBC News UK edition, 'Iraq War Illegal, Says Annan: The United Nations Secretary-General Kofi Annan has told the BBC the US-led invasion of Iraq was an illegal act that contravened the UN Charter' 16 September 2004 <http://news.bbc.co.uk/1/hi/world/middle_east/3661134.stm> (18 October 2004).

11 SEPTEMBER, ISLAMOPHOBIA AND THE FUTURE FOR MUSLIMS

One unfortunate consequence of the events of 11 September 2001 has been a growth in Islamophobia, that is, fear or hatred of Muslims and Islam. The attacks were condemned by the whole of the international community, including Muslims living in every part of the globe. Despite that, there was an immediate backlash against Muslims, many in the west associating Islam with violence and terrorism.[21] The consequences for Muslim minorities in the United States, the United Kingdom and many parts of the western world have been particularly deplorable. The United States and Western Europe witnessed a serious public and political reaction to the attacks of 11 September. In many quarters, Muslim minorities were immediately castigated. Their physical presence was questioned and their loyalties were doubted. There were attacks on Muslim communities, leading to loss of life. There was a dramatic rise in hate crimes against Muslims in the United States, with the Federal Bureau of Investigation reporting a dramatic escalation of 1600 per cent in incidents largely consisting of assaults and intimidation.[22] Hundreds of young men were detained, interned, incarcerated or deported. Having not itself been the subject of an attack, a more sober response from the United Kingdom was anticipated.[23] However, there was an unprecedented surge in violence against Muslims in the aftermath of 11 September 2001 within the United Kingdom. According to one Muslim organisation, the Islamic Human Rights Commission, during September 2001 a total of 206 incidents of assault, violence, verbal and physical abuse and other forms of malicious acts were recorded in Britain.[24]

---

[21] Note Comments made by the Special Rapporteur of the Commission on Human Rights on Contemporary Forms of Racism, Racial Discrimination, Xenophobia and Related Intolerance (E/CN.4/2002/24), paras 12–38, available at <http://ods-dds-ny.un.org/doc/UNDOC/GEN/G02/108/31/PDF/G0210831.pdf?OpenElement> (11 October 2004).

[22] See PA Thomas, 'September 11th and Good Governance' (2002) 53 *Northern Ireland Legal Quarterly* 366, at 389.

[23] *Ibid.*

[24] Islamic Human Rights Commission, *UK Today: The Anti-Muslim Backlash in the Wake of 11th September 2001* (London, 2001). Expanding on some of these incidents, a recent report notes that in the aftermath of 11 September 2001 'Muslim adults and children were attacked, physically and verbally. They were punched, spat at, hit with umbrellas at bus stops, publicly doused with alcohol and pelted with fruits and vegetables. Dog excrement and fireworks were pushed through their letterboxes and bricks were thrown through their windows. They were called murderers and excluded from social gatherings. One woman in Swindon was hospitalised after being beaten with a metal baseball bat; two Cambridge University students had their headscarves ripped off, in broad daylight outside a police station; Saba Zaman, who, in July 2001, had her scarf pulled off and two of her ribs broken in Tooting, London was stopped and searched by the police three times in two weeks following the terrorist attacks in the United States of America (USA). In west London, an Afghani taxi driver Hamidullah Gharwal, was attacked shortly after 11 September, and left paralysed from the neck down . . . Vandals attacked mosques and Asian-run businesses around the

Peoples within Muslim majority States have also felt uncomfortable at the manner in which their governments have acquiesced and supported United States foreign policy. The United States and United Kingdom governments have brought forth evidence which, according to them, justifies the continual bombing of Afghanistan as well as the invasion and occupation of Iraq. The arguments for invading Iraq having been discredited (and with the loss of credibility in all western intelligence gathering services) there are at present huge masses of Muslim peoples who have developed misgivings about the motives behind prosecution of the 'war on terrorism'—they are demanding transparency, fairness and justice in providing evidence, and absolute compliance with human rights standards in the case of trials and convictions.

A further deeply disturbing feature has been the torture, abuse and humiliation of Muslim men, women and children. Evidence has now been brought of the continual torture and violation of fundamental rights of the detainees of Guantánamo Bay in Cuba (also known as Camp X-Ray).[25] Since 11 January 2002, when the first twenty captives from Afghanistan were transferred to the camp, over 600 captives (including women and children) have been sent to this base. A vast majority of adults have since been detained, and held incommunicado without charges being brought against them.[26] Men are held in wire 'cages' measuring eight feet by six feet and in circumstances described by Amnesty International as 'falling below minimum standards for humane behaviour'.[27]

Since the detainees are predominantly Muslim by faith, their continued detention is also a major concern for British minority communities. Their detention has heightened concerns over a foreign policy based on racial and religious discrimination. Muslim human rights organisations regard the Guantánamo captivities as evidence of the United Kingdom government pursing an Islamophobic agenda.[28] Representations and legal challenges against many of the detainees have ended largely in

country. Nine pigs' heads were dumped outside a mosque in Exeter. Many [Muslims] were said not to have reported attacks because of fear of reprisals'. H Ansari, *Muslims in Britain* (London, Minority Rights Group, 2002) at 4.

[25] E Katselli and S Shah, 'September 11 and the UK Response' (2003) 52 *International & Comparative Law Quarterly* 245, at 250.

[26] See Amnesty International, 'Hundreds Still Held by US government in Guantánamo Bay' (April 2004) <http://web.amnesty.org/wire/April2004/guantanamo> (2 October 2004); Amnesty International, 'Guantánamo Bay: a human rights scandal' <http://web.amnesty.org/pages/guantanamobay-index-eng> (2 October 2004).

[27] Cited in P Thomas, n 22 above, at 379; also see United States of America, Memorandum to the US Government on the rights of people in US custody in Afghanistan and Guantánamo Bay AI Index 51/053/2002 http://web.amnesty.org/library/Index/ENGAMR510532002 (15 April 2002).

[28] See Islamic Human Rights Commission, 'Failure to Repatriate Britons Masks Islamophobic Policy', London, 11 August 2003.

disappointment. Although the last four British detainees were released from Guantánamo in January 2005, they have complained of torture and abuse.[29]

In detaining individuals at Guantánamo, the United States has expressed disdain for norms of international human rights laws and international humanitarian laws.[30] The US administration refuses to apply Article 4 of the third Geneva Convention 1949, which defines 'prisoners of war'.[31] The provision of prisoner of war status remains critical for the captured detainees. They are entitled to a series of rights, including exemption for lawful acts of war, humane treatment and the right to be given a fair trial.[32] At the same time the current US administration has decided to hold trials for some individuals in military commissions specially constituted under a Presidential Order of 13 November 2001.[33] The military commissions undermine the fundamental principles of law and contradict sacrosanct norms of separation of powers. The Order authorises the President to be the Prosecutor, Judge and Jury at the same time. The commissions lack independence and impartiality. They are therefore a travesty of justice, violating the United States' own commitment to international human rights laws. They have been likened to 'kangaroo courts'.[34] The detention of individuals and the setting up of the military commissions has been condemned by a variety of sources as a gross violation of international law. In its report issued on 5 September 2002, Amnesty International stated that the continued detention of individuals in Guantánamo Bay was a violation of international law.[35] The organisation demanded that the detainees be entitled to fundamental rights as provided by international humanitarian and human rights laws. Similar views were echoed by

---

[29] See *Abbasi (R on application of) v Secretary of State for Foreign and Commonwealth Office* [2002] EWCA Civ 1316.

[30] Katselli and Shah, n 25 above, at 250.

[31] See the Geneva Convention III Relative to the Treatment of Prisoners of War (adopted 12 August 1949, entered into force 21 October 1950) TIAS No 3364, 6 UST 3316. Text of the treaty is available at the website of the Office of the High Commissioner for Human Rights <http://www.unhchr.ch/html/intlinst.htm> (26 September 2004).

[32] *Ibid.*

[33] The Military Order is entitled 'Detention, Treatment and Trial of Certain Non-Citizens in the War Against Terrorism' (Military Order) 66 Fed Reg 57,833 (16 November 2001).

[34] HH Koh, 'Agora: Military Commissions—The Case against Military Commissions' (2002) 96 *American Journal of International Law* 337–44, at 339.

[35] See Amnesty International's Memorandum to the US Government on the Rights of Individuals in US Custody in Afghanistan and Guantánamo Bay of 15 April 2002 at <http://web.amnesty.org/ai.nsf/recent/AMR510532002> (22 September 2004). Also see the allegations made by the three British detainees of Guantánamo; V Dodd and T Branigan, 'Questioned at Gunpoint, Shackled, Forced to Pose Naked: British Detainees tell their Stories of Guantánamo Bay' Special Report, Guantánamo Bay, *Guardian Unlimited* 4 August 2004 <http://www.guardian.co.uk/guantanamo/story/0,13743,1275560,00.html> (27 September 2004).

the then High Commissioner, Mary Robinson,[36] and leading international law experts.[37]

There is an increasing amount of evidence of maltreatment, abuse and degradation in Iraq.[38] It has now been established that many innocent individuals were taken into custody, with little or no evidence of their involvement in international terrorism. These policies reflect a disdain on the part of the United States towards the fundamental human rights of the Iraqi people. The ultimate responsibility for accountability for these violations and injustices is placed upon the international community led by the world's great powers. With such disregard for human rights values, critics from the Islamic world are bound to agree with Strawson's view that '[t]he West's responses to September 11 demonstrate that the shallowness of its human rights culture does not grant it the podium to lecture the world on democracy and rule of law'.[39]

---

[36] See the statement made by the (former) High Commissioner for Human Rights on the Detention of Taliban and al-Qaeda prisoners at the US Base in Guantánamo Bay, Cuba, 16 January 2002. For further details see the Office of the UN High Commissioner for Human Rights <http://www.unhchr.ch/html/hchr.htm> (30 March 2004).

[37] Professor Koh in his thought-provoking paper makes the observation that 'should those culprits [involved in the 11 September attacks] be captured, the United States must try, not lynch, them to promote four legal values higher than vengeance: holding them *accountable* for their crimes against humanity; *telling the world the truth* about these crimes; reaffirming that such acts violate all *norms* of civilized society; and demonstrating that law abiding societies, unlike terrorists *respect human rights* by channelling retribution into criminal punishment for even the most heinous outlaws. The Military Order undermines each of these values' Koh, n 34 above, at 340–1.

[38] Note the evidence of abuse conducted by the US military in Abu Ghraib prison, Iraq.

[39] Strawson, 'Introduction: In the name of Law' in J Strawson (ed), n 12 above, at xx.

Select Bibliography

BOOKS

ABU-LUGHOD, I, (1996) (ed), *The Arab-Israeli Confrontation of June 1967: An Arab Perspective* (Ann Arbor, UMI Books on Demand).

ADAMEC, LW, (2001) *Historical Dictionary of Islam* (Maryland and London, The Scarecrow Press, Lanham).

AGRAWALA, SK, (1973) *Aircraft Hijacking and International Law* (Bombay, NM Tripathi Private Limited).

ALEXANDER, Y (ed), (1976) *International Terrorism: National, Regional and Global Perspectives* (New York, Praeger).

—— (1992) *International Terrorism: Political and Legal Documents* (Dordrecht, Martinus Nijhoff Publishers).

ALEXANDROWICZ, CH, (1973) *The European—African Confrontation: A Study in Treaty Making* (Leiden, Sijthof).

ALI, SS, (2000) *Gender and Human Rights in Islam and International Law: Equal Before Allah, Unequal Before Man?* (The Hague, Kluwer Law International).

AL-KĀSĀANI, ALĀ AL-DĀN, (1910) *Kitāb Badai' al-Sana'i fi Tartib al Shar'ia* vol 7 (Cairo: al-Mtaba 'a al-Jamaliyya).

AL-MŪSAWI, SH, (1997) *Manhajul-Fiqhil-Islami, A Course in the Islamic Jurisprudence* (Tehran, Islamic Culture and Relations Organisation).

ALSTON, P (ed), (1992) *The United Nations and Human Rights: A Critical Appraisal* (Oxford, Clarendon Press).

AN-NA'IM, AA, (1990) *Toward an Islamic Reformation: Civil Liberties, Human Rights and International Law* (Syracuse NY, Syracuse University Press).

ANSARI, H, (2002) *Muslims in Britain* (London, Minority Rights Group).

ASAD, M, (1980) *The Message of the Qur'an: Translated and Explained by Muhammad Asad* (Gibraltar, Dar Al-Andalus).

ATAÖV, T, (2001) *Kashmir and Neighbours: Tale, Terror, Truce* (Aldershot, Ashgate).

AZMI, A, (1990) *Kashmir: An Unparalleled Curfew* (Karachi, Panfwain Printing Press).

BADAWI, MAZ, (1978) *The Reformers of Egypt*, (London, Croom Helm).

BADERIN, MA, (2003) *International Human Rights and Islamic Law* (Oxford, Oxford University Press).

BAILEY, SD, (1988) *The Procedure of the UN Security Council* (Oxford, Clarendon Press).

BALJON, JMS, (1968) *Modern Muslim Koran Interpretation* (Leiden, EJ Brill).

BANTEKAS, I and NASH, S (2003) *International Criminal Law* 2nd edn (London, Cavendish).

BARKER, JC, (1996) *The Abuse of Diplomatic Privileges and Immunities: A Necessary Evil* (Aldershot, Dartmouth).

BASSIOUNI, MC (ed), (1982) *The Islamic Criminal Justice System* (London, Oceana Publications).

—— (1988) *Legal Responses to Terrorism: US Procedural Aspects* (Dordrecht, Martinus Nijhoff Publishers).

—— (2001) *International Terrorism: Multilateral Conventions (1937–2001)* (Ardsley NY, Transnational Publishers).

BEINART, W and DUBOW, S (ed), (1995) *Segregation And Apartheid in Twentieth-Century South Africa* (London, Routledge).

BELL, C, (2000) *Peace Agreements and Human Rights* (Oxford, Oxford University Press).

BOOTH, K and DUNNE, T (eds), (2002) *Worlds in Collision: Terror and the Future of Global Order* (London, Palgrave).

BRÖLMANN, C, LEFEBER, R and ZIECK, M (eds), (1993) *Peoples and Minorities in International Law* (Dordrecht, Martinus Nijhoff Publishers).

BROWNLIE, I, (2003) *Principles of Public International Law*, 6th edn (Oxford, Oxford University Press).

CALLARD, K, (1957) *Pakistan: A Political Study* (London, Allen and Unwin).

CAPOTORTI, F, (1991) *Special Rapporteur: Study on the Rights of Persons Belonging to Ethnic, Religious and Linguistic Minorities*, United Nations Sales No.E.78.XIV.I 1978, reprinted, New York, United Nations Centre for Human Rights, United Nations Sales No E.91.XIV.2.

CARTER, BE, (1988) *International Economic Sanctions: Improving the Haphazard US Legal Regime* (Cambridge, Cambridge University Press).

CASSESE, A, (1989) *Terrorism, Politics and Law: The Achille Lauro Affair* (Cambridge, Polity Press).

—— (1995) *Self-Determination of Peoples: A Legal Reappraisal* (Cambridge, Cambridge University Press).

CATTAN, H, (1973) *Palestine and International Law: the Legal Aspects of Arab-Israeli Conflict* (London, Longman).

CHADWICK, E, (1996) *Self-determination, Terrorism and the International Humanitarian Law of Armed Conflict* (The Hague, Martinus Nijhoff Publishers).

CHAUDHRI, MA, (1994) *The Muslim Ummah and Iqbal* (Islamabad, National Institute of Historical and Cultural Research).

COULSON, NJ, (1964) *A History of Islamic Law* (Edinburgh, Edinburgh University Press).

COURBAGE Y and FARGUES, P, (1997) *Christians and Jews Under Islam* (London, IB Tauris).

DEMBINSKI, L, (1988) *The Modern Law of Diplomacy: External Mission of States and International Organizations* (Dordrecht, Martinus Nijhoff Publishers).

DENNY, FM, (1994) *An Introduction to Islam* (New York, Macmillan Pub Co).

DOI, AR, (1997) *Sharíah: The Islamic Law* (London, Taha Publishers).

DUBOW, S, (2000) *The African National Congress* (Sutton, Stroud).

EATON, G, (1994) *Islam and the Destiny of Man* (Cambridge, Islamic Text Society).

ELAGAB, OY, (1995) *International Law Documents Relating to Terrorism* (London, Cavendish).

EL-ASHKER, AA, (1987) *The Islamic Business Enterprise* (London, Wolfboro, NH, Croom Helm).

EPRILE, C, (1972) *Sudan: The Long War* (London, Institute for the Study of Conflict).

ESPOSITO, JL (ed), (1999) *The Oxford History of Islam* (Oxford, Oxford University Press).

—— (1992) *The Islamic Threat: Myth or Reality?* (Oxford, Oxford University Press).

—— (1995) *The Oxford Encyclopaedia of the Modern Islamic World* vols II and III (New York, Oxford University Press).

EVANS, MD (ed), (2003) *International Law* (Oxford, Clarendon Press).

—— (1997) *Religious Liberty and International Law in Europe* (Cambridge, Cambridge University Press).

FASSBENDER, B, (1998) *UN Security Council Reform and the Right of Veto: A Constitutional Perspective* (The Hague, Kluwer Law International).

FEIN, H (ed), (1992) *Genocide Watch* (New Haven and London, Yale University Press).

FERRARI, S and BRADNEY, A (eds), (2000) *Islam and European Legal Systems* (Aldershot, Ashgate).

FREEDMAN, L *et al*, (1986) *Terrorism and International Order* (London, Routledge and Kegan Paul).

FREY, LS and FREY, ML, (1999) *The History of Diplomatic Immunity* (Columbus, Ohio State University Press).

GASCOIGNE, B, (1991) *The Great Moghuls* (London, Cape).

GIBB, HAR and KRAMERS, JH (eds), (1953) *Shorter Encyclopaedia of Islam* (Ithaca, NY, Cornell University Press).

GIBB, HAR, (1949) *Mohammedanism: An Historical Survey* (London, Oxford University Press).

GLEDHILL, A, (1957) *Pakistan, The Development of its Laws and Constitution* (London, Stevens and Sons Ltd).

GLENN, HP, (2000) *Legal Traditions of the World: Sustainable Diversity in Law* (Oxford, Oxford University Press).

GOHARI, MJ, (2000) *The Taliban: Ascent to Power* (Karachi, Oxford University Press).

GUYATT, N, (1998) *The Absence of Peace: Understanding the Israeli-Palestinian Conflict* (London, Zed Books).

HAIDER, SM (ed), (1978) *Islamic Concept of Human Rights* (Lahore, Book House).

HALLAQ, WB, (2001) *Authority, Continuity and Change in Islamic Law* (Cambridge, Cambridge University Press).

HALM, HH, (1991) *Shiism* (Edinburgh, Edinburgh University Press).

HAMIDULLAH, M, (1977) *Muslim Conduct of State: Being a Treaties on Siyar, that is Islamic Notion of Public International Law, Consisting of the Laws of Peace, War and Neutrality, Together with precedents from Orthodox Practices and Precedent by a Historical and General Introduction* (Lahore, Sh Muhammad Ashraf).

HANNUM, H, (1990) *Autonomy, Sovereignty and Self-Determination: The Accommodation of Conflicting Rights* (Philadelphia, University of Pennsylvania Press).

HARDY, M, (1968) *Modern Diplomatic Law* (Manchester, Manchester University Press).

HARDY, P, (1972) *The Muslims of British India* (London, Cambridge University Press).

HARRIS, DJ, (1998) *Cases and Materials on International Law* 5th edn (London, Sweet & Maxwell).

HASAN KS (ed), (1966) *Documents on the Foreign Relations of Pakistan: The Kashmir Question* (Karachi, Institute of International Affairs).

HASSAN, A, (1982) *The Early Developments of Islamic Jurisprudence* (Islamabad).

HENKIN, L (ed), (1981) *The International Bill of Rights: The Covenant on Civil and Political Rights* (New York, Columbia University Press).

HIGGINS, R and FLORY, M (eds), (1997) *Terrorism and International Law* (London, Routledge).

HIGGINS, R, (1994) *Problems and Process: International Law and How we use it* (Oxford, Clarendon Press).

HUFBAUER, GC, *et al,* (1985) *Economic Sanctions Reconsidered: History and Current Policy* (Washington DC, Institute for International Economics).

HUNTINGTON, SP, (1996) *The Clash of Civilizations and the Remaking of World Order* (London, Simon & Schuster).

HUREWITZ, JC (ed), (1975) *The Middle East and North Africa in World Politics: A Documentary Record—European Expansion 1535–1914* (New Haven, Yale University Press).

HUSSAIN, I, (1988) *Issues in Pakistan's Foreign Policy: An International Law Perspective* (Lahore, Progressive Publishers).

—— (1998) *Kashmir Dispute: An International Law Perspective* (Islamabad, National Institute of Pakistan Studies).

IKRAM, SM, (1969) *Muslim Civilization in India* (New York, Columbia University Press).

INALCIK, H, (1994) *The Ottoman Empire: the Classical Age 1300–1600* (London, Phoenix).

JAHAN, R, (1972) *Pakistan: Failure in National Integration* (New York, Columbia University Press).

JALAL, A, (1985) *The Sole Spokesman: Jinnah, the Muslim League, and the Demand for Pakistan* (Cambridge, Cambridge University Press).

KAMAL, A, (1987) *Pakistan: Political and Constitutional Dilemmas* (Karachi, Pakistan Law House).

KAMALI, MH, (1991) *Principles of Islamic Jurisprudence* (Cambridge, Islamic Text Society).

KARANDIKAR, MA, (1968) *Islam in India's Transition to Modernity* (Bombay, Orient Longmans).

KAUSER, Z, (1994) *Islam and Nationalism: An Analysis of the Views of Azad, Iqbal and Maududi* (Kuala Lumpur, AS Noordeen).

KEDOURIE, E, (1997) *Afghani and Abduh: An Essay on Religious Unbelief and Political Activism in Modern Islam* (London, Frank Cass & Co Ltd).

KENNEDY, CH (ed), (1993) *Pakistan: 1992* (Oxford, Westview Press).

KHADDURI, M, (1955) *War and Peace in the Law of Islam* (Baltimore and London, Johns Hopkins University Press).

—— (1966) *The Islamic Law of Nations—Shaybānī's Siyar: Translated with an Introduction, Notes and Appendices by M Khadduri* (Baltimore, Maryland, Johns Hopkins University Press).

KHALILIEH, HS, (1998) *Islamic Maritime Law: An Introduction* (Brill, Leiden).

KHAN, R, (1999) *The American Papers: Secret and Confidential India-Pakistan-Bangladesh Documents 1965–1973* (Karachi, Oxford University Press).

KHARE, RS (ed), (1999) *Perspectives on Islamic Law, Justice and Society* (Lanham, Md, Rowman and Littlefield Publishers).

KOSKENNIEMI, M, (2002) *The Gentle Civilizer of Nations: The Rise and Fall of International Law, 1870–1960* (Cambridge, Cambridge University Press).

KRAMER, MS (ed), (1987) *Shi'ism, Resistance and Revolution* (Boulder, Col, Westview Press).

KUPER, L, (1981) *Genocide: Its Political Use in the Twentieth Century* (New Haven and London, Yale University Press).

—— (1984) *International Action Against Genocide* (London, Minority Rights Group).

—— (1985) *The Prevention of Genocide* (New Haven, Yale University Press).

LAMB, A, (1991) *Kashmir: A Disputed Legacy, 1846–1990* (Hertingfordbury, Roxford Books).

LAMBERT, J, (1990) *Terrorism and Hostages in International Law: A Commentary on the Hostages Convention 1979* (Cambridge, Grotius Publishers).

LANDAU, R, (1958) *Islam and the Arabs* (London, George Allen and Unwin Ltd).

LAPONCE, JA, (1960) *The Protection of Minorities* (Berkeley and Los Angeles, University of California Press).

LAQUEUR, W and ALEXANDER, Y (eds), (1987) *The Terrorism Reader: A Historical Anthology* (New York, New American Library, Penguin).

—— (1968) *The Road to War, 1967: The Origins of the Arab-Israel Conflict* (London, Weidenfeld & Nicolson).

LEE, RS (eds), (2001) *The International Criminal Court: Elements of Crimes and Rules of Procedure and Evidence* (Ardsley NY, Transnational Publishers).

LEWIS, B, (1984) *The Jews of Islam* (Princeton, NJ, Princeton University Press).

LITTLE, D et al (eds), (1988) *Human Rights and Conflict of Cultures: Western and Islamic Perspectives on Religious Liberty* (Columbia, University of South Carolina Press).

LODGE, J (ed), (1981) *Terrorism: A Challenge to the State* (Oxford, Martin Robertson).

MACGOLIOUTH, DS, (1905) *Muhammad and the Rise of Islam* (London and New York, GP Putnam Sons).

MACLAGAN, E, (1972) *The Jesuits and the Great Mogul* (New York, Octagon Books).

MAHMASSANI, S, (1979) *Arkan Huquq-al-Insan* (Beirut, Dar-'ilmli'-Malayin).

MAHMOOD, S, (1989) *Constitutional Foundations of Pakistan* (Lahore, Jang Publishers).

MAHMOUDI, S et al (eds), (1990) *Festskrift Till Lars Hjerner: Studies in International Law* (Stockholm, Norstedt).

MALANCZUK, P, (1997) *Akehurst's Modern Introduction to International Law* 7th rev edn (London, Routledge) 224.

MALEKIAN, F, (1994) *The Concept of Islamic International Criminal Law: A Comparative Study* (London, Graham & Trotman).

MANSFIELD, P, (1973) *The Ottoman Empire and Its Successor* (London, Macmillan).

MANZOOR, IBN, (1955) *Lisān Al-Arab* vol XII (Beriut, Dar Sader).

MAS'UD, MK, (1995) *Iqbal's Reconstruction of Ijtihad* (Islamabad, Islamic Research Institute).

MATTINGLY, G, (1988) *Renaissance Diplomacy* (New York, Dover Publications).

MAYER, AE, (1995) *Islam and Human Rights: Tradition and Politics,* 2nd edn (Boulder, Col, Westview Press).

McCARTHY, J, (2000) *The Ottoman Peoples and the End of Empire* (London: Hodder and Stoughton).

McCOUBREY, H, (1998) *International Humanitarian Law: Modern Developments in the Limitation of Warfare* 2nd edn (Aldershot, Ashgate).

McGOLDRICK, D, (2004) *From '9–11' to the 'Iraq War 2003': International Law in an Age of Complexity* (Oxford, Hart).

McKEAN, W, (1983) *Equality and Discrimination under International Law* (Oxford, Clarendon Press).

McNAIR, AD, (1956) *International Law Opinions: Selected and Annotated* vol 1, (Cambridge, Cambridge University Press).

McWHINNEY, E, (1975) *The Illegal Diversion of Aircraft and International Law* (Leyden, Sijthoff).

—— (1987) *Aerial Piracy and International Terrorism: The Illegal Diversion of Aircraft and International Law* 2nd rev edn (Dordrecht, Martinus Nijhoff Publishers).

MEENAI, SA, (1989) *The Islamic Development Bank: A Case-Study of Islamic Co-operation* (London and New York, Kegan Paul International).

MERRILLS, JG, (1998) *International Dispute Settlement* (Cambridge, Cambridge University Press).

MINORITY RIGHTS GROUP (ed), (1997) *World Directory of Minorities* (London, Minority Rights Group).

MOINUDDIN, H, (1987) *The Charter of the Islamic Conference and Legal Framework of Economic Cooperation Among its Member States: A Study of the Charter, the General Agreement for Economic, Technical and Commercial Co-operation and the Agreement for Promotion, Protection and Guarantee of Investments Among Member States of the OIC* (Oxford, Clarendon Press).

MORRISON, G, (1973) *The Southern Sudan and Eritrea: Aspects of Wider African Problems* (London, Minority Rights Group).

MULLA, DF, (1990) *Principles of Mahamedan Law* 18th edn (Lahore, PLD Publishers).

NUSSBAUM, A, (1954) *A Concise History of the Law of Nations,* revised edn (New York, Macmillan Co).

O'CONNOR, JF, (1991) *Good Faith in International Law* (Aldershot, Hants).

PACKER, J and MYNTTI, K (eds), (1993) *The Protection of Ethnic and Linguistic Minorities in Europe* (Turku/Åbo, Åbo Akademi, Institute for Human Rights, Åbo Akademi University).

PARWEZ, GA, (1960) *Lughat-ul-Quran: Lexicon of the Qur'an—In Four Volumes* (Lahore).

PATTERSON, H, (1997) *The Politics of Illusion: A Political History of the IRA* (London, Serif).

PAYNE, JL, (1989) *Why Nations Arm* (Oxford: Basil Blackwell).

PLANT, G, (1992) *Environmental Protection and the Law of War: A 'Fifth Geneva' Convention on the Protection of the Environment in the Time of Armed Conflict* (London, John Wiley).

POMERANCE, M, (1982) *Self-Determination in Law and Practice: The New Doctrine in the United Nations* (The Hague, Martinus Nijhoff Publishers).

PORTER, J (ed), (1982) *Genocide and Human Rights: A Global Anthology* (Washington, DC, University Press of America).

POULOSE, T, (1974) *Succession in International Law: A Study of India, Pakistan, Ceylon and Burma* (New Delhi, Orient Longman).

QURESHI, AH (ed), (2002) *Perspectives in International Economic Law* (The Hague, Kluwer Law International).

RAHIM, A, (1911) *The Principles of Muhammadan Jurisprudence According to the Hanafi, Maliki, Shafi'i and Hanbali Schools* (London, Luzac).

RASHID, A, (2000) *Taliban: Militant Islam, Oil and Fundamentalism in Central Asia* (New Haven and London, Yale University Press).

RAY, ND, (1995) *Arab Islamic Banking and the Renewal of Islamic Law* (London, Graham and Trotman).

REHMAN, J, (2000) *The Weaknesses in the International Protection of Minority Rights* (The Hague, Kluwer Law International).

Report by the International Bar Association's Task Force on International Terrorism, (2003) *International Terrorism: Legal Challenges and Responses* (Ardsley NY, Transnational Publishers).

RICHARDS, DS (eds), (1970) *Islam and the Trade of Asia: A Colloquium* (Oxford, Bruno Cassirer).

RIGO-SUREDA, A, (1973) *The Evolution of the Right of Self-Determination: A Study of United Nations Practice* (Leiden, Sijthoff).

ROBERTSON, AH and MERRILLS, JG, (1996) *Human Rights in the World: An Introduction to the Study of the International Protection of Human Rights* (Manchester, Manchester University Press).

SAEED, A, (1999) *Islamic Banking and Interest: A Study of the Prohibition of Riba and its Contemporary Interpretation* (Leiden, Brill).

SAID, EW, (1994) *The Politics of Dispossession: the Struggle for Palestinian Self-Determination 1969–1994* (London, Chatto & Windus).

SALEH, NA, (1986) *Unlawful Gain and Legitimate Profit in Islamic Law: Riba, Gharar and Islamic Banking* (Cambridge, Cambridge University Press).

SAROOSHI, D, (1999) *The United Nations and the Development of Collective Security: The Delegation by the UN Security Council of its chapter VII Powers* (Oxford, Clarendon Press).

SCHACHT, J and BOSWORTH, CE (eds), (1974) *The Legacy of Islam* (Oxford, Clarendon Press).

—— (1964) *An Introduction to Islamic Law* (Oxford, Clarendon Press).

SCHACHTER, O, (1991) *International Law in Theory and Practice* (Dordrecht, Martinus Nijhoff Publishers).

SEN, B, (1988) *A Diplomat's Handbook of International Law and Practice* 3rd edn (Dordrecht, Martinus Nijhoff Publishers).

SHARMA, SK and BAKSHI, SR (eds), (1995) *Kashmir and the United Nations* (New Delhi, Anmol Publications).

SHAW, MN, (1986) *Title to Territory in Africa: International Legal Issues* (Oxford, Oxford University Press).

—— (2003) *International Law* 5th edn (Cambridge, Cambridge University Press).

SIDDIQI, MN, (1981) *Muslim Economic Thinking: A Survey of Contemporary Literature* (Jeddah, International Centre for Research in Islamic Economics, King Abdul Aziz University).

SMITH, MLR, (1995) *Fighting for Ireland?: The Military Strategy of the Irish Republican Movement* (London, Routledge).

SOONS, AHA (ed), (1990) *International Arbitration: Past and Prospects, A Symposium to Commemorate the Centenary of the Birth of Professor JHW Verzijl* (Dordrecht, Martinus Nijhoff Publishers).

STRAWSON, J (ed), (2002) *Law After Ground Zero* (London, GlassHouse Press).

STUYT, AM, (1990) *Survey of International Arbitration 1794–1989* (Dordrecht, Martinus Nijhoff Publishers).

SULLIVAN, JG (ed), (1995) *Embassies Under Siege: Personal Accounts by Diplomats on the Front Line* (Washington, Brassey's).

TAHZIB, BG, (1996) *Freedom of Religion or Belief: Ensuring Effective International Legal Protection* (The Hague, Martinus Nijhoff Publishers).

TAKKENBERG, L, (1998) *The Status of Palestinian Refugees in International Law* (Oxford, Clarendon Press).

TALAL, HB, (1981) *Palestinian Self-Determination: A Study of the West Bank and Gaza Strip* (London, Quartet Books).

THORNBERRY, P, (1991) *International Law and the Rights of Minorities* (Oxford, Clarendon Press).

TOMLINSON, BR, (1976) *The Indian National Congress and the Raj, 1929–1942: The Penultimate Phase* (London, Macmillan).

VAJPEYI, D and MALIK, Y (eds), (1989) *Religious and Ethnic Minority Politics in South Asia* (Glendale, Riverdale Company Publishers).

VAN DYKE, VV, (1985) *Human Rights, Ethnicity and Discrimination* (Westport, Conn and London, Greenwood Press).

VERCHER, A, (1992) *Terrorism in Europe: An International Comparative Legal Analysis* (Oxford, Clarendon Press).

VOGEL, FE, and HAYES III, SL, (1998) *Islamic Law and Finance: Religion, Risk and Return* (The Hague, Kluwer Law International).

WALKER, CP, (2002) *Blackstone's Guide to Anti-Terrorism Legislation* (Oxford, Oxford University Press).

WALLIULLAH, M, (1982) *Muslim Jurisprudence and the Quranic Law of Crimes* (Lahore, IBS).

WEERAMANTRY, CG, (1988) *Islamic Jurisprudence: An International Perspective* (London, Macmillan Press).

WEISS, BG, (1998) *The Spirit of Islamic Law* (Athens, GA, University of Georgia Press).

WELLS, HG, (1925) *The Outline of History: Being a Plain History of Life and Mankind* (London, Cassell).

WOLPERT, S, (1989) *A New History of India* (Oxford, Oxford University Press).

YE'OR, B, (1985) *The Dhimmi: Jews and Christians Under Islam* (London and Toronto, Associated University Press).

ZAWATI, HM, (2001) *Is Jihād a Just War? War, Peace, and Human Rights Under Islamic and Public International Law* (Lewiston, NY, Edwin Mellen Press).

ZWEIGERT, K and KÖTZ, H, (1998) *Introduction to Comparative Law* 3rd edn (Oxford, Clarendon Press).

ARTICLES

ABEYRATNE, RIR, (1985) 'Hijacking and the Tehran Incident—A World in Crisis' 10 *Air Law* 120.

AFSHARI, R, (1994) 'An Essay on Islamic Cultural Relativism in the Discourse of Human Rights' 16 *Human Rights Quarterly* 235.

AHMAD, M, (1975) 'Umma—The idea of a Universal Community' *Islamic Studies* 27.

AKINSANYA, A, (1985) 'The Dikko Affair and Anglo-Nigerian Relations' 34 *International & Comparative Law Quarterly* 602.

ALEXANDROWICZ, CH, (1965–66) 'Kautilyan Principles and the Law of Nations' 41 *British Yearbook of International Law* 301.

—— (1968) 'The Afro-Asian World and the Law of Nations' 123 (I) *Recueil des Cours de l'Académie de Droit International* 121.

ALI SS, (1997) 'The Conceptual Foundations of Human Rights: A Comparative Perspective' 3 *European Public Law* 261.

—— and REHMAN, J, (2003) 'Freedom of Religion versus Equality in International Human Rights Law: Conflicting Norms or Hierarchical Human Rights (A Case Study of Pakistan)' 21 *Nordic Journal of Human Rights* 404.

AN-NA'IM, AA, (1986) 'The Islamic Law of Apostasy and its Modern Applicability: A Case from the Sudan' *Religion* 16, 197.

—— (1987) 'Religious Minorities under Islamic Law and the Limits of Cultural Relativism' 9 *Human Rights Quarterly* 1.

AUST, A, (2000) 'Lockerbie: The Other Case' 49 *International & Comparative Law Quarterly* 278.

AZRT, DE, (2002) 'The Role of Compulsion in Islamic Conversion: Jihad, Dhimma and Rida' 8 *Buffalo Human Rights Law Review* 15.

BADR, GM, (1978) 'Islamic Law: Its Relations to Other Legal Systems' 26 *American Journal of Comparative Law* 188.

BALDWIN, FN Jr, (2002) 'Organised Crime, Terrorism, and Money Laundering in the Americas' 15 *Florida Journal of International Law* 3.

BANTEKAS, I, (2003) 'The International Law of Terrorist Financing' 97 *American Journal of International Law* 315.

BASSIOUNI, CM, (2000) 'Foreword: Assessing "Terrorism" into the New Millennium' 12 *De Paul Business Law Journal* 1.

BASSIOUNI, MC, (1980) 'Protection of Diplomats under Islamic Law' 74 *American Journal of International Law* 609.

BAXTER, R, (1974) 'A Sceptical Look at the Concept of Terrorism' 7 *Akorn Law Review* 380.

BILAL, G, (1999) 'Islamic Finance: Alternatives to the Western Model' 23 *Fletcher Forum of World Affairs* 145.

BLACK, R, (1999) 'Analysis: The Lockerbie Disaster' 3 *Edinburgh Law Review* 85.

BLAKESLEY, CL, (1989) 'Terrorism, Law and our Constitutional Order' 60 *University of Colorado Law Review* 471.

BLEICHER, SA, (1969) 'The Legal Significance of Re-Citation of General Assembly Resolutions' 63 *American Journal of International Law* 444.

BLUM, Y, (1975) 'Reflections on the Changing Concept of Self-Determination' 10 *Israel Law Review* 509.

BOISARD, MA, (1980) 'On the Probable Influence of Islam on Western Public and International Law' 11 *International Journal of Middle East Studies* 429.

BRAND, RA, (1976) 'Security Council Resolutions: When do they Give Rise to Enforceable Legal Rights? The United Nations Charter, the Byrd Amendment and a Self Executing Treaty Analysis' 9 *Cornell International Law Journal* 298.

BROWN, D, (2003) 'Use of Force against Terrorism after September 11th: State Responsibility, self-defense and other Responses' 11 *Cordozo Journal of International and Comparative Law* 1.

BROWN, J, (1988) 'Diplomatic Immunity: State Practice under the Vienna Convention on Diplomatic Relations' 37 *International & Comparative Law Quarterly* 53.

BYERS, M, (2002) 'Terrorism, the Use of Force and International Law after 11 September' 51 *International & Comparative Law Quarterly* 401.

CASSESE, A, (1989) 'The International Community's "Legal" Response to Terrorism' 38 *International & Comparative Law Quarterly* 589.

CHARNOVITZ, S, (1998) 'The Moral Exception in Trade Policy' 38 *Virginia Journal of International Law* 689.

CHENG, B, (1965) 'United Nations Resolutions on Outer Space: "Instant" International Customary Law?' 5 *Indian Journal of International Law* 23.

CHENUMOLU, S, (2003) 'Revamping International Securities Law to Break the Financial Infrastructure of Global Terrorism' 31 *The Georgia Journal of International and Comparative Law* 385.

CLARK, B, (1991) 'The Vienna Convention Reservations Regime and the Convention on Discrimination against Women' 85 *American Journal of International Law* 281.

COCKAYNE, J, (2002) 'Islam and International humanitarian law: From a Clash to a Conservation between Civilizations' 84 *International Review of the Red Cross* 597.

COOK, RJ, (1990) 'Reservations to the Convention on the Elimination of All forms of Discrimination against Women' 30 *Virginia Journal of International Law* 643.

DEMPSEY, PS, (2003) 'Aviation Security: The Role of Law in the War Against Terrorism' 41 *ColJTL* 649.

DINSTEIN, Y, (1989) 'Terrorism as an International Crime' 19 *IYBHR* 55.

DOWNES, C, (2004) '"Targeted Killings" in an Age of Terror: The Legality of the Yemen Strike' 9 *Journal of Conflict and Security Law*, 277.

EHRENBERG, DS, (1995) 'The Labor Link: Applying the International Trading System to Enforce Violations of Forced and Child Labor' 20 *Yale Journal of International Law* 361.

EL-AYOUTY, Y, (1999) 'International Terrorism under the Law' 5 *ILSA Journal of International and Comparative Law* 485.

ELGAVISH, D, (2000) 'Did Diplomatic Immunity Exist in the Ancient Near East? 2 *Journal of the History of International Law* 73.

EMANUELLI, C, (1975) 'Legal Aspects of Aerial Terrorism: The Piecemeal vs. the Comprehensive Approach' 10 *Journal of International Law and Economics* 503.

EMERSON, R, (1971) 'Self-Determination' 65 *American Journal of International Law* 459.

ENTELIS, J, (1997) 'International Human Rights: Islam's Friend or Foe? Algeria as an Example of the Compatibility of International Human Rights regarding Women's Equality and Islamic Law' 20 *Fordham International Law Journal* 1251.

EVANS, AE, (1969) 'Aircraft Hijacking: Its Causes and Cure' 63 *American Journal of International Law* 695.

EVANS, SE, (1994) 'The Lockerbie Incident Cases: Libyan-Sponsored Terrorism, Judicial Review and the Political Question Doctrine' 18 *Maryland Journal of International Law and Trade* 21.

FALK, R, (1980) 'The Iran Hostage Crisis: Easy Answers and Hard Questions' 74 *American Journal of International Law* 411.

FIORITA, D, (1995) 'Aviation Security: Have All the Questions Been Answered' 20 *Annals Air Space Law* 69.

FITZGERALD GF, (1969) 'Development of International Legal Rules for the Repression of the Unlawful Seizure of Aircraft' 7 *Canadian Yearbook of International Law* 269.

FRANK, JA, 'A Return to Lockerbie and the Montreal Convention in the Wake of September 11th Terrorist Attacks: Ramifications of Past Security Council and the International Court of Justice' (2002) 30 *Denver Journal of International Law and Policy* 532.

FRANK, JNB and REHMAN, J, (2003) 'Assessing the legality of the Attacks by the International Coalition against Terrorism against Al-Qaeda and Taliban in Afghanistan: An Inquiry into the Self-Defence Argument under Article 51 of the United Nations Charter' 67 *Journal of Criminal Law* 415.

GARCIA-MORA, M, (1962) 'The Nature of Political Offenses: A Knotty Problem of Extradition Law' 48 *Virginia Law Review* 1226.

GHANDHI PR, and BARKER JC, (2000) 'The Pinochet Judgment: Analysis and Implications' 40 *Indian Journal of International Law* 657.

GILL, TD, (1988) 'The law of armed attack in the Nicaragua case' 1 *Hague Yearbook of International Law* 30.

GOODING, GV, (1987) 'Fighting Terrorism in the 1980's: The Interception of the Achille Lauro Hijackers' 12 *Yale Journal of International Law* 158.

GREEN, LC, (1976) 'Rescue at Entebbe—Legal Aspects' 6 *IHYBR* 312.

—— (1988) 'Terrorism, the Extradition of Terrorists and the "Political Offence" Defence' 31 *German Yearbook of International Law* 337.

—— (1989) 'Terrorism and Armed Conflict: The Plea and the Verdict' 19 *IYBHR* 131.

GROSS, L, (1948) 'The Peace of Westphalia 1648–1948' 42 *American Journal of International Law* 20.

—— (1980) 'The Case Concerning United States Diplomatic and Consular Staff in Tehran: Phase of Provisional Measures' 74 *American Journal of International Law* 395.

GRZYBOWSKI, K, (1981) 'The Regime of Diplomacy and the Tehran Hostages' 30 *International & Comparative Law Quarterly* 42.

HALBERSTAM, M, (1988) 'Terrorism on the High Seas: The Achille Lauro, Piracy, and the IMO Convention on Maritime Safety' 82 *American Journal of International Law* 269.

—— (1989) 'Terrorist Acts against and on Board Ships' 19 *IYBHR* 331.

—— (2003) 'The Evolution of the United Nations Position on Terrorism: From Exempting National Liberation Movements to Criminalizing Terrorism Whenever and Wherever and by Whom Committed' 41 *ColJTL* 573.

HARGROVE, JL, (1987) 'The Nicaragua judgment and the Future of the Law of force and self-defence, 81 *American Journal of International Law* 135.

HIGGINS, R, (1970) 'The Place of International Law in the Settlement of Disputes by the Security Council' 64 *American Journal of International Law* 1.

—— (1985) 'The Abuse of Diplomatic Privileges and Immunities: Recent United Kingdom Experience' 79 *American Journal of International Law* 641.

IQBAL, Z, (1997) 'Islamic Financial Systems' 34 *Finance and Development* 42.

JOYNER, CC (1989) 'Suppression of Terrorism on the High Seas: The 1988 IMO Convention on the Safety of Maritime Navigation' 19 *IYBHR* 343.

KATSELLI, E and SHAH S, (2003) 'September 11 and the UK Response' 52 *International & Comparative Law Quarterly* 245.

KELLMAN, B, (2001) 'Biological Terrorism: Legal Measures for Preventing Catastrophe' 24 *Harvard Journal of Law and Public Policy* 417.

KHADDURI, M, (1956) 'Islam and the Modern Law of Nations' 50 *American Journal of International Law* 358.

—— (1959) 'The Islamic System: Its Competition and Co-existence with Western Systems' *Proceedings of the American Society of International Law* 49.

KHAN, CN, (1963) 'Commonwealth of Muslim States' *Voices of Islam* 41.

KIRGIS JR. FL, (1994) 'The Degrees of Self-Determination in the United Nations Era' 88 *American Journal of International Law* 304.

KLIP, A and MACKAREL M, (1999) 'The Lockerbie Trial—A Court in the Netherlands' 70 *Revue International de Droit Penale* 777.

KOH, HH, (2002) 'Agora: Military Commissions—The Case against Military Commissions' 96 *American Journal of International Law* 337.

KOSKENNIEMI, M, (1994) 'National Self-Determination Today: Problems of Legal Theory and Practice' 43 *International & Comparative Law Quarterly* 241.

LAGODNY, O, (1989) 'The European Convention on the Suppression of Terrorism: A Substantial Step to Combat Terrorism' 60 *University of Colorado Law Review* 583.

LAQUEUR, W, (1986) 'Reflections on Terrorism' 65 *Foreign Affairs* 86.

LARSEN, MD, (1987) 'The Achille Lauro Incident and the Permissible Use of Force' 9 *Loyola of Los Angeles Journal of International and Comparative Law* 481.

LEADER, S and WIENCEK, D (2000) 'Drug Money: The Fuel for Global Terrorism' 12 *Jane's Intelligence Review* 49.

LEE, BA, (1964) 'The Legal Ramifications of Hijacking Airplanes' *American Bar Association* 1034.

LEVITT, G, (1986) 'Is "Terrorism" Worth Defining?' 13 *Ohio Northern University Law Review* 97.

LEVITT, M, (2003) 'Iraq, US and the War on Terror: Stemming the Flow of Terrorist Financing Practical and Conceptual Challenges' 27 *The Fletcher Forum of World Affairs Journal* 59.

LOMBARDI, CB, (1998) 'Islamic Law as a Source of Constitutional Law in Egypt: The Constitutionalization of the *Sharia* in a Modern Arab State' 37 *ColJTL* 81.

MACDONALD, RStJ, (1986) 'The Nicaragua Case: New Answers to Old Questions?' *Canadian Year Book of International Law* 127.

MAHMASSANI, S, (1966) 'The Principles of International Law in the Light of Islamic Doctrine' 117(I) *Recueil des Cours de l'Académie de Droit International* 205.

MANNING, S, (1996) 'The United States Response to International Air Safety' 61 *Journal of Air Law and Commerce* 505.

MARCELLA, D, (1999) 'Passport to Justice: Internationalizing the Political Question Doctrine for Application in the World Court' 40 *Harvard International Law Journal* 81.

McCREDIE, J, (1986) 'Contemporary Uses of Force against Terrorism: The United States Response to Achille Lauro—Question of Jurisdiction and its Exercise' 16 *Georgia Journal of Comparative and International Law* 435.

McGINLEY, GP, (1985) 'The Achille Lauro Affair—Implications for International Law' 52 *Tennesse Law Review* 691.

MELLOR, JSC, (2002) 'Missing the Boat: The Legal and Practical Problems of the Prevention of Maritime Terrorism'. 18 *American University International Law Review* 341.

MURPHY, JF, (1986). 'The Future of Multilateralism and Efforts to Combat International Terrorism' 25 *ColJTL* 35.

—— (1989) 'Defining International Terrorism: A Way Out of the Quagmire' 19 *IYBHR* 13.

MURPHY, SD, (2003) 'Contemporary Practice of the United States Relating to International Law: Settlement of Dispute—Libyan Payment to Families of Pan Am Flight 103 Victims' 97 *American Journal of International Law* 987.

MUSHKAT, R, (1987) 'Is War Ever Justifiable? A Comparative Survey' 9 *Loyola of Los Angeles International and Comparative Law Journal* 227.

NALDI, GJ, (1987) 'The Case Concerning the Frontier Dispute (Burkina Faso/Republic of Mali): *Uti Possidetis* in an African Perspective' 36 *International & Comparative Law Quarterly* 893.

NICHOLS, PM, (1996) 'Trade without Values' 90 *North Western University Law Review*, 658.

OBA, AA, (2002) 'Islamic Law as Customary Law: The Changing Perspective in Nigeria' 51 *International & Comparative Law Quarterly* 817.

Pancracio, J-P, (1985) 'L'affaire de L'Achille Lauro et Le Droit International' 31 *Annuarie Français de Droit International* 219.

Panter-Brick, SK, (1968) 'The Right to Self-Determination: Its Application to Nigeria' 44 *International Affairs* 254.

Paust, JJ, (1987) 'Extradition and United States Prosecution of Achille Lauro Hostage-Takers: Navigating the Hazards' 20 *Vanderbilt Journal of Transnational Law* 235.

—— (2002) 'Use of Armed Force against Terrorists in Afghanistan, Iraq, and Beyond' 35 *Cornell International Law Journal* 533.

Quigley, J, (2002) 'International Law violations by the United States in the Middle East as a factor behind Anti-American Terrorism' 63 *University of Pittsburg Law Review* 815.

Ramzani, RK, (1959) 'The Shi'i System: Its Conflict and Inter-action with Other Systems' *Proceedings of the American Society of International Law* 53.

Rehman, J, (1994) 'Self-Determination, State Building and the Muhajirs: An International Legal Perspective of the Role of the Indian Muslim Refugees in the Constitutional Development of Pakistan' 3 *Contemporary South Asia* 111.

—— (1998) 'International Law and Indigenous Peoples: Definitional and Practical Problems' 3 *Journal of Civil Liberties* 224.

—— (1998) 'Minority Rights in International Law: Raising the Conceptual Issues' 72 *Australian Law Journal* 615.

—— (1999) 'Accommodating National Identity: New Approaches to International and Domestic Law—Concluding Reflections' 6 *International Journal on Minority and Group Rights* 267.

—— (2000) 'Accommodating Religious Identities in an Islamic State: International Law, Freedom of Religion and the Rights of Religious Minorities' 7 *International Journal on Minority and Group Rights* 139.

—— (2000) 'Reviewing the Right of Self-Determination: Lessons from the Experience of the Indian Sub-Continent' 29 *Anglo America Law Review* 454.

—— (2001) 'Minority Rights and Constitutional Dilemmas of Pakistan' 19 *Netherlands Quarterly Human Rights* 417.

—— (2005) 'International Terrorism, *Sharia* and Muslim Minorities in Europe: Islamophobia after 9/11' 3 *European Yearbook of Minority Issues* 217.

Reinisch, A, (2001) 'Developing Human Rights and Humanitarian Law Accountability of the Security Council for the Imposition of Economic Sanctions' 95 *American Journal of International Law* 851.

Rhee, JL, (2000) 'Rational and Constitutional Approaches to Airline Safety in the face of Terrorist Threats' 49 *DePaul Law Review* 847.

Riga, PJ, (1991) 'Islamic Law and Modernity: Conflict and Evolution' 36 *American Journal of Jurisprudence* 103.

Rodley, NS, (1989) 'Human Rights and Humanitarian Intervention: The Case Law of the World Court' 38 *International & Comparative Law Quarterly* 321.

Rogers, J, (1997) 'Bombs, Borders and Boarding: Combating International Terrorism at US Airports and the Fourth Amendment' 20 *Suffolk Transnational Law Review* 501.

ROMERO, J, (2003) 'Prevention of Maritime Terrorism: The Container Security' 4 *Chicago Journal of International Law* 597.

ROSAND, E, (2003) 'Security Council Resolution 1373, the Counter-Terrorism Committee, and the Fight Against Terrorism' 97 *American Journal of International Law* 333.

ROSENSTOCK, R, (1980) 'International Convention against the Taking of Hostages: Another International Community Step Against Terrorism' 9 *Journal of International Law and Policy* 169.

ROZAKIS, CL, (1974) 'Terrorism and the Internationally Protected Persons in the light of ILC Draft Article' 23 *International & Comparative Law Quarterly* 32.

SCHABAS, WA, (1996) 'Reservations to the United Nations Convention on the Rights of the Child' 18 *Human Rights Quarterly* 472.

SCHACHT, J, (1959) 'Islamic law in Contemporary States' 8 *American Journal of Comparative Law* 133.

SCHEWELB, E, (1967) 'Some Aspects of International *Jus Cogens* as Formulated by International Law Commission' 61 *American Journal of International Law* 946.

SCHMID, AP, (1996) 'The Links Between Transnational Organized Crimes and Terrorist Crimes' 2 *Transnational Organised Crime* 40.

SENIAWSKI, BL, (2001) 'Note—Riba Today: Social Equity, the Economy and Doing Business under Islamic Law' 39 *ColJTL* 701.

SEZNEC, J-F, (1999) 'Ethics, Islamic Banking and the Global Financial Market', 23 *Fletcher Forum of World Affairs* 161.

SHAABAN, HS, (1999) 'Commercial Transactions in the Middle East: What Law Governs'? 31 *Law and Policy International Business* 157.

SHAW, MN, (1978) 'Some Legal Aspects of the Entebbe Incident' 1 *Jewish Law Annual* 232.

SHUBBER, S, (1968–1969) 'Is Hijacking of Aircraft Piracy in International Law?' 43 *British Yearbook of International Law* 193.

SHUBBER, S, (1973) 'Aircraft Hijacking under the Hague Convention 1970—A New Regime' 22 *International & Comparative Law Quarterly* 687.

SLOAN, B, (1987) 'General Assembly Resolutions Revisited: (Forty Years Later)' 58 *British Yearbook of International Law* 39.

STOVALL, HL, (2000) 'Arab Commercial Laws—Into the Future' 34 *International Law* 839.

SUBEDI, SP, (2002) 'The UN Response to International Terrorism in the Aftermath of the Terrorist Attacks in America and the Problem of the Definition of Terrorism in International Law' 4 *International Law Forum du droit International* 159.

TAYLOR, JM, (2003) 'Islamic Banking—The Feasibility of Establishing an Islamic Bank in the United States' 40 *American Business Law Journal* 385.

THOMAS, PA, (2002) 'September 11th and Good Governance' 53 *Northern Ireland Legal Quarterly* 366.

THOMPSON, D, (1983) 'The Evolution of the Political Offense Exception in an Age of Modern Political Violence' 9 *Yale Journal of World Public Order* 315.

THORNBERRY, P, (1989) 'Self-Determination, Minorities, Human Rights: A Review of International Instruments' 38 *International & Comparative Law Quarterly* 867.

TOMUSCHAT, C, (1983) 'Protection of Minorities under Article 27 of the International Covenant on Civil and Political Rights' *Völkerrecht als Rechtsordnung, Internationale Gerichtsbarkeit, Menschenrechte, Festschrift für Herman Mosler*, 949.

TRAHAN, J, (2002) 'Terrorism Conventions: Existing Gaps and Different Approaches' 8 *New England Journal of International and Comparative Law* Annual 215.

TROOBOFF, PD, (1989) 'Aircraft Piracy, Federal Jurisdiction, Non-Resident Aliens on Foreign Soil' 83 *American Journal of International Law* 94.

VAN DEN WYNGAERT, C, (1989) 'The Political Offence Exception to Extradition: How to Plug the "Terrorists Loophole" without Departing from Fundamental Human Rights' 19 *IYBHR* 297.

VEROSTA, S, (1964) 'International Law in Europe and West Asia between 100 and 650 AD' 113 (III) *Recueil des Cours de l'Académie de Droit International* 491.

VERWEY, WD, (1981) 'The International Hostages Convention and the National Liberation Movements' 75 *American Journal of International Law* 69.

VOGAL, FE (2002) 'The Trial of Terrorists Under Classical Islamic Law' 43 *Harvard International Law Journal* 53.

VON MEHREN, RB and KOURIDES, PN, (1981) 'International Arbitration Between States and Foreign Private Parties: The Libyan Nationalization Cases' 75 *American Journal of International Law* 478.

WEISS, B, (1978) 'Interpretation in Islamic Law: The Theory of Ijtihad' 26 *American Journal of Comparative Law* 367.

WHITEMAN, M, (1977) 'Jus Cogens in International Law with a Projected List' 7 *Georgia Journal of International and Comparative Law* 607.

WOOD, MC, (1996) 'Security Council Working Methods and Procedures: Recent Developments' 45 *International & Comparative Law Quarterly* 150.

WOUTERS, J and NAERT, F, (2003) 'The European Union and "September 11"' 13 *Indiana International and Comparative Law Review* 719.

YOUNG, E, (1964) 'The Development of the Law of Diplomatic Relations' *British Yearbook of International Law* 141.

ZAGARIS, B, (2002) 'Financial Aspects of the War on Terror: The Merging of the Counter-Terrorism and Anti-Money Laundering Regimes' 34 *Law and Policy International Business* 45.

—— (2002) 'G-20 Nations Agree to Freeze Terrorist Assets and IMF will Provide Technical Aid' 18 *International Enforcement Law Reports* 29.

ZAPPALÀ, S, (2001) 'Do Heads of State in Office Enjoy Immunity from Jurisdiction for International Crimes: The Ghaddafi Case Before the French Cours de Cassation' 12 *European Journal of International Law* 595.

ZUBEL, E, (1999) 'The Lockerbie Controversy: Tension Between the International Court of Justice and the Security Council' 5 *Annual Survey of International and Comparative Law* 259.

Index

Abbas, Abul, 154
Abbassids, 22
Abu Bakar, 19
Abu Hanifa, 20, 48
Achille Lauro, 6, 109, 153–5, 156, 159
aerial terrorism:
  accountability, 151
  aircraft definition, 134
  conventions, 82, 92–3, 132–9
  cooperation, 136
  dispute settlement, 161
  generally, 130–151
  hijacking, 79, 81, 131–2
  history, 131–2
  and Islamic states, 141–2
  jurisdiction, 115, 135, 137–8
  Lockerbie *see* Lockerbie bombing
  Trans-World incident, 142
  UTA incident, 142, 145
Afghanistan:
  economic inequities, 226
  Hanafi school, 20
  history, 26
  Islamisation, 222
  Muslim empire, 22
  permanent sovereignty over natural
    resources, 102
  ratification of aerial terrorism
    conventions, 140
  support for terrorism, 166
  Taliban, 74, 141, 142–3, 166–7, 221
  use of force against, 143–4, 228
African Union/ OAS, 81–2, 83, 93, 149
aggression, definition, 86–7
Agrawala, SK, 131
ahal al-kitab (peoples of the Book), 61, 62, 63,
  69
Akbar, Emperor, 64–5
Al Barakaat, 184
Al Taqwa, 184
Alamgir, Emperor, 65
al-Aqsa mosque, 27, 38, 194
Albania, 187
Al-Barudy, Mr, 67
Alexander, King of Yugoslavia, 85
Alexander the Great, 60–1
Alexandrowicz, CH, 64
Algeria:
  exclusion of ICJ jurisdiction, 117
  and extradition of hostage takers, 110
  independence war, 105
  and liberation movements, 84, 104, 107
  and Morocco, 194
  ratification of aerial terrorism
    conventions, 139, 140
  and territorial integrity, 111
  terrorism finance, 187–8
Algiers, 81, 93
Alī Ibn Abī Tālib, 19, 50, 58
Al-Kāsāani, Ală al-Dān, 52
Al-Megrahi, Abdel Basset, 145, 147, 150
al-Qaeda, 141, 142, 143, 166, 176, 184, 185,
  200
Al-Quds Committee, 41
Al-Quds Fund, 32
amân, 49–50, 117
Amnesty International, 229–230
analogy, 14–15, 18
Anasar-al-Islam, 184
'Anduk, Muhammad, 15
An-Na'im, AA, 56
apartheid, 195, 196, 197, 198
apostasy, 67, 68
Arab League, 79–80, 83, 93, 140, 149
Arabia, 21, 50, 60
Arabic, teaching, 29
Arafat, Yassar, 154, 159
arbitration, Islamic tradition, 50–1
Asad, Muhammed, 179–180
assignment of debts, 47
Assyrians, 83
Austria, 155, 159
aut dedere aut judicare, 77, 109, 115, 155, 157,
  171–2
aval, 47
aviation *see* aerial terrorism

Babur, 64
Badawi, Zaki, 58
Baghdad, 20, 47
Bahrain, 128, 139, 140, 188
Balfour Declaration, 206
Bangladesh, 102, 184
banking:
  hawala, 182–3
  Islamic banking system, 2, 178–181
Bantekas, I, 183
Barthou, Louis, 85
Basra, 47
Bassiouni, Cherif, 19, 117–118, 125

Baxter, R, 73
Benghazi, 35
Berlin, fall of Berlin Wall, 7
Berlusconi, Silvio, 1
Biaharis, 184
bills of exchange, 47
Bilquis, Queen of Sheba, 117
Bin Laden, Usama, 7, 74, 85, 143, 166, 176,
    178, 183, 200, 228
Brownlie, Ian, 196–7, 225–6
Buddhists, 64
Burkino-Faso, ratification of aerial terrorism
    conventions, 140
Bush, George W, 183, 209

Cairo, 22, 39, 154
caliphs, 11
Cameroon, 140
Carter, Jimmy, 124
Carthage, 83
Cassese, A, 155
Cassin, René, 66
Chad, 140, 194
charitable institutions, 181–2
Chechnya, 182, 199, 226
chemical weapons, 94, 225
children, human rights, 177–8
China, 96, 148
Christianity, religious intolerance, 62,
    63
civil war, 193, 194
clash of civilisations, 7–9, 57, 223–6
Cold War, end, 89–92
Colombia, 183
colonialism, 24–6, 84, 195
Comoros, 140
conflict resolution:
    Islamic tradition, 50–1
    OIC principles, 28
    United Nations, 199, 202
Constantinople, 22
constitutions, and Islam, 27
consular immunities *see* internationally
    protected persons
cooperation:
    aerial terrorism, 136
    financing terrorism, 172–4
    Islamic counter-terrorism, 214–217
    Maritime Terrorism Convention, 158
    protection of internationally protected
        persons, 115
Cordoba, 22
corruption, 193
Coulson, NJ, 13
Council of Europe, terrorism convention,
    80
criminal law, and *Qur'an*, 17
culture, 30, 41

Dakar, 34
Damascus, 22, 55
Dar-ul-Harb, 55
Dar-ul-Islam, 49, 50, 55
deduction, 18
Delhi, 64
Dembinski, L, 114
Dempsey, PS, 136
dhimmis, 61, 63
Dikko incident, 128
diplomatic immunities *see* internationally
    protected persons
discrimination:
    fair trial of hostage takers, 110
    and OIC objectives, 195
    race discrimination, 196–8
    and United Nations, 195–6
    women, 178
dispute settlement:
    aerial terrorism, 161
    Financing Terrorism Convention,
        174–5
Doha, 89, 210, 218
Druses, 67

Eaton, G, 60–1, 62–3
Egypt:
    and *Achille Lauro*, 109, 154
    Camp David agreement, 208
    Fatimids, 22
    Hanafi school, 20
    and liberation movements, 104
    and Libya, 194
    Maliki school, 20
    Rome embassy, 128
    Shafi school, 21
    and territorial integrity, 111
    and terrorism conventions, 139, 155,
        159
Egyptian Study, 39
Elagab, OY, 97
El-Ayouty, Yassin, 59, 178
enemy aliens, 50
Entebbe raid, 99, 141–2
environmental protection, 212
error, *Hadith*, 21
espionage, 119
Ethiopia, 166, 194
eurocentricism, 44
European Union, 26, 80–1
explosives, 94
extradition:
    aerial terrorism, 135, 137, 138
    aut dedere aut judicare, 77, 109, 115, 155,
        157, 171–2
    crimes against internationally protected
        persons, 115–116
    and fair trial, 110

financing terrorism, 171–2
hostage-takers, 101, 108–112
maritime terrorism, 157, 161

fair trials, 110, 116, 229
Falk, Richard, 124
FAO, 27
Fatimids, 22
Fez, 33, 34
Fhimah, Al-Amin Khalifa, 145, 147
financial institutions:
    financing terrorism, 2
    hawala system, 182–3
    Islamic systems, 176–183
financing terrorism:
    9/11, impact on Islamic communities,
        183–6
    1999 Convention, 165, 168–183
    cooperation obligations, 172–4
    criminal offences, 168–170
    debate, 6–7
    dispute settlement, 174–5
    extradition or prosecution, 171–2
    freezing funds, 171, 183–6
    and Islamic financial systems, 2, 176–183
    Islamic states, 186–9
    jurisdiction, 171
    legal persons, 170
    options, 163
    and Palestinians, 32, 182
    prevention obligations, 173–4
    and United Nations, 165–8
France, 24, 47, 84, 85, 105, 153
Francis I, King of France, 48
Franz Ferdinand, Archduke, 84
freedom of movement, 98–9
freezing funds, 171, 183–6
Friedman, TL, 1

Gambia, 140
Geneva Conventions *see* humanitarian law
genocide, 59, 223
Germany, 99, 154
Ghaddafi, Colonel, 127
good faith, 12
Greece, 142, 154
Guantánamo, 226, 228
Guinea, 104, 140
Guinea-Bissau, 140
Guyana, 140
Guyatt, N, 206

Hadith, 13, 20, 21
Halberstam, M, 156
Hamas, 184
Hamidullah, Muhammad, 98
Hamza, 118
Hanafi school, 19, 20

Hanbali school, 19, 21
hawala, 2, 47, 182–3
heads of state, 115
Hindus, 62, 64
Hirabah, 59
Hitler, Adolf, 206
Hizbollah, 184
hostage-taking:
    1979 Convention, 77, 79, 99–101, 103
    definition, 100, 108
    denial of human rights, 98–9
    EU Framework Decision on Terrorism, 81
    European Convention on Terrorism, 80
    extradition, 101, 108–12
    fair trial, 110
    and humanitarian law, 105–8
    internationally protected persons, 97–8,
        113–114
    Islamic perspectives, 101–112
    jurisdiction, 108–12
    liberation movements, 101–4
    SAARC Convention, 82
    Sharia, 98
    and territorial integrity principle, 111–112
    war crime, 108
Hoveida, Fereydoun, 66
Hudood, 119
human rights:
    children, 177–8
    fair trial, 110, 116, 229
    and hostage-taking, 98–9
    and Islam, 221
    Islamic state practices, 2, 221
    and Israel, 224
    jus cogens, 196
    and Maritime Terrorism Convention,
        157–9
    occupied Iraq, 230
    Palestinians, 206, 208
    private life, 185
    property rights, 185
    Universal Declaration, 66–8
    US troops in Iraq, 9
    and war on terrorism, 95
humanitarian law:
    conventions, 94–5
    and hostage-taking, 105–8
    Islamic contribution, 105
    Islamic origins, 53
    and Islamic states, 105–8
Huntingdon, SP, 57
Hussein, Saddam, 74, 225

Ibn al-Nawwāha, 118
Ibn Äthāl, 118
Ibn Hanbal, Ahmad, 21
Ibn Taimiya, 21
ICTVTR, 31

identity, Islamic identity, 5, 26–7, 43, 191
ijma, 11, 14, 21
ijtihad, 11, 14–15, 18, 19, 21, 51, 216, 223
Imam, 19
imperialism, 24–6, 84, 195
inân, 47–8
India:
  Hanafi school, 20
  Independence Act 1947, 201
  Indian National Congress, 85
  Indo-Pakistan conflict, 105
  Jammu state, 201, 202
  Kashmir, 85, 89, 105, 182, 183, 192, 199,
    204–5
  minority rights, 65
  Muslim empire, 22, 23, 24, 63–5
  Muslim League, 85
  partition, 202
  Penal Code, 25
  religious tolerance, 64–5
  Shafi school, 21
Indonesia, 21, 25, 102, 140
Infra-Structure Fund, 39
interest *see riba* (usury)
international armed conflicts, 107
International Association of Islamic Banks,
  34
International Bar Association, 185–6
International Civil Aviation Authority, 92,
  132, 134, 136, 144
International Commission for the
    Preservation of Islamic Cultural
    Heritage (ICPICH), 32
International Court of Justice:
  and discrimination, 197
  exclusions of jurisdiction, 116–117, 139,
    140, 141, 204
  Lockerbie, 148–9
  Nicaragua case, 166
International Crescent, 35
International Islamic Court of Justice, 29,
  199
International Islamic News Agency, 38, 40
international law:
  enforcement mechanisms, 85
  Islamic tradition, 45–51
  and *Jihad*, 53–60
  milestones, 7
  sources, 13, 14
International Law Commission, 86, 114
International Maritime Organisation, 92,
  155, 159
International Monetary Fund (IMF), 164,
  177
internationally protected persons:
  abuse of immunity, 126–9
  cooperation, 115
  definition, 115

diplomatic bags, 128
generally, 112–129
hostage-taking, 97–8, 113–114
and Islamic states, 116–123, 120–3
jurisdiction, 115
New York Convention, 112, 113–117
origins of immunities, 49
Sharia, 6, 98, 117, 123, 125
Vienna Conventions, 112, 119–120, 122,
  125–8
vulnerability, 112–113
Interpol, 174
Iqbal, Muhammad, 15
Iran:
  American embassy hostages, 99, 112,
    120–6
  and human rights, 66
  Iran-Iraq war, 193, 212, 225
  Islamisation, 222
  Safavids, 23
  Shah, 120, 121, 124
  terrorism of liberation movements, 103
  and US state terrorism, 74
  USS Vincennes incident, 144–5, 226
Iran Aid, 182
Iraq:
  attacks on UN personnel, 113
  economic inequities, 226
  and extradition of hostage takers, 110
  and ICJ jurisdiction, 117
  invasion *see* Iraq invasion 2003
  invasion of Kuwait, 193, 212
  Iran-Iraq war, 193, 212, 225
  Iraq/Pakistan incident 1973, 126–7
  and Lockerbie, 140
  non-recognition of Israel, 117, 139
  victim of terrorism, 74
Iraq invasion 2003:
  and definition of terrorism, 88
  double standards, 224–5
  human rights abuses, 9, 230
  illegality, 226
  justification, 228
  Muslim issue, 199
  and terrorism, 108
  and United Nations, 8
Ireland, IRA, 84
Islam:
  assassinations, 58
  banking system, 178–181
  civilisation, 2, 223
  and diplomatic immunities, 117–119, 123,
    125
  dissemination of culture, 29
  expansion, 22, 60
  financial systems, 176–183
  history of violence, 58–60
  and human rights, 221

meaning, 10
Meccan stage, 17–18
Medina stage, 17
Muslim empire, 60
origins, 53
schools of thought, 18–21
and state constitutions, 27
violent image, 2, 44
Islamabad, 35
Islamaphobia, 2–3, 141, 227–230
Islamic Banking Portfolio, 39
Islamic Centre for the Development of
    Trade (ICDT), 31
Islamic Chamber of Commerce, Industry
    and Community Exchange (ICCI),
    33
Islamic Council, 68
Islamic Development Bank, 38–9, 180
Islamic Educational, Scientific and Cultural
    Organisation (ISESCO), 38, 40
Islamic Fiqh Academy, 31
Islamic Institute for Technology (ITT), 31
Islamic Research and Training Institute
    (IRTI), 39
Islamic Shipowners Association (ISA),
    36
Islamic Solidarity Fund, 31–2
Islamic states:
    and *Achille Lauro*, 153–5, 159
    aerial terrorim incidents, 141–2
    and aerial terrorism, 139–141
    antagonism among, 192–4
    colonial impact, 24–6
    contribution to humanitarian law, 105
    diplomatic immunities, 117–123
    domination by western world, 5
    and financing terrorism, 186–9
    history, 21–4
    and hostage-taking, 98
    human rights records, 221
    and international law, 26–7
    and internationally protected persons,
        116–117, 120–3
    Islamic identity, 5, 26–7, 43, 191
    and liberation movements, 102–5
    and maritime terrorism, 159–161
    post-9/11 counter-terror, 217–219
    and religious tolerance, 65–9
    and right of self-determination,
        102–4
Islamic States Broadcasting Organisation
    (ISBO), 38, 39–40
Israel:
    apartheid policy, 198
    Arab-Israeli conflict, 105
    definition of terrorism, 88
    Entebbe raid, 141–2
    extradition to, 161

imperialist agenda, 9
non-recognition by Arab states, 117, 139,
    140, 141
and Palestine, 205–9
race discrimination, 198
violation of human rights, 224
Istanbul, 36
istihsan, Malaki school, 20
Italy, 24, 128, 154, 155, 159

Jacobins, 83–4
Jafar al-Sadiq, 19
Jaffari school, 19
Jaish-e-Mohammad, 200, 203–4
Jeddah, 33, 34, 38
Jehangir, Emperor, 64
Jerusalem, al-Aqsa mosque, 27, 38, 194
Jerusalem Committee, 41
Jews, 62
Jihad:
    financing, 181–2
    meaning, 45, 51–2, 222
    and modern international law, 53–60
    Qur'an, 51, 54–5
    terminology, 51, 52
    use of force, 51, 53–60
Jordan, 110, 117, 161, 192, 194, 207
Joyner, CC, 160
jus cogens, 99, 101, 196, 197, 198
just war, 45, 104

Kadi, Yassin, 184–5
Karachi, 33
Kashmir:
    financing cause, 182, 183
    Muslim issue, 199
    and OIC, 204–5
    self-determination, 85, 89, 105, 200–5
    terrorism, 192
    UNCIP, 203
    and United Nations, 202–3
Kenya, 166, 183
Khadduri, Majid, 52, 55–6, 57–8, 61, 62
Khalid-ibn-al-walid, 55
Khalifas, 11
Khan, Muhammad Zafarullah, 67
Khomeini, Ayatollah, 120, 121, 124, 125
Klinghoffer, Leon, 154, 156
Kötz, H, 22
Kuala Lumpur Declaration, 218, 219
Kuwait, 117, 128, 140, 141, 160, 161, 192,
    193, 212

Lambert, J, 110–111, 183
Landau, Rom, 55
League of Nations, 7, 75, 86
Lebanon, 67, 142
legal persons, 170

Levitt, M, 163
liberation movements:
  and hostage-taking, 98, 101–8
  international armed conflicts, 107
  and Islamic states, 105
  Palestinian movements, 184
  and terrorism, 84–5, 87, 88–90, 213
Libya:
  and *Achille Lauro*, 153–4
  and aerial terrorism convention, 140
  diplomatic bags, 128
  and Egypt, 194
  and liberation movements, 104
  Lockerbie *see* Lockerbie bombing
  London embassy incident, 127–8
  and Sudan, 194
  support for terrorism, 166
  and territorial integrity, 111
  and US state terrorism, 74, 226
  UTA incident, 142, 145
Lockerbie bombing:
  accountability, 6, 161
  extradition from Libya, 138
  generally, 144–150
  gross violation of international law, 137
  ICJ jurisdiction, 140
  impact, 142
  trial, 149–150
  UN sanctions, 147–8
  and United Nations Security Council,
    145–8, 151
Losotho, 104

madrisas, 36–7, 182
Mahmassani, S, 12, 47, 49, 50, 69–70
Makkah Al Mukarramah Tarif, 35, 36
Malaysia, 21, 26, 78
Mali, 140
Malik ibn Anas, 20
Maliki school, 19, 20
maritime terrorism:
  Achille Lauro, 153–5
  conventions, 93, 152–3, 155–7
  definition, 156
  extradition, 157, 161
  generally, 152–161
  history, 130
  human rights issues, 157–9
  and Islamic states, 159–161
  jurisdiction, 115, 157
  murder, 156
  offshore installations, 158
  piracy, 152
Mauritania, 140, 194
McKean, W, 197
Mecca, 33, 37, 118
mediation, 50–1
Medina, 20, 54

minority rights, 45, 61, 65
Mjutahid, meaning, 15
Moinuddin, H, 23, 58
Morocco, 139, 140, 194
Muawiyah ibn Abi Sufyan, 19, 59
mudaraba, 180
mufawada, 47
Mughals, 23, 63–5
Muhammad Bin-Qasim, 64
Muhammad, Prophet:
  arbitration, 50
  charity, 181
  death, 18, 60
  diplomatic immunity, 118–19
  Hijrat, 58
  international agreements, 46
  Jihad, 51, 58
  persecution, 54, 58
  source of law, 11, 12, 14
  succession, 19
  trade, 47
Munich Olympics 1972, 88, 99
murder, 156
Musaylama the liar, 118
Musharaka, 180
Musharraf, Pervez, 184
Mushkat, Roda, 56–7
Muslim World League, 68

Najran, 46, 118, 119
Naskh, 17, 18
natural resources, permanent sovereignty
  over, 102
Nazism, 84
nepotism, 193
Netherlands, 25, 114, 149, 150
new world order, 7–9, 221
Nicaragua, 166
Niger, 32, 140, 142, 205
Nigeria, 102, 104, 111, 128, 140
Nimeiri, Ja'far, 221
Nizammiyya courts, 24
nuclear materials, Convention, 79
Nuremberg Tribunal, 86, 99

occupied territories, and terrorism, 78, 88–9
OCOSOC, 26
offshore installations, 158
Oman, 88, 139, 140, 194
OPEC, 114
Organisation of Islamic Capitals and Cities,
  34–5
Organisation of the Islamic Conference (OIC):
  affiliated institutions, 33
  Al-Quds Committee, 41
  Charter, 28, 43, 195
  counter-terror policy, 210–217
  culture, 41–2

definition of terrorism, 89
draft UN Terrorism Convention, 88–9,
    200
institutions, 28–30
investment guarantees, 37
and Islamic identity, 5, 27
and Kashmir, 204–5
and Lockerbie, 149
membership, 27
objectives, 28, 43, 191
origins, 27
post-9/11 counter-terror, 217–219
principles, 28, 195, 199
reaction to external aggression, 194–200
role, 7
science and technology, 42
standing committees, 37, 40–2
subsidiary organisations, 30–42
terrorism convention, 93, 191, 210–217
and terrorism finance, 186
trade cooperation, 37, 42
and Usama Bin Laden, 143
Ottoman empire, 22, 24, 48–9, 63

pagans, 61, 62
Pakistan:
    1986 Pan American hijacking, 100
    counter-terrorism legislation, 96
    and extradition of hostage takers, 110
    and ICJ jurisdiction, 117
    Indo-Pakistan conflict, 105
    Iraq/ Pakistan incident 1973, 126–7
    Islamisation, 221, 222
    and Kashmir *see* Kashmir
    secession claims, 102
    terrorism finance, 189
    and Universal Declaration of Human
        Rights, 66–7
Palestinian Islamic Jihad, 184
Palestinians:
    1967 war, 207
    Achille Lauro, 153–5
    Al-Quds Fund, 32
    economic inequalities, 226
    financing cause, 32, 182
    human rights, 9, 208
    and humanitarian law, 105
    jurisdiction, 109
    OIC support, 198
    right to self-determination, 88–9, 205–9
    'security wall', 208
    and terrorism, 85, 88–9, 192, 224
    and United Nations, 206–7, 208–9
partnerships, 47
Parwez, GA, 16
Payne, JL, 57, 194
piracy, 130, 152
polytheists, 61, 62

Port Said, 153, 154
Portugal, 140
Postal Union, 94
prisoners of war, 229
prisoners, *Sharia*, 98
private life, respect for, 185

qadis, origins, 23–4
Qatar, 140, 188
Qisas, 119
qiyas, 11, 14, 15, 20
Qur'an:
    diplomatic immunity, 117–118, 125
    finance, 178
    and genocide, 59
    injustice, 179
    and international law, 45–6
    Jihad, 51, 54–5
    nature, 17
    persecution of Muslims, 54
    primary source of law, 11–13, 16, 18
    riba, 180
    Zakat, 181
Qutbudin Aibak, 64

Rabat, 27, 28, 38
Rabita Trust, 184
Rajputs, 64
religious tolerance:
    and Christianity, 62, 63
    India, 63–5
    Islamic tradition, 60–5
    modern state practice, 65–9
    stereotypes, 45
    Universal Declaration of Human Rights,
        66–8
reprisals, 155
Research Centre for Islamic History, Art
        and Culture (IRCICA), 30
riba (usury), 23, 46, 177, 178–181
right to liberty, 98–9, 157
right to life, 157
right to security, 157
Robinson, Mary, 230
Romans, 83
rule of law, 193, 199

Sabil Allah, 181
Saeed, Abduallah, 179
Safavids, 23
Saudi Arabia, 192
    diplomatic bags, 128
    and Kashmir, 205
    permanent sovereignty over natural
        resources, 102
    and terrorism, 59
    and terrorism conventions, 140, 160,
        188

Saudi Arabia (*cont.*):
  and Universal Declaration of Human
    Rights, 67, 68
Schwelb, E, 197
science and technology, 42
self-defence, 58
self-determination, right to:
  international law, 101
  interpretation by Islamic states, 102–4
  jus cogens, 198
  Kashmir, 200–5
  OIC principle, 28
  Palestinians, 205–9, 224
  permanent sovereignty over natural
    resources, 102
  secession claims, 102
  and terrorism, 98, 101–4, 213
Senegal, 42, 140
September 11 attacks:
  impact on Islamic communities, 183–6
  and Islamaphobia, 2, 227–230
  Islamic counter-terrorism, 217–219
  milestone, 8, 130, 141
  new world order, 221
  use of retaliatory force, 142–4
SESRTCIC, 30
Shafi, Muhammad ibn Idris al-, 20
Shafi'i school, 19, 20–21
Shajahan, Emperor, 64, 65
Sharia:
  and 9/11 hijackers, 217–218
  controversy, 1–2
  diplomatic immunities, 6, 98, 117, 123,
    125
  evolution, 16–17, 43
  finance guidelines, 176
  and hostage taking, 98
  and international law, 45–51
  interpretations, 4
  and Islamic identity, 5
  legal norms, 17–18
  meaning, 10
  and modern banking, 179
  and modernity, 2, 179, 222
  scope, 10–11, 15–17
  sources of law, 11–15
  and Taliban, 221
  and terrorism, 3–4
Shias, 18, 19, 23
shipping *see* maritime terrorism
Shiraz, 122, 123
Sierra Leone, 140
Siyar:
  development, 11
  diplomatic immunities, 117, 123, 125
  and international law, 45–51
  interpretations, 23
  sources, 11–15, 23

  and terrorism, 3–4
slavery, 223
Somalia, 102, 177, 194
sources of law:
  primary sources, 11–13
  secondary sources, 14–15
South Africa, 84, 140, 197
South Asian Association for Regional
  Cooperation (SAARC), 82, 94
Soviet Union, 110
Spain, 22
Sports Federation of Islamic Solidarity
  Causes, 35
Stalinism, 84
state sovereignty:
  equality, 199
  and global order, 72
  OIC principle, 28, 199
  permanent sovereignty over natural
    resources, 102
  territorial integrity, 111–112, 142, 199
Strawson, J, 25
Sudan, 74, 221
  civil war, 194
  Islamisation, 221, 222
  and Libya, 194
  and Lockerbie, 140
  Penal Code, 25
  Peoples Liberation Army, 89
  ratification of aerial terrorism conven-
    tions, 140
  secession claims, 102
  support for terrorism, 166
  US bombing, 226
Suez crisis, 105
suicide bombings, 59–60
Sulaiman, Prophet, 117–118
Sulayman the Magnificent, 48
Sunna, 11, 12–13, 16, 18, 21, 45, 125
Sunnis, 14, 18, 19, 19–21
Suriname, 140
Surras, 18
Sweden, 113–114
Syria, 103, 110, 111, 117, 139, 153, 193, 194

Tabriz, 122, 123
tahkim, 50–1
Taliban, 74, 141, 142–3, 166–7, 221
Tamil Tigers, 89
Tanzania, 104, 111, 166, 183
taqlid, 15
Tartus, 153
Tazir, 119, 120
territorial integrity, 111–112, 142, 199
terrorism:
  1937 Convention, 75, 86
  African Union Convention, 81–2, 83
  Arab League Convention, 79–80, 83

aviation *see* aerial terrorism
causes, 88
counter-terrorism, 84
  breaches of international law, 8
  excuse for repression, 83, 225
  and human rights, 95
  Islamic cooperation, 214–17
  OIC, 210–217
  subjectivity, 100
definition, 5–6, 71–83, 210, 210–214
draft UN Convention, 77–9, 200
end of Cold War, 89–92
EU framework decision, 80–1
European Convention, 80
financing *see* financing terrorism
history, 83–4
hostages *see* hostage-taking
international conventions, 92–5
and Islam, 3–4, 59–60
and *Jihad*, 51
liberation movements, 84–5, 87, 88–90,
  213
motivations, 72, 88
and occupied territories, 78, 88–9
OIC Convention, 88–9, 191
and post-9/11 Islamic states, 217–219
regional conventions, 79–83
SAARC Convention, 82, 94
shipping *see* maritime terrorism
state terrorism, 74–5, 84
threat, 71
UN Counter-Terrorism Committee, 91,
  168, 185
and United Nations, 86–7, 90–2
Togo, 140
torture debate, 96
trade, 42, 47–9
Trahan, J, 137–8
Trans-World incident, 142
treaties, and Islam, 45–6
Tunisia, 117, 139, 140, 154
Turkey, 20, 24, 26, 205
Turks, 22, 63

Udovitch, AL, 47
Uganda, 32–3, 140, 142
Uhud, battle of, 118
Ummah, 14, 21–2, 43, 178
Ummayids, 19, 22, 23
UNCTAD, 26
UNDP, 27
UNESCO, 29
Unit Trust Investment Fund, 39
United Arab Emirates, 139, 140
United Kingdom:
  and *Achille Lauro*, 154
  colonialism, 24
  counter-terrorism legislation, 96

Dikko incident, 128
financing of terrorism, 7
freezing funds, 184–5
invasion of Iraq, 228
Islamaphobia, 227, 228
Libyan embassy incident, 127–8
Lockerbie *see* Lockerbie bombing
support for US, 8
United Nations:
  anti-discrimination, 195–6
  definition of terrorism, 88
  and internationally protected persons,
    114
  and Palestine, 206–7, 208–9
  prohibition of use of force, 45, 60, 199
  and terrorism, 76, 77–9, 86–7, 90–2
  and terrorism finance, 165–8
United Nations Security Council:
  and 9/11, 143
  Counter-Terrorism Committee, 91, 168,
    185
  and Iraq invasion, 8
  and Iraq-Iran war, 225
  and Kashmir, 202–3
  and Lockerbie, 145–8, 151
  Resolution 1373, 78–9, 91–2, 167–8, 187,
    219
  western world dominance, 5
United States:
  and *Achille Lauro*, 154, 155
  bombing of Libya, 226
  bombing of Sudan, 226
  breach of international law, 229–230
  counter-terrorism legislation, 96
  draft terrorism convention, 76
  embassy bombings, 166
  financing of terrorism, 7
  freezing funds, 183–5
  imperialism, 8–9
  internal repression of Muslims, 8
  Iran hostages, 99, 112, 120–6
  Iraq Liberation Act, 74
  Israel policy, 209
  Lockerbie *see* Lockerbie bombing
  use of force, 142–4, 155
  USS Cole, 153
  USS Vincennes incident, 144–5, 226
  war on terrorism, 8, 225
use of force:
  against hostage takers, 100
  and *Jihad*, 51, 53–60
  OIC principles, 28, 199
  reprisals, 155
  self-defence, 58
  UN prohibition, 45, 60, 199
  US resort to, 142–4, 155
UTA incident, 142, 145
Uthmān ibn 'Affān, 12, 19, 58

Vieira de Mello, Sergio, 113
Vienna Congress 1815, 7
violence:
    history of Islam, 53, 58–60
    image of Islam, 2, 44
    and Muslim culture, 57
    use of force *see* use of force
    violent history, 53, 58–60

Wahabi reformation, 21
Wahshí, ambassador, 118
war crimes, hostage-taking, 108
Wells, HG, 223
Wervey, WD, 106
Westphalia treaty, 7

women, discrimination, 178
World Bank, 164, 177, 180
World Federation of International Arabo-
        Islamic Schools, 36
WTO, 39, 177

Yemen, 88, 117, 140, 153, 193, 194, 226
Yugoslavia, murder of ambassador,
        113–114

Zakat, 181–2
Zawati, Hilmi, 52, 118–119
Zia-ul-Haq, General, 221
Zweigert, K, 22